French Verbs Made Simple(r)

David Brodsky

French VERBS MADE Simple(r)

University of Texas Press Austin

Printed in the United States of America
First edition, 2006

Requests for permission to reproduce material from this work should be sent to:
Permissions, University of Texas Press, P.O. Box 7819, Austin, TX 78713-7819
www.utexas.edu/utpress/about/bpermission.html

∞ The paper used in this book meets the minimum requirements of
ANSI/NISO Z39.48-1992 (R1997) (Permanence of Paper).

Library of Congress Cataloging-in-Publication Data

Brodsky, David, 1950–
French verbs made simple(r) / David Brodsky.—1st ed.
p. cm.
Includes bibliographical references.
ISBN-13: 978-0-292-71472-4
ISBN-10: 0-292-71472-6 (paperback : alk. paper)
1. French language—Verb. 2. French language—Textbooks for foreign speakers—English. I. Title: French verbs made simple. II. Title: French verbs made simpler. III. Title.

PC2271.B76 2006
448.2′421—dc22 2005030902

For Daniel, Michael, and Beatriz

Contents

Preface

The fundamental aim of this book is to provide:

(a) easily understood—yet comprehensive—tools to recognize and learn the patterns that govern the large majority of "irregular" verbs in French; and
(b) clear and systematic illustrations of the use of all the principal French verb forms, with particular emphasis on the subjunctive.

It is intended both for the relatively new student grappling with the apparent complexities of French verbs and for the more advanced practitioner seeking to "perfect" his or her understanding.

The book is divided into three parts, which to a certain extent are independent:

Part I provides a description of the various verb tenses and forms, with a focus on establishing patterns and rules which can assist in learning (and remembering) the conjugations of the so-called Class III (irregular) verbs. Chapter 8 provides a comprehensive treatment of the *regular orthographic* changes which affect approximately 15 percent of *-er* (Class I) verbs. For example:

tu appe**ll**es	*versus*	tu appe**l**ais
je c**è**de	*versus*	nous c**é**dons
je p**è**se	*versus*	nous p**e**sons
je lance	*versus*	nous lan**ç**ons
il emplo**i**e	*versus*	vous emplo**y**ez

Chapter 9 provides an overall summary of verb forms and shows that (at most) six key conjugations determine the complete conjugation of any verb. The few exceptions are specifically highlighted.

Part II illustrates the use of the various verb tenses and forms. Special consideration is given to two of the thorniest problems for students of French: (1) whether a verb is to be conjugated with *avoir* or *être;* and (2) the conditions under which the past participle is variable (e.g., *Marie s'est lavé**e**, Marie s'est lavé les mains, les mains que Marie s'est lavé**es***). Chapter 11 is devoted to the use of the subjunctive. While no longer an element of spoken French, the *passé simple* remains an important element of the written language, and its use is covered in Chapter 12.

Annexes: By reviewing **Annex A**, the student can become familiar with the various "model" verbs (or classes) and their unifying features. Complete conjugations are presented for each of the models, including those displaying purely orthographic modifications. The key elements for each are highlighted, and all other verbs with analogous conjugations are explicitly identified. A summary table provides in concise form *all* of the key elements required to conjugate completely *all* French verbs. **Annex B** provides an alphabetical index of 6,200 verbs, showing the model class to which each verb belongs. **Annex C** presents the conjugations of "defective" verbs, which exist in only a limited number of forms.

A more advanced student has the option of reading the book sequentially or "à la carte". A student at a more elementary level may find it preferable to concentrate initially on those chapters dealing with the indicative (excluding the *passé simple*)—both forms and uses—before moving on to the subjunctive and then to the *passé simple.* In this case the following order of chapters is suggested:

1–3, 5	indicative verb forms, other than *passé simple*
7	compound verb forms
8	orthographic modifications
9	summary and presentation of verb classes
10	uses of indicative
6	subjunctive and imperative forms
11	uses of subjunctive
4	simple past (*passé simple*)
12	use of simple past and imperfect subjunctive

Alternatively, the relatively new student may wish to concentrate initially on the presentation of verbs and verb forms in Annexes A and B, before venturing into the more analytical presentations in Parts I and II.

French Verbs Made Simple(r)

Introduction

The structure of French verbs is not difficult to comprehend for a native English speaker, since most of the forms parallel or are very close in meaning to those employed in English. One seeming major difference is that French employs two "moods": the *indicative* and the *subjunctive.* The mood of the verb does not refer (at least directly) to the mood of the speaker but rather to the type of statement that he or she is making. The indicative can be thought of as the "normal" verb mood (or mode), while the subjunctive is used in a number of special circumstances—in connection with orders, desires, uncertainty, etc. Contrary to what many might think, the subjunctive also exists in English, though its existence generally passes unnoticed, since subjunctive and indicative verb forms in Modern English are almost always the same. But a sentence like

I insist that he *be* punished

provides an illustration that there is at times a difference between the two.

In addition to the indicative and subjunctive, there is a third verbal "mood" in both French and English—the imperative (e.g., "Go!" "Run!").

For any English verb there are essentially only five "simple" forms:

infinitive	(to) write
present	write(s)
past	wrote
past participle	written
present participle	writing

All other verb forms are *compound* ones created from the simple ones by using various auxiliaries or "helping" verbs (e.g., *I was writing, I will write, I would have written*). For French, there are *eleven* simple verb forms—the five English ones, plus:

indicative	subjunctive	imperative
imperfect	present	present
future	imperfect	
conditional		

Each French verb has 48 basic "simple" conjugations. For example, for the verb *parler* ("to speak"):

infinitive	parler
present indicative	parle, parles, parle, parlons, parlez, parlent
imperfect	parlais, parlais, parlait, parlions, parliez, parlaient
simple past	parlai, parlas, parla, parlâmes, parlâtes, parlèrent
past participle	parlé
present participle	parlant
future	parlerai, parleras, parlera, parlerons, parlerez, parleront
conditional	parlerais, parlerais, parlerait, parlerions, parleriez, parleraient
present subjunctive	parle, parles, parle, parlions, parliez, parlent
imperfect subjunctive	parlasse, parlasses, parlât, parlassions, parlassiez, parlassent
imperative	parle, parlons, parlez (*you* singular, *we*, *you* plural)

In addition there are a number of *compound* verb forms, most with close English counterparts.

The French future and conditional tenses are each equivalent to very specific English *compound* forms (*I will write, I would write*). For the imperfect tense, there is no one-to-one correspondence with a specific English verb form, which probably is why among the various indicative verb forms it often causes the greatest difficulty.

The table below illustrates basic English equivalents for the simple and principal compound French *indicative* verb forms. In each case the name in boldface (e.g., **simple past**) is the name by which the form will be referred to throughout the text; for several of the forms, common alternative names are shown in parentheses.

SIMPLE FORMS (INDICATIVE)

infinitive	*To live* is *to love.*
present	He *writes* in the book.
simple past *(preterite)*	He *wrote* a book about Shakespeare (in 1974).
imperfect	When I *was* young I *played* baseball every day. When the phone rang I *was leaving* the house.
future	Someday I *will write* a book about Shakespeare.
conditional	If I were not so lazy, I *would write* a book about Shakespeare.
present participle	I saw your brother *crossing* the street.
past participle	The book, *written* in the Middle Ages, is now in the British Museum.

COMPOUND FORMS (INDICATIVE)	
compound past *(present perfect)*	He *has written* a number of best-sellers.
past perfect *(pluperfect)*	By the age of 30, he *had written* a number of best-sellers.
future perfect	By the time I retire, I *will have worked* 40 years.
conditional perfect *(past conditional)*	I *would have done* it, if only I had had the chance.

For the simple and compound pasts we will frequently use their respective French names, *passé simple* and *passé composé.*

Verb Classes

French verbs can be divided into four groups according to the endings of their infinitives:[1]

1. *-er* verbs	parl**er**	"to speak"
2. *-oir* verbs	recev**oir**	"to receive"
3. *-re* verbs	répond**re**	"to respond"
4. *-ir* verbs	fin**ir**	"to finish"

The *-er* verbs are by far the most numerous, as shown in the following breakdown based on the 6,444 verbs contained in *Le Petit Robert:*[2]

DISTRIBUTION OF FRENCH VERBS

-er	*-oir*	*-re*	*-ir*
5,756	40	252	396
89%	1%	4%	6%

[1]As we will see in Chapter 1, these four groups are traditionally reduced to three, based on the type of ending used in the present indicative.

[2]*Le Petit Robert de la langue française* is generally considered to be the "standard" French reference dictionary. It is now available in a CD-rom version, which also contains complete verb conjugations. The six-volume *Grand Robert* has an additional 3,000 verbs.

The *-er* verbs are also the most dynamic, in the sense that "new" verbs virtually without exception take this ending. For example:

téléphoner	"to telephone"
skier	"to ski"
photocopier	"to photocopy"
scanner	"to scan"
boycotter	"to boycott"
digitaliser	"to digitize"

Irregular Verbs

In French, as in most languages, a "Murphy's law of verbs" seems to hold:

1. Regular verbs are infrequently used.
2. Frequently used verbs are irregular.

There is actually a simple explanation apart from that of *monsieur* Murphy: frequently used verbs simply have much greater capacity to resist the constant pressure to become uniform. Consider, for example, the English verb *to crow,* whose historical past tense was *crew:*

> Then began he to curse and to swear, saying, I know not the man. And immediately the cock *crew.* (Matthew 26:74, King James Version)

> And, as the Cock *crew,* those who stood before
> The Tavern shouted—"Open then the Door!" (*Rubáiyat of Omar Khayyám*)

Yet the verb was so infrequently used that most people assumed, or were easily convinced, that the past tense must be *crowed,* and so it has become.

> Then he began to invoke a curse on himself and to swear, "I do not know the man." And immediately the cock *crowed.* (Revised Standard Version)

The verb *to mow* (old past tense *mew*) had a similar experience, while the much more commonly used verbs *to know, to blow, to grow* have been able to resist such uniformizing tendencies and still have "irregular" past tenses: *knew, blew, grew.*

Of course if one goes back far enough in the history of English (and its predecessors), one will discover that most irregular verbs are really quite regular, following archaic patterns that have become obscured by several thousand years of gradual phonetic (and other) changes. In French a similar situation prevails, but with one important advantage: *a very large number of (seemingly) irregular verbs follow easily understood and readily remembered patterns.* This applies in particular to virtually all of the nearly 800 "irregular" *-er* verbs: only two do not follow precise patterns throughout their conjugations.

Recognizing and learning these patterns is a far more efficient way to learn French verbs than simply attempting to memorize what may at first seem like almost random irregularities.

Additional Observations

1. Etymology

The common heritage of English and French—approximately 60 percent of English words have a Latin, often via French, origin—can be a useful tool for remembering certain irregularities that otherwise might appear mysterious. Consider, for example, the *-ou**d**re* verbs, whose present tense plurals offer a stem consonant (or consonants) which differs from the *-d* of the infinitive:

infinitive	"we"	
cou**D**re	cou**S**ons	*sew*
mou**D**re	mou**L**ons	*grind*
résou**D**re	reso**LV**ons	*resolve*

For *résoudre* the connection with English *resolve* is apparent. Perhaps not so obvious is that the *-l* in *mou**l**ons* is the same as in English *molar* and *mill,* both descended from Latin MOLERE ("to grind"). Via an Indo-European root common to Latin and the Germanic languages, it is also the same *-l* which appears in *mea**l**.* Similarly, the *-s* in *cou**s**ons* is the same *-s* which appears in English ***s**uture*—from Latin (CON)SUERE ("to sew")—and, via a common Indo-European root, in ***s**ew* and ***s**eam.*

For these three verbs it is thus the seemingly irregular plurals which have in fact preserved the historically "correct" forms, the *-d* in the infinitive in place of *-s* being a relatively recent innovation.

Throughout the text (frequently in footnotes to avoid disrupting the flow) we have included etymological references which can serve as aids for remembering certain "irregular" elements and which are often of interest in their own right.

2. Pronunciation

A number of irregularities—real or apparent—can only be understood by examining the correspondence between the written form and the actual pronunciation. While most language manuals and English/French bilingual dictionaries make use of the International Phonetic Alphabet (IPA), many students are not familiar with such notation. We have therefore chosen to use a highly simplified notation which requires little explanation.

	representation	IPA
savons	[savon]	[savɔ̃]
mouvoir	[mouvoir]	[muvwar]
meuvent	[meuv]	[mœv]
meus	[meu]	[mø]
brute	[brut]	[bryt]
rompt	[rom]	[rɔ̃]
parte	[part]	[part]
part	[par]	[par]

Our sole objective in introducing such notation is to indicate: (a) which consonants are actually pronounced; and (b) whether the vowel "E" is *pronounced* or is *mute*. Hence, apart from "E" we simply reproduce the vowel combinations as they appear: *-ou, -eu,* etc. Where a vowel is nasalized, as in *sav**on**s* and *r**om**pt,* we include the succeeding consonant in the phonetic transcription to indicate this nasalization, rather than placing a tilde over the vowel as is customary.

The contrasting pronunciations of *parte* and *part* illustrate that the final *-e* (unless it has a written accent) and most final consonants are not pronounced. Word-final *-e* thus serves generally only as a marker that the preceding *consonant* is pronounced. A common example of this is the feminine form of nouns and adjectives—e.g., *verte* ("green", feminine) pronounced [*vert*], *vert* (masculine) pronounced [*ver*].

In French there are two different types of *pronounced* "E": the *closed -e* of *libert**é*** and the *open -e* of *f**ê**te,* essentially corresponding to the vowels in English *m**a**te* and *m**e**t.*[3] In phonetic transcriptions we will mark both with capital letters—[É] and [È]—to highlight their contrast with the unpronounced ("mute") *-e.*

	representation	IPA
aime	[Èm]	[ɛm]
fête	[fÈt]	[fɛt]
cédons	[cÉdon]	[sedɔ̃]
cèdes	[cÈd]	[sɛd]
moulez	[moulÉ]	[mule]

[3] There are in fact *five* other types of "E" with which we will not be directly concerned, exemplified by the vowels in the following words—***le**, p**eu**, p**eu**r, pl**ei**n, **un***—and represented symbolically (IPA) by ə, ø, œ, ɛ̃, œ̃.

There is ambiguity—or controversy—with regard to the pronunciation of -*ai* when it appears as the final sound in a word: in "Parisian" French it is generally [È] (and this is what is normally shown in dictionaries), while in most forms of "non-Parisian" French it is [É]:

	É	È
Parisian	—	f**ai**t, f**ai**te, f**ê**te, j'**ai**, av**ai**s
"Other"	f**ai**t, j'**ai**, av**ai**s	f**ai**te, f**ê**te

We will mark this sound [É], since for our purposes the fundamental distinction is whether or not a final -*e* is pronounced, not which variety it is. Hence:

	representation	IPA
fait	[fÉ]	[fɛ] or [fe]

Where the distinction in pronunciation of the final syllable -*ai* has relevance for the verbal system, we will make note of it.

At several points we will use the terminology *open syllable* and *closed syllable.* An *open* syllable is one in which the vowel is the last (spoken) element—e.g., all three syllables in *avocat:*

[**a**•v**o**•c**a**]

A *closed* syllable is one in which the final (spoken) element is a consonant—e.g., the first syllables in both *parler* and *taxer:*

[pa**r**•lÉ]
[ta**k**•sÉ]

3. Terminology and Numbers

There will frequently be statements like: "*prendre* is the only verb . . ." These should be understood as shorthand for the more long-winded forms: "*prendre* and other verbs sharing the same conjugation (*apprendre, comprendre, surprendre,* etc.)". When like-sounding verbs differ in a particular conjugation—for example, *vous dites* (infinitive *dire*) compared to *vous prédisez* (*prédire*)—this will be indicated.

At various points, reference will be made to the number of verbs in a particular class—e.g., 47 verbs (among those listed in *Le Petit Robert*) are conjugated like *rendre.* These numbers by themselves have no importance, since using a different set of verbs would produce an entirely different set of numbers. Nonetheless, the relative numbers are significant: *céder* and *rapiécer* are "model" verbs for particular classes of orthographic modifications; yet while there are 211 other verbs conjugated like *céder,* no other verb is conjugated like *rapiécer.*

The notation *1s, 2s, 3s, 1p, 2p,* and *3p* will be used as follows:

1s	first person singular (*je*)
2s	second person singular (*tu*)
3s	third person singular (*il, elle*)
1p	first person plural (*nous*)
2p	second person plural (*vous*)[4]
3p	third person plural (*ils, elles*)

4. Definitions and Dictionaries

Brief definitions (one or two words) are given for a number of the verbs presented in the text. These definitions are meant to be suggestive only and are in no manner a substitute for fuller definitions to be found in a dictionary. As early as possible, it is recommended that the student use a French-French dictionary. When purchasing such a dictionary it is important to confirm that it has both pronunciations and examples of use (not only definitions).

5. Simple Past and Imperfect Subjunctive

Many students pay little or no attention to the *passé simple* and *subjonctif imparfait* since these forms have long since disappeared from the spoken language. This neglect is ill-advised, however, particularly with regard to the *passé simple,* which remains alive and well in the written language—from *Le Petit Prince* to the French edition of *National Geographic.* Contrary to its reputation, the *passé simple* is not difficult to learn. At a minimum one should learn to recognize its forms, something which can be accomplished with relatively little effort.

In contrast to the *passé simple,* the contemporary use of the imperfect subjunctive is very restricted. However, since it is equally easy to learn—or at least recognize—why deny oneself the opportunity to appreciate classical French literature, in which its use was not infrequent?

> Le nez de Cléopâtre: s'il **eût** été plus court, toute la face de la terre aurait changé. (Blaise Pascal, *Pensées* [1660])
>
> Cleopatra's nose: had it been shorter, the whole face of the world would have been different.

---

[4] *Vous* is also used as a "formal" second person singular.

PART I

FORMS OF VERBS

CHAPTER 1

Present Tense

The present tense is by far the most difficult of all French verb tenses, reflecting the very large number of different "models" which exist. In many cases verbs which look similar (e.g., *revoir* and *devoir*) have markedly different conjugations, while apparently unrelated verbs (e.g., *suivre* and *écrire*) have very similar ones. Although these variations might appear quite random, they often reflect the *etymological origin* of the verbs in question. For this reason we frequently provide information on the Latin (or Old French) word from which the modern verb is derived. These generally correspond to well-known *English* words and hence can be a useful tool for helping to remember conjugations which might otherwise seem highly irregular.

> **Definition. The *infinitive stem* is equal to the infinitive minus the final *-er, -oir, -re,* or *-ir*.**

-er	*-oir*	*-re*	*-ir*
parl-er	*mouv*-oir	*rend*-re	*fin*-ir
chant-er	*recev*-oir	*écri*-re	*part*-ir

For *-er* verbs, the unmodified infinitive stem serves as the basis for constructing the six present tense conjugations, while for most other verbs it undergoes various modifications. We will use the term *stem consonant(s)* to refer to the consonant(s) which follow the *stem vowel:* for the verbs in the first line above, *-rl, -v, -nd,* and *-n.*

Three Completely Irregular Verbs

We will begin with the three truly irregular verbs, *être* ("to be"), *avoir* ("to have"), and *aller* ("to go"):

	être	*avoir*	*aller*
je	suis	ai	vais
tu	es	as	vas
il, elle	est	a	va
nous	sommes	avons	allons
vous	êtes	avez	allez
ils, elles	sont	ont	vont

For *aller,* two separate verbs have joined to form the present tense.[1] We will subsequently see that a third verb was used for the future and conditional tenses. Note that the first person singular for *avoir* is *j'ai* (not **je ai*).[2]

-*er* Verbs (Class I)

Apart from the irregular *aller,* for *-er* verbs life is very simple. A set of standard endings, which we will call the **-*e* endings,** is added to the infinitive stem. Thus for the model verb *parler* the present tense is as follows:

-*e* endings		pronunciation	
-e	je parl**e**	[parl]	1 syllable
-es	tu parl**es**	[parl]	1 syllable
-e	il, elle parl**e**	[parl]	1 syllable
-ons	nous parl**ons**	[par•**lon**]	2 syllables
-ez	vous parl**ez**	[par•**lÉ**]	2 syllables
-ent	ils, elles parl**ent**	[parl]	1 syllable

The three singulars and third person plural are pronounced identically. The first and second person plurals have an additional syllable, on which the word accent (stress) falls.[3]

In Old French (as in Latin and Old English), verbs were generally used *without* personal pronouns. In Modern French (as in Modern English), the coalescence of forms has made obligatory the use of personal pronouns, in contrast to the other major Romance languages (Spanish, Portuguese, and Italian), in which personal pronouns are added only when emphasis is required. For a verb beginning with a consonant, it is impossible even with the use of personal pronouns to distinguish between the pronunciation of the third person singular and plural:

donner	il donne	[il don]	ils donnent	[il don]
adorer	il adore	[il ador]	ils adorent	[ilS ador]

---

[1] VADERE—as in in***vade*** and cognate with Germanic *wade*—and probably AMBULARE (English *amble*). English *alley* comes from the past participle (*allé*) of *aller.*

[2] An asterisk (*) placed immediately before a particular (verb) form indicates that the form is not a correct one.

[3] All French words have a (light) stress on the final syllable. This is discussed further in the appendix to this chapter.

Other examples of *-er* verbs:

	chanter chant-	*gouverner* gouvern-	*oser* os-
je	chante	gouverne	ose
tu	chantes	gouvernes	oses
il, elle	chante	gouverne	ose
nous	chantons	gouvernons	osons
vous	chantez	gouvernez	osez
ils, elles	chantent	gouvernent	osent

Note that for verbs beginning with a vowel, *je* becomes *j'*—thus *j'ose* (not **je ose*).

About 15 percent of *-er* verbs display *orthographic* modifications in their conjugations. For example, for the verb *appeler* ("to call"):

j'appelle	double *-l*
tu appelles	double *-l*
il appelle	double *-l*
nous appelons	one *-l*
vous appelez	one *-l*
ils appellent	double *-l*

All such orthographic modifications follow regular patterns and will be dealt with in Chapter 8.

-oir, -re, and *-ir* Verbs: General Observations

The present tense of these verbs is considerably more complicated than for the *-er* verbs, due to the following factors.

(a) For the *-ir* verbs there are two sets of endings: ***-e* endings** (as for *-er* verbs) and, far more commonly, ***-s* endings.** This is illustrated below for the verbs *rompre* ("to break") and *couvrir* ("to cover"):

-s endings	*-e* endings
-s	-e
-s	-es
-t	-e
-ons	-ons
-ez	-ez
-ent	-ent

	romp-	*couvr-*
je	romp**s**	couvr**e**
tu	romp**s**	couvr**es**
il, elle	romp**t**	couvr**e**
nous	romp**ons**	couvr**ons**
vous	romp**ez**	couvr**ez**
ils, elles	romp**ent**	couvr**ent**

(b) Many verbs use two different stems for forming the present tense singulars and plurals. A relatively small number of verbs use *three* different stems: one for the singulars, a second for the first and second person plurals, and a third for the third person plural. Examples of two- and three-stem verbs are *partir* ("to leave") and *boire* ("to drink"):

	2 stems		3 stems		
	par-	*part-*	*boi-*	*buv-*	*boiv-*
je	par-**s**		boi-**s**		
tu	par-**s**		boi-**s**		
il, elle	par-**t**		boi-**t**		
nous		part-**ons**		buv-**ons**	
vous		part-**ez**		buv-**ez**	
ils, elles		part-**ent**			boiv-**ent**

(c) While many verbs with multiple stems modify only the stem consonant and/or vowel, a very large group of verbs *extends* the infinitive stem by adding *-i* to the singulars, *-iss* to the plurals. *Finir* ("to finish") is an example of such a verb with ***extended -s* endings,** and its conjugation below contrasts with the conjugation of *courir* ("to run"), which uses the same endings but does not extend its infinitive:

	finir fin-	*courir* cour-
je	fin-**i-s**	cour-**s**
tu	fin-**i-s**	cour-**s**
il, elle	fin-**i-t**	cour-**t**
nous	fin-**iss-ons**	cour-**ons**
vous	fin-**iss-ez**	cour-**ez**
ils, elles	fin-**iss-ent**	cour-**ent**

The overall situation can be summarized as follows, where the numbers represent the number of verbs in each category:[4]

	-oir verbs	*-re* verbs	*-ir* verbs
-*s* endings (1, 2, or 3 stems)	39	249	72
-*e* endings (1 stem)	—	—	16
***extended* -*s* endings**	—	2	308

Thus:

(1) With two exceptions, *-oir* and *-re* verbs only use the basic *-s* endings. *For the large majority of these verbs the stem is non-uniform.*

(2) Approximately 80 percent of *-ir* verbs use *extended -s* endings. Of the others, most use (basic) *-s* endings, while a relatively small number use *-e* endings.

For further information on the historical reasons for the existence of multiple stems and endings, see the appendix to this chapter.

The traditional breakdown of French verbs is as follows:

Class I	*-er* verbs other than *aller*	(5,755)
Class II	verbs with *extended -s* endings	(310)
Class III	all other verbs:	
	(a) *-s* endings	(360)
	(b) *-ir* verbs with *-e* endings	(16)
	(c) *être, avoir, aller*	(3)

Classes I and II are completely regular in all conjugations—taking into account the "regular" orthographic modifications for Class I verbs to be discussed in Chapter 8.[5] Class III verbs, by contrast, display irregularities throughout their conjugations and present the major difficulty in learning French verbs.

The fundamental distinction between the Class I and II verbs—with uniform or extended stems which always preserve stem consonants—and Class III

---

[4] Of the verbs presented in *Le Petit Robert.*

[5] And apart from the irregular future/conditional of the verbs *envoyer* and *renvoyer.*

verbs—whose singular stems are frequently truncated—is illustrated below for three verbs whose infinitive stem ends in *-rt:*

	Class I *porter* porT-	Class II *divertir* diverT-	Class III *sortir* sor- / sorT-
je	porte	divertis	sors
tu	portes	divertis	sors
il, elle	porte	divertit	sort
nous	portons	divertissons	sortons
vous	portez	divertissez	sortez
ils, elles	portent	divertissent	sortent
je	[porT]	[diverTi]	**[sor]**
tu	[porT]	[diverTi]	**[sor]**
il, elle	[porT]	[diverTi]	**[sor]**
nous	[porTon]	[diverTisson]	[sorTon]
vous	[porTÉ]	[diverTissÉ]	[sorTÉ]
ils, elles	[porT]	[diverTis]	[sorT]

Class II Verbs: *-ir* Verbs (+ *Maudire, Bruire*) with *Extended -s* Endings

The only difficulty with Class II verbs is recognizing which ones they are! There are several basic aids:

(1) The 20 percent of *-ir* verbs which do *not* have *extended -s* endings fall into several basic groups, which can easily be learned:

(a) 16 verbs with *-e* endings + *bouillir*
(b) *venir/tenir*[6]
(c) *partir, sortir, sentir/mentir/repentir, servir, dormir*
(d) *courir, mourir*
(e) *fuir, vêtir, -quérir* (e.g., *acquérir/conquérir*).

---

[6] In this listing a slash ("/") between two verbs indicates that their respective conjugations follow the same model.

In the large majority of cases, compounds (e.g., *détenir, recourir*) have the same conjugations. Exceptions include

impartir	"to impart"
répartir	"to distribute"
asservir	"to enslave"
assortir	"to match"
désassortir	"to unmatch"
réassortir	"to match up (with)", "to replenish"

which are conjugated as Class II verbs with *extended -s* endings.[7] In addition, *sortir* and *ressortir,* which are normally conjugated as Class III verbs, can be used with different meanings as Class II verbs.

(2) Any *-ir* verb formed directly from an adjective or noun has *extended -s* endings. Examples:

adjective/noun		verb	
clair	"clear"	éclaircir	"to clarify"
doux	"soft"	adoucir	"to soften"
dur	"hard"	durcir	"to harden"
faible	"feeble"	faiblir	"to get weaker"
		affaiblir	"to weaken"
fin	"end"	finir	"to finish"
fleur	"flower"	fleurir	"to flower", "to decorate"
franc	"frank"	franchir	"to cross (over)"
		affranchir	"to stamp (a letter)"
froid	"cold"	refroidir	"to cool"
garant	"guarantor"	garantir	"to guarantee"
grand	"tall", "large"	grandir	"to grow"
large	"wide"	élargir	"to widen"
maigre	"thin", "skinny"	maigrir	"to lose weight"
mou/mol	"soft"	mollir	"to weaken"
		amollir	"to soften"
noble	"noble"	ennoblir	"to ennoble"
noir	"black"	noircir	"to blacken"
obscur	"dark", "obscure"	obscurcir	"to darken, make obscure"
orgueil	"pride"	enorgueillir	"to make proud"
riche	"rich"	enrichir	"to enrich"
vieux/vieil	"old"	vieillir	"to age"

[7] Other compounds of *partir,* including *repartir* (without written accent, "to leave again"), are conjugated like *partir.* The distinction is thus between *-partir* verbs which involve "leaving"—with *-s* endings—and those which involve "distributing"—with *extended -s* endings. *Asservir* is not a compound form of *servir* but is instead derived from *serf. Assortir* and compounds are not derived from *sortir* but rather from the noun *sorte* ("sort," i.e., "kind" or "type").

(3) There are two *-re* verbs which belong to Class II—*maudire* ("to curse") and *bruire* ("to rustle", "to murmur").[8]

For Class II verbs the regular *-s* endings are added to the *extended* infinitive stem—i.e., with *-i* added for the singulars, *-iss* for the plurals.[9]

	durcir durc-	*garantir* garant-	*polir* ("to polish") pol-
je	durc-**i-s**	garant**is**	pol**is**
tu	durc-**i-s**	garant**is**	pol**is**
il, elle	durc-**i-t**	garant**it**	pol**it**
nous	durc-**iss-ons**	garant**issons**	pol**issons**
vous	durc-**iss-ez**	garant**issez**	pol**issez**
ils, elles	durc-**iss-ent**	garant**issent**	pol**issent**

Note that unlike Class I (*-er*) verbs, the third person plural can always be distinguished from the third person singular, even for verbs beginning with consonants:

il durcit [il durci] ils durcissent [il durciS]

Class III Verbs

The presentation will be organized as follows:

1. *-e* endings (all with uniform stems) + *bouillir*
2. *-s* endings, uniform stems
3. *-s* endings, non-uniform stems
   (a) two stems—consonant variations or *i* → *y*
   (b) three stems—consonant + vowel variations
4. a mixed bag of exceptions.

1. *-e* Present Tense Endings + *Bouillir*

The 16 *-ir* verbs which have *-e* present-tense endings (and uniform stems) consist of:

(a) all *-ir* verbs whose stem ends in *-vr* or *-fr*
(b) verbs ending in *-cueillir* and *-saillir,* plus *défaillir:*[10]

---

[8] *Bruire* is a "defective" verb used only in certain conjugations (see the end of this chapter and Annex C).

[9] For the *-re* verbs *maudire* and *bruire,* whose infinitive stems are *maudi-* and *brui-*, there is no extension for the singulars, while *-ss* is added for the plurals.

[10] For *faillir,* see Annex C.

-fr	*-vr*	*-ill*
of**fr**ir	cou**vr**ir	accue**ill**ir
souf**fr**ir	décou**vr**ir	cue**ill**ir
	entrou**vr**ir	recue**ill**ir
	ou**vr**ir	assa**ill**ir
	recou**vr**ir	sa**ill**ir[11]
	redécou**vr**ir	tressa**ill**ir
	rou**vr**ir	défa**ill**ir

Other verbs ending in *-illir* are Class II verbs, apart from *bouillir,* which has *-s* endings and separate stems for the singular (*bou-*) and plural (*bouill-*). Thus:

	offrir	*couvrir*	*accueillir*
je	offr**e**	couvr**e**	accueill**e**
tu	offr**es**	couvr**es**	accueill**es**
il, elle	offr**e**	couvr**e**	accueill**e**
nous	offr**ons**	couvr**ons**	accueill**ons**
vous	offr**ez**	couvr**ez**	accueill**ez**
ils, elles	offr**ent**	couvr**ent**	accueill**ent**

but

	vieillir (Class II)	*bouillir*
je	vieillis	*bous*
tu	vieillis	*bous*
il, elle	vieillit	*bout*
nous	viellissons	bouill**ons**
vous	vieillissez	bouill**ez**
ils, elles	vieillissent	bouill**ent**

2. *-s* Present Tense Endings, Uniform Stems

The only Class III (model) verbs with *-s* endings and uniform stems are:

-oir	*-re*	*-ir*
—	-clure, rendre, rompre, rire	courir, vêtir

[11] As noted at the end of the chapter, *saillir* can also be conjugated (generally with different meaning) as a Class II verb.

Thus:

	exclure exclu-	*rendre* rend-	*rompre* romp-
je	exclus	rends	romps
tu	exclus	rends	romps
il, elle	exclut	**rend** (*not* *rend**t**)	rompt
nous	excluons	rendons	rompons
vous	excluez	rendez	rompez
ils, elles	excluent	rendent	rompent

	courir cour-	*vêtir* vêt-	*rire* ri-
je	cours	vêts	ris
tu	cours	vêts	ris
il, elle	court	**vêt** (*not* *vêt**t**)	rit
nous	courons	vêtons	rions
vous	courez	vêtez	riez
ils, elles	courent	vêtent	rient

The third person singulars for *rendre* and *vêtir* are accounted for by the following orthographic rule:

> **Rule. If the singular stem ends in *-d* or *-t*, the third person singular omits the final *-t*.**

For *ren**d**re, rom**p**re,* and *vê**t**ir* the uniformity in stems is orthographic only, since the (final) stem consonants *-d, -p,* and *-t* are pronounced in the three plurals but not in the three singulars:

PRONUNCIATION

	rendre	*rompre*	*vêtir*
je	[ren]	[rom]	[vÈ][12]
tu	[ren]	[rom]	[vÈ]
il, elle	[ren]	[rom]	[vÈ]
nous	[ren•**don**]	[rom•**pon**]	[vÈ•**ton**]
vous	[ren•**dÉ**]	[rom•**pÉ**]	[vÈ•**tÉ**]
ils, elles	[ren**d**]	[rom**p**]	[vÈ**t**]

[12] Many speakers pronounce the singulars with a *closed -e* rather than an *open* one—i.e., [É] instead of [È].

Note that for *il rompt* the final *-t* is maintained but, like the preceding *-p*, is not pronounced.

The other *-clure* verbs (*conclure, inclure, occlure*[13]) are conjugated like *exclure*, while there is a large class of verbs conjugated like *rendre:*

> **Rule. Verbs ending in *-endre, -andre, -ondre, -erdre, -ordre* are conjugated like *rendre*.**
> ***Exception: prendre* (three stems)**

	prend-	*pren-*	*prenn-*
je	prends		
tu	prends		
il, elle	**prend** (*not* *prendt)		
nous		prenons	
vous		prenez	
ils, elles			prennent

Prendre used to be regular (with plural forms *prendons, prendez, prendent*) before the *-d* was removed from the plurals, possibly due to the influence of the verbs *venir* and *tenir.*[14]

3. *-s* Endings, Non-uniform Stems

(a) Two stems: consonant variations or *i* → *y*

These can be divided among the following 11 basic groups, where "C" represents a consonant:

	-oir	*-re*	*-ir*
(i)	-voir ("see")	croire, -raire	fuir
(ii)		battre, mettre	
(iii)			-CCir
(iv)		-ivre, écrire	
(v)		-indre	
(vi)		-oudre	
(vii)		dire, lire, suffire, -uire	
(viii)		faire, taire, plaire	
(ix)		-aître, croître	
(x)	valoir, falloir		
(xi)	savoir		

[13] *Occlure* ("to occlude", i.e., to close or obstruct) is rare, used only in a medical sense.

[14] In a somewhat ironic twist, as *-d* was disappearing from the plurals, it was reintroduced into the spelling of the singulars, where it had long since ceased to be pronounced. The double *-n* in the third person plural is an orthographic device used to show that the preceding *-e* is not mute (see Chapter 8).

(i) *-voir* ("see"), *croire, -raire;* also *fuir*

	voir voi- (voy-)	*croire* croi- (croy-)	*abstraire* abstrai- (abstray-)
je	vois	crois	abstrais
tu	vois	crois	abstrais
il, elle	voit	croit	abstrait
nous	voyons (*not* *voions)	croyons	abstrayons
vous	voyez (*not* *voiez)	croyez	abstrayez
ils, elles	voient	croient	abstraient

These verbs in fact have a *single* stem which undergoes a regular orthographic modification (see Chapter 8 for an explanation):

> **Rule. Whenever *-i* appears between two vowels—both of which are pronounced—it changes to *-y.***

Thus in the first and second person plurals the following vowel is pronounced, while in *voient, croient,* and *abstraient* it is silent. Note that *boire,* which rhymes with *croire,* uses three completely different stems (as illustrated earlier).

The *-voir* verbs can present difficulties, since there are five different categories, depending on the origin of *-voir,* each with its own conjugation pattern:

(a) Latin VIDERE ("to see"): *voir, entrevoir, revoir, pourvoir, prévoir*
(b) the irregular *avoir* (Latin HABERE "to have")
(c) *savoir* (Latin SAPERE "to know")[15]
(d) *devoir* (Latin DEBERE "to owe") plus verbs ending in *-cevoir* (from Latin CAPERE "to seize")[16]
(e) *mouvoir* (Latin MOVERE "to move"), *pouvoir* (Vulg. Lat. POTERE "to be able"), and *pleuvoir* (Vulg. Lat. PLOVERE "to rain").

Fuir is conjugated as if its infinitive were **fuiir* (or **fuyir*) so that its stem is *fui-,* with the *-i* changing to *-y* in the first and second person plurals, where the following vowel is pronounced:[17]

---

[15] Latin SAPERE meant "to taste" (hence English *savor, insipid*) as well as "to be wise" (*savant*).

[16] English cognates of DEBERE include *debt, debit,* and *due,* while *-cevoir* verbs correspond to English verbs ending in *-ceive* (*receive, conceive,* etc.).

[17] It is in fact likely that at a very early stage *fuir* had the form *fuyir. Fuir* comes from Vulgar Latin FUGIRE (Classical FUGERE)—source of English *fugue, fugitive, refuge*—and Latin G between vowels typically became *-y* in French (e.g., *loyal* and *royal* compared to their "classical" forms *legal* and *regal*).

	fuir fui- (fu**y**-)
je	fuis
tu	fuis
il, elle	fuit
nous	fu**y**ons
vous	fu**y**ez
ils, elles	fuient

(ii) *battre, mettre*

	battre bat- / bat**t**-	*mettre* met- / met**t**-
je	bats	mets
tu	bats	mets
il, elle	**bat** (*not* *batt)	**met** (*not* *mett)
nous	bat**t**ons	met**t**ons
vous	bat**t**ez	met**t**ez
ils, elles	bat**t**ent	met**t**ent

The double -*t* of the plural stem is shortened to a single -*t* in the singulars. The third person singular is explained by the orthographic rule above which provided *il vêt* rather than *il *vêtt.*

(iii) *-(CC)ir: partir, sortir, sentir/mentir/repentir, servir, dormir*

The conjugations for four of these are shown below:

	partir par- / par**t**-	*sortir* sor- / sor**t**-	*dormir* dor- / dor**m**-	*sentir* sen- / sen**t**-
je	pars	sors	dors	sens
tu	pars	sors	dors	sens
il, elle	part	sort	dort	sent
nous	par**t**ons	sor**t**ons	dor**m**ons	sen**t**ons
vous	par**t**ez	sor**t**ez	dor**m**ez	sen**t**ez
ils, elles	par**t**ent	sor**t**ent	dor**m**ent	sen**t**ent

In each case the singular stems lose a consonant: e.g.,

je/tu part-s → pars rts → rs

These are the only *-(CC)ir* verbs which are in Class III; the majority are Class II verbs with *extended -s* endings (e.g., *conve**rt**ir, rale**nt**ir, rem**pl**ir*)

(iv) *-ivre, écrire*

	suivre sui- / sui**v**-	*vivre* vi- / vi**v**-	*écrire* écri- / écri**v**-
je	suis	vis	écris
tu	suis	vis	écris
il, elle	suit	vit	écrit
nous	sui**v**ons	vi**v**ons	écri**v**ons
vous	sui**v**ez	vi**v**ez	écri**v**ez
ils, elles	sui**v**ent	vi**v**ent	écri**v**ent

The truncated singulars are explained by the word-final *vs* → *s* and *vt* → *t.* Note that *suis* is also the first person singular of *être,* so that *je suis* can mean "I follow" or "I am". *Écrire* was formerly *escrivre* (from Latin SCRIBERE, source of English *scribe* and *scribble*) before the *-v* also disappeared from the infinitive, due to the influence of the infinitives *dire* ("to speak") and *lire* ("to write"), with which *écrire* is frequently associated.[18] Verbs ending in *-scrire,* corresponding to English *-scribe* verbs (*décrire, inscrire, transcrire,* etc.) are conjugated like *écrire.*

(v) *-indre*

	plaindre plain- / plai**gn**-	*peindre* pein- / pei**gn**-	*joindre* join- / joi**gn**-
je	plains	peins	joins
tu	plains	peins	joins
il, elle	plaint	peint	joint
nous	plai**gn**ons	pei**gn**ons	joi**gn**ons
vous	plai**gn**ez	pei**gn**ez	joi**gn**ez
ils, elles	plai**gn**ent	pei**gn**ent	joi**gn**ent

All *-indre* verbs follow the same pattern: singular stem *-in,* plural stem *-ign.*[19]

---

18 For a time there were competing forms *nous écrisons* and *ils écrisent*—with *-s* from the corresponding conjugations of *dire* and *lire*—before the forms with *-v* triumphed.

19 French *-indre* verbs are derived from Latin verbs ending in -NGERE. In the plurals where -NG was followed by a vowel it became a *palatalized* "N," written *-gn* and pronounced as in *Espa**gn**e,* while in the singulars and infinitive the result was a nasalization of the preceding vowel. The infinitive passed from **plainre* to *plaindre*—the *-dre* ending evidently being found easier to pronounce—so it is actually the infinitive that is "irregular".

(vi) *-oudre*

	absoudre absou- / absol**v**-	*coudre* cou**d**- / cou**s**-	*moudre* mou**d**- / mou**l**-
je	absous	cou**d**s	mou**d**s
tu	absous	cou**d**s	mou**d**s
il, elle	absout	**coud** (*not* *coudt)	**moud** (*not* *moudt)
nous	absol**v**ons	cou**s**ons	mou**l**ons
vous	absol**v**ez	cou**s**ez	mou**l**ez
ils, elles	absol**v**ent	cou**s**ent	mou**l**ent

The *-d* from the infinitive appears in the singular stems for *coudre* and *moudre* but not for *absoudre.* The third person singulars for *coudre* and *moudre* show the same reduction *dt* → *d* as in *il ren**d**.*

For all three verbs it is the plurals rather than the infinitive which preserve the original Latin stem consonant(s)—ABSOLVERE, CO(N)SUERE, and MOLERE.[20] For *absoudre* the singular stem represents a normal phonetic development of *-ol + consonant* → *-ou* (e.g., *fou* "crazy" from earlier *fol*).[21] The explanation for the singular stems of the other two verbs is more complex and is intertwined with the history of the infinitives. The old infinitives *cosre* and *molre* were found difficult to pronounce, so a "helping" *-d* was added, thus giving *cos**d**re* and *mol**d**re.* These subsequently became *cou**d**re* and *mou**d**re.* At a much later stage the *-d* was added (erroneously) to the spellings of the singulars, where, in complete contrast to the infinitive, it had *never* been pronounced.

Not surprisingly, the conjugations of these verbs have caused great difficulty and uncertainty, with forms like *je *cous/*mous* not infrequently found, as well as *nous *cou**d**ons/*mou**d**ons.*

Note also that the three plurals of *moudre* are homonyms with those of *mouler* ("to mold, cast").

(vii) *dire, lire, suffire, -uire*

	dire di- / di**s**-	*lire* li- / li**s**-	*suffire* suffi- / suffi**s**-
je	dis	lis	suffis
tu	dis	lis	suffis
il, elle	dit	lit	suffit
nous	di**s**ons	li**s**ons	suffi**s**ons
vous	**dites** (*not* *disez)	li**s**ez	suffi**s**ez
ils, elles	di**s**ent	li**s**ent	suffi**s**ent

[20] As noted in the Introduction, an aid to remembering the plural stem consonants is to keep in mind the etymological connection to cognate English words: *absol**v**e, **s**uture/**s**ew, mo**l**ar/mi**ll**.*

[21] Cognate with English *foo**l*** and *fo**ll**y.*

	conduire condui- / condui**s**-
je	conduis
tu	conduis
il, elle	conduit
nous	conduis**ons**
vous	conduis**ez**
ils, elles	conduis**ent**

Confire and *circoncire* have analogous conjugations.[22]

The second person plural *vous dites* is exceptional, *dire* being one of only three French verbs not using the *-ez* ending (along with *être* and *faire*). *Redire* has a similar conjugation, while other composites of *dire* have the normal *-disez*—with the exception of *maudire,* which as we have noted earlier is a Class II verb.

	dire	vous **dites**
	redire	vous re**dites**
	contredire	vous contre*disez*
	dédire	vous dé*disez*
	interdire	vous inter*disez*
	médire	vous mé*disez*
	prédire	vous pré*disez*
(Class II)	maudire	vous mau***dissez***

Note that in *maudissez* the *-ss* is pronounced "S", while in *médisez* the *-s* is pronounced "Z".

(viii) *faire, taire, plaire*

	faire fai- / fai**s**-	*taire* tai- / tai**s**-	*plaire* plai- / plai**s**-
je	fais	tais	plais
tu	fais	tais	plais
il, elle	fait	tait	plaît (*not* *plait)
nous	fais**ons**	tais**ons**	plais**ons**
vous	**faites** (*not* *faisez)	tais**ez**	plais**ez**
ils, elles	**font** (*not* *faisent)	tais**ent**	plais**ent**

[22] The *-s* in the plural conjugations for *dire, conduire, suffire,* and *confire* has an etymological basis, as the corresponding Latin verb had a -c in its stem (DICERE, CONDUCERE, SUFFICERE, CONFICERE) which in French became *-s* (pronounced "Z" between vowels). *Lire* took its *-s* by analogy from *dire,* while that of *circoncire* came from *circoncision.*

As for group (vii), the *-s* in the plural conjugations has an etymological explanation.[23]

Faites and *font* are exceptional: *faire* is one of only three verbs with the second person plural ending in *-tes* (along with *vous êtes, vous dites*), and one of only four with the third person plural ending in *-ont* (*ils sont, ils ont, ils vont*). *Plaire* and its compound forms (*complaire, déplaire*) have a circumflex (ˆ) over the *-i* in the third person singular. As in many French words,[24] this circumflex represents an *-s* which has disappeared: e.g.,

il plai**s**t (Old French) → il pla**î**t

The same transformation (*st* → *t*) occurred with *faire* and *taire* but is not marked with a circumflex.[25]

(ix) *-aître, croître*

	connaître connai- / connai**ss**-	*accroître* accroi- / accroi**ss**-	*croître* croî- / croi**ss**-
je	connais	accrois	croîs
tu	connais	accrois	croîs
il, elle	connaît	accroît	croît
nous	connaissons	accroissons	croissons
vous	connaissez	accroissez	croissez
ils, elles	connaissent	accroissent	croissent

The *-ss* in the plural conjugations is again etymological, reflecting a Latin -SC (COGNOSCERE, CRESCERE). In the infinitives, the former presence of an *-s* is marked by a circumflex: e.g.,

conoi**s**tre (Old French) → conna**î**tre[26]
(ac)croi**s**tre (Old French) → (ac)cro**î**tre

All three verbs have a circumflex in the third person singular, marking a former *-s*, analogous to that of *plaire* in group (viii). For *croître* the circumflex has been

[23] In Latin all three verbs had a -C in their stem (FACERE, TACERE, PLACERE) which subsequently became *-s* in the plurals, while disappearing from the infinitive and the singular stem. Cognate English words reflecting the same phonetic change (*hard* "C" → *soft* "C") include *facile, tacit, placid.*

[24] E.g., *forêt, hôpital, rôtir* (corresponding to English *forest, hospital, roast*).

[25] This was also the case with the verbs in group (vii) whose plural stem *-s* is etymological.

[26] Old French *-oi* split into two in Modern French, some shifting to *-ai,* others remaining *-oi.* English *conn**oi**sseur* and *reconn**oi**ter* (Modern Fr. *conn**ai**sseur* and *reconn**aî**tre*) reflect the older French forms.

extended to the first and second person singulars as well. This has no etymological basis but is to distinguish the spelling—though not the pronunciation!—from the corresponding forms of *croire* in group (i).

	croire	*croître*
je	crois	cro**î**s
tu	crois	cro**î**s

Other *-aître* verbs include *naître, paraître,* and *paître. Décroître* is conjugated like *accroître.*

(x) *valoir, falloir*

	valoir vau- / val-	*falloir* fau- / (fall-)
je	vau**X**	—
tu	vau**X**	—
il, elle	vaut	faut
nous	valons	—
vous	valez	—
ils, elles	valent	—

The transformations *als* → *aux* and *alt* → *aut* are regular occurrences in French. For example:

m**al** (sing.)		m**aux** (plur.)
le journ**al**		les journ**aux**
altre (Old Fr.)	→	**aut**re (Mod. Fr.)
s**alt** (Old Fr.)	→	s**aut** (Mod. Fr.)

Valoir is one of three French verbs with endings *-x* in the first and second person singulars (along with *pouvoir* and *vouloir*). *Falloir* ("it is necessary") is an *impersonal* verb used only in the third person singular.

(xi) *savoir*

	savoir sai- / sav-	*avoir*
je	sais	ai
tu	sais	[as]
il, elle	sait	[a]
nous	savons	avons
vous	savez	avez
ils, elles	savent	[ont]

The conjugation of the irregular verb *avoir* is shown alongside *savoir,* since there are certain similarities. We will subsequently see that the similarities between these two verbs carry over to some of the other verb forms as well.

(b) Three stems: consonant + vowel variations

In addition to a variation in stem *consonant,* a number of verbs also display a variation in stem *vowel.* As a result, such verbs use three separate stems for forming their present tense:

Stem 1	3 singulars	vowel no. 1, consonant no. 1
Stem 2	1st and 2nd person plural	vowel no. 2, consonant no. 2
Stem 3	3rd person plural	vowel no. 1, consonant no. 2

When the infinitive has stem consonant *-r,* consonants numbers 1 and 2 are the same, so that the three stems are reduced to two.

There are four groups to be considered.

(i) Vowel alternation *eu – ou*

	mouvoir meu- / mouv- / *meuv-*	*pouvoir* peu- / pouv- / *peuv-*	*vouloir* veu- / voul- / *veul-*	*pleuvoir* pleu- / — / *pleuv-*
je	meus	peu**X**, puis	veu**X**	—
tu	meus	peu**X**	veu**X**	—
il, elle	meut	peut	veut	pleut
nous	mouvons	pouvons	voulons	—
vous	mouvez	pouvez	voulez	—
ils, elles	*meuvent*	*peuvent*	*veulent*	*pleuvent*

Apart from the vowel alternation, the singulars lose the stem consonant (*-v* or *-l*) of the plurals. *Pouvoir* and *vouloir* have first and second personal singulars ending in *-x* rather than *-s,* the only verbs besides *valoir* with this characteristic. *Puis* is in fact the historically "correct" form but much to the consternation of grammarians has been largely replaced in common use by *peux.* It remains obligatory, however, in direct interrogation:

Puis-je entrer?	"Can / may I enter?"

Pleuvoir ("to rain") is generally used only impersonally in the third person singular (*it rains*) but can also be used intransitively, most frequently in the plural ("the shells *rain* down on the battlefield").

Mourir offers the same vowel variation but no consonant variation, so that it has only two stems:

	mourir meur- / mour-
je	meurs
tu	meurs
il, elle	meurt
nous	mourons
vous	mourez
ils, elles	*meurent*

Note that *mourir* differs from all other two-stem verbs in that the vowel of the third person plural is that of the singulars, not that of the other two plurals.

(ii) Vowel alternation *oi – e*

	recevoir (-cevoir) reçoi- / recev- / *reçoiv-*	*devoir* doi- / dev- / *doiv-*
je	reçois	dois
tu	reçois	dois
il, elle	reçoit	doit
nous	recevons	devons
vous	recevez	devez
ils, elles	*reçoivent*	*doivent*

Apart from the vowel alternation, the singulars lose the stem consonant *-v* (analogous to *suivre* and *vivre*). For *recevoir,* the *cédille* (¸) is a normal orthographic modification to indicate that *-c* followed by *-a, -o,* or *-u* maintains its "soft" (i.e., "S") pronunciation (see Chapter 8). Other *-cevoir* verbs include *apercevoir, concevoir,* and *décevoir.*

(iii) Vowel alternation *oi – u*

	boire boi- / bu- / *boiv-*
je	bois
tu	bois
il, elle	boit
nous	buvons
vous	buvez
ils, elles	*boivent*

Boire is an anomaly, as it used to belong to group (ii) with first and second person plural *nous **be**vons* and *vous **be**vez*. After much vacillation, and perhaps influenced by the past participle (*bu*), the forms were altered to *nous **bu**vons* and *vous **bu**vez*. The original vowel is maintained in English ***be**verage*.[27]

(iv) Vowel alternation *ie* – *e*

	tenir tien- / ten- / *tienn-*	*venir* vien- / ven- / *vienn-*	*acquérir* acquier- / acquér- / *acquièr-*
je	tiens	viens	acquiers
tu	tiens	viens	acquiers
il, elle	tient	vient	acquiert
nous	tenons	venons	acquérons
vous	tenez	venez	acquérez
ils, elles	*tiennent*	*viennent*	*acquièrent*

Tenir and *venir* have identical conjugations—in all verb tenses and forms. Note that the *-n* in the singular is not pronounced but serves instead to signal that the preceding *-e* is nasalized. The three plurals have identical stem consonant "N", though this is written *-nn* for the third person plural. For *acquérir*, which has stem consonant *-r*, there is no consonant variation; but in its stead there is an alternation of *accent* marks: (a) an *acute* accent on the infinitive and the first two plurals; (b) a *grave* accent on the third person plural.[28] Conjugated like *acquérir* are *conquérir, enquérir, reconquérir,* and *requérir.*

4. A Mixed Bag of Exceptions

(i) *Haïr* ("to hate")

	hai- / haïss-	*pronounced as*
je	**hais** (*not* *haïs)	[É]
tu	**hais** (*not* *haïs)	[É]
il, elle	**hait** (*not* *haït)	[É]
nous	haïssons	[a•i•son]
vous	haïssez	[a•i•sÉ]
ils, elles	haïssent	[a•is]

[27] The vacillations in vowel are also reflected in Old Fr. *bevrage*/Mod. Fr. *br**eu**vage* ("beverage"), ***boi**sson* ("beverage"), and ***bu**vable* ("drinkable").

[28] The accent *grave* in *acqui**è**rent* and the doubling of *-n* in *tie**nn**ent* and *vie**nn**ent*—analogous to *ils pre**nn**ent*—are two different ways of marking the non-mute pronunciation of the stem vowel *-e* (see Chapter 8).

Haïr is of Germanic origin (cognate with English *hate*) and could not make up its mind whether to become a Class II or III verb. The final compromise adopted was that it is Class III in the three singulars, while in the plurals—and in all other tenses and forms—it is Class II. Note that this is not a purely orthographic distinction: the *dieresis* (2 dots over the -*i*) indicates that -*ai* in the plurals is to be pronounced as two separate vowels (cf. *naïve*) whereas in the singular it has the value [É].

(ii) *Asseoir* ("to sit")

Asseoir offers two completely different conjugations:

	(A) assied- / assey-	(B) assoi- (asso**y**-)
je	assieds	assois
tu	assieds	assois
il, elle	**assied** (*not* *assied**t**)	assoit
nous	asseyons	asso**y**ons
vous	asseyez	asso**y**ez
ils, elles	asseyent	assoient

The first conjugation displays a vowel alternation *ie* – *e* as well as an unpronounced etymological -*d* in the singulars,[29] with the third person singular displaying the normal reduction *dt* → *d*. The second conjugation is entirely parallel to that of *voir*. Some speakers offer a mixture of the two forms, employing the second for the singulars and the first for the plurals.

Rasseoir ("to sit down again") is conjugated like *asseoir*, with (A) and (B) conjugations. *Surseoir* ("to postpone") offers only conjugation (B). *Messeoir*[30] and the basic *seoir* are "defective" verbs, which exist only in a limited number of conjugations (see [v] below).

(iii) *Vaincre* ("to defeat", i.e., *vanquish*)

	vainc-/vainqu-	*pronounced as*
je	vaincs	[vain]
tu	vaincs	[vain]
il, elle	**vainc** (*not* *vainc**t**)	[vain]
nous	**vainquons** (*not* *vain**c**ons)	[vain•kon]
vous	vainquez	[vain•kÉ]
ils, elles	vainquent	[vaink]

[29] The Old French singular forms were *j'assié, tu assiés, il assiet.*

[30] "To not sit well with" (rare use other than literary).

The second and third person plurals require the orthographic modification *c* → *qu* in order to conserve the *hard* "C" sound in front of the "front" vowel *-e* (Chapter 8). According to the normal orthographic rules, *vain**qu**ons* should be spelled **vaincons,*[31] but the *-qu* from the other forms has triumphed. The three singulars have an unpronounced *-c,* and the final *-t* is dropped from the third person.

(iv) Verbs belonging to two conjugations

There are a few verbs which, with different meanings, can be conjugated either as Class II or as Class III. Among these are:

	Class II	Class III
sortir	to obtain (legal term) (3s/3p only)	*to go out*
ressortir	to concern, to be relative to	*to go out again*
saillir	to gush, to mate/couple (3s/3p only)	*to jut out, bulge* (3s/3p only)[32]

The more common use (and form) is italicized.

(v) "Defective" verbs

A number of verbs are "defective" in the sense that they are normally used only in certain conjugations: e.g., both forms of *saillir* in (iv) above. We have noted earlier that the "impersonal" verbs *falloir* and *pleuvoir* are used only with *il.* Other defective verbs are presented in Annex C.

Appendix
It Could Have Been Worse . . .

Some questions which occur to many students:

1. Why do many Class III verbs have different stem vowels (*je **meu**s – nous **mou**vons, je **vie**ns – nous **ve**nons*)?

In the "Vulgar"[33] Latin, which was the origin of French and the other Romance languages, the three singulars and the third person plural were stressed on the *stem* syllable, the first

[31] As in the past participle *vaincu.*

[32] Although in literary use with this meaning, *saillir* is not infrequently found with a Class II conjugation: "Sa poitrine abondante *saillissait* sous sa chemise" (Gustave Flaubert).

[33] "Vulgar" means simply "of the people" (Latin VULGUS, also the basis for *divulge*) and initially, at least, had no negative connotation.

and second person plural on the *post-stem* syllable—exactly as in Modern French. A general phenomenon in French was that vowels in *stressed open* syllables[34] underwent major modifications, while those in closed and/or unstressed syllables were much less affected and in many cases were left intact. As a result, virtually all verbs whose stem vowel was in an open syllable found themselves in Old French with two different vowels, one for the four conjugations with the stress on the stem, the other for the two conjugations with the stress on the post-stem syllable.

The table below illustrates the Old French conjugations for five *-er* verbs—paragons of regularity in Modern French—whose stem vowel was in an open syllable.

Latin vowel	A	E (short)	E (long)	O (short)	O (long)
Modern French	*laver*	*crever*	*espérer*	*prouver*	*pleurer*
Old French					
infinitive	laver	crever	esperer	prover	plorer
je	l**e**f	cr**ie**f	esp**oi**r	pr**ue**ve[35]	pl**eu**r
tu	l**e**ves	cr**ie**ves	esp**oi**res	pr**ue**ves	pl**eu**res
il, elle	l**e**ve	cr**ie**ve	esp**oi**re	pr**ue**ve	pl**eu**re
nous	lavons	crevons	esperons	provons	plorons
vous	lavez	crevez	esperez	provez	plorez
ils, elles	l**e**vent	cr**ie**vent	esp**oi**rent	pr**ue**vent	pl**eu**rent

For each of the verbs, the infinitive and first and second person plurals preserved the original stem vowel, while in the other four conjugations (highlighted in bold) it was altered in a uniform manner. In Modern French all such *-er* verbs have been completely regularized—in most cases using the *nous-vous* stem, in a few cases (including *pleurer*) using the *je-tu-il-ils* stem.[36] For all *-er* verbs an *-e* has been added in Modern French to the first person singular.

By contrast, verbs whose stem vowel was in a *closed* syllable generally had completely regular conjugations in Old French. For example (with stem vowels essentially

[34] Recall that an open syllable is one ending in a vowel, while a closed syllable ends in a (pronounced) consonant.

[35] The more common form was *pruis* (perhaps analogous to *je puis*).

[36] For *pleurer* ("to cry", "to weep"), regularization using the *je-tu-il-ils* stem was no doubt favored by the existence of the frequently used noun *pleurs* ("tears"). In contrast, *déplorer* ("to deplore", literally "to weep on someone"), which in Old French had the same conjugation (*je depleur*), was regularized using the *nous-vous* stem.

corresponding to the five examples above): *chanter, verser, fermer, porter, fonder.* A very interesting exception was *parler*—today's archetypal regular verb:

Old French

	parler (*infinitive*)
je	parol
tu	paroles
il, elle	parole
nous	parlons
vous	parlez
ils, elles	parolent

Parler's problem was that initially it had been a very long word

Vulgar Latin *parabolare,* later shortened to *parolare.*

Reflecting the influence of the Church, early residents of France (and Italy) spoke in *parables* (literally *parabolas*).[37] *Parolare* became Old French *parler;* however, for the three singulars and third person plural—where the stress fell on the *-o* of *parolare*—the Old French forms had the stem *parol-*. Modern French has regularized the verb with the plural stem *parl-*, while the longer stem remains in French (and English) *parole.*

All Class I and II verbs which had multiple stems in Old French now have completely regular conjugations. Most but not all Class III verbs which had *vowel* variation in Old French have also been regularized in Modern French. The failure to eliminate completely such variation is probably linked to the fact that Class III verbs also frequently had *consonant* variations, whereas Class I verbs generally did not, so that regularization for Class III verbs was overall a far more difficult process.

2. How do the French verb endings *-er, -oir, -re, -ir* correspond to the three-fold division *-ar, -er, -ir* characteristic of most other major Romance languages?

Latin verbs were divided into four groups, depending on the infinitive ending. In the first, second, and fourth groups, the vowel of the ending was *stressed* and hence was subject in French to the various vowel modifications which we have noted above (A → *e,* long E → *oi*).[38] In the third group, the vowel of the infinitive ending was *unstressed* and simply disappeared in French, giving rise to the *-re* verbs. The contrasting evolution of four different Latin verbs is presented below (the stressed syllable in the Latin verb is italicized).

---

[37] By contrast, Spanish and Portuguese residents spoke in *fables* (Mod. Spanish *hablar,* Mod. Portuguese *falar*).

[38] Since it was in an open syllable.

Verb Group	I	II	III	IV
Ending	-ARE	-ERE	-ERE	-IRE
	CAN•*TA*•RE	VA•*LE*•RE	*PER*•DE•RE	DOR•*MI*•RE
Italian	cant**are**	val**ere**	perd**ere**	dorm**ire**
Spanish	cant**ar**	val**er**	perd**er**	dorm**ir**
Portuguese	cant**ar**	val**er**	perd**er**	dorm**ir**
French	chant**er**	val**oir**	perd**re**	dorm**ir**
French	**-er**	**-oir**	**-re**	**-ir**
Other Romance	**-ar**(e)	**-er**(e)	**-er**(e)	**-ir**(e)

French *-er* verbs thus correspond to *-ar* verbs in the other Romance languages and *-oir* and *-re* verbs to other Romance *-er* verbs,[39] while *-ir* verbs are common to all Romance languages.

3. Why do some *-ir* verbs use "plain" *-s* endings, while others (the majority) use *extended -s* endings, and still others *-e* endings?

The *-s* endings are in fact the "classical" ones. A comparison with the other Romance languages is instructive:

	3s	1p
Latin	SERV-IT	SERV-IMUS
Italian	ser-**ve**	serv-iamo
Spanish	sir-**ve**	serv-imos
Portuguese	ser-**ve**	serv-imos
French	ser-t	serv-ons

In French, the vowel disappeared from the ending of the singulars,[40] providing a marked contrast with the other major Romance languages. This led directly to the loss of a stem consonant, since **servt* would have been unpronounceable, and hence to the creation of a separate stem for the singulars, a process replicated in the majority of verbs with *-s* endings.

Partly to combat this erosion of the stem, in the very earliest days of the language many *-ir* verbs were "strengthened" by adding an element *-isc* immediately after the stem. This was in fact an extension of the Latin practice of adding -SCERE to indicate the beginning of an action or process: e.g.,

FLORERE	"to bloom or flower", i.e., *to flower*
FLORESCERE	"to begin to bloom or flower", i.e., *to flourish*

[39] The other Romance languages have combined the second and third groups into a single category of *-er* verbs, while in French these remain distinct.

[40] As did all nonstressed vowels in final syllables apart from Latin A, which became *-e* (hence the *-e* endings of French Class I verbs).

Connaître and *naître* are examples of Latin verbs which had the -*sc* element from a very early stage (COGNOSCERE and NASCERE). Over time many additional *inceptive* verbs were created, referring to the process itself, not necessarily only to its beginning. Eventually they were created from adjectives and nouns as well (e.g., *noble* → *ennoblir*).

In Old French, the -*isc* element became -*iss* in the three plurals (e.g., *finiss-*) while in the singulars it was reduced to -*i:*

je	fin + isc + s	→	finis
tu	fin + isc + s	→	finis
il, elle	fin + isc + t	→	finist (Old French) → finit

A large number of "old" verbs switched to the new style, and over time verbs with extended -*is* endings came to represent 80 percent of all -*ir* verbs. Such (French) verbs are the basis for the -*ish* endings of *English* verbs: e.g.,

> abolish, accomplish, blemish, brandish, cherish, demolish, embellish, establish, finish, flourish (from FLORESCERE), furbish, furnish, garnish, impoverish, languish, nourish, perish, polish, ravish, relinquish, replenish, tarnish, vanish, etc.

The -*ish* ending in English became so popular that it was applied to a number of verbs which had not been inceptive in either Latin or French: e.g., *admonish, diminish, distinguish, famish, publish, vanquish.*

Finally, with regard to the 16 -*ir* verbs which use -*e* endings (e.g., *couvrir, cueillir*), these have to be considered in two separate groups:

(a) Those whose stem ends in -*vr* or -*fr* were able to maintain the pronunciation of *both* stem consonants throughout the conjugation (as compared, for example, to *partir,* where in the singulars the -*t* did not survive). This required the addition of a "supporting" -*e:*

*je couvr	→	je couvre
*tu couvrs	→	tu couvres
*il couvr	→	il couvre

(b) Those ending in -*illir* could have been spelled either with one -*l* and no -*e* (e.g., **je cueil*) or with two -*l*s and an -*e* (*je cueille*), with no effect on the pronunciation. The latter form was chosen in order to maintain orthographic consistency with the plural conjugations (*nous cueillons*).

4. Why do French verbs (and words in general) appear to have no stress accent (i.e., stressed syllable)? Why are they usually shorter than the corresponding words in other Romance languages?

As in English, in Latin each word had a syllable which was stressed. All of the major Romance languages have (generally) maintained the word stress on the same syllable on which it fell in Latin, with the following important refinement for French:

> **In French, all vowels and consonants following the stressed syllable generally disappeared, with the exception of "A", which became a *mute* (i.e., unpronounced) -*e*.**

The "truncated" appearance of French words is thus due to the fact that everything which came after the stressed syllable simply vanished. Some attribute this to Germanic influence, as the Germanic Franks were the ruling class in the northern French territories in which the language developed.[41] In Modern French the stress remains—always on the final syllable—but it has diminished to such an extent that many are unaware that it even exists.

A comparison of *il chante,* the past participles *chanté/parti,* and the noun *page* with the corresponding forms in other Romance languages is instructive. In each case, the stressed syllable is highlighted in bold.

Latin	French	Spanish	Italian
CAN•TA	**chante** [chant]	**can**•ta	**can**•ta
CAN•**TA**•TUS	chan•**té**	can•**ta**•do	can•**ta**•to
PAR•**TI**•TUS	par•**ti**	par•**ti**•do	par•**ti**•to
PA•GI•NA	**page**	**pá**•gi•na	**pa**•gi•na

[41] The pervasive Germanic influence is reflected in the fact that France is the only "Romance" country which uses a Germanic word for both its name and language. The term "frank" (Fr. *franc*), meaning "free", owes its origin to the fact that only the ruling Franks, and those locals accorded equal status, possessed full freedom.

CHAPTER 2

Imperfect Tense and Present Participle

The imperfect tense and present participle are both constructed using the same stem:

> **Rule. The stem used for both the imperfect tense and the present participle is the stem of the first person plural (*nous*) present tense conjugation, obtained by removing the ending *-ons.***
>
> ***Exceptions:* *être* (both), *avoir,* and *savoir* (present participle only).**

Note that for all Class I—and some Class III—verbs, this stem is equal to the infinitive stem, while for all Class II verbs it is the infinitive stem plus the "extra" element *-iss.*

Imperfect Tense

The imperfect is among the most perfect of all French verb forms: for all verbs apart from *être,* standard endings are added to the stem defined above. Thus for *parler:*

endings (present)	*parler* (Class I) nous *parl*-ons	pronunciation
-ais	je parl**ais**	[par•lÉ]
-ais	tu parl**ais**	[par•lÉ]
-ait	il, elle parl**ait**	[par•lÉ]
-ions	nous parl**ions**	[par•li•on]
-iez	vous parl**iez**	[par•li•É]
-aient	ils, elles parl**aient**	[par•lÉ]

Similarly,

(1p present)	*finir* (Class II) *finiss*-ons	*partir* *part*-ons	*prendre* *pren*-ons
je	finiss**ais**	part**ais**	pren**ais**
tu	finiss**ais**	part**ais**	pren**ais**
il, elle	finiss**ait**	part**ait**	pren**ait**
nous	finiss**ions**	part**ions**	pren**ions**
vous	finiss**iez**	part**iez**	pren**iez**
ils, elles	finiss**aient**	part**aient**	pren**aient**

(1p present)	*moudre* *moul*-ons	*vaincre* *vainqu*-ons	*joindre* *joign*-ons
je	moul**ais**	vainqu**ais**	joign**ais**
tu	moul**ais**	vainqu**ais**	joign**ais**
il, elle	moul**ait**	vainqu**ait**	joign**ait**
nous	moul**ions**	vainqu**ions**	joign**ions**
vous	moul**iez**	vainqu**iez**	joign**iez**
ils, elles	moul**aient**	vainqu**aient**	joign**aient**

(1p present)	*aller* *all*-ons	*asseoir* (A) *assey*-ons	*avoir* *av*-ons
j'	all**ais**	assey**ais**	av**ais**
tu	all**ais**	assey**ais**	av**ais**
il, elle	all**ait**	assey**ait**	av**ait**
nous	all**ions**	assey**ions**	av**ions**
vous	all**iez**	assey**iez**	av**iez**
ils, elles	all**aient**	assey**aient**	av**aient**

For *être* the regular endings are added to the stem *ét-*, which has an acute accent rather than a circumflex:[1]

	être
j'	ét**ais**
tu	ét**ais**
il, elle	ét**ait**
nous	ét**ions**
vous	ét**iez**
ils, elles	ét**aient**

Note that for *all* verbs, the imperfects for the three singulars and third person plural are pronounced identically. For impersonal (or defective) verbs which do

[1] Despite the apparent similarity in form to the infinitive *être,* the imperfect tense (as well as the present and past participles) comes from an entirely different verb—Latin STARE ("to stand"). STARE is also the source for the (now) defective verb *ester* (Annex C), which is in turn the origin of the English verb *to stay.*

not have first person plural (*nous*) conjugations, the imperfect endings are added to the infinitive stem:

pleuvoir	pleuv-	il pleuv**ait**, ils/elles pleuv**aient**
falloir	fall-	il fall**ait**

The imperfects of *rire* and of all verbs ending in *-ier* are completely regular but nonetheless look a bit "odd" since they have *-ii* in the first and second person plurals (see Chapter 8):

	rire	*prier*
(1p present)	*ri*-ons	*pri*-ons
je	riais	priais
tu	riais	priais
il, elle	riait	priait
nous	r**ii**ons	pr**ii**ons
vous	r**ii**ez	pr**ii**ez
ils, elles	riaient	priaient

Present Participle

For all verbs except *être, avoir,* and *savoir* the present participle is obtained by adding *-ant* to the same stem used to form the imperfect. Thus:

infinitive	1p present	stem	present participle
parler	parlons	parl-	parl**ant**
finir	finissons	finiss-	finiss**ant**
offrir	offrons	offr-	offr**ant**
courir	courons	cour-	cour**ant**
partir	partons	part-	part**ant**
croire	croyons	croy-	croy**ant**
boire	buvons	buv-	buv**ant**
abstraire	abstrayons	abstray-	abstray**ant**
rendre	rendons	rend-	rend**ant**
mettre	mettons	mett-	mett**ant**
prendre	prenons	pren-	pren**ant**
écrire	écrivons	écriv-	écriv**ant**
peindre	peignons	peign-	peign**ant**
absoudre	absolvons	absolv-	absolv**ant**
moudre	moulons	moul-	moul**ant**
dire	disons	dis-	dis**ant**

faire	faisons	fais-	fais**ant**
connaître	connaissons	connaiss-	connaiss**ant**
valoir	valons	val-	val**ant**
pouvoir	pouvons	pouv-	pouv**ant**
recevoir	recevons	recev-	recev**ant**
tenir	tenons	ten-	ten**ant**
acquérir	acquérons	acquér-	acquér**ant**
haïr	haïssons	haïss-	haïss**ant**
vaincre	vainquons	vainqu-	vainqu**ant**
asseoir (A)	asseyons	assey-	assey**ant**
asseoir (B)	assoyons	assoy-	assoy**ant**

Être uses the same stem as for its imperfect, while the stems for *avoir* and *savoir* are those of their *present subjunctive* (Chapter 6):

être	ét-	ét**ant**
avoir	ay-	ay**ant**
savoir	sach-	sach**ant**

Appendix

"Old" Present Participles

The present participle has not always been as regular as it is today, and numerous older forms replaced by more "regular" ones have continued to exist as adjectives or nouns. These include:

verb	modern present participle	"old" present participle	
aimer	aimant	amant	"lover"
fleurir	fleurissant	florissant	"flourishing"[2]
pouvoir	pouvant	puissant	"powerful"
recevoir	recevant	récipient[3]	"container"
savoir	sachant	savant	"learned", "savant"
servir	servant	sergent	"sergeant"
valoir	valant	vaillant	"valiant"
vouloir	voulant	bienveillant	"benevolent"

[2] Flourishing flowers are *fleurissant,* but things which flourish figuratively (people, countries, poetry, etc.) are *florissant.* The verb *fleurir* theoretically has a second form of the imperfect using the stem *flor-*, which applies figuratively (Voltaire: *Homère fl**o**rissait deux générations après la guerre de Troie*).

[3] *Récipient* is a relatively "modern" (sixteenth century) borrowing of the original Latin present participle.

Present participles ending in *-guant* and *-quant* have maintained these forms even though they should be written *-gant* and *-cant* according to the normal rules of French orthography (see Chapter 8, Rule O-10). In a number of cases a verbal adjective or noun with a "regular" spelling has been created, existing alongside the present participle:

verb	present participle	"regular" verbal adjective or noun	
communiquer	communi**qu**ant	communi**c**ant	"communicating"
convaincre	convain**qu**ant	convain**c**ant	"convincing"
fabriquer	fabri**qu**ant	fabri**c**ant	"manufacturer"
fatiguer	fati**gu**ant	fati**g**ant	"fatiguing"
fringuer	frin**gu**ant	frin**g**ant	"spirited", "dashing"
intriguer	intri**gu**ant	intri**g**ant	"devious", "scheming"
naviguer	navi**gu**ant	navi**g**ant	"seagoing"
provoquer	provo**qu**ant	provo**c**ant	"provocative"
suffoquer	suffo**qu**ant	suffo**c**ant	"suffocating"
vaquer	va**qu**ant	va**c**ant	"vacant"
zigzaguer	zigza**gu**ant	zigza**g**ant	"zigzagging"

Many Latin present participles ended in *-ent,*[4] and a number of these have entered French as "learned" verbal adjectives or nouns alongside the *-ant* present participles.[5]

verb	present participle	"learned" verbal adjective or noun	
adhérer	adhér**ant**	adhér**ent**	"adherent"
affluer	affl**uant**	affl**uent**	"tributary"
coïncider	coïncid**ant**	coïncid**ent**	"coincident", "coinciding"
converger	converg**eant**[6]	converg**ent**	"convergent"
déférer	défér**ant**	défér**ent**	"deferential"
déterger	déterg**eant**	déterg**ent**	"detergent"
différer	différ**ant**	différ**ent**	"different"
diverger	diverg**eant**	diverg**ent**	"divergent"
émerger	émerg**eant**	émerg**ent**	"emergent", "emerging"
équivaloir	équival**ant**	équival**ent**	"equivalent"
excéder	excéd**ant**	excéd**ent**	"surplus", "excess"

[4] Latin present participles of verbs in group 1 ended in *-ant,* while those in groups 2–4 ended in *-ent* (see the Appendix to Chapter 1 for a description of the groups).

[5] The traditional British preference for *depend**a**nt* (noun) is based on the French spelling, while the preferred American spelling *depend**e**nt* reflects the original Latin form. Note that in French the pronunciation of *-ant* and *-ent* is identical (in both cases, nasalized "A").

[6] The *-e* following the *-g* in *convergeant*—and in *détergeant, divergeant, émergeant, négligeant*—is a normal orthographic modification to preserve the soft "G" (see Chapter 8).

exceller	excell**a**nt	excell**e**nt	"excellent"
expédier	expédi**a**nt	expédi**e**nt	"expedient"
influer	influ**a**nt	influ**e**nt	"influential"
négliger	néglig**ea**nt	néglig**e**nt	"negligent"
précéder	précéd**a**nt	précéd**e**nt	"preceding", "precedent"
présider	présid**a**nt	présid**e**nt	"president"
résider	résid**a**nt	résid**e**nt	"resident"
somnoler	somnol**a**nt	somnol**e**nt	"somnolent", "drowsy"

Note that the *-ent* verbal adjective or noun is identical in appearance—but not in pronunciation!—to the third person plural of the corresponding verb:

noun	président	[prÉ•si•**den**]	3 syllables
verb 3p	ils président	[prÉ•**sid**]	2 syllables

The contrasting use of *present participles* and *verbal adjectives,* which can give rise to confusion, will be considered in Chapter 10.

CHAPTER 3

Past Participle

For purposes of classifying past participles, we will define the *ending* of the past participle to be

(a) *-t* if it ends in consonant + *-t*—*plain**t**, mor**t**, couver**t***
(b) otherwise, the final vowel plus final consonant (if any)—*parl**é**, fin**i**, acqu**is**, incl**us***.

The remainder of the past participle (*plain-, mor-, couver-, parl-, fin-, acqu-, incl-*) will be called the *past participle stem.*[1] The past participle stem for most verbs is the same as the infinitive stem; in such cases we will say that the stem is "normal" or "regular".

We will begin with an overall summary.

Past Participle Endings, Grouped by Infinitive Types

-er		*-oir*		*-re*		*-ir*	
parl-**É**	(Class I)	val-**U**	(*valoir*)	rend-**U**	(*rendre*)	fin-**I**	(Class II)
all-**É**	(*aller*)	ass-**IS**	(*asseoir* only)	fa-**IT**	(*faire*)	part-**I**	(*partir*)
				m-**IS**	(*mettre*)	acqu-**IS**	(*acquérir*)
				n-**É**	(*naître*)	cour-**U**	(*courir*)
				plain-**T**	(*plaindre*)	mor-**T**	(*mourir*)
				incl-**US**	(*inclure*)		

1. **All** *-er* verbs have past participles equal to the infinitive stem plus the ending *-é* (*parler* → *parl**é***).
2. **All** *Class II* verbs[2] (i.e., those with *extended -s* present tense endings) have past participles equal to the infinitive stem plus the ending *-i* (*finir* → *fin**i***).
3. For *Class III verbs* the situation is far more complex. Nonetheless, by grouping these verbs by their infinitive endings, we can simplify things somewhat, particularly for *-oir* verbs.

[1] This definition is for classification purposes only and in many cases does not represent the actual historical/etymological manner in which past participles were created. In the case of *acquis,* for example, the *-is* was historically part of the stem (Lat. ACQUISITUS), likewise the *-us* for *inclus* (Lat. INCLUSUS).

[2] Except *maudire* (see below).

(a) Apart from *asseoir,* all *-oir* verbs have past participles ending in *-u.* For *-voir* ("to see") verbs and those whose infinitives end in *-loir, -u* is added to the infinitive stem (e.g., *valoir* → *val**u***); in all others it is added to a truncated stem (e.g., *pouvoir* → *p**u***).
(b) For *-re* verbs there are six different types of past participle endings: *-u, -it, -is, -é, -t, -us.* In some cases these endings are added to the infinitive stem, in others to a truncated or otherwise altered one.
(c) Class III *-ir* verbs are almost evenly divided between *-i* and *-u* past participles, with a few *-is* and *-t* endings. All *-i* and *-u* endings are added to the infinitive stem: *part(ir)* → *part**i***, *ven(ir)* → *ven**u***.

Before proceeding to a detailed presentation, we need to take note of the fact that most past participles have plural and feminine forms.

Plural and Feminine Forms of the Past Participle

The basic forms of the past participle presented above refer to the *masculine singular* past participle. The vast majority of verbs also have three other forms of the past participle: feminine singular, masculine plural, and feminine plural. With only one exception, the feminine singular is formed by adding *-e* to the corresponding masculine past participle. The plurals are formed by adding an additional *-s* (so that a feminine plural has an additional *-es*); however, no *-s* is added to the plural of masculine *-is* or *-us* participles. These rules are illustrated below for the seven types of participle endings (*-é, -i, -u, -is, -it, -t, -us*).

	masculine		feminine	
	singular	*plural*	*singular*	*plural*
parler	parl**é**	parl**és**	parl**ée**	parl**ées**
finir	fin**i**	fin**is**	fin**ie**	fin**ies**
valoir	val**u**	val**us**	val**ue**	val**ues**
prendre	pr**is**	*pris*	pr**ise**	pr**ises**
faire	fa**it**	fa**its**	fa**ite**	fa**ites**
plaindre	plain**t**	plain**ts**	plain**te**	plain**tes**
inclure	incl**us**	*inclus*	incl**use**	incl**uses**

The single exception is *absoudre:*

absoudre	absous	*absous*	absou**te**	absou**tes**

The Académie Française has tried to regularize the situation by changing the masculine participle to *absout* (and hence masculine plural to *absouts*), thus far without success.

There are a relatively small number of verbs (e.g., *nuire, plaire, être, suffire*) which have neither feminine nor plural past participles. It is neither necessary nor particularly useful to memorize which verbs these are: if a verb can be used in a situation in which a plural or feminine past participle is required (see Chapter 10), it is almost certain that such a form exists.

Several verbs have a circumflex over the masculine past participle which, rather confusingly, is not extended to the other forms:

	masculine		feminine	
	singular	*plural*	*singular*	*plural*
croître	crû	crus	crue	crues
devoir	dû	dus	due	dues
mouvoir	mû	mus	mue	mues

For *devoir* the circumflex distinguishes *dû* from the article *du,* while for *croître* it distinguishes *crû* from the (masculine singular) past participle of *croire.* There is no justification for the exceptional treatment accorded to *mû,* which nonetheless continues to survive all efforts to regularize it.

Note also that verbs like *créer* which end in *-éer* have feminine past participles ending in *-éée* and *-éées:*

l'organisation ***créée*** en 1945	"the organization *created* in 1945"

Now we turn to a detailed presentation.

A. *-er* Verbs (Class I plus *Aller*)

Without exception, *-er* verbs (including the irregular *aller*) form their past participle by adding *-é* to the infinitive stem.

	infinitive stem	past participle
aller	all-	all**é**
appeler	appel-	appel**é**
commencer	commenc-	commenc**é**
céder	céd-	céd**é**
jeter	jet-	jet**é**

B. Class II: *-ir* Verbs with Extended *-s* Present Tense Endings, plus *Maudire*

Apart from *maudire,* all Class II verbs form their past participle by adding *-i* to the infinitive stem. This includes *haïr,* whose present tense offers a mixture of Class II and III forms. The past participle for *maudire* is ***maudit,*** analogous to that of the other *-dire* verbs.

		infinitive stem	past participle
	finir	fin-	fin**i**
	durcir	durc-	durc**i**
	garantir	garant-	garant**i**
	polir	pol-	pol**i**
	haïr	ha-	ha**ï** (not *ha**i**)
exception	*maudire*	maudi-	maudi**t**[3]

Note that the past participle for *haïr* is pronounced [a•i].

C. Class III Verbs: All Others

C1. *-oir* Verbs

All *-oir* verbs have *-u* past participles, apart from *asseoir.* Infinitives ending in *-loir* and *-voir* ("to see") add *-u* to the full infinitive stems. All other verbs add *-u* to a truncated stem.

	infinitive stem	past participle
falloir	fall-	fall**u**
valoir	val-	val**u**
vouloir	voul-	voul**u**
voir	v-	v**u**
entrevoir	entrev-	entrev**u**
pourvoir	pourv-	pourv**u**
prévoir	prév-	prév**u**
revoir	rev-	rev**u**

[3] The opposing verb *bénir* ("to bless", from Latin BENEDICERE) has lost all connection to *dire* and has been assimilated completely to Class II, with regular past participle *béni.* The old form *bénit* of the past participle remains as an adjective, however. Thus it is *pain bénit* ("blessed bread"), not **pain béni.*

		truncated stem	past participle
	mouvoir	m-	m**û** (not *m**u**)
	pleuvoir	pl-	pl**u**
	pouvoir	p-	p**u**
	recevoir	rec-	reç**u**
	devoir	d-	d**û** (not *d**u**)
	savoir	s-	s**u**
	avoir	(e)	e**u**
exception	*asseoir*	ass-	ass***is***

The *e-* in *eu* is a historical relic and has no phonetic value but has remained, since otherwise the word would look a bit odd (**u*).[4] We have noted earlier that the past participles for *devoir* and *mouvoir* have circumflexes, but only for the masculine singular forms. This is the case as well for the compound *redevoir* (*redû*), but in contrast both *émouvoir* (*ému*) and *promouvoir* (*promu*) have past participles with no circumflex. The *cédille* in **reçu** is a normal orthographic change required to preserve the soft "C" sound (see Chapter 8).

C2. *-re* Verbs

This is by far the most difficult group. There are six different endings used for the past participle (*-u, -it, -is, -é, -t, -us*), and the pattern of their distribution is not as consistent as one might hope. A number of verbs with similar present tense conjugations (*dire-lire, battre-mettre, suivre-vivre*) have markedly different past participles.

(1) Two *-re* verbs have the past participle ending *-é: naître → né* and *être → été.* These are the only non-*er* verbs with this past participle ending.[5]

(2) *-indre* verbs have *-t* past participles, with the past participle stem ("p.p. stem") equal to the infinitive minus the final *-dre:*

		p.p. stem	past participle[6]
-*t*	*plaindre*	plain-	plain**t**
	peindre	pein-	pein**t**
	joindre	join-	join**t**

[4] All of the truncated *-u* past participles ended in *-eü* in Old French (*meü, pleü, peü, receü, deü, seü, eü*), where the *-e* and *-u* were initially pronounced as separate vowels. When the *-e* ceased to be pronounced, it was removed from the spelling (apart from *eu*), with a circumflex placed on the *-u* to "commemorate" the vanished *-e* (e.g., *reçû-reçûe*). This now remains only for *dû* and *mû.*

[5] The name *René* literally means "reborn". English *puny* comes from *puis**ne*** (= puis + **né**) which initially meant "born after". *Puisne* continues to be used in "British" English to refer to lower-ranking judges. Modern French *aîné* ("elder", "eldest") literally means "born before".

[6] Compare English *complain**t**/plain**t**iff, pain**t*** (originally *pein**t***), *join**t**.*

(3) Verbs like *rendre, rompre, battre* (with two stem consonants but no preceding *-i*) have past participles with a *-u* added to the infinitive stem. **Exceptions:** *prendre* and *mettre,* which add *-is* to a truncated stem consisting of the initial consonant or consonant combination.[7]

		infinitive stem	past participle
-u	*rendre*	rend-	rend**u**
	rompre	romp-	romp**u**
	battre	batt-	batt**u**

		truncated stem	past participle
-is	*prendre*	pr-	pr**is**
	mettre	m-	m**is**

(4) *-oudre* verbs, apart from *-soudre,* have *-u* past participles formed using the stem of the present tense plurals:[8]

		present plural stem	past participle
-u	*coudre*	cous-	cous**u**
	moudre	moul-	moul**u**
-s / -te	*absoudre*	absolv-	abso**us** (feminine: abso**ute**)

As noted earlier, *absoudre* is the only French verb whose feminine past participle is not formed in a regular manner from the masculine. The past participles for *dissoudre* are analogous, while for *résoudre* the situation is more complex, as it offers two completely different past participles:

(a) the analogous *résous* (feminine: *résoute*) representing "to change or convert (into)", as in "fog resolved (changed) into rain".

(b) the *normal* past participle, however, is *résolu* in the sense of "to resolve a problem", "to resolve to do something".

(5) *-oire* and *-ître* verbs—and *-aire* verbs other than *faire* and *traire*—have *-u* past participles, with the *-u* added to a truncated consonant stem. The past participles of *faire* and *traire* are *fait* and *trait.*[9]

---

[7] Corresponding to English ***pris**on* and ***mis**sion.*

[8] The past participles for *coudre* and *moudre* thus preserve the "etymological" stem consonants (see the Introduction).

[9] Corresponding etymologically to *feat/fact* and *trait/tract.*

		truncated stem	past participle
-u	*boire*	b-	b**u**
	croire	cr-	cr**u**
	croître	cr-	cr**û** (not *cr**u**)
	accroître	accr-	accr**u**
	connaître	conn-	conn**u**
	plaire	pl-	pl**u**[10]
	taire	t-	t**u**
-it	*faire*	fa-	fa**it**
	traire	tra-	tra**it**

(6) *Suivre* and *vivre,* which have identical present tense conjugations, have markedly different past participles:

		infinitive stem	past participle
-i	*suivre*	suiv-	suiv**i**

		irregular stem	past participle
-u	*vivre*	véc-	véc**u**

(7) *-(C)ire* verbs use a reduced stem equal to the infinitive minus *-ire.* The endings can be *-it, -i, -is,* or *-u:*

		reduced stem	past participle
-it	*dire*	d-	d**it**
	écrire	écr-	écr**it**
	confire[11]	conf-	conf**it**
-i	*suffire*	suff-	suff**i**
	rire	r-	r**i**
-is	*circoncire*	circonc-	circonc**is**
-u	*lire*	l-	l**u**

[10] Note that the past participle of *plaire* is identical to that of *pleuvoir: le fait qu'il a* ***plu*** *m'a* ***plu*** ("the fact that it *rained pleased* me"). The simple past and imperfect subjunctive of *pleuvoir* (*il plut, il plût*) are likewise identical to the corresponding forms of *plaire.*

[11] In practical terms, *confire* exists only through the past participle *confit* ("pickled", "preserved", "crystallized")—e.g., *confit de canard, des cerises confites.* It corresponds to English *comfit* and *confit.*

Within this category, there is a useful "rule" for distinguishing between (and remembering) verbs which have past participles that end in *-i* and *-it: -it* past participles are associated with *transitive* verbs, *-i* past participles with *intransitive* ones. Since past participles of transitive verbs can be used as *feminine* adjectives (see Chapter 10), one can take advantage of the following memory aids (where the final *-t* of the feminine past participle is pronounced):[12]

à l'heure *di**te***	"at the *stated* (agreed) time"
la langue *écri**te***	"the *written* language"
cerise *confi**te***	"cherry *comfit*"

(8) *-uire* verbs also use a reduced stem equal to the infinitive minus *-ire.* The past participle ending is most commonly *-it,* the exceptions being *nuire* and *luire,* whose past participles end in *-i.*

		reduced stem	past participle
-it	*conduire*	condu-	condu**it**
	construire	constru-	constru**it**
	détruire	détru-	détru**it**
	cuire	cu-	cu**it**
-i	*nuire*	nu-	nu**i**
	luire	lu-	lu**i**

As in (7) above, in this group one can also distinguish between *-it* and *-i* verbs according to whether they are *transitive* or *intransitive,* respectively. For the *-it* past participles, one can make use of the following memory aids:[13]

une voiture *condui**te*** par le roi	"a car *driven* by the king"
une maison bien *construi**te***	"a well-*constructed* house"
une maison *détrui**te***	"a *destroyed* house"
terre *cui**te***	"*baked* clay", "terra *cotta*"

For *cuire* an additional aid is Fr./Eng. *biscuit,* which literally means "twice *cooked*".

[12] In the "old" days, the past participles of *suffire* and *rire* also ended in *-it.* However, as intransitive verbs they could not be used in (feminine) adjectival constructions, leading to the eventual disappearance of the final *-t.*

[13] While the English counterpart of *nuire* ("to harm") is a transitive verb, in French the object which is *harmed* is preceded by the preposition *à,* so that the object is *indirect* (see Chapter 10) and cannot be used in adjectival expressions: *Fumer* ***nuit À*** *la santé* ("Smoking *harms* health"). *Luire* ("to shine", "to glow") is purely intransitive. In Old French, the past participles of both verbs ended in *-it.*

(9) *-clure* verbs have past participles ending in *-us* or *-u*, added to a reduced stem equal to the infinitive minus *-ure:*

		reduced stem	past participle
-us	*inclure*	incl-	incl**us**
	occlure	occl-	occl**us**
-u	*conclure*	conclu-	conclu
	exclure	exclu-	exclu

The past participles for *inclure* and *exclure* are easily remembered: *inclure* includes the *-s*, *exclure* excludes it. In Old French, the past participles for all of these verbs had *-us*, but a competing form without the *-s* eventually drove out the "classical" forms for *conclure* and *exclure*. Remnants of the old past participles with *-s* can be seen in the derived words *conclu**s**ion* and *exclu**s**ion*, as well as in English *sluice.*[14]

(10) *Vaincre* has a *-u* past participle, with infinitive stem:

		infinitive stem	past participle
-u	*vaincre*	vainc-	vainc**u**

C3. *-ir* Verbs (Not of Class II)

(1) *-illir* verbs have *-i* past participles with a regular stem:

		infinitive stem	past participle
-i	*assaillir*	assaill-	assailli
	bouillir	bouill-	bouilli
	cueillir	cueill-	cueilli
	défaillir	défaill-	défailli

Note that *bouillir*—whose present tense differs from other Class III *-illir* verbs—is no exception.

[14] Initially *eau excluse* ("excluded water"), taken into English in the fourteenth century as *scluse.* In modern French the noun has become *écluse.*

(2) "Classical" *-ir* verbs having the form *-(CC)ir* have *-i* past participles and normal stems; also *fuir:*

		infinitive stem	past participle
-i	*partir*	part-	part**i**
	sortir	sort-	sort**i**
	sentir	sent-	sent**i**
	mentir	ment-	ment**i**
	repentir	repent-	repent**i**
	servir	serv-	serv**i**
	dormir	dorm-	dorm**i**
	fuir	fu-	fu**i**

(3) *Acquérir* is the only *-ir* verb with an *-is* past participle; like other *-is* participles (*mis, pris*), the stem is truncated:

		truncated stem	past participle
-is	*acquérir*	acqu-	acqu**is**

It is easily remembered because of its similarity to English ***acquis****ition.*

(4) *Mourir* and *couvrir* have *-t* past participles, added to the stems *mor-* and *couver-:*

		p.p. stem	past participle
-t	*mourir*	mor-	mor**t**
	couvrir	couver-	couver**t**

Mort is easily remembered because of the related word ***mort****al* (*mortel* in French), while *couvert* corresponds to English *covert* and *covered.* Using the infinitive stem for *couvrir* would give the unpronounceable **couvrt,* hence the addition of an *-e.*

(5) *Tenir/venir, courir,* and *vêtir* have *-u* past participles, using the infinitive stem:

		infinitive stem	past participle
-u	*tenir*	ten-	ten**u**
	venir	ven-	ven**u**
	courir	cour-	cour**u**
	vêtir	vêt-	vêt**u**

CHAPTER 4

Simple Past (*Passé Simple*)

There are four different sets of endings for the simple past:

	"*bare*" endings	-*a* endings	-*i* endings	-*u* endings
je	-s	-*ai*	-is	-us
tu	-s	-as	-is	-us
il, elle	-t	-*a*	-it	-ut
nous	-^mes	-âmes	-îmes	-ûmes
vous	-^tes	-âtes	-îtes	-ûtes
ils, elles	-rent	-*èrent*	-irent	-urent

For the "bare" endings the ^ indicates that a circumflex is placed on the preceding vowel (e.g., *vin*- + ^*mes* → *vînmes*).[1] Note that the -*i* and -*u* endings are derived directly from the corresponding "bare" endings, while for the -*a* endings there are three differences:

(a) first person singular -*ai*
(b) third person singular -*a* (not *-*at*)
(c) third person plural -*èrent.*

There is generally a very close link between the form of the past participle and that of the simple past. For the purpose of the simple past, it is useful to partition verbs into the following six groups:

1. -*er* verbs (Class I + *aller*)
2. -*i past participle* verbs—past participles ending in -*i*, -*is*, or -*it*
3. -*u past participle* verbs—past participles ending in -*u* or -*us*
4. -*rt past participle* verbs—past participles ending in -*rt*
5. -*indre* verbs (*plaindre, peindre, joindre*)
6. *être* and *naître*—the only non-*er* verbs with past participles ending in -*é*.

[1] For the second person plurals, the circumflex represents a "real" -*s* which disappeared—e.g., for the -*a* endings the Old French form was -*astes*. For the first person plurals, the -*s* was introduced in imitation of the second person plural *written* form at a time (thirteenth century) when the latter's pronunciation of -*s* had already been lost: the initial Old French form for the -*a* endings was -*ames,* later -*asmes.*

Using this partition, we can establish the following patterns for the simple past tense endings:

group #	simple past endings (type)
1.	*-a*
2.	*-i*
3.	*-u, -i, "bare"*
4.	*-u, -i*
5.	*-i*
6.	*-u, -i*

The appropriate endings are in the large majority of cases added to the *past participle stem.*

Group 1: *-er* Verbs

All *-er* verbs, including *aller,* use *-a* simple past endings added to the *past participle stem* ("p.p. stem").[2] Examples:

	parler	*céder*	*aller*
p.p. stem	parl-	céd-	all-
je	parl**ai**	céd**ai**	all**ai**
tu	parl**as**	céd**as**	all**as**
il, elle	parl**a**	céd**a**	all**a**
nous	parl**âmes**	céd**âmes**	all**âmes**
vous	parl**âtes**	céd**âtes**	all**âtes**
ils, elles	parl**èrent**	céd**èrent**	all**èrent**

Group 2: Past Participles Ending in *-i, -is,* or *-it*

These verbs use *-i* simple past tense endings which, with three exceptions, are added to the *past participle stem.* Note that all Class II verbs—i.e., those which have extended *-s* present tense endings—are included in this group.[3] Examples:

	finir (Class II)	*partir*	*bouillir*
p.p. stem	fin-	part-	bouill-
je	fin**is**	part**is**	bouill**is**
tu	fin**is**	part**is**	bouill**is**

[2] For *-er* verbs the past participle stem is equal to the infinitive stem.

[3] For *haïr,* the first and second person plurals (*haïmes, haïtes*) have no circumflex, since the *-i* already has a dieresis (¨).

il, elle	fin**it**	part**it**	bouill**it**
nous	fin**îmes**	part**îmes**	bouill**îmes**
vous	fin**îtes**	part**îtes**	bouill**îtes**
ils, elles	fin**irent**	part**irent**	bouill**irent**

	asseoir[4]	*prendre*	*mettre*
p.p. stem	ass-	pr-	m-
je	ass**is**	pr**is**	m**is**
tu	ass**is**	pr**is**	m**is**
il, elle	ass**it**	pr**it**	m**it**
nous	ass**îmes**	pr**îmes**	m**îmes**
vous	ass**îtes**	pr**îtes**	m**îtes**
ils, elles	ass**irent**	pr**irent**	m**irent**

	dire	*suffire*	*suivre*
p.p. stem	d-	suff-	suiv-
je	**dis**	suff**is**	suiv**is**
tu	**dis**	suff**is**	suiv**is**
il, elle	**dit**	suff**it**	suiv**it**
nous	**dîmes**	suff**îmes**	suiv**îmes**
vous	**dîtes**	suff**îtes**	suiv**îtes**
ils, elles	**dirent**	suff**irent**	suiv**irent**

The second person plural for *dire* is pronounced identically to the present (*vous dites*).

The three exceptions—in terms of their stems, not the endings used—are *faire* with stem *f-* and *conduire* and *écrire*, which use their *present plural stem* (*nous* ***conduis****ons*, ***écriv****ons*).

	faire	*conduire*	*écrire*
stem	f-	condui**S**-	écri**V**-
je	**fis**	conduis**is**	écriv**is**
tu	**fis**	conduis**is**	écriv**is**
il, elle	**fit**	conduis**it**	écriv**it**
nous	**fîmes**	conduis**îmes**	écriv**îmes**
vous	**fîtes**	conduis**îtes**	écriv**îtes**
ils, elles	**firent**	conduis**irent**	écriv**irent**

[4] *Asseoir*, which in most other tenses has two forms, has only one for its simple past.

Note that for all Class II verbs, the three singulars have identical present and simple pasts:

	present	*simple past*
je	finis	finis
tu	finis	finis
il, elle	finit	finit

This is also the case for *dire* (*je dis, tu dis, il dit*) and *rire* (*je ris, tu ris, il rit*).

Group 3: Past Participles Ending in *-u* or *-us*

The majority of verb types within this group use *-u* simple past endings, in each case added to the past participle stem.

	vouloir	*mouvoir*	*devoir*	*avoir*
p.p. stem	voul-	m-	d-	(e)-
je	voul**us**	m**us**	d**us**	e**us**
tu	voul**us**	m**us**	d**us**	e**us**
il, elle	voul**ut**	m**ut**	d**ut**	e**ut**
nous	voul**ûmes**	m**ûmes**	d**ûmes**	e**ûmes**
vous	voul**ûtes**	m**ûtes**	d**ûtes**	e**ûtes**
ils, elles	voul**urent**	m**urent**	d**urent**	e**urent**

	moudre	*croire*	*croître*	*courir*
p.p. stem	moul-	cr-	cr^-	cour-
je	moul**us**	cr**us**	*cr**ûs***	cour**us**
tu	moul**us**	cr**us**	*cr**ûs***	cour**us**
il, elle	moul**ut**	cr**ut**	*cr**ût***	cour**ut**
nous	moul**ûmes**	cr**ûmes**	cr**ûmes**	cour**ûmes**
vous	moul**ûtes**	cr**ûtes**	cr**ûtes**	cour**ûtes**
ils, elles	moul**urent**	cr**urent**	*cr**ûrent***	cour**urent**

Note that for *croître* a circumflex is placed on *all* conjugations in order to distinguish it from *croire*—to no avail in the first and second person plurals. The other verbs which have circumflexes in their past participles (*devoir* and *mouvoir*) do not carry these over to the simple past. For *avoir*, as for its past participle *eu*, the initial *e-* in the simple past is a relic and is not pronounced.

Seven verbs (or verb types) in this group shift to *-i* simple past endings, and one uses "bare" endings. For all of the verbs shifting to *-i* endings, the past participle stem is used:

	voir	*rendre*[5]	*rompre*
p.p. stem	v-	rend-	romp-
je	v**is**	rend**is**	romp**is**
tu	v**is**	rend**is**	romp**is**
il, elle	v**it**	rend**it**	romp**it**
nous	v**îmes**	rend**îmes**	romp**îmes**
vous	v**îtes**	rend**îtes**	romp**îtes**
ils, elles	v**irent**	rend**irent**	romp**irent**

	battre	*coudre*	*vaincre*
p.p. stem	batt-	cous-	vainc- (vainqu-)
je	batt**is**	cous**is**	vainqu**is**
tu	batt**is**	cous**is**	vainqu**is**
il, elle	batt**it**	cous**it**	vainqu**it**
nous	batt**îmes**	cous**îmes**	vainqu**îmes**
vous	batt**îtes**	cous**îtes**	vainqu**îtes**
ils, elles	batt**irent**	cous**irent**	vainqu**irent**

	vêtir
p.p. stem	vêt-
je	vêt**is**
tu	vêt**is**
il, elle	vêt**it**
nous	vêt**îmes**
vous	vêt**îtes**
ils, elles	vêt**irent**

Note that *je vis, tu vis, il vit* can be either the simple past of *voir* or the present of *vivre.* The other *-voir* ("see") verbs also shift to *-i* endings, except for *pourvoir,* which maintains *-u* endings.[6] For *vaincre,* the *-qu* in place of *-c* is a normal orthographic change to maintain the hard "C" sound (Chapter 8).

[5] Simple pasts like *rendre:* all verbs ending in *-endre* (other than *prendre*), *-andre, -ondre, -erdre,* and *-ordre.*

[6] All of the "nonseeing" *-voir* verbs follow the general rule and have *-u* endings.

Tenir/venir use "bare" endings, with the past participle stem changing its vowel from *-e* to *-i:*

	tenir	*venir*
e → i	tIn-	vIn-
je	tin**s**	vin**s**
tu	tin**s**	vin**s**
il, elle	tin**t**	vin**t**
nous	tîn**mes**	vîn**mes**
vous	tîn**tes**	vîn**tes**
ils, elles	tin**rent**	vin**rent**

Note the circumflex on the preceding stem vowel for the first and second person plurals.

Group 4: Past Participles Ending in *-rt*

Couvrir (and related verbs) uses *-i* endings; *mourir* uses *-u* endings. In both cases the endings are added to the *infinitive stem* rather than to the past participle stem.

	couvrir (I)	*mourir* (U)
(past participle	couvert	mort)
infinitive stem	couvr-	mour-
je	couvr**is**	mour**us**
tu	couvr**is**	mour**us**
il, elle	couvr**it**	mour**ut**
nous	couvr**îmes**	mour**ûmes**
vous	couvr**îtes**	mour**ûtes**
ils, elles	couvr**irent**	mour**urent**

Group 5: *-indre* Verbs

All of these verbs have *-i* simple past endings, added to the *present plural stem* (*nous* ***plaign****ons*, ***peign****ons*, ***joign****ons*) rather than to the past participle stem:

	plaindre	*peindre*	*joindre*
(past participle	plaint	peint	joint)
present plural stem	plaign-	peign-	joign-
je	plaign**is**	peign**is**	joign**is**
tu	plaign**is**	peign**is**	joign**is**

il, elle	plaign**it**	peign**it**	joign**it**
nous	plaign**îmes**	peign**îmes**	joign**îmes**
vous	plaign**îtes**	peign**îtes**	joign**îtes**
ils, elles	plaign**irent**	peign**irent**	joign**irent**

Group 6: *être/natre*

Être has *-u* endings added to the stem *f-; naître* uses *-i* endings and the stem *naqu-:*

	être (U)	*naître* (I)
stem	f-	naqu-
je	f**us**	naqu**is**
tu	f**us**	naqu**is**
il, elle	f**ut**	naqu**it**
nous	f**ûmes**	naqu**îmes**
vous	f**ûtes**	naqu**îtes**
ils, elles	f**urent**	naqu**irent**

The *-qu* in the simple past for *naître* is really a hard "C". The *f-* in the simple past for *être* goes back to the original Latin, where the verb ESSE ("to be"), like its English counterpart, took elements from different sources.

Summary

The simple past for 97 percent of verbs is provided by the following *basic rule:*

BASIC RULE FOR SIMPLE PAST

simple past group	simple past endings	stem
1. *-er* verbs	*-a*	past participle
2. *-i* past participle verbs	*-i*	past participle
3. *-u* past participle verbs	*-u*	past participle

Exceptions to the basic rule—and cases not covered by it—are shown below:

SIMPLE PAST: EXCEPTIONS TO *BASIC RULE*

	-oir	***-re***		***-ir***	
-*u* past participle → -*i* or "*bare*" endings	voir (v**I**-)	rendre	(rend**I**-)	venir	(v**in**-)
		rompre	(romp**I**-)	tenir	(**tin**-)
		battre	(batt**I**-)	vêtir	(vêt**I**-)
		coudre	(cous**I-**)		
		vaincre	(vain**quI**-)		
stem ≠ pp. stem		faire	(**fI**-)		
		écrire	(écri**vI**-)		
		conduire	(condui**sI**-)		
simple past groups 4–6		naître	(na**quI**-)	couvrir	(couvr**I**-)
		plaindre	(plai**gnI**-)	mourir	(mour**U**-)
		être	(**fU**-)		

Note that the simple past is almost always immediately recognizable by its similarity to the past participle, infinitive, or present plural. There are only six exceptions: ***être, faire, voir, tenir, venir, naître:*** **f-, fi-, v-, tin-, vin-, naqu-.**

CHAPTER 5

Future and Conditional Tenses

The future and conditional endings for *all* verbs are as follows:

future	conditional
-ai	-ais
-as	-ais
-a	-ait
-ons	-ions
-ez	-iez
-ont	-aient

To form the future and conditional tenses, these endings are added to a common stem, which we will call the *future stem.*

General patterns for the future stem:

1. for Class I and II verbs, it is the infinitive;
2. among *-oir* verbs, only *pourvoir, prévoir,* and *surseoir* use the infinitive, while all others use a shortened or otherwise modified stem;
3. for *-re* verbs, it is the infinitive *minus* the final *-e* (e.g., *rendre* → *rendr-*);
4. for Class III *-ir* verbs, it is generally the infinitive.

Rule. If we define the *infiitivẹ)* to be the infinitive minus the final *-e,* if any, then the situation is as follows:

FUTURE STEMS WHICH ARE *NOT* THE *infinitiv(e)*

-er	*-oir*	*-re*	*-ir*
aller	ALL except *pourvoir,*	être	acquérir
envoyer	*prévoir, surseoir*	faire	courir
			cueillir
			mourir
			tenir/venir

Examples of regular futures and conditionals, using the *infinitiv(e)* as stem:

	parler (Class I)		finir (Class II)	
	future	*conditional*	*future*	*conditional*
je	parler**ai**	parler**ais**	finir**ai**	finir**ais**
tu	parler**as**	parler**ais**	finir**as**	finir**ais**
il, elle	parler**a**	parler**ait**	finir**a**	finir**ait**
nous	parler**ons**	parler**ions**	finir**ons**	finir**ions**
vous	parler**ez**	parler**iez**	finir**ez**	finir**iez**
ils, elles	parler**ont**	parler**aient**	finir**ont**	finir**aient**

	prévoir		prendre	
	future	*conditional*	*future*	*conditional*
je	prévoir**ai**	prévoir**ais**	prendr**ai**	prendr**ais**
tu	prévoir**as**	prévoir**ais**	prendr**as**	prendr**ais**
il, elle	prévoir**a**	prévoir**ait**	prendr**a**	prendr**ait**
nous	prévoir**ons**	prévoir**ions**	prendr**ons**	prendr**ions**
vous	prévoir**ez**	prévoir**iez**	prendr**ez**	prendr**iez**
ils, elles	prévoir**ont**	prévoir**aient**	prendr**ont**	prendr**aient**

Note that:

1. The endings for the future tense are essentially equal to the *present* tense of the verb *avoir:*

j'	ai	=	-ai
tu	as	=	-as
il, elle	a	=	-a
nous	(av)ons	→	-ons
vous	(av)ez	→	-ez
ils, elles	ont	=	-ont

2. The endings for the conditional tense are *identical* to those of the *imperfect* tense (of *avoir* and all other verbs). Note that for most verbs these endings added to the *infinitive stem* give the *imperfect,* added to the *infinitiv(e)* give the *conditional.*

3. For the future, the second and third person singulars have the same pronunciation, as do the first and third person plurals.

4. For the conditional, the three singulars and third person plural are pronounced the same.

5. For the first person singular, the future and conditional are pronounced identically.[1]

We will see in the appendix to this chapter that 1 and 2 did not arise by coincidence but instead reflect the historical development of these verb forms.

The table below gives the future stem—the conditional stem is always the same—for verbs which do not use the *infinitiv(e)*. Also shown is the first person singular future and conditional.

	infinitive	future stem	future (je)	conditional (je)
-*er* verbs	aller	ir-	irai	irais
	envoyer	enverr-	enverrai	enverrais
-*oir* verbs	voir	verr-	verrai	verrais
	avoir	aur-	aurai	aurais
	savoir	saur-	saurai	saurais
	mouvoir	mouvr-	mouvrai	mouvrais
	devoir	devr-	devrai	devrais
	recevoir	recevr-	recevrai	recevrais
	pleuvoir	pleuvr-	*il* pleuvra	*il* pleuvrait
	pouvoir	pourr-	pourrai	pourrais
	falloir	faudr-	*il* faudra	*il* faudrait
	valoir	vaudr-	vaudrai	vaudrais
	vouloir	voudr-	voudrai	voudrais
	asseoir (A)	assiér-	assiérai	assiérais
	asseoir (B)	assoir-	assoirai	assoirais
-*re* verbs	être	ser-	serai	serais
	faire	fer-	ferai	ferais
-*ir* verbs	acquérir	acquerr-	acquerrai	acquerrais
	courir	courr-	courrai	courrais
	mourir	mourr-	mourrai	mourrais
	cueillir	cueill**er**-	cueillerai	cueillerais
	venir	viendr-	viendrai	viendrais

[1] In the not-too-distant past, it was taught that the pronunciation of the final vowel in the first person singular future could be distinguished from that in the conditional, the former being "closed" [É] and the latter "open" [È].

-er Verbs

The future stem for *aller* comes from the infinitive of the Latin verb "to go": IRE. The irregular future stem for *envoyer* (and *renvoyer*) arose from the perceived relationship with *voir*, whose future stem is *verr-*. Thus, when trying to figure out what the future stem of *envoyer* was (or should be),

	present			*future*
voir	tu vois	[voi]		tu verras
	nous voyons	[voy•on]		nous verrons
envoyer	tu envoies	[en•voi]	→	[???]
	nous envoyons	[en•voy•on]	→	[???]

the deduction made was that it was *enverr-*.[2]

-oir Verbs

Only *pourvoir, prévoir,* and *surseoir* use the infinitive as their future stem. *Entrevoir* and *revoir* follow the example of *voir,* with irregular stems *entreverr-* and *reverr-*. In both *avoir* and *savoir,* the *avoir* becomes *aur-*. The other "non-seeing" *-voir* verbs have shortened stems ending in *-vr,* apart from *pouvoir,* whose stem ends in *-rr.* For *falloir, valoir,* and *vouloir* the stem is shortened and a "helping" *-d* is added.[3] *Asseoir* offers two different future stems, the second of which is regular in pronunciation but does not reproduce the extraneous *-e* of the infinitive. By contrast, *surseoir* uses the full infinitive stem (*je surseoirai, je surseoirais*).

-re Verbs

Only two verbs have irregular future stems: *être* (*ser-*) and *faire* (*fer-*). All others use the infinitive minus final *-e.*

---

[2] There is in fact no relationship between the two verbs: *envoyer* comes from Latin VIA ("way", "road"), *voir* from VIDERE ("to see").

[3] In Old French the *-au* of the stem was still *-al.* Thus, *falr-* became *faldr-* and eventually *faudr-*, and similarly for the other two.

-ir Verbs

Five verbs have irregular future stems. For *acquérir, courir,* and *mourir,* the final *-rir* of the infinitive becomes *-rr,* and for *acquérir* the *-é* loses its accent.[4]

Cueiller- has successfully resisted efforts at regularization, thus leading to the contrast:

infinitive	*future stem*
assaillir	assaillir-
bouillir	bouillir-
défaillir	défaillir-
cueillir	cueiller- (*not* *cueillir-)

Tenir/venir takes the vowel *-ie* from its irregular present tense stem (*je **tiens**, **viens***) and adds a "helping" *-d* to facilitate the pronunciation of the combination *-nr.*[5]

Appendix
Historical and Methodological Note

The Latin future tense died, leaving almost no trace in the successor Romance languages.[6] The main reason for its disappearance was that phonetic developments during the post-Classical period had created confusions between it and other verb tenses.

A new Romance future tense arose as a refinement of a construction which had already existed in Classical Latin: the combination of the verb *to have* (or "have to") with another verb to convey an idea of what will happen (or has to happen) in the future. Thus, Cicero wrote to his friend Atticus:

DE RE PUBLICA NIHIL HABEO AD TE SCRIBERE

"Of public matters I have nothing to write you."

---

[4] As explained in Chapter 8, since the *-e* now finds itself in a *closed* syllable, its pronunciation changes to [È]; accordingly, it must surrender its *acute* accent.

[5] Analogous to the *-d* in English *thunder* (Middle English *thunre*).

[6] Among the few exceptions: (a) Eng./Fr. *placebo,* from Latin PLACEBO ("I will please"); and (b) Eng./Fr. *lavabo* ("washbowl", "sink"), from the use of Latin LAVABO ("I will wash") in the liturgical expression:

LAVABO IN INNOCENTIA MANUS MEAS . . .

I will wash mine hands in innocency . . . (Psalms 26:6)

The meaning of this differs very little from the straightforward future:

> "Of public matters I *will write* nothing to you."

Similarly, *I have to go to Rome tomorrow* is not too distant in meaning from *I am going* (will go) *to Rome tomorrow.*

The modern form of the Romance future arose from the custom of placing the verb "to have" (present tense) after the infinitive. Thus:

partir + ai	→	partirai
partir + as	→	partiras
partir + a	→	partira
partir + (av)ons	→	partirons
partir + (av)ez	→	partirez
partir + ont	→	partiront

Classical Latin had no single verb form corresponding to the notion of a "future in the past" (e.g., *he said he* ***would leave*** *Rome the next day*). The Romance development of the future tense led naturally to the development of a future *in the past* by replacing the present of the verb *avoir* with the imperfect. Thus, the natural progression in meaning was:

"I told you that I *had to leave.*" → "I told you that I *would leave.*"

In French and most of the other Romance languages the *conditional* tense—originally limited to the past—was thus formed through a fusion of the infinitive with the imperfect of *avoir.*

partir + (av)ais	→	partirais
partir + (av)ais	→	partirais
partir + (av)ait	→	partirait
partir + (av)ions	→	partirions
partir + (av)iez	→	partiriez
partir + (av)aient	→	partiraient

While Class I and II verbs continue to use the full infinitive as their future stem, many Class III verbs have shortened or otherwise modified the stem. For example, for *mourir* and *suivre:*

mourir + ai	→	*mourirai	→	mourrai
suivre + ai	→	*suivreai	→	suivrai

CHAPTER 6

Subjunctive and Imperative

Present Subjunctive

The present subjunctive endings for all but two verbs (*être, avoir*) are:

	subjunctive endings
je	-e
tu	-es
il, elle	-e
nous	-ions
vous	-iez
ils, elles	-ent

The formation of the present subjunctive is governed by the following rule.

Rule. The present subjunctive for the three singulars and third person plural uses the 3p (*ils*) present stem, while the 1p (*nous*) stem is used for the first and second person plurals.

Exceptions (9): *être, avoir, savoir, pouvoir, faire, aller, falloir, valoir, vouloir.*

Present subjunctives are thus divided into two groups, according to whether they have one or two stems.

A. One Stem: Identical Stems for *Nous* and *Ils* Forms of Present Indicative

This group includes all Class I and II verbs and most Class III verbs.

		parler (Class I)	*finir* (Class II)	*partir*
	ils	parl-ent	finiss-ent	part-ent
	nous	parl-ons	finiss-ons	part-ons
je		parl**e**	finiss**e**	part**e**
tu		parl**es**	finiss**es**	part**es**
il, elle		parl**e**	finiss**e**	part**e**

nous		parl**ions**	finiss**ions**	part**ions**
vous		parl**iez**	finiss**iez**	part**iez**
ils, elles		parl**ent**	finiss**ent**	part**ent**

		asseoir (A)	*moudre*	*joindre*
	ils	assey-ent	moul-ent	joign-ent
	nous	assey-ons	moul-ons	joign-ons
je		assey**e**	moul**e**	joign**e**
tu		assey**es**	moul**es**	joign**es**
il, elle		assey**e**	moul**e**	joign**e**
nous		assey**ions**	moul**ions**	joign**ions**
vous		assey**ez**	moul**iez**	joign**iez**
ils, elles		assey**ent**	moul**ent**	joign**ent**

		rendre	*dire*	*couvrir*
	ils	rend-ent	dis-ent	couvr-ent
	nous	rend-ons	dis-ons	couvr-ons
je		rend**e**	dis**e**	couvr**e**
tu		rend**es**	dis**es**	couvr**es**
il, elle		rend**e**	dis**e**	couvr**e**
nous		rend**ions**	dis**ions**	couvr**ions**
vous		rend**iez**	dis**iez**	couvr**iez**
ils, elles		rend**ent**	dis**ent**	couvr**ent**

B. Two Stems: Different Stems for *Nous* and *Ils* Forms of Present Indicative

This group consists of Class III verbs that have orthographic *i* – *y* alternation in their present indicative stems, as well as those displaying *vowel* variation. Examples:

		voir	*croire*	*mouvoir*
	ils	voi-ent	croi-ent	meuv-ent
	nous	*voy*-ons	*croy*-ons	*mouv*-ons
je		voie	croie	meuve
tu		voies	croies	meuves
il, elle		voie	croie	meuve

nous		*voy**ions***	*croy**ions***	*mouv**ions***
vous		*voy**iez***	*croy**iez***	*mouv**iez***
ils, elles		voi**ent**	croi**ent**	meuv**ent**

		devoir	*prendre*	*boire*
	ils	doiv-ent	prenn-ent	boiv-ent
	nous	*dev*-ons	*pren*-ons	*buv*-ons
je		doiv**e**	prenn**e**	boiv**e**
tu		doiv**es**	prenn**es**	boiv**es**
il, elle		doiv**e**	prenn**e**	boiv**e**
nous		*dev**ions***	*pren**ions***	*buv**ions***
vous		*dev**iez***	*pren**iez***	*buv**iez***
ils, elles		doiv**ent**	prenn**ent**	boiv**ent**

		acquérir	*mourir*	*venir*
	ils	acquièr-ent	meur-ent	vienn-ent
	nous	*acquér*-ons	*mour*-ons	*ven*-ons
je		acquièr**e**	meur**e**	vienn**e**
tu		acquièr**es**	meur**es**	vienn**es**
il, elle		acquièr**e**	meur**e**	vienn**e**
nous		*acquér**ions***	*mour**ions***	*ven**ions***
vous		*acquér**iez***	*mour**iez***	*ven**iez***
ils, elles		acquièr**ent**	meur**ent**	vienn**ent**

Note that (apart from the nine exceptions given below):

(a) The present subjunctive for the third person plural is *always* equal to the corresponding *present indicative.*

(b) For Class I verbs this equality extends to the three singulars, thus giving four forms which are identical to the present indicative. This is also the case for the 16 *-ir* verbs which have *-e* endings in the present indicative (e.g., *couvrir, cueillir*).

(c) For all verbs, the present subjunctives for the first and second person plural are equal to the corresponding *imperfect* (indicative).

(d) For all verbs, the present subjunctives for the three singulars and third person plural are *pronounced* identically.

C. Nine Verbs with Irregular Present Subjunctives

	être soi- / *soy-*	*avoir* ai- / *ay-*	*savoir* sach-
je	soi**S**	ai**e**	sach**e**
tu	sois	ai**es**	sach**es**
il, elle	soi**T**	ai**T**	sach**e**
nous	*soyons*	*ayons*	sach**ions**
vous	*soyez*	*ayez*	sach**iez**
ils, elles	soi**ent**	ai**ent**	sach**ent**

	pouvoir puiss-	*faire* fass-	*aller* aill- / *all-*
je	puiss**e**	fass**e**	aill**e**
tu	puiss**es**	fass**es**	aill**es**
il, elle	puiss**e**	fass**e**	aill**e**
nous	puiss**ions**	fass**ions**	*all**ions***
vous	puiss**iez**	fass**iez**	*all**iez***
ils, elles	puiss**ent**	fass**ent**	aill**ent**

	falloir faill-	*valoir* vaill- / *val-*	*vouloir* veuill- / *voul-*
je	—	vaill**e**	veuill**e**
tu	—	vaill**es**	veuill**es**
il, elle	faill**e**	vaill**e**	veuill**e**
nous	—	*val**ions***	*voul**ions***
vous	—	*val**iez***	*voul**iez***
ils, elles	—	vaill**ent**	veuill**ent**

Note that:

(a) Normal subjunctive endings are used *except* for *être* and *avoir: je sois, il soit/il ait,* and the first two plurals (*-ons* and *-ez* rather than **-ions* and **-iez*).

(b) *Savoir, pouvoir,* and *faire* have uniform stems.

(c) The verbs with *-l* in the infinitive have two subjunctive stems, apart from the impersonal verb *falloir,* which is used only in the third person singular. The first and second person plurals are the same as the corresponding *imperfect* (indicative).

(d) While *équivaloir* and *revaloir* have subjunctives analogous to those of *valoir, prévaloir* has a completely regular subjunctive (*je prévale, tu prévales,* etc.).

Subjunctive: Imperfect Tense

The imperfect subjunctive is completely determined by the corresponding form of the simple past:

(1) the stem is identical to that of the simple past;
(2) the endings correspond to those used for the simple past, as indicated in the table below.

There are no exceptions.[1]

	"*bare*" endings	-*a* endings	-*i* endings	-*u* endings
je	-sse	-asse	-isse	-usse
tu	-sses	-asses	-isses	-usses
il, elle	-ˆt	-ât	-ît	-ût
nous	-ssions	-assions	-issions	-ussions
vous	-ssiez	-assiez	-issiez	-ussiez
ils, elles	-ssent	-assent	-issent	-ussent

Examples:

	tenir	*parler* (Class I)	*finir* (Class II)	*valoir*
past stem	tin-	parl-	fin-	val-
je	tinsse	parlasse	finisse	valusse
tu	tinsses	parlasses	finisses	valusses
il, elle	tînt	parlât	finît	valût
nous	tinssions	parlassions	finissions	valussions
vous	tinssiez	parlassiez	finissiez	valussiez
ils, elles	tinssent	parlassent	finissent	valussent

	venir	*aller*	*rendre*	*être*
past stem	vin-	all-	rend-	f-
je	vinsse	allasse	rendisse	fusse
tu	vinsses	allasses	rendisses	fusses
il, elle	vînt	allât	rendît	fût
nous	vinssions	allassions	rendissions	fussions
vous	vinssiez	allassiez	rendissiez	fussiez
ils, elles	vinssent	allassent	rendissent	fussent

[1] For *haïr*, the third person singular (*haït*) has no circumflex, since the -*i* already has a dieresis (¨).

	revenir	*ressasser*	*conduire*	*avoir*
past stem	revin-	ressass-	conduis-	e-
je	revinsse	ressassasse	conduisisse	eusse
tu	revinsses	ressassasses	conduisisses	eusses
il, elle	revînt	ressassât	conduisît	eût
nous	revinssions	ressassassions	conduisissions	eussions
vous	revinssiez	ressassassiez	conduisissiez	eussiez
ils, elles	revinssent	ressassassent	conduisissent	eussent

Note that:

(a) The third person singular has no *-s* but instead a circumflex. For verbs using "bare", *-i,* and *-u* endings this circumflex is all that distinguishes it from the third person singular *simple past.*

(b) For Class II verbs, all forms apart from the third person singular are identical to those of the *present subjunctive.* The third person plural is identical to *both* the *present subjunctive* and the *present indicative* (e.g., *ils finissent, finissent, finissent*).

(c) Verbs with *-s* in the infinitive (e.g., *ressasser*) or simple past stem (e.g., *conduire*) have forms which are awkward to write (and to pronounce).

Imperative

Imperative statements are direct orders or commands:

you	Get out!
we	Let's go!

In French "you" commands can involve *tu* or *vous,* so that there are three grammatical persons in which the imperative is possible. Unlike other conjugated verb forms, personal pronouns are not used with the imperative:[2]

Viens avec moi!	"Come with me!" (*you* singular)
Allons à la plage!	"Let's go to the beach!"
Ne *faites* pas de bruit!	"Don't make noise!" (*you* plural)

[2] All three imperative forms have distinct pronunciations, so that, unlike the present indicative (*je chante, tu chantes, il chante, ils chantent*), there is no possibility of confusion.

Rule. 1. Imperatives for the first and second person plurals are identical to the corresponding present tense (indicative).

2. For the second person singular, *-er* verbs (including *aller*) lose the final *-s* of the present indicative. The same occurs for the 16 *-ir* verbs which use *-e* endings for their present tense. For all other verbs, the second person singular imperative is identical to the corresponding present indicative.

Exceptions (4): ***être, avoir, savoir, vouloir.***

Examples:

		parler (Class I)	*finir* (Class II)	*partir*	*couvrir*
2s present		parles	finis	pars	couvres
	(tu)	*parle*	finis	pars	*couvre*
	(nous)	parlons	finissons	partons	couvrons
	(vous)	parlez	finissez	partez	couvrez

		aller	*dire*	*faire*	*répondre*
2s present		vas	dis	fais	réponds
	(tu)	*va*	dis	fais	réponds
	(nous)	allons	disons	faisons	répondons
	(vous)	allez	***dites***	***faites***	répondez

Note that:

(a) The second person plural for *dire* and *faire* reproduces the irregularity of the present tense and hence is consistent with the above rule.

(b) *Pouvoir* and *valoir*, whose second person singular present tense ends in *-x*, are not used in the imperative.

(c) Verbs which "lose" *-s* from the second person singular imperative have the *-s* restored when followed by one of the pronouns *y* or *en* (to which they are then connected by a hyphen):[3]

Va**s**-y tout de suite.	"Go there right away."
Mange**s**-en la moitié.	"Eat half of it."

[3] So long as an infinitive does not directly follow the *y* or *en*—*Va **y chercher** du repos* ("Go try to find some rest there").

Exceptions:

		être	*avoir*	*savoir*	*vouloir*
subjunctive stem		soi- / soy-	ai- / ay-	sach-	veuill- / voul-
	(tu)	sois	aie	sache	veuille, veux
	(nous)	soyons	ayons	sachons	——, voulons
	(vous)	soyez	ayez	sachez	veuillez, voulez

Note that:

(a) For *être,* the imperatives are identical to the corresponding present subjunctives.

(b) For *avoir,* the imperatives correspond to the present subjunctive, apart from the second person singular, which loses its final *-s.*

(c) For *savoir,* the subjunctive stem is used with endings *-e, -ons, -ez.*

(d) *Vouloir* offers two imperatives. The more common form uses the stem *veuill-* (the *nous* form does not exist).[4] It is typically used in forms of courtesy—for example, at the end of a letter:

Veuillez agréer l'expression de nos sentiments distingués et dévoués.

(literally: "Please accept the expression of our distinguished and devoted sentiments.")

The second form—identical to the present indicative—is essentially used only in negative imperatives: *ne m'en veux pas, ne m'en voulez pas* ("don't be angry with me").

[4] Note that the present subjunctive is not **vous veuilliez* (although it used to be) but *vous vouliez.*

CHAPTER 7

Compound Verb Forms

Compound verb tenses are formed by using the *past participle,* along with the appropriate form of an *auxiliary verb.* Depending on the verb and its use, the auxiliary verb can be either *avoir* or *être.*

	verb form	=	(form of) *avoir/être* + past participle
indicative			
	1. compound past		present
	2. past perfect		imperfect
	3. [past anterior]		simple past
	4. [double compound past]		compound past
	5. future perfect		future
	6. conditional perfect		conditional
subjunctive			
	7. past subjunctive		present subjunctive
	8. [past perfect subjunctive]		imperfect subjunctive
imperative			
	9. [past imperative]		imperative

With the virtual disappearance from the (spoken) language of the simple past and imperfect subjunctive, the past anterior and past perfect subjunctive have likewise fallen out of use. The double compound past (*passé surcomposé*) is considered nonstandard by many speakers (and authorities). The past imperative is very rare.

Two features (and challenges for the student) of French compound verbs are that:

(1) There are two different auxiliary verbs: *avoir* and *être*—some verbs use *avoir,* others *être.* In some cases, the same verb can be used (in different contexts) with either auxiliary:

Il est sorti.	"He went out."
Il a sorti les valises.	"He took out the suitcases."

(2) Used with *être*, the past participle agrees in gender and number with the subject; used with *avoir*, it agrees in gender and number with a preceding direct object:

Elle est sorti**e.**	"She went out."
Ils sont sorti**s.**	"They went out."
Les *valises* qu'il a sorti**es** . . .	"The suitcases which he took out . . ."

These issues are discussed in Chapter 10.

1. Compound Past

The compound past (*le passé composé*) is formed using the *present* tense of the auxiliary verb—*avoir* or *être,* as appropriate—with the past participle.

with *avoir*	with *être*		
j'ai chanté	je suis parti(**e**)	I *have*	sung/left
tu as chanté	tu es parti(**e**)	you *have*	sung/left
il (elle) a chanté	il (elle) est parti(**e**)	he (she) *has*	sung/left
nous avons chanté	nous sommes parti(**e**)**s**	we *have*	sung/left
vous avez chanté	vous êtes parti(**e**)(**s**)	you *have*	sung/left
ils (elles) ont chanté	ils (elles) sont parti(**e**)**s**	they *have*	sung/left

The *(e)* is included if the subject is feminine,[1] the *(s)* if *vous* is plural.[2] For *vous êtes* there are thus four possibilities for the ending of the past participle:

vous êtes parti	vous êtes parti**s**	masculine singular/plural
vous êtes parti**e**	vous êtes parti**es**	feminine singular/plural

As the *passé composé* has supplanted the *passé simple*—at least in the spoken language—it can also be translated as *I sang/I left*, etc.

2. Past Perfect (Pluperfect)

The past perfect (*le plus-que-parfait*), like its English counterpart, refers to situations existing prior to a fixed point in the past. It is formed analogously to the

[1] E.g., *Nous les femmes, nous sommes parti**es**.*

[2] *Vous* is used as a "general" second person *plural* and as a "formal" second person *singular.*

compound past, except that the present tense of *avoir* or *être* is replaced by the imperfect.

avoir/être (present)	+	past participle	→	compound past
avoir/être (imperfect)	+	past participle	→	past perfect

with *avoir*	with *être*		
j'avais chanté	j'étais parti(**e**)	I *had*	sung/left
tu avais chanté	tu étais parti(**e**)	you *had*	"
il (elle) avait chanté	il (elle) était parti(**e**)	he (she) *had*	"
nous avions chanté	nous étions parti(**e**)**s**	we *had*	"
vous aviez chanté	vous étiez parti(**e**)(**s**)	you *had*	"
ils (elles) avaient chanté	ils (elles) étaient parti(**e**)**s**	they *had*	"

3. [Past Anterior]

The past anterior (*le passé antérieur*) marks a past event *completed* prior to another past event and is formed using the simple past (*passé simple*) of the auxiliary verb. It is frequently accompanied by conjunctions of time (*quand, aussitôt que, dès que,* etc.). The past anterior can therefore often be translated by "had just (done something)". It is rarely used in modern speech (or writing), almost always being replaced by the *passé composé,* by a construction using the infinitive, or by the *passé surcomposé* (no. 4, below).

with *avoir*	with *être*			
j'eus chanté	je fus parti(**e**)	I	*had* just	sung/left
tu eus chanté	tu fus parti(**e**)	you	"	"
il (elle) eut chanté	il (elle) fut parti(**e**)	he (she)	"	"
nous eûmes chanté	nous fûmes parti(**e**)**s**	we	"	"
vous eûtes chanté	vous fûtes parti(**e**)(**s**)	you	"	"
ils (elles) eurent chanté	ils (elles) furent parti(**e**)**s**	they	"	"

4. [Double Compound Past]

Like the past anterior, the *passé* ***sur****composé* marks a past event *completed* prior to another past event. It is formed using the *passé composé* of the auxiliary verb, so that two past participles follow in succession. The *passé surcomposé* is frequently accompanied by time conjunctions (*quand, aussitôt que, dès que,* etc.) and can also often be translated by "had just (done something)". While its use is shunned by many authorities and speakers, it is widely used in certain regions.

with *avoir*	with *être*			
j'**ai eu** chanté	j'**ai été** parti(**e**)	I	*had* just	sung/left
tu **as eu** chanté	tu **as été** parti(**e**)	you	"	"
il (elle) **a eu** chanté	il (elle) **a été** parti(**e**)	he (she)	"	"
nous **avons eu** chanté	nous **avons été** parti(**e**)**s**	we	"	"
vous **avez eu** chanté	vous **avez été** parti(**e**)(**s**)	you	"	"
ils **ont eu** chanté	ils (elles) **ont été** parti(**e**)**s**	they	"	"

5. Future Perfect

The future perfect (*le futur antérieur*) consists of the future of the auxiliary verb plus the past participle:

with *avoir*	with *être*			
j'aurai chanté	je serai parti(**e**)	I	*will have*	sung/left
tu auras chanté	tu seras parti(**e**)	you	"	"
il (elle) aura chanté	il (elle) sera parti(**e**)	he (she)	"	"
nous aurons chanté	nous serons parti(**e**)**s**	we	"	"
vous aurez chanté	vous serez parti(**e**)(**s**)	you	"	"
ils (elles) auront chanté	ils (elles) seront parti(**e**)**s**	they	"	"

6. Conditional Perfect

The conditional perfect (*le conditionnel passé*) is formed by the conditional of the auxiliary verb plus the past participle.

with *avoir*	with *être*			
j'aurais chanté	je serais parti(**e**)	I	*would have*	sung/left
tu aurais chanté	tu serais parti(**e**)	you	"	"
il (elle) aurait chanté	il (elle) serait parti(**e**)	he (she)	"	"
nous aurions chanté	nous serions parti(**e**)**s**	we	"	"
vous auriez chanté	vous seriez parti(**e**)(**s**)	you	"	"
ils (elles) auraient chanté	ils (elles) seraient parti(**e**)**s**	they	"	"

7. Past Subjunctive

The past subjunctive (*le subjonctif passé*)[3] is analogous in formation to the *passé composé,* with the present subjunctive of the auxiliary used in place of the present indicative.

with *avoir*	with *être*	. . . *that*	
j'aie chanté	je sois parti(**e**)	I *have*	sung/left
tu aies chanté	tu sois parti(**e**)	you *have*	"
il (elle) ait chanté	il (elle) soit parti(**e**)	he (she) *has*	"
nous ayons chanté	nous soyons parti(**e**)**s**	we *have*	"
vous ayez chanté	vous soyez parti(**e**)(**s**)	you *have*	"
ils (elles) aient chanté	ils (elles) soient parti(**e**)**s**	they *have*	"

8. [Past Perfect Subjunctive]

The past perfect (or pluperfect) subjunctive (*le subjonctif plus-que-parfait*)[4] is analogous in formation to the *plus-que-parfait,* with the imperfect subjunctive of the auxiliary used in place of the imperfect indicative.

with *avoir*	with *être*	. . . *that*	
j'eusse chanté	je fusse parti(**e**)	I *had*	sung/left
tu eusses chanté	tu fusses parti(**e**)	you *had*	"
il (elle) eût chanté	il (elle) fût parti(**e**)	he (she) *had*	"
nous eussions chanté	nous fussions parti(**e**)**s**	we *had*	"
vous eussiez chanté	vous fussiez parti(**e**)(**s**)	you *had*	"
ils (elles) eussent chanté	ils (elles) fussent parti(**e**)**s**	they *had*	"

9. [Past Imperative]

The rarely used *impératif passé* is formed using the imperative of the auxiliary followed by the past participle.

---

[3] Or *le passé du subjonctif.*

[4] Or *le plus-que-parfait du subjonctif.* This is sometimes referred to as *le conditionnel passé deuxième forme,* in which case the *première forme* denotes the conditional perfect (no. 6).

with *avoir*	with *être*
aie chanté	sois parti(**e**)
ayons chanté	soyons parti(**e**)**s**
ayez chanté	soyez parti(**e**)(**s**)

Past imperative is somewhat of a misnomer, since as an imperative it can refer only to the future. The "past" indicates that the action referred to must take place *prior* to another *future* action /event:

> *Soyez partis* avant midi, sinon vous n'arriverez pas à l'heure.
>
> "*Leave* before noon, otherwise you will not arrive in time."
> ["*Be* in the position of *having left* before noon . . ."]

CHAPTER 8

Orthographic Modifications

One out of every seven *-er* verbs—nearly 800 in all—"looks" irregular. However, apart from *envoyer* (irregular future) and *aller* (truly irregular), all of these "irregularities" are due to a series of *orthographic changes* obeying very precise and easily learned rules. They can be divided into the following categories:

	type of modification		example	# verbs
A.	stem consonant change when followed by "back" vowel (*-a, -o, -u*)			
	c → *ç*	(18 conjugations)	lan**c**er	111
	g → *ge*	(18 conjugations)	man**g**er	172
B.	doubling of stem consonant			
	l → *ll*	(21 conjugations)	appe**l**er	54
	t → *tt*	(21 conjugations)	je**t**er	55
C.	change in written accent on stem vowel *-e*			
	e → *è*	(21 conjugations)	p**e**ser	71
	é → *è*	(9 conjugations)	c**é**der	212
D.	combinations of A and C			
	c → *ç* and *e* → *è*		dép**ec**er	2
	c → *ç* and *é* → *è*		rapi**éc**er	1
	g → *ge* and *é* → *è*		prot**ég**er	12
E.	*y* → *i* before unpronounced vowel		emplo**y**er	52
			essu**y**er	5
			pa**y**er	31

While the focus in this chapter is on orthographic modifications affecting *-er* verbs, at the same time some light will be shed on certain peculiarities associated with the following "Class III" verbs: *recevoir, prendre, venir, acquérir, voir, croire, -traire* verbs, *rire,* and *vaincre.*

A. Consonant Changes When Followed by "Back" Vowel (*-a, -o, -u*)

Verbs whose stems end in *-cer* or *-ger* face a problem in those conjugations in which the vowel immediately following the stem consonant is *-a* or *-o,*[1] since the normal pronunciation of *-c* and *-g* in this situation—as in English—is hard, rather than the soft "C" or "G" of the infinitive. In the case of *-c,* the solution adopted was to add a *cédille* (¸); for *-g,* to add an immediately following *-e,* which marks the soft pronunciation of the *-g* but is itself not pronounced.

Such modifications are required in 18 conjugations, as illustrated below for the verbs *lancer* and *manger.*

present (1)	nous lan**ç**ons
imperfect (4)	je lan**ç**ais, tu lan**ç**ais, il lan**ç**ait, ils lan**ç**aient
simple past (5)	je lan**ç**ai, tu lan**ç**as, il lan**ç**a, nous lan**ç**âmes, vous lan**ç**âtes
imperfect subjunctive (6)	je lan**ç**asse, tu lan**ç**asses, il lan**ç**ât, nous lan**ç**assions, vous lan**ç**assiez, ils lan**ç**assent
present participle (1)	lan**ç**ant
imperative (1)	lan**ç**ons
present	nous mang**e**ons
imperfect	je mang**e**ais, tu mang**e**ais, il mang**e**ait, ils mang**e**aient
simple past	je mang**e**ai, tu mang**e**as, il mang**e**a, nous mang**e**âmes, vous mang**e**âtes
imperfect subjunctive	je mang**e**asse, tu mang**e**asses, il mang**e**ât, nous mang**e**assions, vous mang**e**assiez, ils mang**e**assent
present participle	mang**e**ant
imperative	mang**e**ons

The same principle governs the replacement of *-c* by *-ç* in *-cevoir* verbs like *recevoir,* in the 22 conjugations in which *-c* is followed by *-a, -o,* or *-u:*

	indicative		subjunctive	
	present	*simple past*	*present*	*imperfect*
je	*reçois*	*reçus*	*reçoive*	*reçusse*
tu	*reçois*	*reçus*	*reçoives*	*reçusses*
il, elle	*reçoit*	*reçut*	*reçoive*	*reçût*
nous	recevons	*reçûmes*	recevions	*reçussions*
vous	recevez	*reçûtes*	receviez	*reçussiez*
ils, elles	*reçoivent*	*reçurent*	*reçoivent*	*reçussent*
past participle:	*reçu*			
2s imperative:	*reçois*			

[1] For these verbs there are no conjugations in which the following vowel is *-u.*

B. Doubling of Stem Consonant in 21 Conjugations (e.g., *appeler, jeter*)

C1. Change in Written Accent on Stem Vowel *-e* in Certain Conjugations

e → *è* 21 conjugations (e.g., *peser*)

Modifications B and C1 are entirely analogous. They affect all *-er* verbs with a stem vowel *-e* which is in an *open syllable* and has no written accent;[2] i.e., all *except those* in which the stem vowel *-e:*

(1) is followed by two consonants[3] (e.g., ***fermer, cesser***) or *-x* (e.g., ***vexer***),[4]
(2) has a circumflex (e.g., ***fêter***), or
(3) has an acute accent (e.g., ***céder***).

Groups (1) and (2) have completely regular conjugations like *parler,* while group (3) has its own series of orthographic modifications described in C2 below. In order to understand the principle which underlies modifications B and C1, as well as C2, we need to make a brief digression.

A Digression on "Mute" *-e*

French pronunciation—in particular certain peculiarities of the verbal system—cannot be understood without an appreciation of the role played by "mute" *-e* (*e muet*): an *-e* whose pronunciation has been totally lost or, if conserved, considerably reduced. The final *-e* at the end of feminine nouns and adjectives is the most prominent example, its modern role being only to indicate that the preceding *consonant* is pronounced.

---

[2] From the Introduction we recall that an *open* syllable is one ending in a vowel, a *closed* syllable one ending in a (pronounced) consonant. The rare, and even more rarely used, verbs ending in *-eyer* (*brasseyer, capeyer, faseyer, grasseyer, langueyer, volleyer*) are exceptions to the general rule: the stem vowel *-e* is in an open syllable yet the verbs undergo no orthographic modification.

[3] Other than the combination *-vr,* in which both elements are pronounced in the following syllable so that the stem vowel *-e* remains in an *open* syllable. *Sevrer* is the only such verb—[se•vrer]—and is conjugated like *peser.*

[4] The letter *-x* has the phonetic value of two consonants (*-ks*) so that the stem vowel is in a closed syllable (*vek•ser*).

Mute -e is normally represented by a phonetic symbol in the form of an inverted, upside down *e*: ə. For our purposes we will use "( )" to represent an *-e* which is never pronounced and "(e)" for one which, if pronounced, has only a reduced pronunciation.

Some examples:

	spelling	*pronounced like*	*no. of syllables*
	brute	brut( )	1
	bête	bet( )	1
	atroce	atros( )	2
	projeter	proj(e)ter	2 (+)
	appeler	app(e)ler	2 (+)
contrast:	accéder	accÉder	3
contrast:	arrêter	arrÉter	3
	refuser	r(e)fuser	2 (+)
contrast:	réfuter	rÉfuter	3

where the (+) serves as a reminder that there may be some residual pronunciation.

With very few exceptions, the following rules apply:

Rule O-1. French *-e* in *open* syllables is always mute, *unless* it has a written accent (acute, grave, or circumflex).

Rule O-2. If the written accent is acute, *-e* has a *closed* pronunciation ([É], as in English *mate*), while a grave accent indicates that the pronunciation is *open* ([È], as in English *met*). With a circumflex the pronunciation can be either closed (*arrêter*) or open (*fête*).

We can illustrate Rule O-1 with reference to the verb *parler*, which is 100 percent regular and has no orthographic modifications. There are nonetheless 21 conjugations in which the *-e* following the stem is mute, as indicated below by "( )" or "(e)", as appropriate:

	present indicative	present subjunctive	future	conditional	imperative
je	parl( )	parl( )	parl(e)rai	parl(e)rais	
tu	parl( )s	parl( )s	parl(e)ras	parl(e)rais	parl( )
il, elle	parl( )	parl( )	parl(e)ra	parl(e)rait	
nous	parlons	parlions	parl(e)rons	parl(e)rions	parlons
vous	parlez	parliez	parl(e)rez	parl(e)riez	parlez
ils, elles	parl( )nt	parl( )nt	parl(e)ront	parl(e)raient	

For verbs like *parler*, the mute *-e* in these 21 syllables creates no difficulty, and the orthography remains unchanged. However, verbs with stem vowel *-e* in an *open* syllable come into conflict with the following basic rule:

Rule O-3. French does not tolerate mute *-e* in successive syllables.

By Rule O-1, the stem vowel *-e* in verbs like *appeler* should *always* have a mute pronunciation—being in an "open" syllable—but by Rule O-3 it is not allowed to have a mute pronunciation in the 21 conjugations in which the *post-stem* vowel is a mute *-e!* To escape from this dilemma, recourse is made to the following rule/remedy:

Rule O-4. For such verbs, the normally mute stem vowel *-e* is *pronounced* in the 21 conjugations in which the *following* vowel is a mute *-e*. To mark the non-mute status of the stem vowel in these conjugations, two alternative methods are employed:

(a) doubling the immediately following consonant so that the stem vowel is no longer in an open syllable; or

(b) placing a *grave* accent (`) on the stem vowel.

Verbs such as *appeler* and *jeter* adopt the first solution, *peser* and *peler* the second.

	appeler	jeter	peser	peler
present indicative				
je	appe**ll**e	je**tt**e	p**è**se	p**è**le
tu	appe**ll**es	je**tt**es	p**è**ses	p**è**les
il, elle	appe**ll**e	je**tt**e	p**è**se	p**è**le
nous	appelons	jetons	pesons	pelons
vous	appelez	jetez	pesez	pelez
ils, elles	appe**ll**ent	je**tt**ent	p**è**sent	p**è**lent
future				
je	appe**ll**erai	je**tt**erai	p**è**serai	p**è**lerai
tu	appe**ll**eras	je**tt**eras	p**è**seras	p**è**leras
il, elle	appe**ll**era	je**tt**era	p**è**sera	p**è**lera
nous	appe**ll**erons	je**tt**erons	p**è**serons	p**è**lerons
vous	appe**ll**erez	je**tt**erez	p**è**serez	p**è**lerez
ils, elles	appe**ll**eront	je**tt**eront	p**è**seront	p**è**leront

The present subjunctive and imperative follow the pattern of the present indicative, the conditional that of the future. Note that in the 27 conjugations (including the infinitive) in which there is no orthographic change, the stem vowel *-e* remains mute (e.g., *nous j(e)tons*).

The contrasting example of *appeler/peler* highlights a potential inconvenience: for a given verb requiring such orthographic remedy, how does one know which of the two remedies is to be applied? A partial answer is provided by the following rule:

Rule O-5. If the stem consonant is *not -l* or *-t,* then the second remedy (grave accent) is used.

In cases in which this rule does not apply (i.e., verbs ending in *-eler* or *-eter*) the first remedy (doubling) is employed in approximately 80 percent of the cases, the second remedy (grave accent) in the remainder. The overall situation is summarized below:

stem consonant	no. of verbs	*doubling*	*e → è*
L	72	54	*18*
T	65	55	*10*
Other	43	—	43
Total	180	109	71

The complete list of 28 "exceptions" (i.e., *-eler* and *-eter* verbs employing the grave accent method) is provided in Annex A,[5] the two most common probably being *acheter* and *geler.* Note that for a verb ending in *-eler* or *-eter,* knowledge of the first person singular present (*je gèle, j'achète*) is sufficient to determine the entire conjugation.[6]

Note also that the above principles account for the apparent irregularities in the third person plurals for the verbs *prendre, venir,* and *acquérir:*

ils, elles	*pre**nn**ent*	*vie**nn**ent*	*acqui**è**rent*

In all three cases it is necessary to indicate that the stem vowel *-e* has a non-mute pronunciation: for the first two verbs the stem consonant is doubled,[7] while a grave accent is used in *acqui**è**rent.*

---

[5] Under the entries for *appeler* (1-3a) and *jeter* (1-3b).

[6] *Interpeller* has a pronunciation entirely analogous to that of *appeler* yet is conjugated with *-ll* in all conjugations (model *parler*). Logically, it should be either: (a) written **interpeler* and conjugated like *appeler* (or *peler*); or (b) pronounced like *exceller* (i.e., with no mute *-e*). Both approaches have their supporters.

[7] The doubling of *-n* is exceptional: based on the pattern observed above (Rule O-5), one would have predicted **ils prènent,* **ils viènent.*

C2. Change in Written Accent on Stem Vowel *-e* in Certain Conjugations

é → è	9 conjugations	(e.g., *céder*)

Verbs like *fêter* with a circumflex over the *-e* avoid the above problems: the circumflex ensures that the stem vowel *-e* is *never* mute, and hence no remedial measure is required for the 21 conjugations in which the following vowel is a mute *-e*. The conjugation is thus entirely analogous to that of *parler*.

One might well think that verbs like *céder* should likewise be safe, since the written accent ensures that the stem vowel *-e* can never be mute. Nonetheless, these verbs encounter problems due to the following rule.

> **Rule O-6.** **(a) *-e* can have a *closed* pronunciation only when it is in an *open* syllable.**
> **(b) an *-é* which finds itself in a *closed* syllable must therefore change its pronunciation to that of an *open -e*, and accordingly its orthography to *-è*.**

Rule O-6 causes no problem for the infinitive, since the stem vowel *-e* is in an *open* syllable—the following consonant is pronounced as the first element of the *next* syllable:

		pronounced like
infinitive	céder	cÉ•dÉ

However, in the conjugations in which there is a *mute -e* in the *final* syllable, the *-d* moves (backward) to the stem syllable, thus making it *closed*. In accordance with part (b) of Rule O-6, *-é* has to change to *-è*. Thus, for the present indicative there is a contrast between the three singulars and third person plural—in which the stem vowel finds itself in a *closed* syllable—and the first two plurals, where it remains in an *open* syllable:

		pronounced like
je	**cède**	cÈd( )
tu	**cèdes**	cÈd( )
il, elle	**cède**	cÈd( )
nous	cédons	cÉ•don
vous	cédez	cÉ•dÉ
ils, elles	**cèdent**	cÈD( )

The written accent is altered in the same four conjugations of the present subjunctive, as well as the *tu* form of the imperative, thus making a total of nine written accent shifts.

These are the *only* orthographic modifications for *céder*-type verbs: unlike *appeler, jeter, peser,* no modifications are required for either the future or conditional. Why not? Because—*at least in theory*—in these conjugations the stem vowel remains in an *open* syllable and thus is entitled to maintain its "closed" pronunciation (and acute accent). Thus for the future:

		(theoretically) pronounced like
je	céderai	cÉ•d(e)rÉ
tu	céderas	cÉ•d(e)ra
il, elle	cédera	cÉ•d(e)ra
nous	céderons	cÉ•d(e)ron
vous	céderez	cÉ•d(e)rÉ
ils, elles	céderont	cÉ•d(e)ron

The "in theory" caveat is necessary because most people seem to pronounce the future and conditionals with the *-d* in the *stem* syllable, and thus (naturally) with an *open -e* rather than a *closed* one:

je cÈd•rÉ *rather than* je cÉ•d(e)rÉ

Most "authorities" now indicate a tolerance for an alternate orthography where the accent *aigu* of the future and conditional is replaced by an accent *grave*[8]—in which case there would be 21 written accent shifts (as for *peser, peler*) rather than the "standard" nine.

Note that there are a number of *céder* type verbs where the stem vowel *-é* is followed by *two* consonants. For example:

sé**ch**er	je s**è**che
ré**gn**er	je r**è**gne
célé**br**er	je cél**è**bre
inté**gr**er	j'int**è**gre
ré**gl**er	je r**è**gle

In each of these cases, the *-é* of the infinitive remains in an *open* syllable despite being followed by two consonants:

(a) *-ch* and *-gn* represent single consonant sounds—corresponding to English *-sh* and Spanish *ñ*—thus *sé•**ch**er* and *ré•**gn**er*

[8] This has also been recommended by the Conseil Supérieur de la Langue Française.

(b) in the other cases, the two consonants are *inseparable combinations* and are pronounced together in the following syllable—thus *cé•lé•**br**er, in•té•**gr**er, ré•**gl**er.* This often happens in English as well—the standard American pronunciation is *in•te•**gr**al* (compared to the more "British" *in•te**g**•**r**al*).

Verbs like *créer* and *agréer* with no stem consonant do not follow the pattern of *céder* but are instead conjugated following the standard model *parler*—the absence of a stem consonant means that the stem vowel *-e* always remains in an *open* syllable. Thus for *créer:*

		pronounced like
je	crée	crÉ
tu	crées	crÉ
il, elle	crée	crÉ
nous	créons	crÉ•on
vous	créez	crÉ•É
ils, elles	créent	crÉ

D. Combinations of A and C

A and C1:	*c* → *ç*	and	*e* → *è*	dép**ec**er
A and C2:	*c* → *ç*	and	*é* → *è*	rapi**éc**er
	g → *ge*	and	*é* → *è*	prot**ég**er

These represent simple combinations of the changes in A above with those of either C1 or C2: combinations A and C1 involve orthographic modifications in 39 conjugations, A and C2 in 27. *Dépecer* and *rapiécer* are effectively the only verbs in their class,[9] while other commonly used verbs conjugated like *protéger* include *abréger, alléger, piéger,* and *siéger.*

The present tense conjugations of the three groups are shown below:

present indicative	dépecer	rapiécer	protéger
je	dép**è**ce	rapi**è**ce	prot**è**ge
tu	dép**è**ces	rapi**è**ces	prot**è**ges
il, elle	dép**è**ce	rapi**è**ce	prot**è**ge
nous	*dépeçons*	*rapiéçons*	*protégeons*
vous	dépecez	rapiécez	protégez
ils, elles	dép**è**cent	rapi**è**cent	prot**è**gent

[9] The defective verb *clamecer* is theoretically conjugated like *dépecer.*

E. *y* → *i* before Unpronounced Vowel: *-oyer, -uyer,* and *-ayer* Verbs

As above, a preliminary digression will be useful and will at the same time provide the basis for understanding several orthographic peculiarities already noted in Chapters 1 and 2 for the verbs *voir, croire, abstraire, rire,* and *-ier* verbs like *prier.*

A Digression on "I", "Y", and "IY"

In French, as in many languages, when *-i* is followed by another vowel there is a natural tendency for it to change its pronunciation to either the consonant "Y" or the combination "IY". The articulation of this "Y" sound can only occur, however, if the *following* vowel is actually *pronounced* (i.e., not a mute *-e*).

Rule O-7. Whenever *-y* is followed by a mute *-e,* it changes its pronunciation and orthography to *-i.*

Rule O-8. Whenever *-i* is followed by a vowel other than mute *-e,* the pronunciation changes to either "Y" or "IY". If there is a preceding vowel, the orthography changes from *-i* to *-y;* otherwise there is no change.

Present indicative

change:	*voir*	nous voi-ons	→	voyons	[vwa•yon][10]
		vous voi-ez	→	voyez	[vwa•yÉ]
	croire	nous croi-ons	→	croyons	[crwa•yon]
		vous croi-ez	→	croyez	[crwa•yÉ]
	abstraire	nous abstrai-ons	→	abstrayons	[ab•strÈ•yon]
		vous abstrai-ez	→	abstrayez	[ab•strÈ•yÉ]
no change:	*nier*	nous ni-ons	→	nions	[nyon]
		vous ni-ez	→	niez	[nyÉ]
	prier	nous pri-ons	→	prions	[pri•yon]
		vous pri-ez	→	priez	[pri•yÉ]
	rire	nous ri-ons	→	rions	[ri•on] or [ri•yon]
		vous ri-ez	→	riez	[ri•É] or [ri•yÉ]

[10] Here we represent the stem vowels *-oi* and *-ai* by [wa] and [È], in order to make the distinction more apparent with the following "Y" sound. The results for *voir, croire,* and *abstraire* might appear to be in conflict with Rule O-8, since in Modern French the *-i* in *-oi* and *-ai* is not a real "I" vowel. However, the additional "Y" in the pronunciation arose at an earlier stage, when the *-i* was still pronounced.

The same process literally occurs twice in combinations of *-ii* plus (pronounced) vowel:

> **Rule O-9. Whenever *-ii* is followed by a vowel other than mute *-e*, the pronunciation changes to either "I•Y" or "IY•Y". If there is a preceding vowel, the orthography of the first *-i* changes to *-y;* otherwise there is no change.**

Imperfect indicative/present subjunctive

change:	*voir*	nous voi-ions	→	voyions	[vwai•yon]
		vous voi-iez	→	voyiez	[vwai•yÉ]
	croire	nous croi-ions	→	croyions	[crwai•yon]
		vous croi-iez	→	croyiez	[crwai•yÉ]
	abstraire	nous abstrai-ions	→	abstrayions	[ab•strÈi•yon]
		vous abstrai-iez	→	abstrayiez	[ab•strÈi•yÉ]
no change:	*nier*	nous ni-ions	→	niions	[ni•yon]
		vous ni-iez	→	niiez	[ni•yÉ]
	prier	nous pri-ions	→	priions	[priy•yon]
		vous pri-iez	→	priiez	[priy•yÉ]
	rire	nous ri-ions	→	riions	[ri•yon] or [riy•yon]
		vous ri-iez	→	riiez	[ri•yÉ] or [riy•yÉ]

In contrast to *voir, croire,* and *abstraire,* the verbs *rire, prier,* and *nier*[11] have no orthographic modifications—only a slightly odd appearance (*-ii*) in the first and second person plurals of the imperfect indicative and present subjunctive.

It should also be noted that verbs ending in *-**u**er* do *not* have orthographic modifications in these forms.[12]

Imperfect indicative/present subjunctive

	remuer	*attribuer*	
nous	rem**uions**	attrib**uions**	*not* *-uyons
vous	rem**uiez**	attrib**uiez**	*not* *-uyez

Now we can return to the *-yer* verbs. In conformity with Rule O-7, *-y* becomes *-i* in the 21 conjugations in which the following vowel is a mute *-e*. For *-ayer*

[11] The large majority of *-ier* verbs follow the pronunciation pattern of *nier* rather than *prier,* but this has absolutely no impact on the written forms, both of which are conjugated like the "standard" verb *parler.*

[12] The technical reason presumably is that the *-u* with which the stem ends is pronounced as a consonant (essentially "W") rather than as a vowel. Note the contrast with the *present* tense of the "irregular" verb *fuir: nous fuyons* and *vous fuyez,* rather than **fuions* and **fuiez.*

verbs, however, this modification is not obligatory: there exists a (rarer) conjugation which maintains *-yer* throughout all 48 forms.

	employer	essuyer	payer (A)	payer (B)
present indicative				
je	emploie	essuie	paie	paye
tu	emploies	essuies	paies	payes
il, elle	emploie	essuie	paie	paye
nous	employons	essuyons	payons	payons
vous	employez	essuyez	payez	payez
ils, elles	emploient	essuient	paient	payent
future				
je	emploierai	essuierai	paierai	payerai
tu	emploieras	essuieras	paieras	payeras
il, elle	emploiera	essuiera	paiera	payera
nous	emploierons	essuierons	paierons	payerons
vous	emploierez	essuierez	paierez	payerez
ils, elles	emploieront	essuieront	paieront	payeront

Similar modifications occur in the present subjunctive, conditional, and second person singular imperative.

Note that *-eyer* verbs, which are few and rarely used, do *not* undergo this orthographic modification.[13]

Two Concluding Points

1. The orthographic modifications in B (*appeler, jeter*), C1 (*peser*), and E (*employer*) affect in each case *the same 21 conjugations*—those in which the vowel following the stem is a mute *-e:*

present indicative and subjunctive	three singulars and 3rd person plural
future and conditional	all six conjugations
imperative	2nd person singular

2. We have seen (A above) that when followed by *-a, -o,* or *-u,* "soft" *-c* becomes *-ç* and "soft" *-g* becomes *-ge.* This is consistent with the following general system, which characterizes French orthography.

[13]The scarcity reflects the fact that *-eyer* is not a naturally occurring phonetic combination in French, having evolved in all "native" words to *-oyer.* Of the six *-eyer* verbs, the most commonly employed is the English import *volleyer.*

	following vowel	(E, I)	(A, O, U)
	hard C	qu	c
	soft C	c	ç
	hard G	gu	g
	soft G	g	ge *or* j
Examples:	hard C	**qu**estion, **qu**i	**c**asser, **c**ode, **c**ube
	soft C	**c**ément, **c**ire	**ç**a, ma**ç**on, re**ç**u
	hard G	**gu**erre, **gu**ide	**g**ala, **g**orille, fi**g**ure
	soft G	**g**eler, **g**ilet	chan**ge**able, pi**ge**on, **j**uger

For *vaincre,* the shift *c* → *qu* accounts for present tense *vain**qu**ez* and *vain**qu**ent* and for the simple past stem *vain**qu**-:* the letter which follows in each case is *-e* or *-i.* Due to the "corrupting" influence of these forms, the present tense first person plural—which should be **vaincons*—has become *vain**qu**ons.*

"Logically," verbs ending in *-guer* should change the *-gu* to *-g* in those conjugations in which the following vowel is *-a* or *-o,* and in the same conditions *-quer* verbs should change the *-qu* to *-c.* However, such "reverse" orthographic changes do not occur in the verbal system:

Rule O-10. ***-guer* and *-quer* verbs maintain *-gu* and *-qu* in all conjugations, even when the following vowel is *-a* or *-o.***

This is illustrated below for the present tenses of *fatiguer* and *marquer:*

je	fatigue	marque
tu	fatigues	marques
il, elle	fatigue	marque
nous	fati**gu**ons *not* *fati**g**ons	mar**qu**ons *not* *mar**c**ons
vous	fatiguez	marquez
ils, elles	fatiguent	marquent

From the point of view of French orthography, these are considered irregular verbs. From the point of view of *appearance,* however, they are completely regular since they have the same stem for all 48 conjugations.

Many adjectives and nouns related to *-guer* and *-quer* verbs display the "correct" orthography, thus providing contrasts such as:

verb	present participle	noun /adjective
navi**gu**er	navi**gu**ant	navi**g**ant, navi**g**able, navi**g**ateur, navi**g**ation
provo**qu**er	provo**qu**ant	provo**c**ant, provo**c**ation, provo**c**ateur

CHAPTER 9

Summary

French verbs can be classified as follows:

Class I **-*er* verbs other than *aller***

About 15 percent of these verbs are subject to one or more orthographic modifications (Chapter 8):

(a) stem consonant change when followed by *-a* or *-o* (*manger, lancer*)

(b) *y* → *i* before a vowel which is not pronounced (*employer*)

(c) changes in written accents for verbs whose stem vowel *-e* is in an *open* syllable (*app**e**ler, c**é**der*), other than those in which the stem vowel has a circumflex (*f**ê**ter*) or in which there is no following consonant (*cr**é**er*).

Envoyer combines (b) with an irregular future stem.

Class II ***extended -s* endings in present**

About 80 percent of *-ir* verbs plus *maudire.* Apart from the past participle of *maudire* and the three present singulars of *haïr,* there are no irregularities.

Class III A **-*e* present endings + *bouillir***

17 *-ir* verbs (*couvrir, offrir, souffrir, cueillir, assaillir, défaillir, bouillir*)[1]

B **-*s* present endings**

(a) all *-oir* verbs, except *avoir*

(b) all *-re* verbs, except *être* and *maudire*

(c) *-ir* verbs not in Class II or Class IIIA

Irregular ***être, avoir, aller***

Defective **Verbs used only in certain conjugations** (Annex C)

---

[1] And 10 other verbs ending in *-ouvrir, -cueillir,* or *-saillir.*

Key Conjugations

For each verb there are six *key conjugations*—seven if one includes the infinitive—which serve as building blocks for the entire verb (all 48 simple forms). These are:[2]

0. infinitive

1. present indicative: first person singular (1s)
2. present indicative: first person plural (1p)
3. present indicative: third person plural (3p)
4. past participle
5. simple past: first person plural (1p)
6. future: first person singular (1s)

Each key conjugation has an associated *stem* obtained by removing the appropriate *ending* (as defined in Chapters 1–5). This is illustrated below for *parler* (Class I), *recevoir* (Class III), and *finir* (Class II):

		key conjugation	stem	
0.	*infinitive*	*parler*	*parl-*	*infinitive stem*
1.	1s present	je parle	parl-	**1s present stem**
2.	1p present	nous parlons	parl-	**1p present stem**
3.	3p present	ils parlent	parl-	**3p present stem**
4.	past participle	parlé	parl-	**past participle stem**
5.	1p simple past	nous parlâmes	parl-	**simple past stem**
6.	1s future	je parlerai	parler-	**future stem**

		key conjugation	stem	
0.	*infinitive*	*recevoir*	*recev-*	*infinitive stem*
1.	1s present	je reçois	reçoi-	**1s present stem**
2.	1p present	nous recevons	recev-	**1p present stem**
3.	3p present	ils reçoivent	reçoiv-	**3p present stem**
4.	past participle	reçu	reç-	**past participle stem**
5.	1p simple past	nous reçûmes	reç-	**simple past stem**
6.	1s future	je recevrai	recevr-	**future stem**

[2] For nos. 5 and 6, *any* of the six conjugations could be selected as the key one. For the simple past we have chosen the first person *plural* because it is much more distinctive than the first person singular, particularly for Class II verbs (*nous finîmes* versus *je finis*).

		key conjugation	stem	
0.	*infinitive*	*finir*	*fin-*	*infinitive stem*
1.	1s present	je finis	fini-	**1s present stem**
2.	1p present	nous finissons	finiss-	**1p present stem**
3.	3p present	ils finissent	finiss-	**3p present stem**
4.	past participle	fini	fin-	**past participle stem**
5.	1p simple past	nous finîmes	fin-	**simple past stem**
6.	1s future	je finirai	finir-	**future stem**

The *key stems* can be used to construct the remaining 41 simple forms, as follows (**all exceptions noted**):

present indicative	2s, 3s = *1s present stem* + *-es, -e* (Class I and 3A) = *1s present stem* + *-s, -t* (all others) 2p = *1p present stem* + *-ez* (3s endings *-dt, -tt, -ct* are reduced to *-d, -t, -c: il rend, met, vainc*—not **ren**dt**, *me**tt**, *vain**ct***) **Exceptions:** *dire, faire—vous dites, vous faites* **Irregular:** *être, avoir, aller*
imperfect	= *1p present stem* + imperfect endings **Exception:** *être* (stem *ét-*)
present participle	= *1p present stem* + *-ant* **Exceptions:** *être, avoir, savoir—**ét**ant, **ay**ant, sa**ch**ant.*
simple past	= *simple past stem* + simple past endings (4 types)
future/conditional	future = *future stem* + future endings conditional = *future stem* + conditional endings
present subjunctive	1s, 2s, 3s, 3p = *3p present stem* + *-e, -es, -e, -ent* 1p, 2p = *1p present stem* + *-ions, -iez* **Exceptions:** *être, avoir, savoir, pouvoir, faire, aller, falloir, valoir, vouloir*
imperfect subjunctive	= *simple past stem* + imperfect subjunctive endings (4 types)

imperative	2s = present indicative, minus final *-s* for Class I, IIIA, *aller* 1p, 2p = present indicative **Exceptions:** *être, avoir, savoir, vouloir*

For Classes I and II considerable additional simplification is possible.

Class I

The first five key conjugations are formed from the infinitive stem; the sixth uses the infinitive itself. For the approximately 15 percent of verbs undergoing orthographic modifications, such changes are completely determined by the rules given in Chapter 8. While there is some ambiguity for *-eler* and *-eter* verbs, the first person singular (present indicative) will confirm whether the verb is of the consonant doubling (*appeler*) or written accent shifting (*peler*) type.

The only "real" irregularity among Class I verbs is the future stem *enverr-* for *envoyer.*

Class II

All of the appropriate forms can be determined from the infinitive: the first three stems are *extended* by *-i* or *-iss.* The only irregularities are the past participle of *maudire* (*maudit*) and the singular stem for *haïr* (*je hais* not **je haïs*).[3]

Class III

As a class of "leftovers", Class III understandably has very few *overall* patterns. There are nonetheless some useful *local* patterns which apply to the *-oir, -re,* and *-ir* subgroups.

(1) *-oir* verbs (including the irregular *avoir*) have past participles in *-u,* apart from *asseoir* (*assis*): *-loir* and *-voir* ("to see") verbs add *-u* to the full infinitive stem, while other verbs add *-u* to a truncated stem.

[3] For *haïr,* there are no circumflexes in the simple past (1p, 2p) and imperfect subjunctive (3s), since the *-i* already has a dieresis (¨).

(2) *-re* verbs apart from *faire* (and the irregular *être*) have future stems equal to the infinitive minus the final *-e*.

(3) The *rendre* group—the largest within Class III—has a completely regular conjugation, taking into account the third person singular *il ren**d***. The group consists of all verbs ending in *-ndre*, apart from the *-prendre* and *-indre* verbs.[4]

(4) "Classical" *-ir* verbs (*partir, sortir, sentir/mentir/repentir, servir, dormir*) are completely "regular". Note that in the present singulars the second consonant is lost (*je pars, sors, sens, sers, dors*).

(5) All of the conjugations for Class IIIA verbs can be determined in a predictable manner from the infinitive, with the exception of the present tense singulars for *bouillir* (*je bous* not **je bouillis*) and the future tense for *cueillir* (*cueill**er**-*).

One important "general" pattern also applies to Class III as a whole.

(6) There are only six verbs whose simple past is not easily *recognizable* by its similarity to the past participle, infinitive, or present plural: *être, faire, voir, tenir, venir, naître: fu-, fi-, vi-, tin-, vin-, naqui-*.

The annexes at the end of the book provide additional information on verb forms.

Annex A is divided into three parts:

A1: a list of model verbs corresponding to categories into which all French verbs can be placed.
A2: a summary table providing the six key conjugations—and "exceptional" irregularities—for each of the model verbs (apart from those with orthographic modifications only).
A3: complete conjugations for each of the model verbs, highlighting particular irregularities and/or orthographic modifications. Other verbs sharing the same model are explicitly identified.

Annex B provides an alphabetical listing of approximately 6,200 verbs, identifying for each the model which it follows.

Annex C presents information on "defective" verbs, which exist only in a limited number of conjugations.

---

[4]The three *-rompre* verbs have a virtually analogous conjugation, differing only in the third person singular present indicative, which maintains the final *-t* (*il romp**t*** versus *il rend*).

PART II

USES OF VERBS

CHAPTER 10

Indicative

In this chapter we will consider all forms of the indicative other than the simple past (*passé simple*) and past anterior, whose discussion will be deferred until Chapter 12. We begin with a brief review of several key grammatical concepts.

> **Definition. A *transitive* verb is one which is capable of having a direct object. Other verbs are *intransitive.***

To throw and *to give* are transitive verbs:

We throw *the ball.*	Nous lançons *le ballon.*
He gives *the book* to his friend.	Il donne *le livre* à son ami.

The ball and *the book* are direct objects, *his friend* an indirect object. In contrast, *to go* and *to yawn* are (at least normally)[1] intransitive verbs.

I go home.	Je vais à la maison.
He yawns.	Il bâille.

While *home* is normally a noun, in this case it is an adverb (*where?*).

Many French intransitive verbs correspond to English transitive ones, the difference being that in French the "object" is introduced by a preposition (*à* or *de*).[2] Some of the more common of these are given below:

déplaire	Cela *déplaît* ***à*** certains.	"That *displeases* some."
désobéir	*désobéir* ***à*** ses parents	"*to disobey* one's parents"
douter	Nous ne *doutons* jamais ***de*** sa parole.	"We never *doubt* his word."
nuire	Fumer *nuit* ***à*** la santé.	"Smoking *harms* health."
obéir	Les enfants doivent *obéir* ***à*** leurs parents.	"Children should *obey* their parents."

---

[1] *To go* is transitive in *I am going* ***swimming****, the pitcher went* ***the distance****; to yawn* in "[he] yawns **a yawn** a yard wide" (Mary Kingsley, *Travels in West Africa*).

[2] In French grammar a special category has been created for these verbs: *les verbes transitifs indirects*—"transitive verbs having indirect objects"—to distinguish them from the "pure" intransitive verbs having no objects at all.

plaire	Il est impossible de *plaire* ***à*** tout le monde.	"It's impossible *to please* everyone."
profiter	Cela *profite* ***à*** lui mais pas **à** moi.	"That *benefits* him but not me."
remédier	pour *remédier* ***à*** cette situation	"to *remedy* this situation"
renoncer	J'ai *renoncé* ***au*** tabac.	"I have *renounced* (given up) smoking."
répondre	Il n'a pas *répondu* ***à*** la question.	"He didn't *answer* the question."[3]
résister	*résister* ***à*** une force hostile	"*to resist* a hostile force"
ressembler	Il *ressemble* ***à*** sa mère.	"He *resembles* his mother."
succéder	L'automne *succède* ***à*** l'été et précède l'hiver.	"Autumn *succeeds* summer and precedes winter."
téléphoner	Elle a *téléphoné* ***à*** son père.	"She *telephoned* her father."

A few verbs are transitive with respect to "things" but intransitive with respect to people (and organizations), notably:

ordonner[4]	Marie *ordonne* ***à*** son fils de travailler.	"Marie *orders* her son to work."
	Le roi *ordonne* son exécution.	"The king *orders* his execution."
pardonner	Nous *pardonnons* ***à*** tous.	"We *pardon* everybody."
	Le roi *pardonne* ses crimes.	"The king *pardons* his crimes."

A relatively small number of French transitive verbs correspond to English intransitive ones, the most common probably being:

attendre	Attendez-moi!	"*Wait* ***for*** me!"
chercher	Je cherche un livre par Gide.	"I am *searching* ***for*** a book by Gide."
écouter	Nous écoutons la musique.	"We are *listening* ***to*** music."

The transitive/intransitive contrast has implications for object pronouns. For example:

Le président **l'**appelle.	"The president calls *him.*"
Le président **lui** téléphone.	"The president phones *him.*"

[3] English *respond* is likewise intransitive: *He didn't respond* ***to*** *the question.*

[4] In the sense of "to ordain", *ordonner* is used transitively with respect to people: *ordonner un prêtre* ("to ordain a priest").

Present Tense

The French present tense *generally* corresponds to that of English:

(1) "True" present:

Il *chante* une chanson.	"He *sings* a song."
Tu *manges* très vite.	"You *eat* in a big hurry."
Nous *montons* les escaliers lentement.	"We *climb* the stairs slowly."
L'enfant *lit* le livre.	"The child *reads* the book."

(2) To describe a permanent situation or habitual actions:

Il ne *fume* jamais.	"He never *smokes.*"
Les chevaux *mangent* de l'herbe.	"Horses *eat* grass."
Chez nous, nous *déjeunons* à midi.	"In our house we *eat* at noon."
En hiver les jours *sont* très courts.	"In winter the days *are* very short."

(3) The *if* verb of *if . . . then* clauses, where the *then* verb is in the future:

S'il *pleut* demain, je resterai à la maison.	"If it *rains* tomorrow, I will stay at home."

If . . . then clauses will be discussed further below.

As in English, the present tense can also on occasion be used to describe future activities.

Où *vas*-tu cet été?	"Where *are* you *going* this summer?"
Je *vais* en France.	"I *(will) go* to France."

The present tense is also used frequently to narrate activities from the past:

Et en ce moment César *prend* sa décision, *passe* le Rubicon et *avance* avec son armée vers Rome.	"And in that moment Caesar *takes* his decision, *crosses* the Rubicon, and *advances* with his army towards Rome."

Probably the most important difference between the French and English present tenses is that the very common English construction *to be + present participle* (*I am washing, she is reading, they are going*) does not exist in Modern French. One has the option of using either the simple verb form (*je lave, elle lit, ils vont*) or a more complicated—and hence relatively infrequent—construction: *je suis en train de laver, elle est en train de lire, ils sont en train d'aller* ("to be in the process of . . .").

Past Participle and *Passé Composé*

Past Participle as Adjective

As in English, the past participle of transitive verbs can be used adjectivally, in which case it agrees with the noun it modifies in both gender and number.[5] For example, for the verb *voler* ("to rob"):

le trésor *volé*	"the *stolen* treasure"
les trésors *volé**s*** par les pirates	"the treasures *stolen* by the pirates"
la voiture *volé**e***	"the *stolen* car"
les voitures *volé**es*** par les voleurs	"the cars *stolen* by the thieves"

Passé Composé

In the spoken language, the *passé composé* translates both the English *past* and *compound past* (*present perfect*):

J'*ai écrit* à ma mère aujourd'hui.	"I *wrote/have written* to my mother today."
Shakespeare *a écrit* Hamlet en 1600.	"Shakespeare *wrote* Hamlet in 1600."

Il *est allé* à l'école aujourd'hui.	"He *went/has gone* to school today."
Franklin *est allé* à Paris en 1776.	"Franklin *went* to Paris in 1776."

These two pairs of sentences illustrate a distinctive element of the *passé composé:* two different auxiliary verbs—*avoir* and *être*—are used, depending on the verb employed. The examples below illustrate a second distinctive element: when the auxiliary is *être* there is agreement in *number* and *gender* with the subject, but when the auxiliary is *avoir* the past participle is usually *but not always* invariable.

Elle est allé**e** à l'école.	"She *went/has gone* to school."
Ils sont allé**s** à l'école.	"They (masc.) *went/have gone* to school."
Elles sont allé**es** à l'école.	"They (fem.) *went/have gone* to school."
Je (*François*) suis allé à l'école.	"I (masc.) *went/have gone* to school."
Je (*Françoise*) suis allé**e** à l'école.	"I (fem.) *went/have gone* to school."
Tu es allé(**e**) à l'école.	"You *went/have gone* to school."

[5] There are certain fine points and exceptions. For example, the participles *attendu, compris, entendu, excepté, supposé,* and *vu* are invariable when placed before the noun, variable if placed after: ***excepté** les enfants,* but *les enfants* ***exceptés.*** This can be viewed as a special case of the rules (introduced later in this chapter) governing agreement with a *preceding direct object.*

Nous sommes allé(**e**)**s** à l'école.	"We *went/have gone* to school."
Vous êtes allé(**e**)(**s**) à l'école.	"You *went/have gone* to school."
Elle m'a donné une pomme.	"She *gave* me an apple."
La pomme qu'il m'a donné**e** était pourrie.	"*The apple* that he gave me was rotten."
Les pommes qu'il m'a donné**es** étaient pourries.	"*The apples* that he gave me were rotten."

In these examples, *(e)* indicates that an additional *-e* is required if the subject (*tu, nous, vous*) is feminine, *(s)* an additional *-s* if the subject *vous* is plural:

tu es allé *or* allé**e**
nous sommes allé**s** *or* allé**es**
vous êtes allé *or* allé**e** *or* allé**s** *or* allé**es**

For a given verb, the same auxiliary—*être* or *avoir*—is used in all of the compound verb forms (Chapter 7); for example, for the *past perfect, future perfect,* and *conditional perfect:*

Elle *avait écrit* un roman.	"She *had written* a novel."
Elle *était allé**e*** à l'école.	"She *had gone* to school."
Elle *aura écrit* un roman.	"She *will have written* a novel."
Elle *sera allé**e*** à l'école.	"She *will have gone* to school."
Elle *aurait* écrit un roman.	"She *would have written* a novel."
Elle *serait allé**e*** à l'école.	"She *would have gone* to school."

Auxiliary Verb and Accord of Past Participle

The choice of auxiliary—*être* or *avoir*—and the accord of the past participle are almost certainly the two issues causing the most difficulties for students of French, at least insofar as the verbal system is concerned. The choice of auxiliary is considerably easier to resolve and is also far more important. Unless the past participle ends in *-s* or *-t,* the differences among the four forms are purely orthographic, since they are pronounced identically:

chanté	chantés	chantée	chantées	[chantÉ]			
sorti	sortis	sortie	sorties	[sorti]			
valu	valus	value	values	[valu]			
mis	mis	mise	mises	[mi]	[mi]	[miS]	[miS]
inclus	inclus	incluse	incluses	[inclu]	[inclu]	[incluS]	[incluS]
mort	morts	morte	mortes	[mor]	[mor]	[morT]	[morT]

With regard to the degree of compliance with the "norm", a comment made more than seventy years ago is equally valid today:

> ...the spoken language shows much fluctuation, the tendency to leave the participle invariable being counteracted by the influence of the schoolmaster and of the written word.[6]

An eminent French historian of the language observed at about the same time:

> Elle n'est point douteuse: la langue tend à l'*invariabilité* du participe construit avec *avoir*... La règle actuelle, toute artificielle, est fondée sur un usage que d'aucuns peuvent trouver respectable, mais qui est complètement illogique et par là même singulièrement fragile.[7]
>
> There can be no doubt: the language tends towards the *invariability* of the (past) participle constructed with *avoir*... The current rule, completely artificial, is based on a usage which some may find respectable, but which is completely illogical and for that reason particularly fragile.

The overall situation can be summarized as follows:

	category	auxiliary	accord of past participle
(1)	certain intransitive verbs	être	with subject
(2)	other verbs	avoir	with *preceding* direct object, if any
(3)	verbs used *pronominally*	être	*generally* with subject

The basic features of these categories are described below, while the appendix to this chapter attempts to shed light on *why* such differences exist.

(1) Intransitive verbs of motion or transformation

These verbs are conjugated using *être* as auxiliary. The past participle *accords* with the *subject* (i.e., agrees in number and gender). The most common are listed below:

infinitive	past participle	
aller	allé	*go*
arriver	arrivé	*arrive*
venir	venu	*come*
revenir	revenu	*come back*

[6] Ewert (1969: 231; first published in 1933).

[7] Brunot and Bruneau (1937: 693). Note that *d'aucuns* means "some", *aucun* normally "not any".

	devenir	devenu	*become*
*	entrer	entré	*enter*
*	rentrer	rentré	*re-enter, go in*
*	sortir	sorti	*go out, exit*
	partir	parti	*leave*
	rester	resté	*remain*
*	retourner	retourné	*return*
*	monter	monté	*climb, mount*
*	descendre	descendu	*descend*
	tomber	tombé	*fall*
	naître	né	*be born*
	mourir	mort	*die*

Less common are:

parvenir	parvenu	*reach, attain*
décéder	décédé	*die*

These are typically remembered by the various things that one can do in a house—or perhaps hospital: enter, go up the stairs, go down the stairs (maybe by falling), go out the door, be born, die, and so forth.

Je *suis allé(**e**)* à Paris en Octobre.	"I *went* to Paris in October."
Nos amis *sont arrivé(**e**)**s*** hier soir.	"Our friends *arrived* last night."
Il *est devenu* un grand acteur.	"He *became/has become* a great actor."
Napoléon *est né* en Corse.	"Napoleon *was born* in Corsica."
Marie Antoinette *est mort**e*** en 1793.	"Marie Antoinette *died* in 1793."

The unifying element is that all of these are *intransitive* verbs of *motion* or *transformation.* The verbs marked with an asterisk in the list above can also be used *transitively* (i.e., with a direct object)[8]—and in such cases the auxiliary is *avoir,* not *être.* This gives rise to the following contrasts:

Est-ce qu'elle *est descendu**e*** de sa chambre?	"*Has* she *come down* from her room?"
Non, mais son mari *a descendu* ses valises.	"No, but her husband *has brought down* her bags."
Elle *a descendu* l'escalier.	"She *came down* the staircase."
Je *suis monté(**e**)* à ma chambre.	"I *went up* to my room."

[8] *Tomber* as well, in sporting and familiar senses: e.g., *il **a tombé** son adversaire* ("he *felled* his adversary"). *Aller* is used transitively in the expression *aller son chemin* ("to continue on his/her way").

J'*ai monté* l'escalier.	"I *went up* the staircase."
Elle a *monté* les valises à sa chambre.	"She *took* the suitcases *up* to her room."
Nous *sommes entré(**e**)**s*** par la fenêtre.	"We *entered* by the window."
Nous *avons entré* le piano par la fenêtre.	"We *brought in* the piano by the window."
Nous *avons entré* les données dans l'ordinateur.	"We *entered* the data in the computer."
Elle est *rentré**e*** dans sa chambre.	"She *went back* into her room."
Elle *a rentré* sa voiture au garage.	"She *put* her car (*back*) in the garage."

For *monter,* the auxiliary can be *avoir* rather than *être* even in *intransitive* use, if the emphasis is on the *action* rather than on the *state:*

La Bourse *a monté.*	"The stock market *has risen.*"
La température *a monté.*	"The temperature *has risen.*"
Les prix *ont monté.*	"Prices *have gone up.*"

Hence the contrast:

J'*ai monté* (à) la tour Eiffel deux fois.	"I *have climbed* the Eiffel Tower twice."
De la tour Eiffel, où je *suis monté(**e**)* hier, il y a une vue splendide.	"From the Eiffel Tower, which *I climbed* yesterday, there is a splendid view."

This is in fact an illustration of a more general phenomenon affecting a relatively large number of intransitive verbs and will be considered further in the appendix to this chapter.

(2) Other verbs

All other verbs—when not used *pronominally* (see [3] below)—are conjugated using *avoir* as auxiliary. There is *no* accord between the past participle and *subject.* On the other hand, when there is a *direct object* which *precedes* the verb there is *normally* accord between the past participle and the *direct object.*

Nous avons acheté *une voiture.*	"We (have) bought *a car.*"
La voiture que nous avons acheté**e** est verte.	"*The car* which we bought is green."
J'ai vu *Marie* ce matin. /J'ai vu *Paul* ce matin.	"I saw *Marie/Paul* this morning."
Je **l'**ai vu**e**/Je **l'**ai vu /Je **les** ai vu**s**.	"I saw *her/him/them.*"

The situation becomes more complicated when there is a preceding direct object *and* a following infinitive. If the preceding direct object is the *active* subject of the infinitive, then there is accord; if it is the *passive* object of the infinitive, there is no accord:

L'actrice que j'ai vu**e** *jouer* était française.	"*The actress* that I saw *perform* was French."
Je *l'*ai vu**e** jouer.	"I saw *her* perform."
La pièce que j'ai vu *jouer* était de Molière.	"*The play* which I saw *performed* was by Molière."
Je *l'*ai vu jouer.	"I saw *it* (the play) performed."

In the first two examples one can say *the actress performs* (active). In the second pair, however, one cannot say *the theatrical work performs:* rather *the theatrical work is performed* (passive).

An exception to the exception occurs for *faire* and *laisser,* in which case there is never accord of the past participle, even when the preceding direct object is the active subject of the infinitive which follows.[9]

Je *les* ai fait partir. (*not* *fait**s**)	"I made *them* leave."	(*they leave*—active)
Je *les* ai laissé partir. (*not* *laissé**s**)	"I let *them* leave."	(*they leave*—active)

There are other fine points and exceptions, but these are the principal ones.

(3) Reflexive/pronominal verbs

Consider the following groups of sentences:

(a)	Marie *se lave* avec du savon.	"Marie *washes herself* with soap."
	Nous *nous lavons* avec du savon.	"We *wash ourselves* (or *each other*) with soap."
	Je *me lève* de bonne heure.	"I *get (myself) up* (out of bed) early."
	Je *me donne* au travail.	"I *devote myself* to work."
(b)	Jean et Marie *s'écrivent.*	"Jean and Marie *write (to) each other.*"
	Nous *nous écrivons.*	"We *write (to) each other.*"
(c)	Jean et Marie *se sourient.*	"Jean and Marie *smile (at each other).*"
	Nous *nous sourions.*	"We *smile (at each other).*"
	Les rois *se succèdent.*	"The kings *succeed (follow) one another.*"

[9] For *laisser* this is a relatively new rule, and there is still much disagreement. When there is no following infinitive, *faire* and *laisser* accord "normally" with a preceding direct object: e.g., *la table qu'il a faite* ("the table which he made").

(d)	Le prisonnier *s'évade.*	"The prisoner *escapes.*"
	Je *m'évade.*	"I *escape.*"
(e)	Cette boisson *se boit* frais.	"This beverage *is (to be) drunk* chilled."
	Ces livres *se vendent* bien.	"These books *sell (are sold)* well."

All five groups represent *verbes pronominaux,* the common element being an "extra" pronoun[10] (*me, te, se, nous, vous*) which corresponds to the subject.

The first two groups illustrate ordinary *transitive* verbs (*laver, lever, donner, écrire*) used *reflexively* (we washed *ourselves*), *reciprocally* (*each other*), or with "new" meaning (e.g., *se donner*). The difference between (a) and (b) is that in (a) the "extra" pronoun represents a *direct* object on which the subject acts (Marie washes *herself,* we wash *ourselves* or *each other,* I devote *myself*), while in (b) it represents an *indirect* object which receives the action:

We write *letters* (dir. obj.) TO *each other* (ind. obj.).

Group (c) consists of intransitive verbs: the extra pronoun represents (in French, though not necessarily always in English) an *indirect* object. In group (d) the pronoun has come to be an *inseparable* element of the verb, without necessarily having any particular reflexive (or object) sense. Thus, verbs like **évader, *exclamer, *méfier, *réfugier, *suicider* exist only in their *pronominal* forms *s'évader, s'exclamer, se méfier, se réfugier, se suicider.* For the purposes of this exposition we will call them *inseparable* verbs.[11] Finally, group (e) represents *pronominal verbs with a passive sense,* and the extra pronoun is essentially a direct object: *cette boisson* ***se*** *bois frais* literally means "this beverage drinks ***itself*** cool".

A verb can often find itself in more than one category, sometimes with altered meaning. Thus, for *donner:*

Je *me donne* un cadeau.	reflexive (ind. obj.)	"I *give myself* a present."
Je *me donne* au travail.	(dir. obj.)	"I *devote myself* to work."

In the first case, the pronoun *me* is an *indirect* object (I am the recipient of the gift), while in the second, *me* is the *direct* object which is given (to my work). In this context *se donner* has essentially become an entirely new verb ("to devote

---

[10] In French grammar books this is called a *pronom personnel réfléchi* ("personal reflexive pronoun"). We will use the less elegant phrasing "extra" pronoun to avoid confusion, since many of the pronominal verbs with which they are used are not reflexive verbs.

[11] The French name is *les verbes essentiellement pronominaux;* alternatively, *les verbes pronominaux de sens lexicalisé.*

oneself"), analogous to the *inseparable* verbs like *s'évader*, but with the important difference that *donner* exists whereas **évader* does not.

All pronominal verbs are conjugated with *être* as auxiliary. The accord of the past participle is more complicated.

Rule 1. All pronominal verbs have auxiliary *être*.

Rule 2. For pronominal verbs, the past participle accords with the pronoun/subject[12] *unless* this "extra" pronoun serves grammatically as an *indirect* object.

These rules can be illustrated with regard to the above partition of pronominal verbs, where *se* represents the "extra" pronoun:

group	*se*	accord with pronoun (= subject)
(a) transitive verbs	(usually) direct object	*unless* there is an *explicit direct* object[13]
(b) transitive verbs	indirect object	never
(c) intransitive verbs	indirect object	never
(d) inseparable verbs	—	always[14]
(e) passive sense	(direct object)	always

When the transitive verb *laver* is conjugated reflexively, there is *normally* accord between the past participle and the object pronoun (subject):

with *avoir*	with *être*
J'ai lavé le linge.	Je *me* suis lavé(**e**) au savon.
Tu as lavé le linge.	Tu *t'*es lavé(**e**) au savon.
Elle a lavé le linge.	Elle *s'*est lavé**e** au savon.
Nous avons lavé le linge.	Nous *nous* sommes lavé(**e**)**s** au savon.
Vous avez lavé le linge.	Vous *vous* êtes lavé(**e**)(**s**) au savon.
Elles ont lavé le linge.	Elles *se* sont lavé**es** au savon.

[12] For pronominal verbs, the "extra" pronoun always corresponds to the subject.

[13] In which case, as we will see below, *se* becomes an *indirect* object pronoun.

[14] There is only one inseparable verb in which *se* is treated as an indirect rather than a direct object: *arroger* ("to appropriate"): thus *elle s'est arrogé le titre* ("she appropriated the title for herself"), not *elle s'est *arrogé***e** *le titre.*

In each of the examples on the right, the object pronoun (*me, te, se, nous, vous, se*) serves as a *direct* object. However, if an explicit direct object is added to the sentence, the reflexive pronoun ceases to be the direct object. In

Marie se lave *les mains* avec du savon.	"Marie washes *her hands* with soap."

les mains is now the direct object, *se* the indirect object (literally: Marie washes *to herself* the hands). Since there is no accord with an *indirect* object pronoun, we have the contrast:

(1) Marie s'est lavé**e** avec du savon.	"Marie washed (herself) with soap."
(2) Marie s'est lavé *les mains* avec du savon.	"Marie washed *her hands* with soap."

As with verbs conjugated with *avoir,* if the direct object *precedes* the verb there *is* accord between the *direct object* and the past participle:

(3) *Les mains* que Marie s'est lavé**es** avec du savon sont toujours sales.	"*The hands* which Marie washed with soap are still dirty."

Note that in (3) it is *lavé**es*** whereas in (1) it is *lavé**e***.

If we consider the pronoun element of an inseparable verb (such as *s'évader*) to be a direct object, then we can reformulate Rule 2 above to cover all cases in which there is accord of the past participle—either with the "extra" pronoun (i.e., subject) or with a preceding direct object like *les mains:*

> **Rule 2′. For pronominal verbs, the past participle accords with a *preceding direct object* (be it "extra" object pronoun or explicit direct object), if any; otherwise there is no accord.**

Further examples are provided below:

(i) accord with pronoun (subject)

—*se* functions as *direct* object
—*inseparable* verbs
—*passive* sense

Elle s'est *regardé**e*** dans un miroir.	"She looked (at) herself in a mirror."
Ils se sont *aperçu**s*** dans la rue.	"They caught sight of each other in the street."
La porte s'est *fermé**e*** toute seule.	"The door closed (itself) by itself."
Je me suis *marié**e*** avec un français.	"I married (myself to) a Frenchman."

Ils se sont *caché**s***.	"They hid (themselves) from each other."
Ils se sont *donné**s*** à leur travail.	"They dedicated themselves to their work."
Elles se sont *souven**ues*** de toi.	"They (fem.) remembered you."
Elle s'est *évanoui**e***.	"She fainted."
La scène s'est *déroulé**e*** sous nos yeux.	"The scene unfolded (itself) before our eyes."
Ces livres se sont bien *vendu**s***.	"These books have sold (themselves) well."

(ii) no accord

—*se* functions as *indirect* object
—*intransitive* verbs
—*following* direct object (FDO)

Elles se sont *écrit*.	"They wrote (to) each other."	(*écrire à quelqu'un*)
Elle s'est *demandé* pourquoi cela ne marchait pas.	"She wondered (asked herself) why it didn't work."	(*demander à quelqu'un*)
Ils se sont *nui*.	"They did each other harm."	(*nuire à*)
Elles se sont *plu*.	"They liked each other."	(*plaire à*)
Ils se sont *souri*.	"They smiled at each other."	(*sourire à*)
Les orages se sont *succédé* sans interruption.	"The storms followed (one after the other) without interruption."	(*succéder à*)
Ils se sont *téléphoné*.	"They telephoned one another."	(*téléphoner à*)
Ils se sont *rendu* compte de leur erreur.	"They realized their mistake."	(FDO)
Ils se sont *donné* des cadeaux.	"They gave each other presents."	(FDO)
Elle s'est *coupé* la main.	"She cut her hand."	(FDO)
Ils se sont *caché* leurs inquiétudes.	"They hid their anxieties from each other."	(FDO)
Ils se sont *construit* une maison.	"They built themselves a house."	(FDO)

(iii) accord with *preceding* direct object

J'ai vu *la maison* qu'ils se sont *construit**e***.	"I saw the house which they built (for) themselves."
La main qu'il s'est *coupé**e*** est sanglante.	"The (his) hand which he cut is bloody."

Imperfect

As noted in the Introduction, the imperfect does not correspond directly to any simple English verb form. It normally refers to an action which took place in the past, without any indication as to whether the action was completed or whether it continued indefinitely: *yesterday it rained two inches* (completed) as opposed to *yesterday it was raining* (imperfect). Its most common uses are in:

(a) *Indefinite* statements about the past:

La famine *régnait* dans tout le pays . . . La famine *augmentait* dans le pays d'Égypte. (Genèse 41:56, version Louis Segond)	"And the famine *was* all over the face of the earth . . . And the famine *waxed* sore in the land of Egypt." (King James Version)
Quand j'*étais* jeune je *jouais* souvent au base-ball.	"When I *was* young *I played* a lot of baseball."
Il y *avait* beaucoup de monde à la fête.	"There *were* a lot of people at the party."

(b) Statements relating to a condition existing at the moment of a specific action in the past (the latter expressed using the *passé composé*):[15]

Je *lavais* le linge quand le téléphone a sonné.	"I *was washing* the laundry when the telephone rang."
J'*étais* en train de laver le linge quand le téléphone a sonné.	"I *was* (in the process of) *washing* the laundry when the telephone rang."
J'*allais* toujours à l'école quand Armstrong a marché sur la lune.	"I *was* still *going* to school when Armstrong walked on the moon."

(c) The *if* part of *if . . . then* clauses where the *then* clause is in the conditional:

Si je *pouvais* le faire, je le ferais.	"If I *were able* to do it, I would do it."

These clauses will be considered in greater detail at a later stage.

(d) Translations for "as if" (*comme si*) phrases in either the present or past:

Il parle ***comme s'il*** *était* fou.	"He speaks ***as if*** *he were* crazy."
Il parlait ***comme s'il*** *était* fou.	"He was speaking ***as if*** *he were* crazy."
Il me traite ***comme si*** *j'étais* son valet.	"He treats me ***as if*** *I were* his valet."

---

[15] Or *passé simple: Je lavais le linge quand le téléphone* ***sonna.***

Past Perfect

The past perfect is used to express an action in the past which occurred prior to another past action or point in time:

J'*avais* déjà *préparé* le repas quand mes invités sont arrivés. — "I *had* already *prepared* the dinner when my guests arrived."
La porte qu'il *avait fermée* en sortant était ouverte quand il est revenu. — "The door which he *had shut* on leaving was open when he returned."
Nous étions contents parce que nous *avions reçu* de bonnes nouvelles. — "We were happy because we *had received* good news."
Je croyais (J'ai cru) que tu *étais* déjà *parti(e)*. — "I thought that you *had already* left."

The verb in the main clause is in the *passé composé* or imperfect, according to the normal rules.

Perhaps the most common use of the past perfect is referring to past hypothetical situations in an *if . . . then* clause:

Si j'*avais su,* je ne serais pas venu(e). — "If I *had known,* I would not have come."

These clauses will be discussed in greater detail at a later stage.

"Immediate" Past: *Venir de + Infinitive*

The construction *venir* (present tense) *de + infinitive* is frequently used in place of the *passé composé* to refer to an event which has just taken place.

Elle *vient d'arriver.* — "She *has just arrived.*"

With reference to something which *had* just occurred, *venir* (imperfect tense) *de + infinitive* is frequently used in place of the past perfect.

Je suis allé(e) le voir mais il *venait de sortir.* — "I went to see him but he *had just left.*"

Present Participle, *Gérondif,* and Verbal Adjective

These are distinguished in both form and use. We use *gérondif* since its use does not correspond directly to the English *gerund.*

	aimer	*exceller*	*provoquer*	*diverger*
present participle	aimant	excellant	provoquant	divergeant
gérondif	*en* aimant	*en* excellant	*en* provoquant	*en* divergeant
verbal adjective	aimant(e)(s)	excell**ent**(e)(s)	provo**cant**(e)(s)	diverg**ent**(e)(s)

In terms of form:

(a) the *gérondif* is equal to the present participle preceded by *en;*
(b) the present participle and the *gérondif* are *invariable;*
(c) the verbal adjective *accords* (in gender and number) with the noun it modifies, and in some cases its form differs from that of the corresponding present participle (see Chapter 2).

The **present participle** expresses action which occurs *simultaneously* with the action of the (conjugated) verb:

J'ai vu votre frère *traversant* la rue.	"I saw your brother *crossing* the street."
C'est une fille *aimant* les chats.	"She is a girl *loving* (who loves) cats."
Une comédie est une pièce de théâtre *ayant* pour but de divertir.	"A comedy is a play *having* the objective to entertain (whose aim is to entertain)."

When placed at the beginning of a sentence, the present participle can be physically separated from its "subject":

Aimant la campagne, la fille ne veut pas vivre en ville.	"*Loving* the country(side), the girl does not want to live in town."
Dormant au deuxième étage, elle n'a rien entendu.	"*Sleeping* on the second floor, she did not hear anything."

It can also be used in *compound* form:

La pluie *ayant cessé,* je suis sorti(e).	"The rain *having stopped,* I went out."
Étant tombée amoureuse de lui, elle lui a envoyé un e-mail.	"*Having fallen* in love with him, she sent him an e-mail."
Je n'étais pas très sale, *m'étant lavé(e)* le matin même.	"I wasn't very dirty, *having washed myself* that very morning."

The first example illustrates an important difference with respect to the *gérondif:* the present participle can have a subject (*la pluie*) which is different from that of the principal clause (*je*).

The **gérondif** functions essentially as an *adverb,* providing information on *when* or *how* something occurs:

En traversant la rue j'ai vu votre frère.	"*While crossing the street,* I saw your brother."
En me promenant j'ai rencontré Marie.	"*While taking a walk,* I met Marie."
J'aime travailler *en écoutant* la musique.	"I like to work *while listening* to music."
Les enfants sont sortis *en courant.*	"The children went out *running.*"
Il a gagné beaucoup d'argent *en travaillant* pendant les vacances.	"He earned a lot of money *by working* during the vacation."
C'est *en forgeant* qu'on devient forgeron.	"It's *by forging* that one becomes a blacksmith."

The last example is the French equivalent of the proverb *practice makes perfect.* The requirement that the *gérondif* be preceded by *en* was not formalized until a relatively late stage, so that a number of "fixed" expressions which violate the rule remain in the language, including:

fixed expression	modern form	
chemin *faisant*	*en faisant* chemin	"on (or along) the way"
tambour *battant*	*en battant* tambour	"briskly", "promptly"
argent *comptant*	*en comptant* argent	*figurative:* "at face value"
ce *faisant*	*en faisant* cela	"in so doing"
ce *disant*	*en disant* cela	"in so saying", "by virtue of this"

A second requirement of the (modern) *gérondif* is that it refer to the *subject* of the verb on which it depends. Thus a sentence like the following is generally not allowed (in either language):

**En sortant* de l'école, il était déjà très tard.	*"*On leaving* school, it was already very late."

since *en sortant* refers to an unnamed person (*he, she, I,* etc.) while the subject of the main clause is the impersonal *il.* Such rules did not apply when proverbs were made, hence:

L'appétit vient *en mangeant.*	"Appetite comes *from eating*" (i.e., *The more one has, the more one wants*).

As its name implies the **verbal adjective** functions (purely) as an adjective and like other adjectives agrees in gender and number with the noun it modifies:

C'est une fille *aimante*.	"She is an *affectionate* girl."
Ces livres sont *intéressants*.	"These books are *interesting*."
Vous n'étiez pas très *convaincant(e)(s)*.	"You were not very *convincing*."

Note the contrast between *une fille aimante* and *une fille . . . aimant les chats*, as well as the fact that the present participle corresponding to *convaincant(e)(s)* is *convainquant*. Other examples contrasting invariable present participle (PP) and variable verbal adjective (VA):

(PP)	une femme *charmant* ses auditeurs	"a woman *charming* her listeners"
(VA)	une femme *charmante*	"a *charming* woman"
(PP)	Les enfants *se méfiant* du chien n'osaient pas pénétrer dans la cour.	"The children, not *trusting* (wary of) the dog, did not dare enter the courtyard."
(VA)	Les enfants étaient *méfiants*.	"The children were *wary*."
(PP)	Pierre *excellant* dans ses études, il a reçu de très bonnes notes.	"Pierre *excelling* in his studies, he obtained very good grades."
(VA)	Pierre est un élève *excellent*.	"Pierre is an *excellent* student."
(PP)	Votre opinion *différant* de la mienne, nous ne nous comprendrons jamais.	"Your opinion *differing* from mine, we will never understand each other."
(VA)	Votre opinion est bien *différente* de la mienne.	"Your opinion is very *different* from mine."

It was not until 1679 that the distinction between *invariable* present participle and *variable* verbal adjective was formalized. As observed earlier with the *gérondif*, a number of "old" uses—incorrect by today's norms—have continued in the language, notably in certain legal expressions.

fixed expression	literally	in other words
la partie *plaignante*	"the party *complaining*"	"the plaintiff"
les *ayants* droit	"those *having* right(s)"	"claimants", "beneficiaries"
les *ayants* cause	"those *having* cause"	"right holders", "successors"
à tous *venants*	"to all *coming*"	"to all comers"
les *tenants* et *aboutissants*	"the *holdings* and *resultings*"	"the ins and outs"
toutes affaires *cessantes*	"all affairs *ceasing*"	"forthwith", "at once"
séance *tenante*	"*holding* session"	"immediately"
à la nuit *tombante*	"at night *falling*"	"twilight", "dusk"

In each of these examples, the italicized expression is used as a present participle and hence by the modern "norm" should be without accord (e.g., **les ayant droit*).

English ***gerunds***—sometimes called *verbal nouns*—are generally translated by French *infinitives:*

J'aime *lire.*	"I like *reading.*"/"I like *to read.*"
Fumer nuit à la santé.	"*Smoking* damages health."
Courir est la meilleure façon d'apprendre la patience.	"*Running* is the best way to learn patience."

Future Tense

The French future tense is used very similarly to the future in English:

Demain j'*irai* chez le médecin.	"Tomorrow I *will go* to the doctor."
Un jour elle *sera* présidente.	"One day she *will be* president."
L'année prochaine nous *achèterons* une nouvelle voiture.	"Next year we *will buy* a new car."

In expressions using *quand, lorsque, dès que,* etc., French uses the future where in English the present tense is more common:

Quand tu *seras* prêt(e), nous *partirons.*	"When you are (*will be*) ready, we *will leave.*"
Dès que la pluie *cessera,* je *partirai.*	"As soon as the rain stops (*will stop*), I *will leave.*"
Appelle-moi quand il *arrivera.*	"Call me when he arrives (*will arrive*)."
Vous pouvez venir quand vous *voudrez.*	"You can come when you like *(will like).*"
Je *retournerai* à Paris dès que je *pourrai.*	"I *will return* to Paris as soon as I can (*will be able to*)."

The future tense is used in the *then* part of *if . . . then* clauses where the *if* verb is in the present:

S'il pleut demain, je *resterai* à la maison.	"If it rains tomorrow, I *will stay* at home."

If . . . then clauses will be discussed further below.

Other uses of the future include:

(a) *futur historique* (or *prophétique*), where from the perspective of the past a historical event is still "to come":

À la mort de son père, il est devenu roi: son règne *durera* cinquante ans.	"Upon the death of his father, he became king: his reign *will* (was to) *last* 50 years."

(b) *futur de politesse* (or *d'atténuation*), where use of the future tense allows the speaker to maintain a certain "distance" from the message he or she is conveying:

Cela *fera* dix euros.	"That *will make* (be) 10 euros."

(c) as a substitute for the *impératif* to express an order or command:

Tu ne *tueras* point.	"Thou *shalt* not *kill.*" (Exodus 20:13)

Alternative Forms of the Future

In English, the future tense is often replaced by a more informal construction using the verb *to go*, particularly when the future being referred to is not too distant:

future:	I *will do* my homework tomorrow.
near-future:	I am *going to do* my homework tomorrow.

An analogous substitution frequently occurs in French, using *aller* plus *infinitive* in place of the more formal future:

future:	Je *ferai* mes devoirs demain.
	L'année prochaine j'*achèterai* une nouvelle voiture.
near-future:	Je *vais faire* mes devoirs demain.
	L'année prochaine je *vais acheter* une nouvelle voiture.

As noted earlier, the *present* tense is used on occasion to replace the future. This is particularly common with regard to the verb *aller:*

future:	Demain nous *irons* à la plage.
present:	Demain nous *allons* à la plage.
	"Tomorrow we will go [*go*] to the beach."

Future Perfect

The French use of the future perfect generally parallels English usage:

Dans deux ans, j'*aurai terminé* mes études.	"In two years I *will have finished* my studies."
Quand j'*aurai lu* ce livre, je te le prêterai.	"When I *(will) have read* this book, I will lend it to you."

Conditional Tense

The conditional tense initially developed to fulfill the role of a future in the past and only later was extended to situations in the present and future. Its major uses include the following.

Future in the Past

He said: *I will be there at noon.* Il a dit qu'il *serait* là à midi.	"He said he *would be* there at noon."

Similarly,

Je pensais que tu *arriverais* plus tôt.	"I thought that you *would arrive* earlier."
Je vous ai dit que je le *ferais!*	"I told you that I *would do* it!"

Present Conditional Meaning

Tu *devrais* te coucher.[16]	"You *should* go to bed."
Je *pourrais* transcrire ici un gros volume de vos ignorances. (Voltaire)	"I *could* fill a big book with examples of your ignorance."
Je *voudrais* aller en France cet été.	"I *would like* to go to France this summer."
J'ai toujours rêvé de vivre à Paris; mon appartement *serait* dans le quartier Latin.	"I have always dreamed of living in Paris; my apartment *would be* in the Latin Quarter."

---

[16] This could be interpreted alternatively as an expression of "politeness", depending on the degree of insistence suggested by the tone of the speaker's voice.

Politeness

J'*aimerais* un café, s'il vous plaît.	"I *would like* a coffee, please."
Accepteriez-vous notre invitation?	"*Would* you accept our invitation?"

Uncertainty

Il y *aurait* une centaine de victimes.	"There *are (reported to be)* 100 victims."
Une nuée de sauterelles *se dirigerait* vers le Midi.	"A swarm of grasshoppers *is (reportedly) moving* towards the South (of France)."

Conditionals of uncertainty are frequent in news reporting.

If . . . Then Clauses

The conditional tense is employed as the second element in *if . . . then* clauses when the *if* verb is in the imperfect. These will be discussed further below.

Si je pouvais le faire, je le *ferais.*	"If I were able to do it, I *would do* it."

Conditional Perfect

J'*aurais* bien *voulu* être médecin, mais je n'ai pas assez étudié quand j'étais jeune.	"I *would have* very much *liked* to be a doctor, but I didn't study enough when I was young."
L'avion *serait tombé* dans la montagne.	"The airplane *would* (i.e., was reported to) *have crashed* in the mountains."

A frequent use of the conditional perfect is as the second element in *if . . . then* clauses in which the first is in the past perfect (*plus-que-parfait*).

Passé Surcomposé

Consider the sentence "When it finished raining, we left." There are two points of importance: (a) the *termination* of the action of raining; and (b) the prior nature (*anteriority*) of such termination in relation to the action expressed in the second verb ("to leave"). Until relatively recently, this would have been expressed unambiguously as:

(1) Quand la pluie *eut cessé,* nous *partîmes.*

where *eut* and *partîmes* are simple pasts (*passé simple*) of the verbs *avoir* and *partir;* the compound form *eut cessé* is the *passé antérieur.* Over time, however, the *passé simple* died out in spoken speech, replaced by the *passé composé.* If one replaces both *eut* and *partîmes* by their corresponding *passé composé—a eu* and *sommes partis*—the result is

(2) Quand la pluie ***a eu*** *cessé,* nous *sommes partis.*[17]

The first verb (*a eu cessé*) is now in the *passé surcomposé* (i.e., the *passé composé* of the auxiliary verb *avoir* followed by the past participle of *cesser*).

The alternative to using the *passé surcomposé* is either the basic *passé composé* itself:

(3) Quand la pluie *a cessé,* nous sommes partis.

or alternative constructions (more "elegant" in the view of some), notably using the present participle of the auxiliary:

(4) La pluie *ayant cessé,* nous sommes partis.

The *passé surcomposé* is used by a large number of French speakers, including (it appears) a majority in the south of France, Switzerland, and Quebec and perhaps up to half of northern France (excluding Paris).[18] It nonetheless occupies a very odd status in Modern French. According to the noted French linguist Henriette Walter:

> Posez donc la question autour de vous et vous constaterez que beaucoup de personnes cultivées l'emploient en toute bonne conscience, aussi bien à l'oral qu'à l'écrit, en étant intimement persuadées que c'est la seule forme correcte. Mais d'autres personnes, tout aussi cultivées, et avec le même sentiment de détenir la vérité, refusent de l'employer, en affirmant avec la même vigueur que ce sont là des formes incorrectes et absolument non conformes à la norme. D'autres encore, dont je suis, tout en les jugeant tout à fait utiles, ne peuvent se résoudre à les utiliser.[19]

> Pose the question about you, and you will observe that many cultured people use it (*passé surcomposé*) in completely good conscience, orally as

---

[17] From this point on, we cease to mark possibilities of accord: *nous sommes partis* rather than *nous sommes parti(e)s.*

[18] There is also a more "dialectical" use of the *passé surcomposé* in independent clauses, as in the oft-quoted phrase of the humorist Fernand Raynaud: *La vigne ça a eu payé, mais ça ne paye plus*—"Wine growing *used to be* (i.e., at one time was, but that time is well past) profitable, but it no longer pays."

[19] Walter (1988: 182).

well as in writing, being intimately persuaded that it is the only correct form. But others, equally cultured, and with the same utter conviction of possessing the truth, refuse to employ it, affirming with the same vigor that these are incorrect forms and absolutely not in compliance with the norm. Others still, of whom I am one, while judging them absolutely useful, are unable to convince ourselves to use them.

Many grammar books dismiss the *passé surcomposé* as "popular" or limited to the spoken language only. Thus, according to *1001 Pitfalls in French:*[20]

> ... cette forme fait un peu trop populaire. Aussi considère-t-on que les deux participes passés (*eu cessé*) font lourd. En tout cas, le passé surcomposé est à déconseiller.
>
> ... this form is a bit too popular. In addition, the two past participles (*eu cessé*) can be regarded as "heavy". In any case, the passé surcomposé is not to be recommended.

However, the Académie Française points out:

> Bien qu'ils appartiennent principalement au langage parlé, les temps surcomposés se rencontrent chez les meilleurs auteurs, de Balzac à Mauriac en passant par Stendhal, Hugo, Renan ou Proust.[21]
>
> Although they belong principally to the spoken language, the "surcomposed" tenses are to be found among the best authors, from Balzac to Mauriac passing through Stendhal, Hugo, Renan, or Proust.

The process of surcomposition can be applied to tenses other than the *passé composé*—hence the reference above to *les temps surcomposés.* For example:

past perfect surcomposé	quand la pluie *avait eu cessé*
future perfect surcomposé	quand la pluie *aura eu cessé*
conditional perfect surcomposé	quand la pluie *aurait eu cessé*

---

[20] James H. Grew and Daniel D. Olivier, *1001 Pitfalls in French* (New York: Barron's Educational Series, 1986), p. 51.

[21] From the web site of l'Académie Française (www.academie-francaise.fr), rubric "La langue française—Questions courantes—Temps surcomposés."

In contrast to the *passé surcomposé,* such forms are used relatively infrequently.

Other examples of the *passé surcomposé:*

Aussitôt qu'il *a eu mangé* le gâteau, il s'est senti mal.	"As soon as *he had eaten* the cake, he felt ill."
Quand elle *a été rentrée,*[22] elle a mis ses pantoufles.	"When she *returned* home, she put on her slippers."
Même lorsqu'il *a eu quitté* la peinture, il est resté peintre avec sa plume.[23]	"Even when he *had abandoned* painting, he remained a painter with his pen."
Dès que *j'ai eu vu* que la lettre ne me concernait pas, je te l'ai renvoyée.	"As soon as I *saw* that the letter didn't concern me, I sent it back to you."

Those who do not use the *passé surcomposé* will in each of these cases substitute either the *passé composé* or an alternative construction:

> Aussitôt qu'il a mangé le gâteau . . .
> Après avoir mangé le gâteau . . .

Finally, it should perhaps be noted that what might appear to a native English-speaker to be a logical construction—and a direct translation of the corresponding English—will not work:

> *Quand *elle était rentrée,* elle a mis ses pantoufles.

With *quand, dès que, lorsque,* etc., the past perfect (*plus-que-parfait*) refers to a *habitual* (or possibly incompleted) action in the past and can be used only when the verb in the principal clause is in the *imperfect:*

(Chaque jour) quand elle *était rentrée,* elle *mettait* ses pantoufles.	(Each day) when she *(had) returned* home, she *would put* on her slippers.

[22] When the *passé surcomposé* is used with a verb which employs *être* as an auxiliary *but which can also be used transitively* with *avoir* (p. 109), a potential problem arises, since the phrase could also be interpreted as a *passive* expression—in this case, "when she (or it) *was brought* in".

[23] A "modernization" of the original by the nineteenth-century author Charles Augustin Saint-Beuve: "Même lorsqu'il *eut quitté* la peinture . . . il *resta* peintre avec sa plume."

If...Then Constructions

In French, as in English, there are essentially three types of conditional phrases: two in the present (possible and purely hypothetical) and one in the past (hypothetical only). The past conditional phrases can in turn be subdivided into two categories, depending upon whether the main (resultant) clause refers to the past or present.

	possible	hypothetical
ENGLISH		
present	If I *win* the lottery I *will buy* a new house.	If I *were* rich I *would buy* a new house.
past	———	(a) If I *had won* the lottery, I *would have bought* a new house. (b) If I *had won* the lottery, today I *would be* a rich man.
FRENCH		
present	Si je *gagne* au loto, j'*achèterai* une nouvelle maison.	Si j'*étais* riche, j'*achèterais* une nouvelle maison.
past	———	(a) Si j'*avais gagné* au loto, j'*aurais acheté* une nouvelle maison. (b) Si j'*avais gagné* au loto, aujourd'hui je *serais* un homme riche.

The use of French verb tenses in such phrases, which to a large extent parallels English usage, is as follows:

	if	*then*
present possible	present	future (less commonly present or imperative)
present hypothetical	imperfect	conditional
past hypothetical	past perfect	(a) conditional perfect (b) conditional

Since

past perfect	=	imperfect of *avoir/être*	+	past participle
conditional perfect	=	conditional of *avoir/être*	+	past participle

the use of verb tenses can be summarized as:

	if	*then*
possible	present	future
hypothetical	imperfect	conditional

Other examples:

S'il *pleut* demain je n'*irai* pas au parc.	"If it *rains* tomorrow I *will* not *go* to the park."
Ce *sera* un désastre s'il *pleut* demain.	"It *will be* a disaster if it *rains* tomorrow."
Ce *serait* un désastre s'il *pleuvait* demain.	"It *would be* a disaster if it *were to rain* tomorrow."
Si tu *as lu* tous ces livres, l'examen *sera* facile pour toi.	"If you *have read* all these books, the test *will be* easy for you."
Cela *aurait été* un désastre si cet homme *avait gagné* les élections.	"It *would have been* a disaster if that man *had won* the elections."
Si tu *avais étudié* plus quand tu étais jeune, aujourd'hui tu *serais* médecin	"If you *had studied* more when you were young, today you *would be* a doctor."
Si j'*ai* le temps, je t'*aiderai*.	"If I *have* (the) time, I *will help* you."
Si j'*avais* le temps, je t'*aiderais*.	"If I *had* (the) time, I *would help* you."
Si j'*avais eu* le temps, je t'*aurais aidé*.	"If I *had had* (the) time, I *would have helped* you."
Il y a des gens qui n'*auraient* jamais *été* amoureux s'ils n'*avaient* jamais *entendu* parler de l'amour. (La Rochefoucauld)	"There are people who *would* never *have been* in love if they *had* never *heard* of love."

It is very important to note that the future and conditional can *never* appear in the "if" part of an *if . . . then* construction:

*Si tu *feras* cela, je serai content.	Si tu **fais** cela . . .
*Si je *serais* riche, j'achèterais une maison.	Si j'**étais** riche . . .

When *si* means "whether" rather than "if", there is no such restriction:

Il me demande **si** je *viendrai*.	"He asks me **whether** I *will come*."
Il m'a demandé **si** je *viendrais*.	"He asked me **whether** I *would come*."
Je ne sais pas **si** je *viendrais* même *si* vous m'*invitiez*.	"I don't know **whether** I *would come* even *if* you *were to invite* me."

In the last example, the first *si* ("whether") is followed by the conditional, while *même si* ("even if ") is followed by the imperfect.

Conditional Phrases with Conjunctions Other Than *If*

As in English, conditional phrases can also be expressed with conjunctions (or phrases) other than *if.* For example:

au cas où	"in case", "in the event that", "if"
en cas que	"in case", "in the event that", "if"
pourvu que	"provided that"
à condition que	"on (the) condition that"

With the notable exception of *au cas où* and related *dans le cas où, pour le cas où, dans l'hypothèse où,* which are accompanied by the conditional, the other expressions require the subjunctive and will be considered in Chapter 11.

Au cas où *il pleuvrait,* le match n'aurait pas lieu.	"If it *were to rain,* the match would not take place."
Au cas où elle *téléphonerait,* dis-lui que je suis sorti.	"If she *telephones,* tell her that I have gone out."
Que faire dans le cas où vous *seriez arrêté* ou *détenu* à l'étranger.	"What to do in case you are (*would be*) *arrested* or *detained* abroad."
Dans l'hypothèse où le montant de votre commande *serait* supérieur à 150 euros, nous vous prions de nous fournir une copie de votre pièce d'identité.	"In the event that your order *is* (*would be*) more than 150 euros, we ask you to furnish us a copy of your identity card."

Passive Constructions

As in English, in French a *transitive* verb can be converted from the *active* to the *passive* "voice" by using its past participle with the verb "to be" (*être*): the *active* object becomes the *passive* subject. In French passive constructions, there is accord (in gender and number) between the subject and past participle.[24]

---

[24] Exceptionally, the intransitive verbs *obéir* and *désobéir* can be used passively, reflecting their origin as transitive verbs: *Les lois son obéi**es** par tous les bons citoyens* ("Laws are *obeyed* by all good citizens"). Similarly for *pardonner,* which is intransitive when used with people: *vous êtes pardonné* ("you are *pardoned*").

Active

Pierre *aime* Marie.	"Pierre *loves* Marie."
Les fleurs *attirent* les abeilles.	"Flowers *attract* bees."
Les Autrichiens *parlent* allemand.	"Austrians *speak* German."
Voltaire *a écrit* Candide au 18ème siècle.	"Voltaire *wrote* Candide in the 18th century."

Passive

Marie est *aimé**e*** par Pierre.	"Marie *is loved* by Pierre."
Les abeilles *sont attiré**es*** par les fleurs.	"Bees *are attracted* by flowers."
L'allemand *est parlé* en Autriche.	"German *is spoken* in Austria."
Candide *a été écrit* au 18ème siècle.	"Candide *was written* in the 18th century."

The *tense* of the passive corresponds to that of the auxiliary *être*. Thus:

present	Marie *est* aimé**e** par Pierre.	"Marie *is* loved by Pierre."
passé composé	Marie *a été* aimé**e**.	"Marie *was/has been* loved."
imperfect	Marie *était* aimé**e**.	"Marie *was* loved." (*did it end?*)
plus-que-parfait	Marie *avait été* aimé**e**.	"Marie *had been* loved."
future	Marie *sera* aimé**e**.	"Marie *will be* loved."
future perfect	Marie *aura été* aimé**e**.	"Marie *will have been* loved."
conditional	Marie *serait* aimé**e**.	"Marie *would be* loved."
conditional perfect	Marie *aurait été* aimé**e**.	"Marie *would have been* loved."
passé simple	Marie *fut* aimé**e**.	"Marie *was* loved." (*it ended*)
passé surcomposé	Marie *a eu été* aimé**e**.	"Marie *had been* loved" (*prior to . . .*)[25]

The passive is used with much less frequency in French than in English. It is commonly replaced by an active construction (*Voltaire a écrit*) or by using:

(a) the pronoun *on* ("one"):

On parle allemand en Autriche.	"*One speaks* German in Austria."

(b) a pronominal construction (encountered earlier):

L'allemand *se parle* en Autriche.	"German is spoken (*speaks itself*) in Austria."

---

[25] Or well in the past.

Use of *On* as Substitute for *Nous*

Admonishments of purists to the contrary, in conversational French *nous* has largely been supplanted by the pronoun *on*. Thus one frequently hears (and not infrequently sees in writing) expressions such as:

On y va.	"Let's go."
Nous, on a gagné.	"We won."
On a notre façon de voir les choses.	"We have our own way of seeing things."
On avait nos idées.	"We had our own ideas."
On est toujours séparé**s** pendant les vacances!	"We're always apart during the holidays!"
On était perdu**s**.	"We were lost."
On est allé**s** au cinéma hier.	"We went to the movies yesterday."
On a vu notre chef hier.	"We saw our leader yesterday."

Note that:

(a) *On* can be used only as a subject; it can never stand alone or be used as an object.[26]

(b) In written form, there is generally agreement in gender and number with "we"—*on est allé**s*** or *on est allé**es***—but it is not infrequent to find it without such accord—*on est allé.*

Such uses of *on* as a substitute for *nous* need to be distinguished from the more "classic" use of *on* as a third person pronoun meaning "one", although in many cases only the context can make clear whether it refers to "one" in general or to "us": e.g.,

On ne sait jamais.	"One (we?) never knows."

Appendix
Questions about the *Passé Composé*

There are a number of basic questions which occur at some stage to many students and to at least some native practitioners of the language as well:

(1) Why are some verbs conjugated with *être,* the rest with *avoir*?

(2) Why is there agreement with the *subject* for verbs conjugated with *être,* but with the *direct object* for those conjugated with *avoir* (and then only when the direct object *precedes* the verb)?

---

[26] This reflects its origin, being derived from the *nominative* case of Latin HOMO ("man"); the *accusative* (direct object) case HOMINEM became the noun *homme.*

(3) Why do *pronominal* verbs—all of which are conjugated with *être*—not have uniform agreement between subject and past participle?
(4) If the 20 or so *intransitive verbs of transformation and motion* (*aller, sortir, venir,* etc.) are conjugated with *être,* why are the 900 or so *other intransitive* verbs conjugated with *avoir?*
(5) Why do some verbs (e.g., *mentir*) have *invariable* past participles (i.e., only the masculine singular form exists)?

To provide at least partial answers to these questions, a brief overview of the origins of the *passé composé* is essential.

The Latin *perfect* tense was used to convey the meanings of both the "remote" and "near" pasts (i.e., *I went* and *I have gone*). During the evolution to Romance languages, the perfect came to specialize in the remote past and gave birth to the Romance simple past tense (French *passé simple*). To express the near past, speakers of the Romance languages came up with a structure entirely analogous to that used in English: the combination of the auxiliary verb *to have* with the past participle. In fact it was a relatively short step from expressions of the form

J'*ai* déjà deux livres *écrits.* "I already *have* two books *written.*"

to the formal compound past

J'*ai* déjà *écrit* deux livres. "I *have written* two books already."

This process worked for *transitive* verbs only, however. For intransitive verbs the passive construction, where the past participle is used *adjectivally,*

she is *gone* (to Paris) he is *dead*

led naturally to the development of a formal compound past with *to be* (*être*) as the auxiliary:

Elle *est allée* à Paris. Il *est mort* à l'âge de 80 ans.

Both of these processes occurred almost simultaneously in English and French, the principal difference being that in Modern English "have" has become the auxiliary for intransitive as well as for transitive verbs. In the early seventeenth century this transition was still incomplete:

Michael Cassio, Lieutenant to the warlike Moor Othello, *Is come* on shore. (Shakespeare, *Othello*)
And the woman said unto them, They *be gone* over the brook of water. (2 Samuel 17:20, King James Version)

For verbs conjugated with *être,* the agreement of the past participle (in gender and number) with the subject thus reflects the past participle's former status as a simple adjective.

For *transitive* verbs, in the very early days of the language the past participle generally accorded with the direct object (which it modified), regardless of whether the object was placed *before* or *after* the verb. Thus, one would have said *j'ai écri**ts** deux livres* ("I wrote two books") as well as *les livres que j'ai écri**ts**.* Over time, as *j'ai écrit* came to be thought of as a single entity (i.e., the *passé composé*), past participles which came *before* the direct object *could* be left invariable (as in Modern French). But this was not a hard and fast rule.[27]

The current formal rule was adopted only in the eighteenth century. It had been proposed two centuries earlier in imitation of Italian by the poet Clément Marot[28] and immortalized in one of his epigrams—whose sense can only with some difficulty be conveyed in English:

Notre langue a cette façon	Our language has this feature
Que le terme qui va devant	That the term which goes before
Volontiers régit le suivant . . .	Willingly determines that which follows . . .
Il faut dire en termes parfaits:	One must say in perfect terms:
Dieu en ce monde *nous a fait**s**;*	God in this world *us has made**s**.*
Faut dire en paroles parfaites:	Must say in perfect words:
Dieu en ce monde *les a fait**es**;*	God in this world *them*[29] *has made**es**;*
Et ne faut point dire en effet:	In fact one must not say:
Dieu en ce monde *les a fait;*	God in this world *them has made;*
Ne *nous a fait* pareillement,	And similarly he has not *us made,*
Mais *nous a fait**s**,* tout rondement.	But, more nimbly, has *us made**s**.*

For *pronominal verbs* in the "old" days there was always agreement between past participle and subject, even in cases where there was an explicit direct object. Molière (1622–1673) could still write:

Oui, ils *se sont donné**s*** l'un à l'autre *une promesse de mariage.* (*L'Avare*)	"Yes, they *have given* one to the other *a promise of marriage.*"

whereas in the modern "sanitized" version of his text, one is likely to find:

Oui, ils se sont *donné* l'un à l'autre *une promesse de mariage.*

---

[27] The fundamental distinction concerning the location of the direct object seems to have arisen from the following consideration: when it was placed *before* the verb, one could easily "adjust" the past participle ending (which had yet to be uttered or written), but when it was placed *after* the verb, it would be "too late" to make such an adjustment.

[28] Official poet to the court of François I (king of France from 1515 to 1547) at a time when all things Italian were the rage. In modern Italian, agreement of the past participle is obligatory only with respect to preceding direct object *pronouns.*

[29] I.e., *les paroles* ("the words"), *parole* being a feminine noun.

At this point we come to the penultimate question: why are the “other” intransitive verbs conjugated with *avoir* rather than *être?* The simple answer is that many of these *can* also (in effect) be conjugated with *être,* thus giving a difference in nuance between the *action* itself and the *result* of that action:

(a) The actual (past) action—with *avoir*

Ce roman *a paru* en 1905.	“This novel *came out* in 1905.”
Votre mari *a* bien *vielli.*	“Your husband *has aged* well.”
L’autobus *a passé* devant chez nous.[30]	“The bus *passed* in front of our house.”
Le temps *a changé* depuis hier.	“The weather *has changed* since yesterday.”
Elle *a divorcé* en 2002.	“She *(got) divorced* in 2002.”
Tous ses amis *ont émigré.*	“All of his friends *have emigrated.*”
Les fêtes *ont commencé.*	“The festivities *have begun.*”

(b) The current *result* of a past action—with *être*

Son nouveau roman *est paru.*	“His new novel *is (has come) out.*”
Votre mari *est vielli.*	“Your husband *is old-looking.*”
L’autobus *est passé* depuis 10 minutes.	“It’s 10 minutes since the bus *went by.*”
Le temps *est changé.*	“The weather *is changed* (different).”
Elle *est divorcée* (depuis 2002).	“She *is divorced* (since 2002).”
Tous ses amis *sont émigrés*	“All of his friends *are emigrants.*”
L’année *est commencée.*	“The year *has (is) begun.*”

Thus, one could say:

Elles *ont paru,* puis *ont disparu;* on ne les voit plus, elles *sont disparu**es**.*	“They appeared, then disappeared; one sees them no more, they *have (are) disappeared.*”

The constructions in (b) can be considered either as *passé composé* or simply as past participles used adjectivally. Indeed, as we have seen above, this latter sense is precisely how the *passé composé* with *être* arose. However, many intransitive verbs have no meaning in this construction and hence can be conjugated only with *avoir:*

	with *avoir*	*not* with *être*	English equivalent
elle a bâillé	“she yawned”	*elle est bâillée	*she is yawned
elle a bavardé	“she chatted”	*elle est bavardée	*she is chatted
elle a joggé	“she jogged”	*elle est joggée	*she is jogged
elle a lutté	“she struggled”	*elle est luttée	*she is struggled
elle a menti	“she lied”	*elle est mentie	*she is lied
la vache a meuglé	“the cow mooed”	*la vache est meuglée	*the cow is mooed

[30] In recent times, the use of *passer* (in an intransitive sense) with the auxiliary *avoir* has become rare.

We are now in a position to answer our final question. Why do some verbs have *invariable* past participles: for example, for the verb *mentir* the only form which exists is *menti* (and not **mentie,* **mentis,* or **menties*)? The answer is really very simple: verbs with invariable past participles are (invariably!) intransitive verbs which are conjugated with *avoir* and which cannot be used adjectivally as past participles—in other words, verbs like *bâiller, bavarder, jogger, lutter, mentir,* and *meugler.* Since these verbs are never used in a situations in which their past participle must agree with a noun, they have no need of a variable past participle. Conversely, as an almost universal rule, one can say that if a verb *can* be used in a position in which a *variable* past participle is (or seems to be) required, such a form exists.[31]

Apparent exceptions, such as:

(1) Les heures difficiles que j'ai véc**ues** . . .	"The difficult hours which I have *lived* . . ."
(2) Les heures que j'ai *dormi* . . . (*not* *dormi**es**)	"The hours that I have *slept* . . ."

generally arise from rather arcane grammatical interpretations, in this case considering *difficult hours* to be a direct object but *hours* slept to be an adverb (i.e., the hours *during which* I slept). The examples above are thus consistent with the fact that the past participle of *vivre* is variable, but not that of *dormir.*[32]

One verb with an invariable past participle worth noting is *être.*

---

[31] Some sources show *émigrer*—one of our earlier examples—as having an invariable past participle, considering *émigré* to be a "separate" adjective/noun (with feminine and plural forms). The practical effect is the same.

[32] Another apparent exception is *fermenter* ("to undergo fermentation"), which theoretically has the invariable past participle *fermenté.* Nonetheless, an Internet search will reveal thousands of references to *fermentée* (*pâte fermentée, boisson fermentée, papaye fermentée,* etc.)—clear proof that any formal list of "invariable" past participles should be regarded with caution.

CHAPTER 11

Present and Past Subjunctive

In this chapter we will consider the present and past subjunctive. The imperfect and past perfect subjunctives—essentially to be found only in classical literature and in a few fixed expressions—will be treated in Chapter 12.

Only traces of the subjunctive remain in Modern English:

(a) the third person singular, where the present indicative ending *-s* contrasts with the "null" subjunctive ending (*he does* versus *he do*);
(b) the verb *to be,* whose present subjunctive for all six conjugations is "be" (*if I be, if you be,* etc.); and
(c) the use of *were* rather than *was* in statements of the form *if I were, if he were, were he to* (past subjunctive of *to be*).

Consider, for example, the following phrase pairs:

Indicative	Subjunctive
He *is* here; he *was* here.	I wish that he *were* here.
He *does* it.	It is essential that he *do* it.
He *is* punished.	I demand that he *be* punished.
He *leaves.*	It is my desire that he *leave* at once.
He *is* elected.	God forbid that he *be* elected.
The king *lives.*	Long *live* the king!
It *is* so; it *was* so.	If only it *were* so!
He *understands.*	In order that he *understand* . . .
I *am* wicked.	"If I *be* wicked, woe unto me . . ." (Job 10:15)
It *pleases* the court.	"If it *please* the court . . ."

If John *was* at the meeting (last night), he certainly maintained a very low profile.

versus

If John *were* at the meeting, it would make a big difference.

Some General Comments on the Use of the Subjunctive

The subjunctive is often explained as representing the expression of an opinion or state of mind of the speaker, in the form of a wish, order, sentiment, or judgment. Its use in French (as well as its traces in English) generally obeys these precepts. The difficulty for the student of French, and the advanced practitioner as well, is that in its finer detail the use of the subjunctive does not represent a fully consistent system. This can perhaps best be illustrated by contrasting the use of subjunctives in French, Spanish, and Italian, all of which derived both the form and use of their subjunctives from a common source. Consider the following sentences:

1. When I *am* rich I will buy a house.
2. I think that you *are* right.
3. He is the richest man that I *know.*
4. I will call you when I *arrive.*
5. Take an umbrella, in case it *rains.*
6. If I *were* rich, I would buy a castle.
7. I wonder if this *is* true.
8. Although it *is raining,* I will go for a walk.
9. Even if it *rains,* I will go for a walk.

Translated into the three languages, these phrases would typically employ the following moods for the italicized verb:

	French	Spanish	Italian
1.	indicative (future)	**subjunctive**	indicative (future)
2.	indicative	indicative	**subjunctive**
3.	**subjunctive**	indicative	**subjunctive**
4.	indicative (future)	**subjunctive**	indicative (future)
5.	indicative (conditional)	**subjunctive**	**subjunctive**
6.	indicative (imperfect)	**subjunctive** (imperfect)	**subjunctive** (imperfect)
7.	indicative	indicative	**subjunctive**
8.	**subjunctive**	indicative	**subjunctive**
9.	indicative	**subjunctive**	**subjunctive**

In each case, French usage differs from one or both of the others; nor is there uniformity between the Spanish and Italian forms. Any "logical" explanation of why the subjunctive is used as it is in one of these languages is unlikely to convince practitioners of the other two.

The uses of the subjunctive in French fall into two general categories, depending upon whether such use is *obligatory* or *optional.* Contrary to what might be one's initial thought, its correct use is more important in the second case than in the first. That is, an error with an obligatory subjunctive does not impede the accurate conveyance of what the person is trying to say, whereas with an optional subjunctive it is likely to do so.

Thus in English if one incorrectly says

*I wish that he *leaves.*

rather than

I wish that he *leave.*

this will not prevent anyone from understanding what the speaker is trying to say. Converse examples (i.e., of optional subjunctives) are rather hard to find in English, but consider the following pair of sentences:

subjunctive	Though I *be* sick I will go to school tomorrow. (i.e., I am not sick at the moment but even if I am sick tomorrow I will still go to school)
indicative	Though I *am* sick I will go to school tomorrow. (i.e., I am sick at the moment but still intend to go to school tomorrow)

While archaic, the first phrase is grammatically correct (native English speakers would almost certainly say "Even if I am sick . . ."). The incorrect use of one of these forms in place of the other would convey inaccurate information as to the current health of the speaker.

As suggested by the earlier comparison, the subjunctive is used considerably less frequently in French than in either Spanish or Italian. In particular, the imperfect subjunctive has completely died out in French—in many cases having been replaced by the imperfect indicative or conditional—while it remains alive and well in the other two languages. "Optional" subjunctives seem to be a particularly endangered species: even in schools the contrast between subjunctive and indicative is generally taught as subject to rigid rules rather than depending on the nuance that one is trying to convey. While this tends to make life easier for the student, it has come at the cost of making the subjunctive appear to be somewhat of a relic—something that one has to do "correctly" in order to speak or write "proper" French, but with little intrinsic value.

Numerous books have been written on the French subjunctive[1] (as well as the Spanish, Italian, etc.) which attempt to develop a coherent theory for its use. The following is a rather typical explanation:[2]

> The Subjunctive is the subjective mood and is employed to convey the attitude of the speaker: something of himself is introduced into the statement (or question), which is put forward, not as something absolute, but as dependent upon the thoughts or feelings of the speaker; he presents the action denoted by the verb as something unfulfilled, possible, probable, hypothetical, desirable, or states it in an attenuated (polite) form. The Subjunctive may therefore with some justice be called the contingent or prospective mood. But, as applied to human speech "subjective" and "objective" are relative terms, and correspond largely to a difference of degree. Thus, in a sentence like *Voilà un livre qui est intéressant,* the relative clause is purely descriptive, and yet the speaker identifies himself with the statement to the extent of putting it forward as being in his opinion correct. On the other hand, if he says *Donnez-moi un livre qui soit intéressant,* the qualification attached to the book is put forward as something desired or demanded by the speaker.

Before turning to a practical consideration of use of the subjunctive, we will note two factors which can impede its understanding.

Frequent Identity of Subjunctive and Indicative Forms

From Chapter 6 we recall that in a number of cases the present subjunctive is *identical* in form to the corresponding present indicative. Specifically:

Class I *parler*	Class II *finir*	Class III *rendre*
je parle	ils, elles finissent	ils, elles rendent
tu parles		
il, elle parle		
ils, elles parlent		

[1] For example: Marcel Cohen, *Le subjonctif en français contemporain* (Paris: SEDES, 1965); Olivier Soutet, *Le subjonctif en français* (Paris: Ophrys, 2000).

[2] Ewert (1969: 238).

For all three classes of verbs, the first and second person plurals *always* have identical present subjunctives and imperfect indicatives:

Class I *parler*	Class II *finir*	Class III *rendre*
nous parlions	nous finissions	nous rendions
vous parliez	vous finissiez	vous rendiez

As a result, it is often difficult to distinguish precisely when a subjunctive is being used. In the following examples, the verbs in (1a) and (1b) look identical, but one is subjunctive while the other is not; the same holds for (2a) and (2b):

(1a)	*subjunctive*	Je veux qu'il *chante.*	"I want him to sing."
(1b)	*present indicative*	Je vois qu'il *chante.*	"I see that he sings."
(2a)	*subjunctive*	Je voulais que vous *chantiez.*	"I wanted you to sing."
(2b)	*imperfect indicative*	Je voyais que vous *chantiez.*	"I saw that you were singing."

The fact that most subjunctives in French go unnoticed has certainly been an important factor contributing to the subjunctive's relative marginalization compared to its use in other Romance languages.[3]

The *Ne Explétif*

This is a *ne* which *can be* added to certain categories of subjunctive phrases and which has no negative meaning—in fact **it has no meaning whatsoever.** Thus the two sentences

Je crains qu'il vienne.
Je crains qu'il ***ne*** vienne.
} "I fear that he will come."

are absolutely identical in meaning and are both to be distinguished from:

Je crains qu'il *ne* vienne *pas.* "I fear that he will *not* come."

The *ne explétif* is *never* obligatory and is frequently omitted, particularly in spoken French. In our examples of the subjunctive we will include the *ne explétif*

[3] Recall that Class I verbs—all of whose subjunctive forms are easily confused with indicative ones—account for nearly 90 percent of French verbs.

wherever it is likely to occur, marking each such example with **. Following the presentation of the subjunctive, we will return to this element in order to summarize its use and to give some idea as to how it developed.

Subjunctive Forms (Tenses)

There are only two forms of the subjunctive in common use in Modern French—the *present* and the (compound) *past: je finisse, j'aie fini.*

In the large majority of cases, the subjunctive appears in *dependent* clauses:

Je veux *qu'il parte immédiatement.*	"I wish *that he leave immediately.*"
Je travaille *afin que tu puisses manger.*	"I work *so that you can eat.*"

Its use in *independent* clauses is generally limited to what could be called the "third person imperative"—expressing wish, request, order, or hypothesis:

Qu'il *entre!*	"*Let* him *enter!*"
Pourvu qu'elle *revienne!*	"Let's hope that she *returns!*"
Que la paix *soit* avec vous!	"*Let* peace *be* with you!"
Vive le roi!	"Long *live* the king!"
Qu'il *fasse* beau demain!	"*Let* it *be* nice weather tomorrow!"
Soit un angle de 30°.	"(Let us) *Assume* an angle of 30°."

A relatively common expression using a first person subjunctive is:

que je *sache* / autant que je *sache*	"as far as I know"

For a subjunctive used in a dependent clause, its tense is governed by the so-called *concordance des temps* ("concordance of tenses"). This has been simplified considerably in Modern French due to the elimination of the imperfect subjunctive: the tense of the subjunctive is now determined solely by the *relative* time of its action vis-à-vis that of the verb in the principal clause:

action is	Previous (P)	Simultaneous (S)	Future (F)
tense used:	*past* subjunctive	*present* subjunctive	*present* subjunctive

(S, F)	Je *regrette* qu'il *soit* absent.	"I regret that he *is/will be* absent."
(P)	Je *regrette* qu'il *ait été* absent.	"I regret that he *was* absent."
(S, F)	Je *regrettais* qu'il *soit* absent.	"I regretted that he *was/would be* absent."
(P)	Je *regrettais* qu'il *ait été* absent.	"I regretted that he *had been* absent."

The first and third examples illustrate that the present subjunctive is used indistinguishably to refer to *present* and *future* events. Note also that the *present* subjunctive is used when the principal verb is in the *past* tense, if the two actions are simultaneous. While this initially might strike one as a bit odd, it also occurs in certain English *subjunctive* constructions:

Il a exigé que j'*écrive* une lettre.	"He insisted that I *write* a letter."

Uses of the Subjunctive in Dependent Clauses

These can be divided into three basic categories:

(a) those governed by the *verb* in the principal clause—e.g., *regretter:*

Je **regrette** qu'il *soit* absent.	"I *regret* that he *is/will be* absent."

(b) those governed by a conjunction—e.g., *afin que:*

Je travaille **afin que** tu *puisses* manger.	"I work *so that* you *can/will be able* to eat."

(c) other particular circumstances—e.g., superlative followed by relative clause:

C'est **la plus belle** femme que je *connaisse*.	"She is the *most beautiful* woman that I *know*."

Subjunctives Governed by the Verb in the Principal Clause

These can be partitioned in turn as follows, depending on whether the verb in the main clause expresses:

1. desire/obligation/prohibition/advice or warning
2. sentiment or judgment
3. possibility, probability, or doubt

1. Desire/obligation/prohibition/advice or warning

Examples:

Il veut qu'elle *revienne* toute de suite.	"He wants her *to return* immediately."
Il voulait qu'elle *revienne* toute de suite.	"He wanted her *to return* immediately."
Il préfère que vous le *fassiez*.	"He prefers that you *do* it."

Je souhaite que ma mère qui est malade *guérisse* vite. "I wish that my mother who is ill *(will) recover* quickly."

Il a proposé que la délégation *se rende* à Nice. "He proposed that the delegation *go* to Nice."

Nous suggérons que vous *utilisiez* le bouton droit de votre souris. "We suggest that you *use* the right mouse button."

Il exige que nous *soutenions* sa candidature. "He insists that we *support* his candidacy."

J'ordonne que vous *vous taisiez.* "I order that you *be silent.*"

Le roi ordonne que le prisonnier *soit* exécuté. "The king orders that the prisoner *be* executed."

Faites attention qu'on ne vous *suive* pas. "Be careful (ensure) that you *are* not *followed.*"

The *ne explétif* is frequently found with *empêcher* and *éviter:*

** Cette raison empêche qu'il ***ne*** *parte.* "This reason prevents *him* from *leaving.*"

** Cette raison n'empêche pas qu'il ***ne*** *parte.* "This reason doesn't prevent *him* from *leaving.*"

** Pour éviter que vous ***ne*** *perdiez* du temps . . . "To avoid that you *lose* time . . ."

As shown above, *faire attention* used with the subjunctive means "to ensure that"; used with the indicative the meaning is "to take notice of":

Faites attention que la route *est* glissante. "Be aware (i.e., keep in mind) that the road *is* slippery."

Prendre garde: three different meanings

A rare case where the *ne explétif* actually makes a difference is *prendre garde,* which offers three different meanings:

(i) "normal": to be attentive, note the fact that, etc.

Prenez garde que nous *sommes* à quinze jours des élections. "Be attentive to the fact that we *are* two weeks from the elections."

with no dependent clause:

Prenez garde aux voitures en tranversant la rue. "Be attentive to the cars while crossing the road."

(ii) dependent clause in the subjunctive, without *ne explétif:*[4] to take care of, ensure

Je prends garde que tout *soit* prêt pour demain soir.	"I will take care (ensure) that everything *is* (*will be*) ready for tomorrow night."

(iii) dependent clause in the subjunctive, with *ne explétif:* to seek to avoid, to take precautions against

** Il prend garde que ses adversaires ***ne soient*** informés de ses intentions.	"He takes care that his adversaries *are* not (*will* not *be*) informed of his intentions."
** Prenez garde qu'on **ne** vous *trompe.*	"Take care that you *are* not (*will* not *be*) deceived."

Infinitive constructions in place of the subjunctive

When the dependent and independent clauses have the same subject, an infinitive construction is used instead:

	Je veux *sortir* d'ici immédiatement.	"I want *to leave* here immediately."
not	*Je veux que je *sorte* d'ici immédiatement.	
	Je préférerais *être* à Paris.	"I would prefer *to be* in Paris."
not	*Je préférerais que je *sois* à Paris.	

When the subjects are different, an infinitive construction is often still possible and in such cases generally preferred:

Je vous ordonne de *vous taire.*	"I order you *to be silent.*"
Ils m'ont ordonné d'y *assister* à sa place.	"They ordered me *to take* his place."
Ils m'ont empêché de *partir.*	"They prevented me from *leaving.*"
Je vous interdis de me *parler* sur ce ton.	"I forbid you *to speak* to me in this tone."
Je vous prie d'*ouvrir* la fenêtre.	"I ask you kindly *to open* the window."
Cette raison ne l'empêche pas de *partir.*	"This reason doesn't prevent him from *leaving.*"

[4] In this usage it has become common (although considered "peu correcte" by some) to replace "que" with "à ce que": *Je prends garde* ***à ce que*** *tout soit prêt . . .*

2. Sentiment or judgment

After verbs expressing sentiment or judgment the subjunctive is generally used:

(a) Sentiment

Ça me fait plaisir que tu *sois venu.*	"I am glad that you *have come.*"
Je suis heureux que tu *puisses* venir.	"I am happy that you *can* come."
Je suis content que nous *ayons pu* trouver un accord rapidement.	"I am happy that we *were (have been) able* to reach an agreement rapidly."
Nous sommes désolés que cela n'*ait* pas *marché.*	"We are sorry that this *has* not *worked.*"
Quel dommage que je n'*aie* pas mes vingt-cinq ans! (Victor Hugo)	"What a pity that I don't *have* my twenty-five years (can't be twenty-five again)!"
Je suis triste que tu *aies passé* Noël toute seule.	"I am sad that you *(have) spent* Christmas all alone."
Il est bizarre qu'il *ait dit* cela.	"It's bizarre that he *(has) said* that."
Cela m'ennuie que vous *disiez* cela.	"It bothers me that you *say* that."
Il est honteux que nous *soyons* exclus.	"It is disgraceful that we *are (will be)* excluded."
Il est regrettable que nous n'*ayons* pas *eu* le temps de le faire.	"It is regrettable that we *have* not *had* the time to do it."
Il est rare qu'il *vienne* sans prévenir.	"It is rare that he *comes* without warning."
Cela ne m'étonne pas qu'il le *fasse.*	"It doesn't surprise me that he *does (would do)* it."
Cela m'étonne que Marie *soit* absente.	"It surprises me that Marie *is* absent."

Note that with the present subjunctive there is often an ambiguity: in the last phrase, for example, I may have just been informed that Marie will not be at the meeting tomorrow, in which case the meaning would be: "It surprises me that Marie *will be* absent."

The *ne explétif* is frequent with expressions of fear—*craindre, avoir peur, redouter:*

** Les Gaulois avaient peur que le ciel **ne** leur *tombe* sur la tête.	"The Gauls feared that the sky *would fall* on their heads."
** Je crains qu'il **ne** *soit* malade.	"I fear that he *is* (*might be*) sick."
** Je redoute qu'il **n'***apprenne* la vérité.	"I dread that he *will learn* the truth."

Infinitive clauses are used when the two subjects are the same:

Je suis désolé d'*être* en retard.	"I am sorry *to be* late."
Je suis désolé de vous *avoir fait* attendre.	"I am sorry *to have made* you wait."

(b) Judgment (or valuation)

These are impersonal expressions of the form "it is . . .", expressing a judgment or valuation concerning the action described in the dependent clause:

Il faut que j'*aille* à Paris.	"It's necessary that I *go* to Paris."
En juillet il a fallu que j'*aille* à Paris.	"In July it was necessary that I *go* to Paris."
Il faut que vous *ayez fini* votre travail avant 19 heures.	"It's necessary that you *finish ([will] have finished)* your work before 7 P.M.
C'est normal qu'il *pleuve* en automne.	"It's normal that it *rains* in autumn."
Il est urgent que tu le *fasses.*	"It's urgent that you *do* it."
Il vaut mieux que tu *partes.*	"It's better that you *leave.*"
Il est essentiel que les enfants *aillent* à l'école.	"It is essential that (the) children *go* to school."
Il convient que vous y *alliez.*[5]	"You should (ought to) *go* there."
Il semble injuste que nous *soyons* si pauvres.	"It seems injust that we *are* so poor."

Espérer and *attendre*

The verb *espérer* ("to hope") merits a special comment. When used affirmatively in the independent clause, the verb in the dependent clause is indicative; however, when *espérer* is used negatively—where it can usually be translated more accurately as "does not expect" rather than "does not hope"[6]—the subjunctive normally follows:

J'espère qu'il *viendra.*	"I hope that he *will come.*"
J'espère qu'il *viendrait* (en ce cas-là).	"I hope he *would come* (in that case)."
J'espère que tu *vas* bien.[7]	"I hope that you *are (go)* well."
J'espère que tu *as* bien *dormi.*	"I hope that you *have slept* well."
J'espérais qu'il *viendrait.*	"I hoped that he *would come.*"
Je n'espère pas qu'il *vienne.*	"I do not expect that he *will come.*"
Je n'espérais pas qu'il *vienne/viendrait.*	"I did not expect that he *would come.*"

---

[5] Used in *personal* expressions, *convenir que* can be followed by the indicative: ***Ils conviennent que*** *ceci* ***s'appliquera*** [future] *aussi aux forces de sécurité* ("They agree that this will also apply to the security forces").

[6] The senses of *hope* and *expect* are closely linked: if one has no *hope* of something, then one does not *expect* it to occur. In the early days of French, the primary meaning of *espérer* even when used positively was "to wait for"/"to expect". This sense is preserved in various expressions, whose use increases the farther south in France one goes; in neighboring Spain *esperar* can mean "to wait", "to expect", or "to hope".

[7] Some purists maintain that when *espérer* is used in the main clause, the verb in the dependent clause can refer only to a future situation, not to a present or past one.

The last example illustrates that when *espérer* is used negatively in the past, the indicative (conditional) can also be used. Used interrogatively, *espérer* can be used with either the indicative or the subjunctive:

Espérez vous qu'il *viendra?* Espérez vous qu'il *vienne?*	"Do you hope that he *will come?*"

A verb frequently associated with *espérer*—and not infrequently confused with it—is *s'attendre* ("to expect").[8] In its "classic" form, *s'attendre que,* the use of the subjunctive follows the same rules as for *espérer*—indicative in the affirmative, subjunctive in the negative.

On s'attend que le président *opposera* son veto à ce projet de loi.	"It is expected that the president *will veto* the law."
Je ne m'attends pas qu'il *vienne* demain.	"I don't expect that he *will come* tomorrow."

In practice, it is far more common to find *s'attendre* ***à ce que***, which is always used with the subjunctive.

On s'attend à ce que le président *oppose* son veto à ce projet de loi.	"It is expected that the president *will veto* the law."

3. Possibility, probability, or doubt

Consider the following hierarchy of likelihood:

impossible → improbable → doubtful → possible → probable → certain

For French the dividing line between subjunctive and indicative is generally located at the beginning of the probable range. Thus:

Il est impossible qu'il ne le *sache* pas.	"It's impossible that he doesn't *know* it."
Aussi invraisemblable que cela *paraisse* . . .	"As unlikely as that *might seem* . . ."
Il est improbable qu'il *vienne* demain.	"It is unlikely that he *will come* tomorrow."
Il est peu probable que la santé mentale du pilote *soit* en cause.	"It is unlikely that the mental health of the pilot *was* a factor."

---

[8] *Attendre,* without the "reflexive" pronoun, means "to wait for".

Je doute que vous la *trouviez* vivante.	"I doubt that you *will find* her alive."
Il se peut que je *vienne.*	"It is possible that I *will come.*"
Il est possible que je *sois* un peu en retard.	"It is possible that I *will be* a little late."
Il est **probable** qu'il *vienne* demain.	"It is likely that he *will come* tomorrow."
or Il est **probable** qu'il *viendra* demain.	"It is likely that he *will come* tomorrow."
Il est évident qu'il *faut* réagir.	"It is evident that it *is necessary* to react."
Il est vrai qu'un triangle *a* trois côtés.	"It is true that a triangle *has* three sides."
Je suis sûr qu'il *viendra* demain.	"I am sure that he *will come* tomorrow."

With *il est probable,* the indicative is generally used, but the subjunctive is possible if a "significant" doubt still remains in the mind of the speaker. The adverb *peut-être* ("maybe") provides an exception to the general pattern: while only "possible", it nonetheless governs the indicative rather than the subjunctive:

Il *viendra* **peut-être** cet après midi.	"He *will* possibly *come* this afternoon."

When one "thinks" something, the process apparently involves fewer doubts in French (and Spanish) than in Italian, and the indicative rather than the subjunctive is therefore used:

Je crois qu'il *viendra* demain.	"I think he *will come* tomorrow."

Similarly, the indicative is used in expressions of the form "it appears that", when this is conveyed by the verb *paraître:*

Il paraît que vous ne *savez* pas lire.	"It appears that you *can*not read."
Il paraît qu'il *pleuvra* demain.	"It looks like it *will rain* tomorrow."
Il me paraît qu'on *devrait* partir maintenant.	"It seems to me that we *should* leave now."

But when *il paraît* is followed by an adjective, the expression becomes one of sentiment or judgment and hence the subjunctive is required.

Il me *paraît* ***étrange*** qu'il *ait pu* vivre dans ces conditions.	"It *seems* ***strange*** to me that he *was able to* live under these conditions."

In contrast to *paraître, sembler* is generally used with the subjunctive, with the nuance "according to appearances":

Il semble que nous *soyons* dans un cercle vicieux.	"It seems that we *are* in a vicious circle."

However, when used to express a more "certain" or "probable" sense, *sembler* can also be used with the indicative:

Il semble qu'il *est* encore vivant.	"It seems that he *is* still alive."

When constructions in the "certain" or "probable" range are put in negative form, they move into the uncertainty range and are *generally* used with the subjunctive. Thus, according to a notice placed by Napoleon in October 1804 in the French press:

> Les gazettes américaines parlent souvent de l'épouse de M. Jérôme Bonaparte. **Il est possible que** M. Jérôme Bonaparte, jeune homme qui n'a pas encore vingt ans, ***ait*** une maîtresse, mais **il n'est pas probable qu**'il ***ait*** une femme, puisque les lois de France sont telles qu'un jeune homme mineur de vingt ans, et même de vingt-cinq ans, ne peut se marier sans le consentement de ses parents . . .[9]
>
> The American newspapers speak often of the wife of Mr. Jerome Bonaparte. **It is possible that** Mr. Jerome Bonaparte, a young man not yet twenty, ***has*** a mistress, but **it is not probable that** he ***has*** a wife, since the laws of France are such that a young man of less than 20 years of age, or even 25, cannot marry without the consent of his parents . . .

Similarly:

Je ne crois pas qu'il *vienne* demain.	"I don't think he *will come* tomorrow."
Il ne paraît pas que tu *aies fait* tes devoirs.	"It doesn't appear that you *have done* your homework."
Il n'est pas certain que tout *soit* incertain. (Pascal)	"It is not certain that all *is* uncertain."
Je ne suis pas sûr que tu *aies* raison.	"I am not sure that you *are* right."

[9] A. Aulard, *Paris sous le premier Empire* (Paris: Léopold Cerf–Noblet–Quantin, 1912), vol. 1, p. 313; boldface added. This citation illustrates another point worthy of mention: until relatively recently it was obligatory to omit the *pas* after *cesser, oser, pouvoir,* and *savoir* (remembered by "COPS") when followed directly by an infinitive: *la pluie ne cesse de tomber, je n'ose vous demander, il ne peut se marier, je ne sais nager.* This omission is now optional.

Il n'est pas vrai que la terre *soit* plate.	"It is not true that the earth *is* flat."
Il n'est pas correcte que Christophe Colomb *ait découvert* l'Amérique.	"It is not correct that Christopher Columbus *discovered* America."

Nonetheless, *je ne crois pas qu'il viendra* is possible if what one really means is that there is (almost) *no* possibility that he will come—effectively transforming the construction back into the certain (or at least probable) range, equivalent to *je crois qu'il ne viendra pas.*[10]

Conversely, when an expression of doubt is put in the negative, it may become a near certainty and hence require the *indicative:*

Je ne doute pas qu'il *viendra* demain.	"I do not doubt that he *will come* tomorrow."

However, in literary use it is not infrequent to see this still in the subjunctive, with a *ne explétif:*

** Je ne doute pas qu'il **ne** *vienne* demain.

One manner of expressing doubt is to deny the existence of something, in which case the verb describing what is denied is put in the subjunctive:

Le suspect nie qu'il *ait* assassiné le roi.	"The suspect denies that he (*has*) assassinated the king."

In this statement the speaker (or writer) is expressing no judgment as to whether the suspect actually assassinated the king but is simply reporting the denial. If, on the other hand, the speaker wishes to emphasize the reality of the fact—thus rejecting the denial—the indicative is used:

Il nie qu'il *a* assassiné le roi.	"He denies that he (*has*) assassinated the king." (But he did.)

Similarly:

Il a nié que la terre *soit* plate.	"He denied that the earth *is* flat."
Il a nié que la terre *est* ronde.	"He denied that the earth *is* round."

---

[10] Used in this manner, *je ne crois pas* is analogous to *il ne faut pas,* which **never** means "it is *not* necessary", but rather "it is necessary that (something) *not* (be done)":

Il ne faut pas qu'elle vienne.	"She *must not* come."

In constructions in which *nier* is used negatively, the subjunctive is generally employed, and a *ne explétif* may occasionally be found:

** Je ne nie pas que ces interprétations ***ne** soient* ingénieuses. (Anatole France)	"I do not deny that these interpretations *are* ingenious."

Other "denial" verbs displaying similar alternation of subjunctive and indicative include *contester, démentir, mettre en doute,* and *ne dire pas.* For example:

Les autorités ont démenti que les suspects *soient* soumis à des mauvais traitements.	"The authorities (have) denied that the suspects *were (are)* subject to ill-treatment."
Je n'ai pas dit que vous *puissiez* sortir.	"I did not say that you *could* leave."

Subjunctives Governed by a Conjunction (or Conjunctive Phrase)

When the dependent clause is introduced by one of the following conjunctions, the subjunctive is (almost) always used, apart from conjunctions marked with a "+", which have preserved the "optional" nature of its use (though they are found far more frequently with the subjunctive than with the indicative).

(a) **Although** (*real* obstacle)

bien que quoique encore que [malgré que]	"although", "even though"

(b) Opposition: **even if, no matter what** (*hypothetical*)

supposé que à supposer que en supposant que	"supposing that", "assuming that"
quoi que, qui que, où que	"whatever", "whoever", "wherever"
si peu que	"no matter how little"

(c) **In order that/for fear that**

afin que pour que	"so that"
+ de (telle) façon que + de (telle) sorte que + de (telle) manière que	"so that" (subjunctive), "in such a manner that" (indicative)
de peur que de crainte que	"for fear that"

(d) **Before/until**

avant que (après que)	"before" ("after")
en attendant que jusqu'à ce que	"until"

(e) **Provided that/in such a case**

pourvu que	"provided that", "as long as"
+ à (la) condition que	"on the condition that"
pour peu que	"even if only to a minimal degree" (i.e., "provided that")
+ moyennant que	"provided that"
en cas que, au cas que	"in case that"

(f) **Unless/without**

à moins que	"unless"
sans que	"without"

(g) **Either . . . or**

soit que . . . soit que	"either this (*happens*) . . . or that (*happens*)"

(h) **Instead of**

au lieu que	"instead of", "rather than"

In the Classical French of the eighteenth century, and to some extent still in literary language, the subjunctive was also "optional" with several conjunctions not marked with a "+", including *encore que* and *jusqu'à ce que.*

(a) Although (*real* obstacle)

Bien que je *sois* riche, je ne suis pas heureux.	"Although I *am* rich, I am not happy."
Il ne pleut pas, **quoique** le ciel *soit* nuageux.	"It isn't raining, although the sky *is* cloudy."
Celui qui croit en moi, **encore qu'**il *soit* mort, vivra. (Jean 11:25, version Darby)	"He that believeth in me, though he *were* dead, yet shall he live." (John 11:25, King James Version)

There remains considerable dispute as to whether *malgré que* is acceptable in the general sense of "although":[11]

Malgré que nous *soyons* de cultures et d'origines différentes . . .	"Despite the fact that we *are* from different cultures and origins . . ."

Note that while French uses the subjunctive in *although* clauses, according to the logic of the subjunctive the indicative would be more appropriate—the condition is real (it *is* raining), not imagined or hypothetical. Indeed, as noted earlier, other Romance languages use the indicative in this case. Conversely, in hypothetical phrases of the type "even if (such condition) were to occur"—where logic would dictate the use of the subjunctive—the situation is reversed: French uses the indicative, other Romance languages—as well as English—the subjunctive. Hence the following contrast:

Même s'il *pleut*, je vais sortir. (IND)	"Even if it *were to rain,* I would go out."[12] (SUBJ)
Bien qu'il *pleuve,* je vais sortir. (SUBJ)	"Although it *is raining,* I will go out." (IND)

(b) Opposition (*hypothetical*)

In contrast to (a), here the opposition is not real but hypothetical or imagined (no matter what, no matter how small, etc.), and the use of the subjunctive appears more "logical".

À supposer que la loi *soit* injuste, il faut néanmoins l'observer.	"(Even) Supposing the law *were* injust, it must nevertheless be obeyed."
Qui que ce soit	"Anybody", "no matter who","whosoever"
Qui que tu sois	"Whoever you *might be*"

---

[11] In the view of purists, the only correct use is in "classical" expressions such as: *Tu dois obéir,* ***malgré que*** *tu en aies* ("You must obey, *despite* your reluctance"). This use in fact goes back to the origin of *malgré* as two separate words: literally, *mal gré que tu en aies* ("bad will that you might have").

[12] In English one can of course also express this without using the subjunctive, in a manner directly parallel to the French: *Even if it rains, I will go out.*

Quoi qu'il *puisse* arriver, nous continuerons.	"Whatever *might* happen, we will continue."
Où que vous *alliez,* je vous suivrai!	"Wherever you *(might) go,* I will follow you!"
Si je peux faire **quoi que** ce *soit* pour vous aider . . .	"If I can do *anything* to help you . . ."
Ne buvez plus d'alcool, **si peu que** ce *soit.*	"Do not drink any more alcohol, no matter how little (it *might be*)."

(c) In order that/for fear that

For *afin que* and *pour que* the essential element is *purpose*—the result of the action is the specific consequence of the will of the actor.

Parlez plus fort **afin que** nous *puissions* vous entendre.	"Speak louder so that we *will be able* to hear you."
Elles sont venues exprès **pour que** nous *parlions* ensemble.	"They have come specifically so that we *(might) speak* together."

De peur que and *de crainte que* refer to hypothetical situations and are frequently accompanied by a *ne explétif:*

** J'ai pris mon parapluie **de peur qu'**il ***ne*** *pleuve.*	"I took my umbrella for fear it *might rain.*"
** Parlez bas, **de crainte qu'**on ***ne*** vous *entende.*	"Speak softly, for fear you *might be heard* (so that you are not heard)."

For *de (telle) manière que, de (telle) façon que,* and *de (telle) sorte que,*[13] the essential element is whether the condition which follows is the specific *objective* of the action of the verb in the main clause, in which case the *subjunctive* is used:

Il tenait ses cartes **de telle manière que** les autres joueurs ne *puissent* pas les voir.	"He was holding his cards in such a manner (specifically) so that the other players *would* not *be able* to see them."

or whether it is simply a (perhaps accidental) *result,* in which case the indicative is used:

Il tenait ses cartes **de telle manière que** les autres joueurs ne *pouvaient* pas les voir.	"He was holding his cards in such a manner that the other players *were* not *able* to see them."

---

[13] The first two forms are frequently employed with *à ce que: de manière* ***à ce que,*** *de façon* ***à ce que.*** This usage is generally viewed as "incorrect et lourd" (Colin 2002: 355).

In the second case nothing is implied about the *intention* of the player, simply that as a *result* of the particular manner in which he was holding his cards, the other players were not able to see them. It may well have been a purposeful action on the part of the player, but the speaker makes no such claim. By contrast, in the first example, it is stated unambiguously that the player was holding his cards in this manner *specifically* so that the other players would not be able to see them.

(d) **Before/until**

The logic underlying the subjunctive is that the verb governed by the conjunction is a (future) *condition* for the realization of the action described by the verb in the main clause. A *ne explétif* frequently accompanies *avant que.*

** Ne parlez pas **avant qu**'elle ***n'****ait fini.*	"Don't speak before (until) she *has finished.*"
** Je partirai **avant qu**'il ***ne*** *revienne.*	"I will leave before he *returns.*"
Reste ici **en attendant que** la pluie *cesse.*	"Stay here until the rain *stops.*"
Je resterai ici **jusqu'à ce que** tu *reviennes.*	"I will remain here until you *return.*"
Je suis resté là **jusqu'à ce qu**'elle *soit revenue.*	"I remained there until she *had returned.*"

In the last sentence, the idea is that I remained "there" specifically *awaiting* her return. To indicate "up to a certain point in time", without any necessary idea of (conditional) waiting, one normally uses the construction *jusqu'au moment où* with the indicative:

Il avait travaillé toute sa vie, **jusqu'au moment où** il *est tombé* malade.	"He had worked all his life, until he *fell* ill."

Theoretically in this case one could use *jusqu'à ce que* with the indicative, but this usage is now considered "vieux ou littéraire"; in normal speech and writing *jusqu'à ce que* is always accompanied by the subjunctive.

Logically, *après que* relates to an action which has already occurred, and the indicative should be used. However, due to "contamination" from its association with *avant que,* it is not rare to find *après que* used with the subjunctive:

Après qu'elle *soit* revenue, je suis parti.	"After she *had* returned, I left."

(e) **Provided that/in such a case**

The subjunctive is used in this case because the action in the main clause is *dependent* upon a (possibly uncertain) condition in the dependent clause—something will happen *provided that* something else does.

Nous vous comprendrons **pourvu que** vous *parliez* lentement.	"We will understand you provided that you *speak* slowly."
Nous partirons demain **à condition que** le temps le *permette.*	"We will leave tomorrow, if the weather *permits.*"
Le berger allemand est un chien qui comprend très vite ce qu'on attend de lui **pour peu qu'**il *ait* un maître compétent.	"The German shepherd is a dog which understands very quickly what is expected of it, if only it *has* a competent master."
Pour peu que nous *fassions* un effort, nous pourrions obtenir une amélioration.	"If we *made* but a small effort, we could obtain an improvement."

À (la) condition que is normally used with the subjunctive. However, in the (rare) case in which the verb expresses a future imperative rather than a hypothesis, the future indicative is used. Hence the contrast:

Je vous donne cet argent	"I (will) give you this money"
—**à (la) condition que** vous *partiez* demain.	—"on the condition that you leave tomorrow."
—**à (la) condition que** vous *partirez* demain.	—"in return for the fact that you WILL leave tomorrow."

Moyennant que is now considered "literary":

Une étude a révélé que les villageois étaient prêts à planter des arbres **moyennant que** ceux-ci *deviennent* leur propriété exclusive.	"A study has revealed that villagers were prepared to plant trees so long as these *become* their exclusive property."

In the above example *deviennent* is a subjunctive, though its form is indistinguishable from that of the present indicative. *En cas que* and *au cas que* have been almost totally supplanted in common French by *au cas où,* which uses the conditional (Chapter 10):

En cas qu'il *pleuve,* je ne sortirai pas. **Au cas où** il *pleuvrait,* je ne sortirai pas.	"In case it *rains,* I will not go out."

(f) Unless/without

In the case of *à moins que,* the subjunctive is used since it expresses a necessary condition for the realization of the action in the main clause, analogous to (e). A *ne explétif* is frequently added.

** Je vais à la piscine cet après-midi **à moins qu**'il ***ne*** *pleuve.*	"I will go to the swimming pool this afternoon, unless it *rains.*"
** **À moins que** je ***ne*** me *trompe,* vous devez être le mari de Marie.	"Unless I *am* mistaken, you must be Marie's husband."

The subjunctive *je trompe* is of course indistinguishable from the present indicative. The subjunctive is used with *sans que* because the action described by the verb is counterfactual (i.e., it does not occur):

Je partirai **sans qu**'il me *voie.*	"I will leave without him *seeing* me."
Il ne se passe pas un jour **sans que** vous *fassiez* une bêtise.	"Not a day passes that you *don't do* something stupid."

Note that with *sans que* the subjunctive does not necessarily imply anything about *intention:* in the first example above, it may or may not be my express intention to leave unnoticed—I am simply offering the observation that I will not be observed.

By "contamination" a *ne explétif* is often added to *sans que* expressions. Though it is no more illogical than others—indeed one could argue that it obeys a certain logic since the event in question does *not* happen—most authorities consider it to be bad form.[14]

(g) Either . . . or

Since both the *either* and *or* clauses describe actions which are uncertain—in principle, *both* cannot occur—the subjunctive is used with each:

Soit qu'il *vienne,* **soit qu**'il ne *vienne* pas.	"Either he *comes* or he *does*n't *come.*"
Elle suggère **soit que** tu *viennes* chez nous, **soit qu**'on *aille* au restaurant.	"She suggests either that you *come* to our place or that we *go* to a restaurant."

(h) Instead of

In Modern French *au lieu que* is used with the subjunctive.[15]

Au lieu que ce *soit* les usagers qui s'adaptent au programme, le programme doit s'adapter aux usagers.	"Instead of it *being* the users who adapt to the program, the program should adapt to the users."

---

[14] Nonetheless the struggle to prevent its use has been abandoned by at least some: *Le Robert & Nathan: Grammaire* gives the example *Je l'ai fait sans qu'il* ***ne*** *le sache,* with nary a mention that some might find this *ne* inappropriate.

[15] In former times it could be used with the indicative as a synonym for *alors que* or *tandis que: Il attend tout d'autrui,* ***au lieu qu'****il devrait agir lui-même* ("He waits for others [to do] everything, *while* [on the contrary] he should act himself").

Other Expressions Requiring the Subjunctive

There are various other constructions where the use of the subjunctive is required and/or customary. These include the following.

(a) Relative clauses relating to a "hypothetical" *object*

Consider the two sentences:

J'aimerais acheter une voiture qui *soit* bleue.	"I would like to buy a car that *is* blue."
J'ai acheté une voiture qui *est* bleue.	"I bought a car that *is* blue."

The distinction here is to some extent analogous to that observed earlier for conjunctions like *de manière que.* In the first case, I am searching specifically for a car that is blue. I am not necessarily sure that such a car even exists, but I have set a blue car as my objective. In the second case, I am simply reporting the result of the outcome of my having purchased a car: it is blue. Perhaps I was searching specifically for a blue car, but the statement provides no information about this. Similarly:

Je cherche un remède qui *puisse* me guérir.	"I am looking for a medicine which *could* cure me."
J'ai un remède qui *peut* te guérir.	"I have a medicine which *can* cure you."

In the first case, I am looking for a "hypothetical" medicine which may or may not exist; in the second, I am speaking of an identified medicine whose effect is not in doubt. If I have doubt about the effectiveness of this (identified) medicine, either the subjunctive or conditional could be used:

J'ai un remède qui *puisse* te guérir. J'ai un remède qui *pourrait* te guérir.	} "I have a medicine which *might* cure you."

(b) Relative clauses following superlatives

The superlative can be introduced by *le plus, le moins, le premier, le dernier, le seul,* etc. If it simply relates an objective fact, the verb in the following dependent clause is generally in the *indicative:*

C'est *le plus bas prix* qu'on nous *a* proposé.	"It is *the lowest price* they (*have*) offered us."
Le Japon est *le seul pays* qui *a* signé l'accord.	"Japan is *the only country* that *has* signed the agreement."

But if the nuance is one of sentiment (wonder, fear, desire, hope, etc.), the subjunctive is often found:

C'est l'homme *le plus riche* que je *connaisse.*	"He is *the richest* man that I *know.*"
C'est *la plus belle* église que j'*aie* jamais *vue.*	"It is *the most beautiful* church that I *have* ever *seen.*"
Elle est *la première* personne avec qui j'*aie eu* une conversation personnelle dans cette ville.	"She is *the first* person with whom I *have had* a personal conversation in this town."
Il est *le seul* qui *puisse* nous aider.	"He is *the only one* who *might be able* to help us."

In the last example, if the meaning refers to a future (possible) eventuality, the conditional would be used instead:

En cas de besoin, il est le seul qui *pourrait* nous aider.	"In case of need, he is the only one who *would be able* to help us."

(c) *Si . . . et que* ("if . . . and also if")

In an "if" statement with two conditions, the second *si* is replaced by *que,* with the accompanying verb obligatorily put into the subjunctive, at least in theory:

Si jamais vous allez à Rome **et que** vous *puissiez* y faire un petit séjour, je vous donnerai des adresses. (Jules Romains)	"**If** you ever go to Rome **and (if)** you *have the possibility* to spend some time there, I will give you some addresses."
S'il fait beau **et que** tu ne *sois* pas trop fatigué nous irons à la plage.	"**If** the weather is nice **and (if)** you *are* not too tired, we will go to the beach."

While examples like this are found in most grammar books, many people use the indicative rather than the subjunctive after *et que.* The most recent edition of *Le Robert & Nathan Grammaire* shows the indicative in the second example above, with no mention that the subjunctive is even a possibility:

S'il fait beau **et que** tu n'*es* pas trop fatigué nous irons à la plage.	"**If** the weather is nice **and (if)** you *are* not too tired, we will go to the beach."

More on the *Ne Explétif*

We have seen above that this is to be found, at least on occasion, in the following contexts:

(1) with verbs of fear (*craindre, avoir peur, redouter*) and dependent clauses introduced by related conjunctions (*de crainte que, de peur que*);
(2) with "inhibiting" verbs—*éviter* and *empêcher;*
(3) with the conjunctions *avant que, à moins que,* and ("erroneously") *sans que;*
(4) in literary constructions with denial or negation (*douter, nier*) expressed in the negative (*je ne doute pas . . .*).

We will see shortly that it can be used in another context as well.

Origin of *ne explétif*

Like the English *expletive*— with which the *ne explétif* is not infrequently compared!—French *explétif* comes from the Latin verb meaning "to fill" (as in *complete* and *deplete*). The French *ne explétif* has at various stages gone by other names, including *ne expressif* and *ne abusif.*

The original idea goes back to Latin, where *ne* was used to introduce dependent clauses following verbs of *fear* and *inhibition.* The origins of this *ne* are obscure, but a possible explanation is that it arose from the "contamination" of two independent phrases: e.g.,

I fear	*and*	Do not come!	→	TIMEO	NE VENIAT
				Je crains qu'il ***ne*** vienne.	

Alternatively, it is not difficult to imagine that a statement like *to ensure that you do not lose time* could become mixed up with *to avoid that you lose time,* resulting in

** Pour éviter que vous ***ne*** *perdiez* du temps . . .	"To avoid that you (****don't***) lose time . . ."[16]

[16] At the early stages of French, negative statements were marked by *ne* only. The addition of *pas* was a later innovation—initially *pas* ("step") had no negative connotation at all, the idea being rather to make the *ne* more emphatic ("not a bit . . ."). Ironically, in common speech today *ne* is frequently omitted (*je sais pas*), leaving the negative to be conveyed entirely by the "positive" *pas.* (English *pace* and *pass* both come from *pas.*)

While abandoned by other Romance languages, the *ne explétif* thrived in Classical French, expanding its orbit from the initial (1) and (2) to include (3) and (4), as well as an additional use described below, this time with the indicative.

Comparisons of inequality

In such comparisons a *ne explétif* can be found if the verb expressing the inequality is in the affirmative. For example:

** C'est plus difficile que je ***ne*** le pensais.	"This is more difficult than I thought."
** C'est pire que je ***ne*** le pensais.	"It's worse than I thought."
** J'ai moins de regrets que tu ***ne*** le crois.	"I have fewer regrets than you think."
** Je suis moins riche que je ***ne*** l'étais.	"I am less rich than I was."
** Il agit autrement qu'il ***ne*** parle.	"He acts differently than he speaks."
** Le temps est meilleur qu'il ***n'***était hier.	"The weather is better than it was yesterday."
** Elle chante mieux que vous ***ne*** le dites.	"She sings better than you say."

Note that all of these verbs are in the *indicative.*

CHAPTER 12

Simple Past and Imperfect Subjunctive

In this chapter we will consider the simple past and imperfect subjunctive, as well as their associated compound forms—past anterior and past perfect subjunctive.

There are two similarities between the simple past and imperfect subjunctive:

(a) in form, they are intimately related (Chapter 6);
(b) both have disappeared from the spoken language.

There is nonetheless a crucial difference: in the written language the imperfect subjunctive has also virtually disappeared, while the simple past remains an essential element.

Simple Past (*Passé Simple*)

The use of the *passé simple* is not restricted to "literature" alone. Thus in the French edition of *National Geographic* (January 2004) one finds:

> Après des débuts modestes comme miliciens et gardes à la cour impériale, les samouraïs **s'emparèrent** du pouvoir en 1185 ... ils **formèrent** une classe privilégiée dont l'autorité était fondée sur la force brute ... de nombreux samouraïs **devinrent** des aristocrates oisifs ... Les anciennes techniques de fabrication des sabres japonais **disparurent** presque totalement au lendemain de la Seconde Guerre mondiale, quand les Alliés **confisquèrent** et **détruisirent** environ 5 millions de lames et en **interdirent** la production.
>
> After their modest beginnings as militiamen and guards at the imperial court, the samurai **seized** power in 1185 ... they **formed** a privileged class whose authority was founded on brute force ... many samurai **became** idle aristocrats ... The ancient techniques of fabricating Japanese sabers **disappeared** almost totally following the Second World War, when the Allies **confiscated** and **destroyed** around 5 million blades and **banned** their production.

In both Old and Classical French there were differences in nuance between the *passé composé* and *passé simple*, essentially analogous to those between the two English past tenses: *they have seized, they seized.* At one stage there was even a precise "24-hour rule": anything within that period was described using the *passé composé,* everything beyond with the *passé simple.*

Eventually, however, the semantic distinction between the two forms disappeared, a factor which facilitated the elimination of the *passé simple* from the spoken language. In the modern written language, the two forms can be used interchangeably and frequently appear within the same text.[1] Thus from the same *National Geographic* article:

> Les samouraïs ***ont dominé*** l'histoire du Japon pendant près de sept cent ans, de 1185 à 1867 ...
>
> The samurai ***(have) dominated*** the history of Japan for nearly seven hundred years, from 1185 to 1867 ...

Similarly, in *Le Petit Prince*—written for children—the author alternates between the two forms:

> J'***ai*** bien ***frotté*** mes yeux. J'***ai*** bien ***regardé.*** Et j'***ai vu*** un petit bonhomme tout à fait extraordinaire ... Je **regardai** donc cette apparition ... Quand je **réussis** enfin à parler, je lui **dis**:"Mais ... qu'est-ce que tu fais là?"[2]
>
> I ***(have) rubbed*** my eyes. I ***(have) looked*** closely. And I ***(have) seen*** a completely extraordinary little fellow ... I therefore **looked** at this apparition ... When I finally **managed** to speak, I **said** to him:"But ... what are you doing there?"

Note that *je dis* and *je réussis* are both *passé simple,* although in form they are identical to the present indicative.

The choice between the two past tenses is thus largely a matter of style, with the *passé simple* generally more frequent in historical recitations, in which frequent uses of the more cumbersome *passé composé* might be awkward:

> Dieu **vit** que la lumière était bonne; et Dieu **sépara** la lumière d'avec les ténèbres. Dieu **appela** la lumière jour, et il **appela** les ténèbres nuit. Ainsi, il y **eut** un soir, et il y **eut** un matin: Ce **fut** le premier jour. (Genèse 1:4–5, version Louis Segond)
>
> And God **saw** that the light was good. And God **separated** the light from the darkness. God **called** the light Day, and the darkness he **called** Night. And there **was** evening and there **was** morning, [this **was**] the first day. (Genesis: 1:4–5, English Standard Version)

---

[1] Some authors certainly try to maintain a distinction between the "near" and "remote" pasts, but this is by no means universal.

[2] Antoine de Saint-Exupéry, *Le Petit Prince* (Paris: Gallimard Jeunesse, 1997).

Learning the *Passé Simple*

Many students familiar with the spoken language are hesitant about trying to read "serious" French because of the frequent use of the *passé simple,* with which they do not feel comfortable. This is unfortunate, since the effort required to become conversant with the *passé simple* is minimal. As we have seen in Part I:

> **There are only six verbs whose simple past is not easily *recognizable* by its similarity to the past participle, infinitive, or present plural: *être, faire, voir, tenir, venir, naître.***

	être *fu-*	faire *fi-*	voir *vi*	tenir *tin-*	venir *vin-*	naître *naqui-*
je	fus	fis	vis	tins	vins	naquis
nous	fûmes	fîmes	vîmes	tînmes	vînmes	naquîmes

The earlier selections illustrate three of these forms: *de**vinrent**, vit,* and *fut.*

Past Anterior (*Passé Antérieur*)

We recall from Chapter 7 that the past anterior is a compound tense formed by adding the past participle to the simple past of the auxiliary verb (*avoir* or *être,* as appropriate): e.g., *j'eus fait.* It is used far less frequently in Modern French than is the simple past, being generally restricted to "literary" works. In the spoken language it has been replaced by the *passé composé,* the *passé surcomposé,* or various alternative constructions (Chapter 10).

To understand the sense of the past anterior, it is useful to consider its relationship to other tenses. For this purpose, the "timeline" below sets out the basic relationships among the present tense and the six indicative tenses relating to the past:[3]

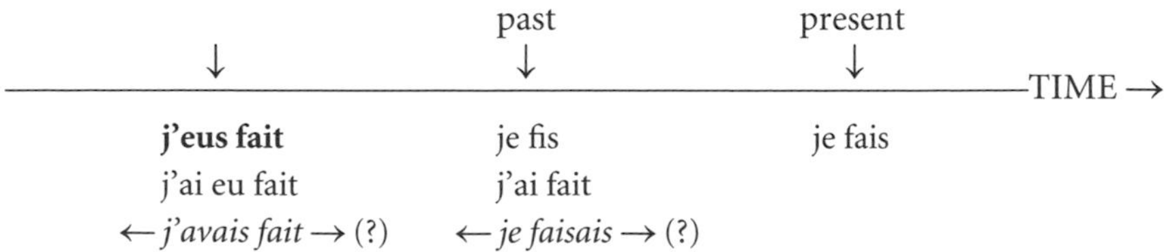

[3] Excluding the conditional and conditional perfect, which can also refer to the past.

The imperfect and past perfect have question marks, since the actions that they describe may or may not have continued (*it was raining yesterday* and *it had been raining the day before* do not give us any information about when, or even whether, the rain subsequently stopped). Like the "modern", though not universally employed, *passé surcomposé,* the past anterior marks an action *completed* prior to another completed action. Its most frequent use is with conjunctions of time (*quand, dès que, à peine,* etc.), in which case it indicates that a particular action occurred *immediately* prior to a second action; this second action is expressed by a verb in the simple past.

Quand elle **eut fini** de travailler, elle ***sortit.***	"When she *had finished* working, she *left.*"
Dès qu'il **eut terminé** son dîner, il ***monta*** dans sa chambre.	"As soon as he *had finished* his dinner, he *went up* to his room."
Édouard n'**eut** pas plutôt **proféré** ces paroles qu'il en **sentit** l'inconvenance. (André Gide)	"Edward *had* hardly *uttered* these words when he *sensed* their impropriety."

The past anterior is also found by itself in expressions with adverbs meaning "soon", "quickly", "all at once" (*bientôt, peu après, en un moment, en un instant,* etc.):

En un instant il **eut rattrapé** le groupe des coureurs de tête.	"In a moment he *had caught up* with the lead group of runners."
Bientôt il **eut retrouvé** son bon aspect de jadis.	"Soon he *had recovered* his past appearance."

And most famously—an example still taught to French *collégiens:*[4]

Ce brouet fut par lui servi sur une assiette:
La Cigogne au long bec n'en put attraper miette,
Et le Drôle **eut lapé** le tout en un moment.
(Jean de la La Fontaine,"Le Renard et la Cigogne")

This soup was served on a platter:
The Stork with long beak was unable to pick up a crumb;
And the sly Fox **had lapped** it all up in an instant.
(Jean de La Fontaine,"The Fox and the Stork")

[4] *Collège* in France is equivalent to U.S. grades six through nine.

Note that there is no inherent value of "quickness" in the past anterior; rather this comes from the accompanying adverb.

Native English-speakers frequently find the distinction between the past anterior (*j'eus fait*) and the past perfect (*j'avais fait*) somewhat confusing, since they are normally translated identically into English: *I had done.*[5]

(1a) Quand j'**eus mangé,** je m'en **allai.**	"When I *had eaten,* I departed."
(2a) Quand j'**avais mangé,** je m'en ***allais.***	"When I *had eaten,* I would depart."
(1b) Dès qu'il **eut parlé,** on lui **obéit.**	"As soon as he *had spoken,* he was obeyed."
(2b) Dès qu'il **avait parlé,** on lui ***obéissait.***	"As soon as he *had spoken,* he would be obeyed."

The difference is that the past anterior always refers to a completed (hence specific) action, while the past perfect *when preceded by a time conjunction* (*quand,* etc.) relates to a series or pattern of actions. For example: "every Thursday I would leave work as soon as I had finished lunch"; "the captain's orders were always obeyed at once".

However, *in the absence of a time conjunction* specifically linking the two phrases, the past anterior *cannot* be used; in this case, the past perfect is employed to refer to the prior (completed) action.

(3a) *J'**eus mangé** et (je) m'en **allai.**	[not possible]
(4a) J'***avais mangé*** et (je) m'en **allai.**	"I *had eaten* and (I) departed."

The difference in nuance between (1a) and (4a) is that the former implies that the action (*eating*) was completed *immediately* prior to that of the second verb (*departing*), while the latter provides no indication of the immediacy of the prior action, simply that I had already eaten at the moment when I departed. The action of eating could, at least in theory, have taken place at any time prior to my departure.

Note that (4a) could also be expressed using the *passé composé*—this would of course be obligatory in spoken French:

(4a′) J'***avais mangé*** et (je) m'en **suis allé.**

[5] In Old French as well, the two forms could often substitute for one another.

Imperfect Subjunctive

In contrast to the simple past (essential to the written language) and past anterior (still exists, but only literary), the use of the imperfect subjunctive in Modern French is essentially dead. Occasional efforts of modern authors to revive its use are generally greeted with derision and ridicule: e.g.,

> Il est pourtant de fins lettrés qui tiennent à l'employer, mais qui feraient peut-être mieux, eux aussi, de s'abstenir car, une fois sur deux, ils l'emploient à tort. L'imparfait du subjonctif devient alors, au XXe siècle, l'ornement superflu qui, se voulant révélateur d'une culture raffinée, n'est bien souvent que l'indice d'une connaissance lacunaire de la norme.[6]

> It is, however, the literary types who insist on using it, but they would perhaps do themselves a service if they resisted the temptation, since half the time they use it incorrectly. The imperfect subjunctive has thus become, in the 20th century, the superfluous ornament which, seeking to be a mark of refined culture, more often serves only to signal deficient knowledge of the rules.

In form, the imperfect subjunctive is by far the most regular of all French verb tenses: it *always* uses the stem of the simple past (Chapter 6). The (minimal) effort required to learn the simple past forms will therefore simultaneously confer familiarity with those of the imperfect subjunctive. Why bother, one might ask? The answer to this is very simple: Why cut oneself off *a priori* from the works of classical French writers and philosophers, particularly when the effort required to learn (or at least recognize) these forms is so small?

The imperfect subjunctive was previously used in past tense expressions requiring the subjunctive, where in Modern French the present subjunctive is used:

	Modern	Classical	*he wished that*
il voulait que	je parte	je partisse	*I would leave*
	je chante	je chantasse	*I would sing*
il voulait que	je sois parti	je fusse parti	*I had (would have) left*
	j'aie chanté	j'eusse chanté	*I had (would have) sung*

It was also used in *past hypothetical* statements, where the imperfect and conditional are used in Modern French (Chapter 10). Thus *If she had lived during that era, she would have been queen* would be:

---

[6] Walter (1988: 122).

Modern	Si elle avait vécu à cette époque, elle aurait été reine.
Classical	Si elle **eût vécu** à cette époque, elle aurait été reine. **Eût-elle** vécu à cette époque, elle **eût été** reine.

The two classical sentences are identical in meaning, the second showing that the imperfect subjunctive could by itself express both the notion *if only–were only* and the conditional *would.*

The compound forms—where the auxiliary verb is in the imperfect subjunctive—are *past perfect* subjunctives: *je fusse parti, j'eusse chanté, elle eût vécu, elle eût été.*

Some examples:

Il aimait la sainte Vierge comme il **eût aimé** sa femme. (Honoré de Balzac)	"He loved the Blessed Virgin as he *might have loved* his wife."
Il convenait que je **fusse** absent de votre mariage. (Victor Hugo)	"It was fitting that I *should be* absent from your marriage."
Si Phileas Fogg manquait, ne **fût**-ce que de quelques heures, le départ d'un paquebot, il serait forcé d'attendre le paquebot suivant . . . (Jules Verne)	"If Phileas Fogg missed, even *were* it only by a few hours, the departure of a steamer, he would be forced to wait for the next steamer . . ."
Supposez que nous **eussions atteint** notre but, n'**eût**-il pas mieux **valu** trouver des continents en pleine lumière au lieu d'une contrée plongée dans une nuit obscure? (Jules Verne)	"Suppose we *had attained* our goal, *would* it not *have been better* to have found continents in broad daylight than a country plunged in utter darkness?"
Son trouble était trop grand pour qu'elle **pût** dormir. (André Maurois, 20th century)	"Her unrest was too great to *allow* her to sleep."
Hitler, alors qu'il **eût pu** arrêter la guerre avant le désastre total, a voulu le suicide général. (Albert Camus, 20th century)	"Hitler, although he *could have* stopped the war before total disaster, preferred collective suicide."

Mais il est rarement arrivé qu'on m'ait objecté quelque chose que je n'**eusse** point du tout **prévue,** si ce n'est qu'elle **fût** fort éloignée de mon sujet; en sorte que je n'ai quasi jamais rencontré aucun censeur de mes opinions qui ne me **semblât** ou moins rigoureux ou moins équitable que moi-même. (René Descartes)

"But it has rarely happened that anything has been objected to me which I *had* not myself completely *anticipated,* unless it *were* something far removed from my subject; so that I have almost never met a single critic of my opinions who did not *appear* to me either less rigorous or less equitable than myself."

Two "relics" of the imperfect subjunctive are not infrequently encountered in Modern French: the essentially equivalent expressions *ne fût-ce que* and *fût-ce,* "not even for", "even if only for."[7] That their use is not only literary is confirmed by the following "real-life" examples:

Ne quittez jamais vos affaires des yeux, **fût-ce** quelques secondes. En cas de délit, prévenez la police au numéro 911.

"Do not take your eyes from your belongings, **not even for** a few seconds. In the event of a crime, notify the police by phoning 911."

Si vous utilisez votre compte privé (**ne fût-ce qu**'une fois) à des fins professionnelles, le fisc aura le droit d'y fouiner.

"If you use your private account (**even if only** a single time) for professional purposes, the tax authorities will have the right to poke their nose into it."

Dans l'histoire, Taiwan n'a jamais été un pays, **ne fût-ce qu**'une seule fois. (Chinese Embassy in France, 2002)

"In all of its history, Taiwan has never been a country, **not even** once."

One final point: for Class II and III verbs, the third person singular forms for the imperfect subjunctive and simple past differ only in that the former has a circumflex (*il finît, il voulût, il fût*), while the latter does not (*il finit, il voulut, il fut*). A good way to remember which form has the circumflex is to recall that a circumflex generally marks an *-s* which has disappeared, and the imperfect subjunctive is the "S" tense par excellence (*je voulusse, tu voulusses,* etc.).

Si tu pouvais écrire, **fût-ce** quelques mots!

"If you could write, (even) **if only** a few words!"

Fut-ce lui ou un autre, je ne sais pas.

"***Was it*** he or another, I do not know."

[7] The "modern" form is *ne serait-ce que.*

Appendix
Why Did Two These Forms (Largely) Disappear?

The more surprising disappearance is that of the simple past from the spoken language. One has difficulty imagining what English would be like if one were restricted to using the "compound" past: *Caesar has been assassinated in 44 BC; after Louis XIV has died, Louis XV has become king;* etc.

Explanations frequently invoke the alleged complexity of the forms of the simple past, but this argument is not very convincing: we have seen in Chapter 4 that there are only a very limited number of verbs whose simple pasts are not determined directly by the form of their past participle. Indeed, any "theory" which seeks to explain the disappearance of the simple past from spoken French will face major difficulties in the face of its survival under virtually identical circumstances in all of the other principal Romance languages.

Limiting the discussion only to Spanish, the first point to observe is that the forms of its simple past are no less irregular or difficult than those of French. Moreover, in complete contrast to French, in the Spanish of Latin America it is the *compound past* which is threatened with extinction by the simple past. In the Spanish of Spain, the division between the two tenses is defined by something very similar to the "24-hour rule" which prevailed at one time in French.

With respect to the French simple past, all one can really say is that during the Old and Middle French periods it was in a continual struggle for "territory" with the compound past, on the one hand, and with the imperfect tense, on the other. At some point the compound past was able to extend its meaning to include the remote as well as the near past. When this occurred the days of the simple past were numbered, at least in the spoken language.

With regard to the even more complete disappearance of the imperfect subjunctive, the situation seems to be of the chicken or egg type: did the imperfect subjunctive disappear because its forms seem so odd—

je chantasse, nous construisissions, tu rassasiasses

or do its forms seem so odd because it has disappeared?

Like the simple past, the imperfect subjunctive continues to be an important element in the other principal Romance languages. To explain its disappearance in French, linguists have come up with various explanations, perhaps the most ingenious (or farfetched) being that it all comes down to the fact that in French it is possible to give a one-word affirmative response to a negative question (Do you not love me? Si!) whereas in the other Romance languages it is not. According to this theory,

> Le *si* du français a une puissance réfutatoire suffisante pour signifier que l 'hypothèse que l'on formule est en quelque sorte mise en cause, mise en débat ... Le français peut alors se dispenser d'avoir recours au mode subjonctif, mode du virtuel. L'indicatif est suffisant: *Si tu m'**avais** tout dit* ... En revanche, l'espagnol doit utiliser le subjonctif car il ne dispose

> pas d'un *si* réfutatoire, capable par avance de mettre en discussion, de renverser l'hypothèse formulée: *Si me lo* ***hubieras*** *dicho todo ...*[8]
>
> The *si* of French has a capacity to refute which is sufficient to indicate that the formulated hypothesis is to a certain extent called into question ... French thus has no need to resort to the subjunctive mood, the mood of the virtual. The indicative is sufficient: *If you* ***had*** *told me everything ...* In contrast, Spanish must utilize the subjunctive since it does not have at its disposition a "refuting" *si,* with the capability [by itself] to call into question, to topple the formulated hypothesis: *If you* ***would have*** *told me everything ...*

---

[8] M. Bénaben, *Manuel de linguistique espagnole* (Paris: Ophrys, 2002), pp. 198–199. In Spanish, *hubieras* is the imperfect subjunctive of *haber,* the Spanish equivalent of *avoir.*

PART III

ANNEXES

ANNEX A

Model Verbs, with Complete Conjugations

A1. List of Model Verbs

Below is a list of "model" verbs representing categories into which all French verbs can be placed: 57 *basic* models plus 27 *variants* (marked "b", "c", and "d"),[1] which differ in only a very limited way from the corresponding model—e.g., by lack of a circumflex (4-3b, 5-19b, 5-22b) or by a past participle ending in *-us* rather than *-u* (5-16b).

A. **Class I**	1-1	parler				
"regular", but noteworthy orthographic modifications	1-1a	fatiguer	1-1b	fabriquer	1-1c	prier
consonant change	1-2a	lancer	1-2b	manger		
consonant doubling	1-3a	appeler	1-3b	jeter		
alternation *e* → *è*	1-4	peser				
alternation *é* → *è*	1-5	céder				
combinations	1-6a	dépecer	1-6b	rapiécer	1-6c	protéger
y → *i*	1-7a	employer	1-7b	payer		
irregular future + *y* → *i*	1-8	envoyer				
B. **Class II**	2-1	finir				
irregular past participle	2-2	maudire				
irregular (singular) present	2-3	haïr				
C. ***-e* present endings + *bouillir***	3-1	couvrir	3-2a	assaillir	3-2b	cueillir
	3-2c	bouillir				
D. ***-s* present endings**						
(i) *-oir* verbs	4-1a	voir	4-1b	prévoir	4-1c	pourvoir
	4-2a	devoir	4-2b	recevoir	4-3a	mouvoir
	4-3b	promouvoir	4-4	pleuvoir	4-5a	valoir
	4-5b	prévaloir	4-5c	falloir	4-6	pouvoir
	4-7	savoir	4-8	vouloir		
	4-9a	asseoir (A)	4-9b	asseoir (B)	4-9c	surseoir

[1] As well as (1-1a) *fatiguer;* all other "a" (1-2a, 1-3a, etc.) represent basic models.

(ii) *-re* verbs	5-1a	rendre	5-1b	rompre	5-2	prendre
	5-3	battre	5-4	mettre	5-5	suivre
	5-6	vivre	5-7	écrire	5-8a	dire
	5-8b	prédire	5-8c	suffire	5-8d	circoncire
	5-9a	conduire	5-9b	nuire	5-10	lire
	5-11	rire	5-12	plaindre	5-13a	absoudre
	5-13b	résoudre	5-14	coudre	5-15	moudre
	5-16a	exclure	5-16b	inclure	5-17	boire
	5-18	croire	5-19a	croître	5-19b	accroître
	5-20	connaître	5-21	naître	5-22a	plaire
	5-22b	taire	5-23	faire	5-24	traire
	5-25	vaincre				
(iii) *-ir* verbs	6-1	partir	6-2	fuir	6-3	acquérir
	6-4	courir	6-5	mourir	6-6	vêtir
	6-7	venir				
E. **Irregular**	7	être	8	avoir	9	aller

Note that C–E correspond to what are traditionally called *Class III* verbs. *Defective* verbs are shown in Annex C.

A2. Summary Table: Six Key Conjugations

Chapter 9 shows that for nearly all verbs the complete conjugations can be determined from a knowledge of (at most) six key conjugations:

1. 1s present indicative
2. 1p present indicative
3. 3p present indicative
4. past participle
5. 1p simple past
6. 1s future

Table 1 provides the six key conjugations (or stem, in the case of the future) for each of the model verb categories presented in A1, apart from those displaying orthographic modifications only (1-2 through 1-7) The final two columns display irregular present subjunctives and information on other irregularities, if any. Blank spaces in columns (1)–(6) indicate that the conjugation is analogous to that of the verb immediately above (e.g., *je vois* → *je prévois* and *je pourvois*, *nous assaillons* → *nous cueillons* and *nous bouillons*). Also shown is the number of verbs (in *Le Petit Robert*) in each category.

Exceptions to general patterns are highlighted in bold, as follows:

(a) the "short" present singular stem *je hais,* the exceptional Class IIIA *je bous,* the verbs whose first (and second) person singular ends in *-x* rather than *-s,* and *je croîs* (where the circumflex is present in all three singulars).
(b) the irregular *vous dites, vous faites, ils font*
(c) *maudit,* the only irregular Class II past participle; *assis,* the sole *-oir* past participle not ending in *-u;* and the three past participles with circumflexes (*dû, mû, crû*)
(d) simple pasts not following the "basic rule" set forth at the conclusion of Chapter 4
(e) verbs having irregular future stems.

A dash (—) indicates that the form in question does not exist—e.g., *absoudre* (5-13a) has no simple past. For *pleuvoir* and *falloir,* in place of the first person plural indicative (which does not exist) the table shows (in brackets) the infinitive stem—used for constructing the imperfect tense (both verbs) and present participle (*pleuvoir* only).

TABLE 1

			(1)	(2)	(3)	(4)	(5)	(6)	Irregular	Other
				Present Indicative		Past	Simple past	Future	present	irregularity
			1s	1p	3p	participle	1p	stem	subjunctive	
1-1	parler	4,972	parle	parlons	parlent	parlé	parlâmes	parler-		
1-2–1-7	*(orthographic)*	*778*								see Chapter 8
1-8	envoyer	2						**enverr-**		
2-1	finir	307	finis	finissons	finissent	fini	finîmes	finir-		
2-2	maudire	1				**maudit**				
2-3	haïr	1	**hais**							no circumflexes
3-1	couvrir	9	couvre	couvrons	couvrent	couvert	**couvrîmes**	couvrir-		
3-2a	assaillir	4	assaille	assaillons	assaillent	assailli	assaillîmes	assaillir-		
3-2b	cueillir	3						**cueiller-**		
3-2c	bouillir	1	**bous**					bouillir-		
4-1a	voir	3	vois	voyons	voient	vu	**vîmes**	**verr-**		
4-1b	prévoir	1						prévoir-		
4-1c	pourvoir	1					pourvûmes	pourvoir-		
4-2a	devoir	2	dois	devons	doivent	**dû**	dûmes	**devr-**		
4-2b	recevoir	6	reçois	recevons	reçoivent	reçu	reçûmes	**recevr-**		*c* → *ç*: 22 conjugations
4-3a	mouvoir	1	meus	mouvons	meuvent	**mû**	mûmes	**mouvr-**		
4-3b	promouvoir	2				promu				
4-4	pleuvoir	2	(il) pleut	[pleuv-]	pleuvent	plu	il plut	**pleuvr-**		
4-5a	valoir	3	**vaux**	valons	valent	valu	valûmes	**vaudr-**	vaill- / val-	
4-5b	prévaloir	1							[regular]	
4-5c	falloir	1	(il) faut	[fall-]	—	fallu	il fallut	**faudr-**	faill-	
4-6	pouvoir	1	**peux, puis**	pouvons	peuvent	pu	pûmes	**pourr-**	puiss-	
4-7	savoir	1	sais	savons	savent	su	sûmes	**saur-**	sach-	sachant + *imperative*
4-8	vouloir	2	**veux**	voulons	veulent	voulu	voulûmes	**voudr-**	veuill- / voul-	*imperative* (2 forms)
4-9a	asseoir (A)	2	assieds	asseyons	asseyent	**assis**	assîmes	**assiér-**		present 3s: assie**d**
4-9b	asseoir (B)	2	assois	assoyons	assoient			**assoir-**		

TABLE 1 (*continued*)

			(1)	(2)	(3)	(4)	(5)	(6)	Irregular	Other
				Present Indicative		Past	Simple past	Future	present	irregularity
			1s	1p	3p	participle	1p	stem	subjunctive	
4-9c	surseoir	1						surseoir-		
5-1a	rendre	47	rends	rendons	rendent	rendu	**rendîmes**	rendr-		present 3s: ren**d**
5-1b	rompre	3	romps	rompons	rompent	rompu	**rompîmes**	rompr-		[present 3s: rompt]
5-2	prendre	12	prends	prenons	prennent	pris	prîmes	prendr-		present 3s: pren**d**
5-3	battre	10	bats	battons	battent	battu	**battîmes**	battr-		present 3s: ba**t**
5-4	mettre	17	mets	mettons	mettent	mis	mîmes	mettr-		present 3s: me**t**
5-5	suivre	3	suis	suivons	suivent	suivi	suivîmes	suivr-		
5-6	vivre	3	vis	vivons	vivent	vécu	vécûmes	vivr-		
5-7	écrire	12	écris	écrivons	écrivent	écrit	**écrivîmes**	écrir-		
5-8a	dire	2	dis	disons	disent	dit	dîmes	dir-		vous **dites**
5-8b	prédire	6								[vous prédisez]
5-8c	suffire	1				suffi				[vous suffisez]
5-8d	circoncire	1				circoncis				[vous circoncisez]
5-9a	conduire	27	conduis	conduisons	conduisent	conduit	**conduisîmes**	conduir-		
5-9b	nuire	5				nui				
5-10	lire	4	lis	lisons	lisent	lu	lûmes	lir-		
5-11	rire	2	ris	rions	rient	ri	rîmes	rir-		
5-12	plaindre	29	plains	plaignons	plaignent	plaint	**plaignîmes**	plaindr-		
5-13a	absoudre	2	absous	absolvons	absolvent	absous/ absoute	—	absoudr-		
5-13b	résoudre	1				résolu	résolûmes			2nd p.p. résous/résoute
5-14	coudre	3	couds	cousons	cousent	cousu	**cousîmes**	coudr-		present 3s: cou**d**
5-15	moudre	1	mouds	moulons	moulent	moulu	moulûmes	moudr-		present 3s: mou**d**
5-16a	exclure	2	exclus	excluons	excluent	exclu	exclûmes	exclur-		

(*continued*)

TABLE 1 (*continued*)

			(1)	(2)	(3)	(4)	(5)	(6)	Irregular	Other
				Present indicative		Past	Simple past	Future	present	irregularity
			1s	1p	3p	participle	1p	stem	subjunctive	
5-16b	inclure	2				inclus				
5-17	boire	1	bois	buvons	boivent	bu	bûmes	boir-		
5-18	croire	1	crois	croyons	croient	cru	crûmes	croir-		
5-19a	croître	1	**croîs**	croissons	croissent	**crû**	crûmes	croîtr-		simple past (all): **crû-**
5-19b	accroître	2	accrois			accru	accrûmes			present 3s: accro**î**t
5-20	connaître	12	connais	connaissons	connaissent	connu	connûmes	connaîtr-		present 3s: conna**î**t
5-21	naître	2	nais	naissons	naissent	né	**naquîmes**	naîtr-		present 3s: na**î**t
5-22a	plaire	3	plais	plaisons	plaisent	plu	plûmes	plair-		present 3s: pla**î**t
5-22b	taire	1								[present 3s: tait]
5-23	faire	10	fais	faisons	**font**	fait	**fîmes**	**fer-**	fass-	vous **faites**
5-24	traire	8	trais	trayons	traient	trait	—	trair-		
5-25	vaincre	2	vaincs	vainquons	vainquent	vaincu	**vainquîmes**	vaincr-		present 3s: vain**c**
6-1	partir	22	pars	partons	partent	parti	partîmes	partir-		
6-2	fuir	2	fuis	fuyons	fuient	fui	fuîmes	fuir-		
6-3	acquérir	5	acquiers	acquérons	acquièrent	acquis	acquîmes	**acquerr-**		
6-4	courir	8	cours	courons	courent	couru	courûmes	**courr-**		
6-5	mourir	1	meurs	mourons	meurent	mort	**mourûmes**	**mourr-**		
6-6	vêtir	3	vêts	vêtons	vêtent	vêtu	**vêtîmes**	vêtir-		present 3s: vê**t**
6-7	venir	28	viens	venons	viennent	venu	**vînmes**	**viendr-**		
7	être	1	[suis-es-est]	[sommes-êtes]	sont	été	**fûmes**	**ser-**	sois-sois-soit-soyons-soyez-soient	*imperfect* étais (etc.) *pres. part.* étant *imperative = subjunc.*
8	avoir	1	[ai-as-a]	avons	ont	eu	eûmes	**aur-**	aie-aies-ait-ayons-ayez-aient	*pres. part.* ayant *imperative* = aie-ayons-ayez
9	aller	1	[vais-vas-va]	allons	vont	allé	allâmes	**ir-**	aill-/all-	

A3. Complete Conjugations of Model Verbs

On the following pages the complete conjugations for all of the model verbs are presented, highlighting the particular irregularities and/or orthographic modifications applicable to each.

For six models, conjugations are shown for several different individual verbs, all of whose conjugations are precisely analogous:

1-7a	employer/essuyer
3-1	couvrir/offrir/souffrir
5-1a	rendre/répandre/répondre/perdre/mordre
5-12	plaindre/peindre/joindre
6-1	partir/sortir/sentir/servir/dormir
6-7	venir/tenir

For each model verb, immediately following the complete conjugations are listed the *stems* for the six *key conjugations*, which nearly always determine the entire conjugation:[2]

present indicative (1s, 1p, 3p)
past participle
simple past (1p)
future (1s)

In this listing the complete past participle is shown, with the ending highlighted in bold. For example:

parler	parl**é**
partir	part**i**
courir	cour**u**
plaindre	plain**t**

Similarly, for the simple past the type of ending is highlighted in bold:

parler	parl**a**-	*-a endings*
partir	part**i**-	*-i endings*
courir	cour**u**-	*-u endings*
venir	vin^-	*"bare" endings*[3]

[2]All exceptions are explicitly identified in the "REMARKS" section following the individual conjugations and are summarized in Chapter 9.

[3]For the "bare" endings, the ^ indicates that a circumflex is placed on the preceding vowel for the first and second person plural: ***vî****nmes* and ***vî****ntes* (for *venir*).

Under "OTHER VERBS" are described and/or listed *all* other verbs conjugated analogously to the model verb.[4] If "OTHER VERBS" does not appear, then the model verb is the *only* one with such conjugation.

1-1	PARLER	TO SPEAK		
INDICATIVE				
	Present	Imperfect	Future	Conditional
je	parle	parlais	parlerai	parlerais
tu	parles	parlais	parleras	parlerais
il, elle	parle	parlait	parlera	parlerait
nous	parlons	parlions	parlerons	parlerions
vous	parlez	parliez	parlerez	parleriez
ils, elles	parlent	parlaient	parleront	parleraient

Simple Past		SUBJUNCTIVE Present	Imperfect
je	parlai	parle	parlasse
tu	parlas	parles	parlasses
il, elle	parla	parle	parlât
nous	parlâmes	parlions	parlassions
vous	parlâtes	parliez	parlassiez
ils, elles	parlèrent	parlent	parlassent

PAST PARTICIPLE	parlé		
PRESENT PARTICIPLE	parlant		
	(tu)	(nous)	(vous)
IMPERATIVE	parle	parlons	parlez
STEMS	parl-, parl-, parl- / parl**é** / parl**a**- / parler-		
OTHER VERBS	all *-er* verbs other than *aller* (9), *envoyer* (1-8), and those with regular orthographic changes (1-2 through 1-7)		

[4] Among those appearing in *Le Petit Robert.* The number of verbs listed does not always coincide with the corresponding number given in Table 1, since *Le Petit Robert* considers to be two separate verbs a single verb form which has separate origins: e.g., *desservir* 1 ("to serve", from Latin DESERVIRE) and *desservir* 2 ("to remove the plates", "to render a disservice", a native French construction formed by combining *des-* and *servir*).

1-1A FATIGUER TO FATIGUE

INDICATIVE

	Present	Imperfect	Future	Conditional
je	fatigue	*fati**gua**is*	fatiguerai	fatiguerais
tu	fatigues	*fati**gua**is*	fatigueras	fatiguerais
il, elle	fatigue	*fati**gua**it*	fatiguera	fatiguerait
nous	*fati**guo**ns*	fatiguions	fatiguerons	fatiguerions
vous	fatiguez	fatiguiez	fatiguerez	fatigueriez
ils, elles	fatiguent	*fati**gua**ient*	fatigueront	fatigueraient

Simple Past		SUBJUNCTIVE Present	Imperfect
je	*fati**guai***	fatigue	*fati**gua**sse*
tu	*fati**guas***	fatigues	*fati**gua**sses*
il, elle	*fati**gua***	fatigue	*fati**guâ**t*
nous	*fati**guâ**mes*	fatiguions	*fati**gua**ssions*
vous	*fati**guâ**tes*	fatiguiez	*fati**gua**ssiez*
ils, elles	fatiguèrent	fatiguent	*fati**gua**ssent*

PAST PARTICIPLE	fatigué		
PRESENT PARTICIPLE	*fati**gua**nt*		
	(tu)	(nous)	(vous)
IMPERATIVE	fatigue	*fati**guo**ns*	fatiguez
STEMS	fatigu-, fatigu-, fatigu- / fatigu**é** / fatigu**a**- / fatiguer-		
REMARKS	Conjugated like *parler.* Noteworthy element is *-gua, -guo* rather than "normal" orthography *-ga, -go.* Hence contrast: *fati**gua**nt—fati**ga**nt* (past participle—adjective).		
OTHER VERBS	verbs ending in *-guer*		

1-1B FABRIQUER TO FABRICATE

INDICATIVE

	Present	Imperfect	Future	Conditional
je	fabrique	*fabri**qua**is*	fabriquerai	fabriquerais
tu	fabriques	*fabri**qua**is*	fabriqueras	fabriquerais
il, elle	fabrique	*fabri**qua**it*	fabriquera	fabriquerait
nous	*fabri**quo**ns*	fabriquions	fabriquerons	fabriquerions
vous	fabriquez	fabriquiez	fabriquerez	fabriqueriez
ils, elles	fabriquent	*fabri**qua**ient*	fabriqueront	fabriqueraient

Simple Past			SUBJUNCTIVE Present	Imperfect
je	*fabri**quai***		fabrique	*fabri**qua**sse*
tu	*fabri**quas***		fabriques	*fabri**qua**sses*
il, elle	*fabri**qua***		fabrique	*fabri**quâ**t*
nous	*fabri**quâ**mes*		fabriquions	*fabri**qua**ssions*
vous	*fabri**quâ**tes*		fabriquiez	*fabri**qua**ssiez*
ils, elles	fabriquèrent		fabriquent	*fabri**qua**ssent*

PAST PARTICIPLE	fabriqué		
PRESENT PARTICIPLE	*fabri**qua**nt*		
	(tu)	(nous)	(vous)
IMPERATIVE	fabrique	*fabri**quo**ns*	fabriquez

STEMS fabriqu-, fabriqu-, fabriqu- / fabriqu**é** / fabriqu**a**- / fabriquer-

REMARKS Conjugated like *parler.* Noteworthy element is *-qua, -quo* rather than "normal" orthography *-ca, -co.* Hence contrast: *fabri**qua**nt—fabri**ca**nt* (past participle—noun).

OTHER VERBS verbs ending in *-quer*

1-1C PRIER TO REQUEST, TO PRAY

INDICATIVE

	Present	Imperfect	Future	Conditional
je	prie	priais	prierai	prierais
tu	pries	priais	prieras	prierais
il, elle	prie	priait	priera	prierait
nous	prions	*pr**ii**ons*	prierons	prierions
vous	priez	*pr**ii**ez*	prierez	prieriez
ils, elles	prient	priaient	prieront	prieraient

Simple Past			SUBJUNCTIVE Present	Imperfect
je	priai		prie	priasse
tu	prias		pries	priasses
il, elle	pria		prie	priât
nous	priâmes		*pr**ii**ons*	priassions
vous	priâtes		*pr**ii**ez*	priassiez
ils, elles	prièrent		prient	priassent

PAST PARTICIPLE	prié		
PRESENT PARTICIPLE	priant		
	(tu)	(nous)	(vous)
IMPERATIVE	prie	prions	priez

STEMS pri-, pri-, pri- / pri**é** / pri**a**- / prier-

REMARKS Conjugated like *parler.* Noteworthy element is *-ii* in imperfect indicative and present subjunctive (1p, 2p).

OTHER VERBS verbs ending in *-ier*

1-2A LANCER TO LAUNCH, THROW

INDICATIVE

	Present	Imperfect	Future	Conditional
je	lance	*lançais*	lancerai	lancerais
tu	lances	*lançais*	lanceras	lancerais
il, elle	lance	*lançait*	lancera	lancerait
nous	*lançons*	lancions	lancerons	lancerions
vous	lancez	lanciez	lancerez	lanceriez
ils, elles	lancent	*lançaient*	lanceront	lanceraient

SUBJUNCTIVE

Simple Past		Present	Imperfect
je	*lançai*	lance	*lançasse*
tu	*lanças*	lances	*lançasses*
il, elle	*lança*	lance	*lançât*
nous	*lançâmes*	lancions	*lançassions*
vous	*lançâtes*	lanciez	*lançassiez*
ils, elles	lancèrent	lancent	*lançassent*

PAST PARTICIPLE	lancé		
PRESENT PARTICIPLE	*lançant*		
	(tu)	(nous)	(vous)
IMPERATIVE	lance	*lançons*	lancez
STEMS	lanc-, *lanç-*, lanc- / lanc**é** / *lanç**a**-* / lancer-		
REMARKS	*c* → *ç*, when followed by *-a* or *-o* (18 conjugations)		
OTHER VERBS	verbs ending in *-cer*		

1-2B MANGER TO EAT

INDICATIVE

	Present	Imperfect	Future	Conditional
je	mange	*mang**e**ais*	mangerai	mangerais
tu	manges	*mang**e**ais*	mangeras	mangerais
il, elle	mange	*mang**e**ait*	mangera	mangerait
nous	*mang**e**ons*	mangions	mangerons	mangerions
vous	mangez	mangiez	mangerez	mangeriez
ils, elles	mangent	*mang**e**aient*	mangeront	mangeraient

SUBJUNCTIVE

Simple Past		Present	Imperfect
je	*mang**e**ai*	mange	*mang**e**asse*
tu	*mang**e**as*	manges	*mang**e**asses*
il, elle	*mang**e**a*	mange	*mang**e**ât*
nous	*mang**e**âmes*	mangions	*mang**e**assions*
vous	*mang**e**âtes*	mangiez	*mang**e**assiez*
ils, elles	mangèrent	mangent	*mang**e**assent*

PAST PARTICIPLE	mangé		
PRESENT PARTICIPLE	*mangeant*		
	(tu)	(nous)	(vous)
IMPERATIVE	mange	*mangeons*	mangez
STEMS	mang-, *mang(e)*-, mang- / mang**é** / *mang(e)**a**-* / manger-		
REMARKS	*g* → *ge,* when followed by *-a* or *-o* (18 conjugations)		
OTHER VERBS	verbs ending in *-ger*		

1-3A APPELER TO CALL

INDICATIVE

	Present	Imperfect	Future	Conditional
j'	*appe**ll**e*	appelais	*appe**ll**erai*	*appe**ll**erais*
tu	*appe**ll**es*	appelais	*appe**ll**eras*	*appe**ll**erais*
il, elle	*appe**ll**e*	appelait	*appe**ll**era*	*appe**ll**erait*
nous	appelons	appelions	*appe**ll**erons*	*appe**ll**erions*
vous	appelez	appeliez	*appe**ll**erez*	*appe**ll**eriez*
ils, elles	*appe**ll**ent*	appelaient	*appe**ll**eront*	*appe**ll**eraient*

Simple Past	
j'	appelai
tu	appelas
il, elle	appela
nous	appelâmes
vous	appelâtes
ils, elles	appelèrent

SUBJUNCTIVE

Present	Imperfect
*appe**ll**e*	appelasse
*appe**ll**es*	appelasses
*appe**ll**e*	appelât
appelions	appelassions
appeliez	appelassiez
*appe**ll**ent*	appelassent

PAST PARTICIPLE	appelé		
PRESENT PARTICIPLE	appelant		
	(tu)	(nous)	(vous)
IMPERATIVE	*appe**ll**e*	appelons	appelez
STEMS	*appe**ll**-*, appel-, *appe**ll**-* / appel**é** / appel**a**- / *appe**ll**er-*		
REMARKS	*l* → *ll,* when followed by *mute -e* (21 conjugations)		
OTHER VERBS	all *-eler* verbs **except** the following, which have conjugation (1-4): *agneler, celer, ciseler, congeler, déceler, décongeler, dégeler, démanteler, écarteler, geler, harceler, marteler, modeler, peler, receler, regeler, remodeler, surgeler*		

1-3B JETER TO THROW

INDICATIVE

	Present	Imperfect	Future	Conditional
je	*je**tt**e*	jetais	*je**tt**erai*	*je**tt**erais*
tu	*je**tt**es*	jetais	*je**tt**eras*	*je**tt**erais*
il, elle	*je**tt**e*	jetait	*je**tt**era*	*je**tt**erait*
nous	jetons	jetions	*je**tt**erons*	*je**tt**erions*
vous	jetez	jetiez	*je**tt**erez*	*je**tt**eriez*
ils, elles	*je**tt**ent*	jetaient	*je**tt**eront*	*je**tt**eraient*

Simple Past		SUBJUNCTIVE Present	Imperfect
je	jetai	*jette*	jetasse
tu	jetas	*jettes*	jetasses
il, elle	jeta	*jette*	jetât
nous	jetâmes	jetions	jetassions
vous	jetâtes	jetiez	jetassiez
ils, elles	jetèrent	*jettent*	jetassent

PAST PARTICIPLE	jeté		
PRESENT PARTICIPLE	jetant		
	(tu)	(nous)	(vous)
IMPERATIVE	*jette*	jetons	jetez
STEMS	*jett-*, jet-, *jett-* / jeté / jeta- / *jetter-*		
REMARKS	*t* → *tt*, when followed by *mute -e* (21 conjugations)		
OTHER VERBS	all *-eter* verbs ***except*** the following which have conjugation (1-4): *acheter, bégueter, caqueter, corseter, crocheter, se duveter, fileter, fureter, haleter, racheter*		

1-4 PESER TO WEIGH

INDICATIVE

	Present	Imperfect	Future	Conditional
je	*pèse*	pesais	*pèserai*	*pèserais*
tu	*pèses*	pesais	*pèseras*	*pèserais*
il, elle	*pèse*	pesait	*pèsera*	*pèserait*
nous	pesons	pesions	*pèserons*	*pèserions*
vous	pesez	pesiez	*pèserez*	*pèseriez*
ils, elles	*pèsent*	pesaient	*pèseront*	*pèseraient*

Simple Past		SUBJUNCTIVE Present	Imperfect
je	pesai	*pèse*	pesasse
tu	pesas	*pèses*	pesasses
il, elle	pesa	*pèse*	pesât
nous	pesâmes	pesions	pesassions
vous	pesâtes	pesiez	pesassiez
ils, elles	pesèrent	*pèsent*	pesassent

PAST PARTICIPLE	pesé		
PRESENT PARTICIPLE	pesant		
	(tu)	(nous)	(vous)
IMPERATIVE	*pèse*	pesons	pesez
STEMS	*pès-*, pes-, *pès-* / pesé / pesa- / *pèser-*		
REMARKS	*e* → *è*, when the following syllable has *mute -e* (21 conjugations)		
OTHER VERBS	*-er* verbs with stem vowel *-e* in *open* syllable— (a) when stem consonant is **not** *-l* or *-t*: 100 percent (b) when stem consonant is *-l* or *-t*: approx. 20 percent (listed in 1-3a and 1-3b)		

1-5	CÉDER	TO CEDE		

INDICATIVE

	Present	Imperfect	Future	Conditional
je	*cède*	cédais	céderai	céderais
tu	*cèdes*	cédais	céderas	céderais
il, elle	*cède*	cédait	cédera	céderait
nous	cédons	cédions	céderons	céderions
vous	cédez	cédiez	céderez	céderiez
ils, elles	*cèdent*	cédaient	céderont	céderaient

Simple Past		SUBJUNCTIVE Present	Imperfect
je	cédai	*cède*	cédasse
tu	cédas	*cèdes*	cédasses
il, elle	céda	*cède*	cédât
nous	cédâmes	cédions	cédassions
vous	cédâtes	cédiez	cédassiez
ils, elles	cédèrent	*cèdent*	cédassent

PAST PARTICIPLE	cédé		
PRESENT PARTICIPLE	cédant		
	(tu)	(nous)	(vous)
IMPERATIVE	*cède*	cédons	cédez
STEMS	*cède*-, céd-, *cède*-/céd**é**/céd**a**-/céder-		
REMARKS	*é* → *è*, when the following syllable has *mute -e*, **except** future and conditional (9 conjugations)		
OTHER VERBS	*-er* verbs with stem vowel *-é*, apart from those having no stem consonant (e.g., *créer, agréer*), which are conjugated like *parler*		

1-6A	DÉPECER	TO TEAR OR CUT UP INTO PIECES		

INDICATIVE

	Present	Imperfect	Future	Conditional
je	dép**è**ce	*dépeçais*	dép**è**cerai	dép**è**cerais
tu	dép**è**ces	*dépeçais*	dép**è**ceras	dép**è**cerais
il, elle	dép**è**ce	*dépeçait*	dép**è**cera	dép**è**cerait
nous	*dépeçons*	dépecions	dép**è**cerons	dép**è**cerions
vous	dépecez	dépeciez	dép**è**cerez	dép**è**ceriez
ils, elles	dép**è**cent	*dépeçaient*	dép**è**ceront	dép**è**ceraient

Simple Past		SUBJUNCTIVE Present	Imperfect
je	*dépeçai*	dépèce	*dépeçasse*
tu	*dépeças*	dépèces	*dépeçasses*
il, elle	*dépeça*	dépèce	*dépeçât*
nous	*dépeçâmes*	dépecions	*dépeçassions*
vous	*dépeçâtes*	dépeciez	*dépeçassiez*
ils, elles	dépecèrent	dépècent	*dépeçassent*

PAST PARTICIPLE dépecé
PRESENT PARTICIPLE *dépeçant*

	(tu)	(nous)	(vous)
IMPERATIVE	dépèce	*dépeçons*	dépecez

STEMS dépèc-, *dépeç-*, dépèc- / dépecé / *dépeça-* / dépècer-

REMARKS
1. *e* → *è*, when following syllable has *mute -e* (21 conjugations)
2. *c* → *ç*, when followed by *-a* or *-o* (18 conjugations)

OTHER VERBS *clamecer* (defective)

1-6B RAPIÉCER TO PATCH

INDICATIVE

	Present	Imperfect	Future	Conditional
je	rapièce	*rapiéçais*	rapiécerai	rapiécerais
tu	rapièces	*rapiéçais*	rapiéceras	rapiécerais
il, elle	rapièce	*rapiéçait*	rapiécera	rapiécerait
nous	*rapiéçons*	rapiécions	rapiécerons	rapiécerions
vous	rapiécez	rapiéciez	rapiécerez	rapiéceriez
ils, elles	rapiècent	*rapiéçaient*	rapiéceront	rapiéceraient

Simple Past		SUBJUNCTIVE Present	Imperfect
je	*rapiéçai*	rapièce	*rapiéçasse*
tu	*rapiéças*	rapièces	*rapiéçasses*
il, elle	*rapiéça*	rapièce	*rapiéçât*
nous	*rapiéçâmes*	rapiécions	*rapiéçassions*
vous	*rapiéçâtes*	rapiéciez	*rapiéçassiez*
ils, elles	rapiécèrent	rapiècent	*rapiéçassent*

PAST PARTICIPLE rapiécé
PRESENT PARTICIPLE *rapiéçant*

	(tu)	(nous)	(vous)
IMPERATIVE	rapièce	*rapiéçons*	rapiécez

STEMS rapièc-, *rapiéç-*, rapièc- / rapiécé / *rapiéça-* / rapiécer-

REMARKS
1. *é* → *è*, when following syllable has *mute -e*, **except** future and conditional (9 conjugations)
2. *c* → *ç*, when followed by *-a* or *-o* (18 conjugations)

1-6C PROTÉGER TO PROTECT

INDICATIVE

	Present	Imperfect	Future	Conditional
je	protège	*protégeais*	protégerai	protégerais
tu	protèges	*protégeais*	protégeras	protégerais
il, elle	protège	*protégeait*	protégera	protégerait
nous	*protégeons*	protégions	protégerons	protégerions
vous	protégez	protégiez	protégerez	protégeriez
ils, elles	protègent	*protégeaient*	protégeront	protégeraient

	Simple Past	SUBJUNCTIVE Present	Imperfect
je	*protégeai*	protège	*protégeasse*
tu	*protégeas*	protèges	*protégeasses*
il, elle	*protégea*	protège	*protégeât*
nous	*protégeâmes*	protégions	*protégeassions*
vous	*protégeâtes*	protégiez	*protégeassiez*
ils, elles	protégèrent	protègent	*protégeassent*

PAST PARTICIPLE protégé

PRESENT PARTICIPLE *protégeant*

IMPERATIVE (tu) protège (nous) *protégeons* (vous) protégez

STEMS protèg-, *protég(e)-*, protèg- / protégé / *protég(e)a-* / protéger-

REMARKS
1. *é* → *è*, when following syllable has *mute -e*, **except** future and conditional (9 conjugations)
2. *g* → *ge*, when followed by *-a* or *-o* (18 conjugations)

OTHER VERBS verbs ending in *-éger*

1-7A (I) EMPLOYER TO EMPLOY

INDICATIVE

	Present	Imperfect	Future	Conditional
j'	*emploie*	employais	*emploierai*	*emploierais*
tu	*emploies*	employais	*emploieras*	*emploierais*
il, elle	*emploie*	employait	*emploiera*	*emploierait*
nous	employons	employions	*emploierons*	*emploierions*
vous	employez	employiez	*emploierez*	*emploieriez*
ils, elles	*emploient*	employaient	*emploieront*	*emploieraient*

Simple Past		SUBJUNCTIVE Present	Imperfect
j'	employai	*emploie*	employasse
tu	employas	*emploies*	employasses
il, elle	employa	*emploie*	employât
nous	employâmes	employions	employassions
vous	employâtes	employiez	employassiez
ils, elles	employèrent	*emploient*	employassent

PAST PARTICIPLE	employé		
PRESENT PARTICIPLE	employant		
	(tu)	(nous)	(vous)
IMPERATIVE	*emploie*	employons	employez
STEMS	*emploi-*, employ-, *emploi-*/employé/employa-/*emploier-*		
REMARKS	*y* → *i* when *mute e* follows (21 conjugations). Conjugation analogous to *essuyer.*		
OTHER VERBS	*-oyer* verbs except *envoyer* and *renvoyer* (1-8)		

1-7A (II) ESSUYER TO WIPE, DRY

INDICATIVE

	Present	Imperfect	Future	Conditional
j'	*essuie*	essuyais	*essuierai*	*essuierais*
tu	*essuies*	essuyais	*essuieras*	*essuierais*
il, elle	*essuie*	essuyait	*essuiera*	*essuierait*
nous	essuyons	essuyions	*essuierons*	*essuierions*
vous	essuyez	essuyiez	*essuierez*	*essuieriez*
ils, elles	*essuient*	essuyaient	*essuieront*	*essuieraient*

Simple Past		SUBJUNCTIVE Present	Imperfect
j'	essuyai	*essuie*	essuyasse
tu	essuyas	*essuies*	essuyasses
il, elle	essuya	*essuie*	essuyât
nous	essuyâmes	essuyions	essuyassions
vous	essuyâtes	essuyiez	essuyassiez
ils, elles	essuyèrent	*essuient*	essuyassent

PAST PARTICIPLE	essuyé		
PRESENT PARTICIPLE	essuyant		
	(tu)	(nous)	(vous)
IMPERATIVE	*essuie*	essuyons	essuyez
STEMS	*essui-*, essuy-, *essui-*/essuyé/essuya-/*essuier-*		
REMARKS	*y* → *i* when *mute -e* follows (21 conjugations). Conjugation analogous to *employer.*		
OTHER VERBS	*-uyer* verbs: *appuyer, désennuyer, ennuyer, ressuyer*		

1-7B PAYER TO PAY

INDICATIVE

	Present	Imperfect	Future	Conditional
je	*paie*/paye	payais	*paierai*/payerai	*paierais*/payerais
tu	*paies*/payes	payais	*paieras*/payeras	*paierais*/payerais
il, elle	*paie*/paye	payait	*paiera*/payera	*paierait*/payerait
nous	payons	payions	*paierons*/payerons	*paierions*/payerions
vous	payez	payiez	*paierez*/payerez	*paieriez*/payeriez
ils, elles	*paient*/payent	payaient	*paieront*/payeront	*paieraient*/payeraient

Simple Past		SUBJUNCTIVE Present	Imperfect
je	payai	*paie*/paye	payasse
tu	payas	*paies*/payes	payasses
il, elle	paya	*paie*/paye	payât
nous	payâmes	payions	payassions
vous	payâtes	payiez	payassiez
ils, elles	payèrent	*paient*/payent	payassent

PAST PARTICIPLE	payé		
PRESENT PARTICIPLE	payant		
	(tu)	(nous)	(vous)
IMPERATIVE	*paie* /paye	payons	payez
STEMS (A)	*pai*-, pay-, *pai*- / pay**é** / pay**a**- / *paier*-		
STEMS (B)	pay-, pay-, pay- / pay**é** / pay**a**- / payer-		
REMARKS	2 different conjugations possible: (A) *y* → *i* when *mute -e* follows (21 conjugations) (B) like *parler*		
OTHER VERBS	*-ayer* verbs other than *bayer* (defective), which has conjugation (B) only		

1-8 ENVOYER TO SEND

INDICATIVE

	Present	Imperfect	Future	Conditional
j'	*envoie*	envoyais	**enverrai**	**enverrais**
tu	*envoies*	envoyais	**enverras**	**enverrais**
il, elle	*envoie*	envoyait	**enverra**	**enverrait**
nous	envoyons	envoyions	**enverrons**	**enverrions**
vous	envoyez	envoyiez	**enverrez**	**enverriez**
ils, elles	*envoient*	envoyaient	**enverront**	**enverraient**

Simple Past		SUBJUNCTIVE Present	Imperfect
j'	envoyai	*envoie*	envoyasse
tu	envoyas	*envoies*	envoyasses
il, elle	envoya	*envoie*	envoyât
nous	envoyâmes	envoyions	envoyassions
vous	envoyâtes	envoyiez	envoyassiez
ils, elles	envoyèrent	*envoient*	envoyassent

PAST PARTICIPLE envoyé
PRESENT PARTICIPLE envoyant

	(tu)	(nous)	(vous)
IMPERATIVE	*envoie*	envoyons	envoyez

STEMS *envoi*-, envoy-, *envoi*- / envoy**é** / envoy**a**- / **enverr-**
REMARKS 1. Irregular future stem **enverr-**
2. *y* → *i* when *mute -e* follows (9 conjugations)
OTHER VERBS *renvoyer*

2-1 FINIR TO FINISH

INDICATIVE

	Present	Imperfect	Future	Conditional
je	finis	finissais	finirai	finirais
tu	finis	finissais	finiras	finirais
il, elle	finit	finissait	finira	finirait
nous	finissons	finissions	finirons	finirions
vous	finissez	finissiez	finirez	finiriez
ils, elles	finissent	finissaient	finiront	finiraient

Simple Past		SUBJUNCTIVE Present	Imperfect
je	finis	finisse	finisse
tu	finis	finisses	finisses
il, elle	finit	finisse	finît
nous	finîmes	finissions	finissions
vous	finîtes	finissiez	finissiez
ils, elles	finirent	finissent	finissent

PAST PARTICIPLE fini
PRESENT PARTICIPLE finissant

	(tu)	(nous)	(vous)
IMPERATIVE	finis	finissons	finissez

STEMS fini-, finiss-, finiss- / fin**i** / fin**i**- / finir-
OTHER VERBS Class II *-ir* verbs (extended *-s* endings for present indicative)

2-2 MAUDIRE TO CURSE

INDICATIVE

	Present	Imperfect	Future	Conditional
je	maudis	maudissais	maudirai	maudirais
tu	maudis	maudissais	maudiras	maudirais
il, elle	maudit	maudissait	maudira	maudirait
nous	maudissons	maudissions	maudirons	maudirions
vous	maudissez	maudissiez	maudirez	maudiriez
ils, elles	maudissent	maudissaient	maudiront	maudiraient

Simple Past		SUBJUNCTIVE Present	Imperfect
je	maudis	maudisse	maudisse
tu	maudis	maudisses	maudisses
il, elle	maudit	maudisse	maudît
nous	maudîmes	maudissions	maudissions
vous	maudîtes	maudissiez	maudissiez
ils, elles	maudirent	maudissent	maudissent

PAST PARTICIPLE *maudit*
PRESENT PARTICIPLE maudissant

	(tu)	(nous)	(vous)
IMPERATIVE	maudis	maudissons	maudissez

STEMS maudi-, maudiss-, maudiss- / ***maudit*** / maud**i**- / maudir-
REMARKS Conjugated like *finir,* apart from past participle (and infinitive)
OTHER VERBS *bruire* (defective)

2-3 HAÏR TO HATE

INDICATIVE

	Present	Imperfect	Future	Conditional
je	**hais**	haïssais	haïrai	haïrais
tu	**hais**	haïssais	haïras	haïrais
il, elle	**hait**	haïssait	haïra	haïrait
nous	haïssons	haïssions	haïrons	haïrions
vous	haïssez	haïssiez	haïrez	haïriez
ils, elles	haïssent	haïssaient	haïront	haïraient

Simple Past		SUBJUNCTIVE Present	Imperfect
je	haïs	haïsse	haïsse
tu	haïs	haïsses	haïsses
il, elle	haït	haïsse	***haït***
nous	***haïmes***	haïssions	haïssions
vous	***haïtes***	haïssiez	haïssiez
ils, elles	haïrent	haïssent	haïssent

PAST PARTICIPLE	haï		
PRESENT PARTICIPLE	haïssant		
	(tu)	(nous)	(vous)
IMPERATIVE	**hais**	haïssons	haïssez
STEMS	**hai**-, haïss-, haïss- / **haï** / **haï**- / haïr-		
REMARKS	Conjugated like *finir* apart from:		
	(1) present tense singular stem **hai**- (not **haï-*)		
	(2) no circumflex (ˆ) in simple past 1p/2p, imperfect subjunctive 3s		

3-1 (I) COUVRIR TO COVER

INDICATIVE

	Present	Imperfect	Future	Conditional
je	couvre	couvrais	couvrirai	couvrirais
tu	couvres	couvrais	couvriras	couvrirais
il, elle	couvre	couvrait	couvrira	couvrirait
nous	couvrons	couvrions	couvrirons	couvririons
vous	couvrez	couvriez	couvrirez	couvririez
ils, elles	couvrent	couvraient	couvriront	couvriraient

	Simple Past	SUBJUNCTIVE Present	Imperfect
je	couvris	couvre	couvrisse
tu	couvris	couvres	couvrisses
il, elle	couvrit	couvre	couvrît
nous	couvrîmes	couvrions	couvrissions
vous	couvrîtes	couvriez	couvrissiez
ils, elles	couvrirent	couvrent	couvrissent

PAST PARTICIPLE	couvert		
PRESENT PARTICIPLE	couvrant		
	(tu)	(nous)	(vous)
IMPERATIVE	couvre	couvrons	couvrez
STEMS	couvr-, couvr-, couvr- / couver**t** / couvr**i**- / couvrir-		
REMARKS	Conjugation analogous to *offrir* and *souffrir*		
OTHER VERBS	verbs ending in *-ouvrir: ouvrir, rouvrir, entrouvrir, découvrir, recouvrir, redécouvrir*		

3-1 (II) OFFRIR TO OFFER

INDICATIVE

	Present	Imperfect	Future	Conditional
j'	offre	offrais	offrirai	offrirais
tu	offres	offrais	offriras	offrirais
il, elle	offre	offrait	offrira	offrirait
nous	offrons	offrions	offrirons	offririons
vous	offrez	offriez	offrirez	offririez
ils, elles	offrent	offraient	offriront	offriraient

Simple Past		SUBJUNCTIVE Present	Imperfect
j'	offris	offre	offrisse
tu	offris	offres	offrisses
il, elle	offrit	offre	offrît
nous	offrîmes	offrions	offrissions
vous	offrîtes	offriez	offrissiez
ils, elles	offrirent	offrent	offrissent

PAST PARTICIPLE	offert		
PRESENT PARTICIPLE	offrant		
	(tu)	(nous)	(vous)
IMPERATIVE	offre	offrons	offrez
STEMS	offr-, offr-, offr- / offer**t** / offr**i**- / offrir-		
REMARKS	Conjugation analogous to *couvrir* and *souffrir*		

3-1 (III) SOUFFRIR TO SUFFER

INDICATIVE

	Present	Imperfect	Future	Conditional
je	souffre	souffrais	souffrirai	souffrirais
tu	souffres	souffrais	souffriras	souffrirais
il, elle	souffre	souffrait	souffrira	souffrirait
nous	souffrons	souffrions	souffrirons	souffririons
vous	souffrez	souffriez	souffrirez	souffririez
ils, elles	souffrent	souffraient	souffriront	souffriraient

Simple Past		SUBJUNCTIVE Present	Imperfect
je	souffris	souffre	souffrisse
tu	souffris	souffres	souffrisses
il, elle	souffrit	souffre	souffrît
nous	souffrîmes	souffrions	souffrissions
vous	souffrîtes	souffriez	souffrissiez
ils, elles	souffrirent	souffrent	souffrissent

PAST PARTICIPLE	souffert		
PRESENT PARTICIPLE	souffrant		
	(tu)	(nous)	(vous)
IMPERATIVE	souffre	souffrons	souffrez
STEMS	souffr-, souffr-, souffr- / souffer**t** / souffr**i**- / souffrir-		
REMARKS	Conjugation analogous to *couvrir* and *offrir*		

3-2A ASSAILLIR TO ASSAIL

INDICATIVE

	Present	Imperfect	Future	Conditional
j'	assaille	assaillais	assaillirai	assaillirais
tu	assailles	assaillais	assailliras	assaillirais
il, elle	assaille	assaillait	assaillira	assaillirait
nous	assaillons	assaillions	assaillirons	assaillirions
vous	assaillez	assailliez	assaillirez	assailliriez
ils, elles	assaillent	assaillaient	assailliront	assailliraient

	Simple Past	SUBJUNCTIVE Present	Imperfect
j'	assaillis	assaille	assaillisse
tu	assaillis	assailles	assaillisses
il, elle	assaillit	assaille	assaillît
nous	assaillîmes	assaillions	assaillissions
vous	assaillîtes	assailliez	assaillissiez
ils, elles	assaillirent	assaillent	assaillissent

PAST PARTICIPLE	assailli		
PRESENT PARTICIPLE	assaillant		
	(tu)	(nous)	(vous)
IMPERATIVE	assaille	assaillons	assaillez
STEMS	assaill-, assaill-, assaill- / assaill**i** / assaill**i**- / assaillir-		
OTHER VERBS	*défaillir, saillir* (defective), *tressaillir*		

3-2B CUEILLIR TO GATHER

INDICATIVE

	Present	Imperfect	Future	Conditional
je	cueille	cueillais	*cueill**er**ai*	*cueill**er**ais*
tu	cueilles	cueillais	*cueill**er**as*	*cueill**er**ais*
il, elle	cueille	cueillait	*cueill**er**a*	*cueill**er**ait*
nous	cueillons	cueillions	*cueill**er**ons*	*cueill**er**ions*
vous	cueillez	cueilliez	*cueill**er**ez*	*cueill**er**iez*
ils, elles	cueillent	cueillaient	*cueill**er**ont*	*cueill**er**aient*

Simple Past			SUBJUNCTIVE Present	Imperfect
je	cueillis		cueille	cueillisse
tu	cueillis		cueilles	cueillisses
il, elle	cueillit		cueille	cueillît
nous	cueillîmes		cueillions	cueillissions
vous	cueillîtes		cueilliez	cueillissiez
ils, elles	cueillirent		cueillent	cueillissent

PAST PARTICIPLE cueilli
PRESENT PARTICIPLE cueillant

	(tu)	(nous)	(vous)
IMPERATIVE	cueille	cueillons	cueillez

STEMS cueill-, cueill-, cueill- / cueilli / cueilli- / *cueiller-*
REMARKS Conjugation analogous to *assaillir* apart from future stem *cueiller-* (not **cueillir-*)
OTHER VERBS *accueillir, recueillir*

3-2C BOUILLIR TO BOIL

INDICATIVE

	Present	Imperfect	Future	Conditional
je	*bous*	bouillais	bouillirai	bouillirais
tu	*bous*	bouillais	bouilliras	bouillirais
il, elle	*bout*	bouillait	bouillira	bouillirait
nous	bouillons	bouillions	bouillirons	bouillirions
vous	bouillez	bouilliez	bouillirez	bouilliriez
ils, elles	bouillent	bouillaient	bouilliront	bouilliraient

Simple Past			SUBJUNCTIVE Present	Imperfect
je	bouillis		bouille	bouillisse
tu	bouillis		bouilles	bouillisses
il, elle	bouillit		bouille	bouillît
nous	bouillîmes		bouillions	bouillissions
vous	bouillîtes		bouilliez	bouillissiez
ils, elles	bouillirent		bouillent	bouillissent

PAST PARTICIPLE bouilli
PRESENT PARTICIPLE bouillant

	(tu)	(nous)	(vous)
IMPERATIVE	bouille	bouillons	bouillez

STEMS *bou-*, bouill-, bouill- / bouilli- / bouilli- / bouillir-
REMARKS Conjugation analogous to *assaillir,* apart from indicative singular present *je bous, tu bous, il bout*

4-1A VOIR TO SEE

INDICATIVE

	Present	Imperfect	Future	Conditional
je	vois	*voyais*	**verrai**	**verrais**
tu	vois	*voyais*	**verras**	**verrais**
il, elle	voit	*voyait*	**verra**	**verrait**
nous	*voyons*	*voyions*	**verrons**	**verrions**
vous	*voyez*	*voyiez*	**verrez**	**verriez**
ils, elles	voient	*voyaient*	**verront**	**verraient**

	Simple Past	SUBJUNCTIVE Present	Imperfect
je	vis	voie	visse
tu	vis	voies	visses
il, elle	vit	voie	vît
nous	vîmes	*voyions*	vissions
vous	vîtes	*voyiez*	vissiez
ils, elles	virent	voient	vissent

PAST PARTICIPLE	vu		
PRESENT PARTICIPLE	*voyant*		
	(tu)	(nous)	(vous)
IMPERATIVE	vois	*voyons*	*voyez*

STEMS voi-, *voy-*, voi- / v**u** / v**i**- / **verr-**

REMARKS
1. *-i* between two vowels → *y,* unless second vowel is *mute -e* (13 conjugations)
2. Future stem **verr-**

OTHER VERBS *entrevoir, revoir*

4-1B PRÉVOIR TO FORESEE

INDICATIVE

	Future	Conditional
je	*prévoirai*	*prévoirais*
tu	*prévoiras*	*prévoirais*
il, elle	*prévoira*	*prévoirait*
nous	*prévoirons*	*prévoirions*
vous	*prévoirez*	*prévoiriez*
ils, elles	*prévoiront*	*prévoiraient*

STEMS prévoi-, *prévoy-*, prévoi- / prév**u** / prév**i**- / *prévoir-*

REMARKS Conjugated like *voir,* apart from future/conditional, which has regular (infinitive) stem

4-1C POURVOIR TO SUPPLY, PROVIDE

INDICATIVE

	Simple Past	Future	Conditional
je	pourv**us**	*pourvoirai*	*pourvoirais*
tu	pourv**us**	*pourvoiras*	*pourvoirais*
il, elle	pourv**ut**	*pourvoira*	*pourvoirait*
nous	pourv**û**mes	*pourvoirons*	*pourvoirions*
vous	pourv**û**tes	*pourvoirez*	*pourvoiriez*
ils, elles	pourv**u**rent	*pourvoiront*	*pourvoiraient*

STEMS pourvoi-, *pourvoy-*, pourvoi- / pourv**u** / pourv**u**- / *pourvoir-*

REMARKS Conjugated like *voir* apart from:
(1) simple past (*-u* endings rather than *-i* endings)
(2) future/conditional, which has regular (infinitive) stem

4-2A DEVOIR TO OWE, MUST

INDICATIVE

	Present	Imperfect	Future	Conditional
je	dois	devais	devrai	devrais
tu	dois	devais	devras	devrais
il, elle	doit	devait	devra	devrait
nous	devons	devions	devrons	devrions
vous	devez	deviez	devrez	devriez
ils, elles	doivent	devaient	devront	devraient

	Simple Past	SUBJUNCTIVE Present	SUBJUNCTIVE Imperfect
je	dus	doive	dusse
tu	dus	doives	dusses
il, elle	dut	doive	dût
nous	dûmes	devions	dussions
vous	dûtes	deviez	dussiez
ils, elles	durent	doivent	dussent

PAST PARTICIPLE *dû* (due, dus, dues)

PRESENT PARTICIPLE devant

	(tu)	(nous)	(vous)
IMPERATIVE	dois	devons	devez

STEMS doi-, dev-, doiv- / d**û** / d**u**- / devr-

REMARKS Circumflex on masculine past participle

OTHER VERBS *redevoir,* including circumflex on masculine past participle (*redû*)

4-2B RECEVOIR TO RECEIVE

INDICATIVE

	Present	Imperfect	Future	Conditional
je	*reçois*	recevais	recevrai	recevrais
tu	*reçois*	recevais	recevras	recevrais
il, elle	*reçoit*	recevait	recevra	recevrait
nous	recevons	recevions	recevrons	recevrions
vous	recevez	receviez	recevrez	recevriez
ils, elles	*reçoivent*	recevaient	recevront	recevraient

Simple Past		SUBJUNCTIVE Present	Imperfect
je	*reçus*	*reçoive*	*reçusse*
tu	*reçus*	*reçoives*	*reçusses*
il, elle	*reçut*	*reçoive*	*reçût*
nous	*reçûmes*	recevions	*reçussions*
vous	*reçûtes*	receviez	*reçussiez*
ils, elles	*reçurent*	*reçoivent*	*reçussent*

PAST PARTICIPLE	*reçu*		
PRESENT PARTICIPLE	recevant		
	(tu)	(nous)	(vous)
IMPERATIVE	*reçois*	recevons	recevez
STEMS	reçoi-, recev-, reçoiv- / re**çu** / re**çu**- / recevr-		
REMARKS	Analogous to *devoir* **except:** (1) regular past participle (no circumflex) (2) *-c* changes to *-ç* when followed by *-a, -o,* or *-u* (22 conjugations)		
OTHER VERBS	verbs ending in *-cevoir: apercevoir, concevoir, décevoir, entrapercevoir, percevoir*		

4-3A MOUVOIR TO MOVE

INDICATIVE

	Present	Imperfect	Future	Conditional
je	meus	mouvais	mouvrai	mouvrais
tu	meus	mouvais	mouvras	mouvrais
il, elle	meut	mouvait	mouvra	mouvrait
nous	mouvons	mouvions	mouvrons	mouvrions
vous	mouvez	mouviez	mouvrez	mouvriez
ils, elles	meuvent	mouvaient	mouvront	mouvraient

Simple Past		SUBJUNCTIVE Present	Imperfect
je	mus	meuve	musse
tu	mus	meuves	musses
il, elle	mut	meuve	mût
nous	mûmes	mouvions	mussions
vous	mûtes	mouviez	mussiez
ils, elles	murent	meuvent	mussent

PAST PARTICIPLE	*mû* (mue, mus, mues)		
PRESENT PARTICIPLE	mouvant		
	(tu)	(nous)	(vous)
IMPERATIVE	meus	mouvons	mouvez
STEMS	meu-, mouv-, meuv- / **mû** / m**u**- / mouvr-		
REMARKS	Circumflex on masculine past participle		

4-3B PROMOUVOIR TO PROMOTE

PAST PARTICIPLE	*promu*
STEMS	promeu-, promouv-, promeuv- / prom**u** / prom**u**- / promouvr-
REMARKS	Conjugated like *mouvoir,* except no circumflex on past participle
OTHER VERBS	*émouvoir* (past participle *ému*)

4-4 PLEUVOIR TO RAIN

INDICATIVE

	Present	Imperfect	Future	Conditional
je	—	—	—	—
tu	—	—	—	—
il	pleut	pleuvait	pleuvra	pleuvrait
nous	—	—	—	—
vous	—	—	—	—
ils, elles	pleuvent	pleuvaient	pleuvront	pleuvraient

Simple Past		SUBJUNCTIVE Present	Imperfect
je	—	—	—
tu	—	—	—
il	plut	pleuve	plût
nous	—	—	—
vous	—	—	—
ils, elles	plurent	pleuvent	plussent

PAST PARTICIPLE	plu		
PRESENT PARTICIPLE	pleuvant		
	(tu)	(nous)	(vous)
IMPERATIVE	—	—	—
STEMS	pleu-, [pleuv-], pleuv- / pl**u** / pl**u**- / pleuvr-		
REMARKS	1. Generally used impersonally ("it rains"); also intransitively in 3p: *Les calomnies pleuvent sur quiconque réussit.* (Voltaire) "Calumnies *rain* on whoever succeeds." 2. *Il a plu, il plut, il plût*—identical for *pleuvoir* and *plaire* (5-22a)		
OTHER VERBS	*repleuvoir*		

4-5A VALOIR TO BE WORTH

INDICATIVE

	Present	Imperfect	Future	Conditional
je	***vaux***	valais	vaudrai	vaudrais
tu	***vaux***	valais	vaudras	vaudrais
il, elle	vaut	valait	vaudra	vaudrait
nous	valons	valions	vaudrons	vaudrions
vous	valez	valiez	vaudrez	vaudriez
ils, elles	valent	valaient	vaudront	vaudraient

	Simple Past	SUBJUNCTIVE Present	Imperfect
je	valus	*vaille*	valusse
tu	valus	*vailles*	valusses
il, elle	valut	*vaille*	valût
nous	valûmes	valions	valussions
vous	valûtes	valiez	valussiez
ils, elles	valurent	*vaillent*	valussent

PAST PARTICIPLE	valu		
PRESENT PARTICIPLE	valant		
	(tu)	(nous)	(vous)
IMPERATIVE (rare)	vaux	valons	valez
STEMS	vau-, val-, val- / val**u** / val**u**- / vaudr-		
REMARKS	1. Irregular *-x* ending in 1s, 2s present indicative 2. Irregular present subjunctive stem *vaill-* (1s, 2s, 3s, 3p) 3. Imperative rarely used		
OTHER VERBS	*équivaloir, revaloir*		

4-5B	PRÉVALOIR	TO PREVAIL
	INDICATIVE Present	SUBJUNCTIVE Present
je	prévau**x**	*prévale*
tu	prévau**x**	*prévales*
il, elle	prévaut	*prévale*
nous	prévalons	prévalions
vous	prévalez	prévaliez
ils, elles	prévalent	*prévalent*

STEMS prévau-, préval-, préval- / prévalu / prévalu- / prévaudr-

REMARKS Conjugated like *valoir,* except for regular present subjunctive

4-5C	FALLOIR	TO BE NECESSARY		
INDICATIVE	Present	Imperfect	Future	Conditional
je	—	—	—	—
tu	—	—	—	—
il	faut	fallait	faudra	faudrait
nous	—	—	—	—
vous	—	—	—	—
ils, elles	—	—	—	—

Simple Past		SUBJUNCTIVE Present	Imperfect
je	—	—	—
tu	—	—	—
il	fallut	*faille*	fallût
nous	—	—	—
vous	—	—	—
ils, elles	—	—	—

PAST PARTICIPLE	fallu		
PRESENT PARTICIPLE	—		
	(tu)	(nous)	(vous)
IMPERATIVE	—	—	—

STEMS fau-, [fall-], — / fall**u** / fall**u**- / faudr-

REMARKS
1. Impersonal verb used only in third person singular
2. Conjugation analogous to *valoir,* including irregular present subjunctive *il faille*

4-6 POUVOIR TO BE ABLE, CAN

INDICATIVE

	Present	Imperfect	Future	Conditional
je	*peux, puis*	pouvais	pourrai	pourrais
tu	*peux*	pouvais	pourras	pourrais
il, elle	peut	pouvait	pourra	pourrait
nous	pouvons	pouvions	pourrons	pourrions
vous	pouvez	pouviez	pourrez	pourriez
ils, elles	peuvent	pouvaient	pourront	pourraient

Simple Past		SUBJUNCTIVE Present	Imperfect
je	pus	*puisse*	pusse
tu	pus	*puisses*	pusses
il, elle	put	*puisse*	pût
nous	pûmes	*puissions*	pussions
vous	pûtes	*puissiez*	pussiez
ils, elles	purent	*puissent*	pussent

PAST PARTICIPLE pu (*invariable*)

PRESENT PARTICIPLE pouvant

	(tu)	(nous)	(vous)
IMPERATIVE	—	—	—

STEMS peu-, pouv-, peuv- / **pu** / **pu**- / pourr-

REMARKS

1. Irregular *-x* ending in 1s, 2s present indicative
2. Alternative 1s present indicative *puis,* used in interrogations
3. Irregular present subjunctive stem *puiss-*
4. Imperative is not used

4-7 SAVOIR TO KNOW

INDICATIVE

	Present	Imperfect	Future	Conditional
je	sais	savais	saurai	saurais
tu	sais	savais	sauras	saurais
il, elle	sait	savait	saura	saurait
nous	savons	savions	saurons	saurions
vous	savez	saviez	saurez	sauriez
ils, elles	savent	savaient	sauront	sauraient

Simple Past		SUBJUNCTIVE Present	Imperfect
je	sus	*sache*	susse
tu	sus	*saches*	susses
il, elle	sut	*sache*	sût
nous	sûmes	*sachions*	sussions
vous	sûtes	*sachiez*	sussiez
ils, elles	surent	*sachent*	sussent

PAST PARTICIPLE	su		
PRESENT PARTICIPLE	*sachant*		
	(tu)	(nous)	(vous)
IMPERATIVE	*sache*	*sachons*	*sachez*
STEMS	sai-, sav-, sav- / **su** / **su**- / saur-		
REMARKS	1. Irregular present subjunctive stem *sach-*		
	2. Irregular present participle stem *sach-*		
	3. Irregular imperative using subjunctive stem		

4-8 VOULOIR TO WANT

INDICATIVE

	Present	Imperfect	Future	Conditional
je	***veux***	voulais	voudrai	voudrais
tu	***veux***	voulais	voudras	voudrais
il, elle	veut	voulait	voudra	voudrait
nous	voulons	voulions	voudrons	voudrions
vous	voulez	vouliez	voudrez	voudriez
ils, elles	veulent	voulaient	voudront	voudraient

Simple Past		SUBJUNCTIVE Present	Imperfect
je	voulus	*veuille*	voulusse
tu	voulus	*veuilles*	voulusses
il, elle	voulut	*veuille*	voulût
nous	voulûmes	voulions	voulussions
vous	voulûtes	vouliez	voulussiez
ils, elles	voulurent	*veuillent*	voulussent

PAST PARTICIPLE	voulu		
PRESENT PARTICIPLE	voulant		
	(tu)	(nous)	(vous)
IMPERATIVE	*veuille,* veu**x**	—, voulons	*veuillez,* voulez
STEMS	veu-, voul-, veul- / voul**u** / voul**u**- / voudr-		
REMARKS	1. Irregular *-x* ending in 1s, 2s present indicative 2. Irregular present subjunctive stem *veuill-* (1s, 2s, 3s, 3p) 3. Two forms of imperative, first used in polite requests, second is rare		
OTHER VERBS	*revouloir*		

1-9A ASSEOIR (A) TO SIT

INDICATIVE

	Present	Imperfect	Future	Conditional
j'	assieds	asseyais	assiérai	assiérais
tu	assieds	asseyais	assiéras	assiérais
il, elle	*assie**d***	asseyait	assiéra	assiérait
nous	asseyons	asseyions	assiérons	assiérions
vous	asseyez	asseyiez	assiérez	assiériez
ils, elles	asseyent	asseyaient	assiéront	assiéraient

	Simple Past	SUBJUNCTIVE Present	SUBJUNCTIVE Imperfect
j'	assis	asseye	assisse
tu	assis	asseyes	assisses
il, elle	assit	asseye	assît
nous	assîmes	asseyions	assissions
vous	assîtes	asseyiez	assissiez
ils, elles	assirent	asseyent	assissent

PAST PARTICIPLE	assis		
PRESENT PARTICIPLE	asseyant		
	(tu)	(nous)	(vous)
IMPERATIVE	assieds	asseyons	asseyez
STEMS	assied-, assey-, assey- / ass**is** / ass**i**- / assiér-		
REMARKS	1. *Asseoir* has two complete conjugations (A and B), having only past participle, simple past, and imperfect subjunctive in common 2. 3rd person singular present indicative ends in *-d* 3. Only *-oir* verb with past participle not ending in *-u*		
OTHER VERBS	*rasseoir* (both A and B)		

4-9B ASSEOIR (B) TO SIT

INDICATIVE

	Present	Imperfect	Future	Conditional
j'	assois	*assoyais*	assoirai	assoirais
tu	assois	*assoyais*	assoiras	assoirais
il, elle	assoit	*assoyait*	assoira	assoirait
nous	*assoyons*	*assoyions*	assoirons	assoirions
vous	*assoyez*	*assoyiez*	assoirez	assoiriez
ils, elles	assoient	*assoyaient*	assoiront	assoiraient

Simple Past		SUBJUNCTIVE Present	Imperfect
j'	assis	assoie	assisse
tu	assis	assoies	assisses
il, elle	assit	assoie	assît
nous	assîmes	*assoyions*	assissions
vous	assîtes	*assoyiez*	assissiez
ils, elles	assirent	assoient	assissent

PAST PARTICIPLE assis

PRESENT PARTICIPLE *assoyant*

	(tu)	(nous)	(vous)
IMPERATIVE	assois	*assoyons*	*assoyez*

STEMS assoi-, *assoy-*, assoi- / as**sis** / as**si**- / assoir-

REMARKS
1. Conjugation would be "regular" if infinitive were **assoir*
2. *-i* between two vowels → *y,* unless second vowel is *mute -e* (13 conjugations)

OTHER VERBS *rasseoir* (both A and B)

4-9C SURSEOIR TO POSTPONE

INDICATIVE

	Future	Conditional
je	*surs**e**oirai*	*surs**e**oirais*
tu	*surs**e**oiras*	*surs**e**oirais*
il, elle	*surs**e**oira*	*surs**e**oirait*
nous	*surs**e**oirons*	*surs**e**oirions*
vous	*surs**e**oirez*	*surs**e**oiriez*
ils, elles	*surs**e**oiront*	*surs**e**oiraient*

STEMS sursoi-, *sursoy-*, sursoi- / surs**is** / surs**i**- / surseoir-

REMARKS Conjugated like *asseoir* (B), except for future stem which uses full infinitive (*surseoir-* not **sursoir-*)

5-1A (I) RENDRE TO RENDER

INDICATIVE

	Present	Imperfect	Future	Conditional
je	rends	rendais	rendrai	rendrais
tu	rends	rendais	rendras	rendrais
il, elle	*ren**d***	rendait	rendra	rendrait
nous	rendons	rendions	rendrons	rendrions
vous	rendez	rendiez	rendrez	rendriez
ils, elles	rendent	rendaient	rendront	rendraient

Simple Past		SUBJUNCTIVE Present	Imperfect
je	rendis	rende	rendisse
tu	rendis	rendes	rendisses
il, elle	rendit	rende	rendît
nous	rendîmes	rendions	rendissions
vous	rendîtes	rendiez	rendissiez
ils, elles	rendirent	rendent	rendissent

PAST PARTICIPLE	rendu		
PRESENT PARTICIPLE	rendant		
	(tu)	(nous)	(vous)
IMPERATIVE	rends	rendons	rendez
STEMS	rend-, rend-, rend- / rend**u** / rend**i**- / rendr-		
REMARKS	3rd person singular present indicative ends in *-d.* Conjugation analogous to *répandre/répondre/perdre/mordre.*		
OTHER VERBS	verbs ending in *-endre,* **except** *prendre* (5-2): *attendre, défendre, dépendre, descendre, détendre, entendre, étendre, fendre, pendre, prétendre, revendre, suspendre, tendre, vendre,* etc.		

5-1A (II) RÉPANDRE TO SPREAD, SCATTER

INDICATIVE

	Present	Imperfect	Future	Conditional
je	répands	répandais	répandrai	répandrais
tu	répands	répandais	répandras	répandrais
il, elle	*répan**d***	répandait	répandra	répandrait
nous	répandons	répandions	répandrons	répandrions
vous	répandez	répandiez	répandrez	répandriez
ils, elles	répandent	répandaient	répandront	répandraient

Simple Past		SUBJUNCTIVE Present	Imperfect
je	répandis	répande	répandisse
tu	répandis	répandes	répandisses
il, elle	répandit	répande	répandît
nous	répandîmes	répandions	répandissions
vous	répandîtes	répandiez	répandissiez
ils, elles	répandirent	répandent	répandissent

PAST PARTICIPLE	répandu		
PRESENT PARTICIPLE	répandant		
	(tu)	(nous)	(vous)
IMPERATIVE	répands	répandons	répandez
STEMS	répand-, répand-, répand- / répand**u** / répand**i**- / répandr		
REMARKS	3rd person singular present indicative ends in *-d*. Conjugation analogous to *rendre/répondre/perdre/mordre.*		
OTHER VERBS	*épandre*		

5-1A (III) RÉPONDRE TO RESPOND, ANSWER

INDICATIVE

	Present	Imperfect	Future	Conditional
je	réponds	répondais	répondrai	répondrais
tu	réponds	répondais	répondras	répondrais
il, elle	*répon**d***	répondait	répondra	répondrait
nous	répondons	répondions	répondrons	répondrions
vous	répondez	répondiez	répondrez	répondriez
ils, elles	répondent	répondaient	répondront	répondraient

Simple Past		SUBJUNCTIVE Present	Imperfect
je	répondis	réponde	répondisse
tu	répondis	répondes	répondisses
il, elle	répondit	réponde	répondît
nous	répondîmes	répondions	répondissions
vous	répondîtes	répondiez	répondissiez
ils, elles	répondirent	répondent	répondissent

PAST PARTICIPLE	répondu		
PRESENT PARTICIPLE	répondant		
	(tu)	(nous)	(vous)
IMPERATIVE	réponds	répondons	répondez
STEMS	répond-, répond-, répond- / répond**u** / répond**i**- / répondr-		
REMARKS	3rd person singular present indicative ends in *-d*. Conjugation analogous to *rendre/répandre/perdre/mordre*.		
OTHER VERBS	verbs ending in *-ondre: confondre, correspondre, fondre, se morfondre, parfondre, pondre, refondre, surtondre, tondre*		

5-1A (IV) PERDRE TO LOSE

INDICATIVE

	Present	Imperfect	Future	Conditional
je	perds	perdais	perdrai	perdrais
tu	perds	perdais	perdras	perdrais
il, elle	*per**d***	perdait	perdra	perdrait
nous	perdons	perdions	perdrons	perdrions
vous	perdez	perdiez	perdrez	perdriez
ils, elles	perdent	perdaient	perdront	perdraient

	Simple Past	SUBJUNCTIVE Present	SUBJUNCTIVE Imperfect
je	perdis	perde	perdisse
tu	perdis	perdes	perdisses
il, elle	perdit	perde	perdît
nous	perdîmes	perdions	perdissions
vous	perdîtes	perdiez	perdissiez
ils, elles	perdirent	perdent	perdissent

PAST PARTICIPLE	perdu		
PRESENT PARTICIPLE	perdant		
	(tu)	(nous)	(vous)
IMPERATIVE	perds	perdons	perdez
STEMS	perd-, perd-, perd- / perd**u** / perd**i**- / perdr-		
REMARKS	3rd person singular present indicative ends in *-d*. Conjugation analogous to *rendre/répandre/répondre/mordre*.		
OTHER VERBS	*reperdre*		

5-1A (V) MORDRE TO BITE

INDICATIVE

	Present	Imperfect	Future	Conditional
je	mords	mordais	mordrai	mordrais
tu	mords	mordais	mordras	mordrais
il, elle	***mord***	mordait	mordra	mordrait
nous	mordons	mordions	mordrons	mordrions
vous	mordez	mordiez	mordrez	mordriez
ils, elles	mordent	mordaient	mordront	mordraient

Simple Past		SUBJUNCTIVE Present	Imperfect
je	mordis	morde	mordisse
tu	mordis	mordes	mordisses
il, elle	mordit	morde	mordît
nous	mordîmes	mordions	mordissions
vous	mordîtes	mordiez	mordissiez
ils, elles	mordirent	mordent	mordissent

PAST PARTICIPLE	mordu		
PRESENT PARTICIPLE	mordant		
	(tu)	(nous)	(vous)
IMPERATIVE	mords	mordons	mordez
STEMS	mord-, mord-, mord- / mord**u** / mord**i**- / mordr-		
REMARKS	3rd person singular present indicative ends in *-d*. Conjugation analogous to *rendre/répandre/répondre/perdre.*		
OTHER VERBS	verbs ending in *-ordre: démordre, détordre, distordre, remordre, retordre*		

5-1B ROMPRE TO BREAK

INDICATIVE

	Present	Imperfect	Future	Conditional
je	romps	rompais	romprai	romprais
tu	romps	rompais	rompras	romprais
il, elle	rompt	rompait	rompra	romprait
nous	rompons	rompions	romprons	romprions
vous	rompez	rompiez	romprez	rompriez
ils, elles	rompent	rompaient	rompront	rompraient

Simple Past		SUBJUNCTIVE Present	Imperfect
je	rompis	rompe	rompisse
tu	rompis	rompes	rompisses
il, elle	rompit	rompe	rompît
nous	rompîmes	rompions	rompissions
vous	rompîtes	rompiez	rompissiez
ils, elles	rompirent	rompent	rompissent

PAST PARTICIPLE	rompu		
PRESENT PARTICIPLE	rompant		
	(tu)	(nous)	(vous)
IMPERATIVE	romps	rompons	rompez
STEMS	romp-, romp-, romp-/rompu/rompi-/rompr-		
REMARKS	Conjugation analogous to *rendre* (5-1a), except *il rompt* maintains final -*t*		
OTHER VERBS	*corrompre, interrompre*		

5-2 PRENDRE TO TAKE

INDICATIVE

	Present	Imperfect	Future	Conditional
je	prends	prenais	prendrai	prendrais
tu	prends	prenais	prendras	prendrais
il, elle	*prend*	prenait	prendra	prendrait
nous	prenons	prenions	prendrons	prendrions
vous	prenez	preniez	prendrez	prendriez
ils, elles	prennent	prenaient	prendront	prendraient

Simple Past		SUBJUNCTIVE Present	Imperfect
je	pris	prenne	prisse
tu	pris	prennes	prisses
il, elle	prit	prenne	prît
nous	prîmes	prenions	prissions
vous	prîtes	preniez	prissiez
ils, elles	prirent	prennent	prissent

PAST PARTICIPLE	pris		
PRESENT PARTICIPLE	prenant		
	(tu)	(nous)	(vous)
IMPERATIVE	prends	prenons	prenez
STEMS	prend-, pren-, prenn- / **pris** / **pri-** / prendr-		
REMARKS	1. *Prendre* is the only *-endre* verb not conjugated like *rendre* 2. 3rd person singular present indicative ends in *-d*		
OTHER VERBS	verbs ending in *-prendre: apprendre, comprendre, se déprendre, désapprendre, entreprendre, s'éprendre, se méprendre, rapprendre, réapprendre, reprendre, surprendre*		

5-3 BATTRE TO BEAT

INDICATIVE

	Present	Imperfect	Future	Conditional
je	bats	battais	battrai	battrais
tu	bats	battais	battras	battrais
il, elle	***bat***	battait	battra	battrait
nous	battons	battions	battrons	battrions
vous	battez	battiez	battrez	battriez
ils, elles	battent	battaient	battront	battraient

Simple Past		SUBJUNCTIVE Present	Imperfect
je	battis	batte	battisse
tu	battis	battes	battisses
il, elle	battit	batte	battît
nous	battîmes	battions	battissions
vous	battîtes	battiez	battissiez
ils, elles	battirent	battent	battissent

PAST PARTICIPLE	battu		
PRESENT PARTICIPLE	battant		
	(tu)	(nous)	(vous)
IMPERATIVE	bats	battons	battez
STEMS	bat-, batt-, batt- / batt**u** / batt**i-** / battr-		
REMARKS	3rd person singular present indicative *ba**t*** (not **bat-t*)		
OTHER VERBS	verbs ending in *-battre: abattre, combattre, contrebattre, débattre, s'ébattre, embattre, rabattre, rebattre*		

5-4 METTRE TO PUT

INDICATIVE

	Present	Imperfect	Future	Conditional
je	mets	mettais	mettrai	mettrais
tu	mets	mettais	mettras	mettrais
il, elle	*met*	mettait	mettra	mettrait
nous	mettons	mettions	mettrons	mettrions
vous	mettez	mettiez	mettrez	mettriez
ils, elles	mettent	mettaient	mettront	mettraient

	Simple Past	SUBJUNCTIVE Present	Imperfect
je	mis	mette	misse
tu	mis	mettes	misses
il, elle	mit	mette	mît
nous	mîmes	mettions	missions
vous	mîtes	mettiez	missiez
ils, elles	mirent	mettent	missent

PAST PARTICIPLE	mis		
PRESENT PARTICIPLE	mettant		
	(tu)	(nous)	(vous)
IMPERATIVE	mets	mettons	mettez
STEMS	met-, mett-, mett- / **mis** / **mi**- / mettr-		
REMARKS	3rd person singular present indicative ***met*** (not **met-t*)		
OTHER VERBS	verbs ending in *-mettre: admettre, commettre, compromettre, décommettre, démettre, émettre, s'entremettre, omettre, permettre, promettre, réadmettre, remettre, retransmettre, soumettre, transmettre*		

5-5 SUIVRE TO FOLLOW

INDICATIVE

	Present	Imperfect	Future	Conditional
je	suis	suivais	suivrai	suivrais
tu	suis	suivais	suivras	suivrais
il, elle	suit	suivait	suivra	suivrait
nous	suivons	suivions	suivrons	suivrions
vous	suivez	suiviez	suivrez	suivriez
ils, elles	suivent	suivaient	suivront	suivraient

Simple Past		SUBJUNCTIVE Present	Imperfect
je	suivis	suive	suivisse
tu	suivis	suives	suivisses
il, elle	suivit	suive	suivît
nous	suivîmes	suivions	suivissions
vous	suivîtes	suiviez	suivissiez
ils, elles	suivirent	suivent	suivissent

PAST PARTICIPLE	suivi		
PRESENT PARTICIPLE	suivant		
	(tu)	(nous)	(vous)
IMPERATIVE	suis	suivons	suivez
STEMS	sui-, suiv-, suiv- / suivi / suivi- / suivr-		
OTHER VERBS	*poursuivre, ensuivre* (defective)		

5-6 VIVRE TO LIVE

INDICATIVE

	Present	Imperfect	Future	Conditional
je	vis	vivais	vivrai	vivrais
tu	vis	vivais	vivras	vivrais
il, elle	vit	vivait	vivra	vivrait
nous	vivons	vivions	vivrons	vivrions
vous	vivez	viviez	vivrez	vivriez
ils, elles	vivent	vivaient	vivront	vivraient

Simple Past		SUBJUNCTIVE Present	Imperfect
je	vécus	vive	vécusse
tu	vécus	vives	vécusses
il, elle	vécut	vive	vécût
nous	vécûmes	vivions	vécussions
vous	vécûtes	viviez	vécussiez
ils, elles	vécurent	vivent	vécussent

PAST PARTICIPLE	vécu		
PRESENT PARTICIPLE	vivant		
	(tu)	(nous)	(vous)
IMPERATIVE	vis	vivons	vivez
STEMS	vi-, viv-, viv- / véc**u** / véc**u**- / vivr-		
OTHER VERBS	*revivre, survivre*		

5-7 ÉCRIRE TO WRITE

INDICATIVE

	Present	Imperfect	Future	Conditional
j'	écris	écrivais	écrirai	écrirais
tu	écris	écrivais	écriras	écrirais
il, elle	écrit	écrivait	écrira	écrirait
nous	écrivons	écrivions	écrirons	écririons
vous	écrivez	écriviez	écrirez	écririez
ils, elles	écrivent	écrivaient	écriront	écriraient

	Simple Past	SUBJUNCTIVE Present	Imperfect
j'	*écrivis*	écrive	écrivisse
tu	*écrivis*	écrives	écrivisses
il, elle	*écrivit*	écrive	écrivît
nous	*écrivîmes*	écrivions	écrivissions
vous	*écrivîtes*	écriviez	écrivissiez
ils, elles	*écrivirent*	écrivent	écrivissent

PAST PARTICIPLE	écrit		
PRESENT PARTICIPLE	écrivant		
	(tu)	(nous)	(vous)
IMPERATIVE	écris	écrivons	écrivez

STEMS écri-, écriv-, écriv- / écr**it** / *écriv**i**-* / écrir-

REMARKS Simple past stem differs from that of past participle: *écr**iv**-* vs. *écr-*

OTHER VERBS verbs ending in *-écrire* or *-scrire: décrire, récrire* (**or** *réécrire*); *circonscrire, inscrire, prescrire, proscrire, réinscrire, retranscrire, souscrire, transcrire*

5-8A DIRE TO SAY

INDICATIVE

	Present	Imperfect	Future	Conditional
je	dis	disais	dirai	dirais
tu	dis	disais	diras	dirais
il, elle	dit	disait	dira	dirait
nous	disons	disions	dirons	dirions
vous	***dites***	disiez	direz	diriez
ils, elles	disent	disaient	diront	diraient

Simple Past		SUBJUNCTIVE Present	Imperfect
je	dis	dise	disse
tu	dis	dises	disses
il, elle	dit	dise	dît
nous	dîmes	disions	dissions
vous	dîtes	disiez	dissiez
ils, elles	dirent	disent	dissent

PAST PARTICIPLE	dit		
PRESENT PARTICIPLE	disant		
	(tu)	(nous)	(vous)
IMPERATIVE	dis	disons	***dites***
STEMS	di-, dis-, dis-/d**it**/di-/dir-		
REMARKS	*Vous **dites**:* present indicative and imperative		
OTHER VERBS	*redire* (*vous **redites***)		

5-8B PRÉDIRE TO PREDICT

INDICATIVE

	Present
je	prédis
tu	prédis
il, elle	prédit
nous	prédisons
vous	*prédisez*
ils, elles	prédisent

	(tu)	(nous)	(vous)
IMPERATIVE	prédis	prédisons	*prédisez*
STEMS	prédi-, prédis-, prédis-/préd**it**/préd**i**-/prédir-		
REMARKS	*Vous prédisez:* regular present indicative and imperative. Otherwise conjugated like *dire.*		
OTHER VERBS	*contredire, dédire, interdire, médire* (all with *-disez*) also *confire:* confi-, confis-, confis-/conf**it**/conf**i**-/confir- (*maudire* is Class II [2-2])		

5-8C SUFFIRE TO SUFFICE

INDICATIVE

	Present	Imperfect	Future	Conditional
je	suffis	suffisais	suffirai	suffirais
tu	suffis	suffisais	suffiras	suffirais
il, elle	suffit	suffisait	suffira	suffirait
nous	suffisons	suffisions	suffirons	suffirions
vous	suffisez	suffisiez	suffirez	suffiriez
ils, elles	suffisent	suffisaient	suffiront	suffiraient

Simple Past		SUBJUNCTIVE Present	Imperfect
je	suffis	suffise	suffisse
tu	suffis	suffises	suffisses
il, elle	suffit	suffise	suffît
nous	suffîmes	suffisions	suffissions
vous	suffîtes	suffisiez	suffissiez
ils, elles	suffirent	suffisent	suffissent

PAST PARTICIPLE	*suffi* (invariable)		
PRESENT PARTICIPLE	suffisant		
	(tu)	(nous)	(vous)
IMPERATIVE	suffis	suffisons	suffisez
STEMS	suffi-, suffis-, suffis- / suffi / suffi- / suffir-		
REMARKS	Conjugation analogous to *prédire,* apart from past participle *suffi*		

5-8D CIRCONCIRE TO CIRCUMCISE

PAST PARTICIPLE	*circoncis*
STEMS	circonci-, circoncis-, circoncis- / circoncis / circonci- / circoncir-
REMARKS	Conjugation analogous to *suffire* (and *prédire*), apart from past participle

5-9A CONDUIRE TO DRIVE, CONDUCT

INDICATIVE

	Present	Imperfect	Future	Conditional
je	conduis	conduisais	conduirai	conduirais
tu	conduis	conduisais	conduiras	conduirais
il, elle	conduit	conduisait	conduira	conduirait
nous	conduisons	conduisions	conduirons	conduirions
vous	conduisez	conduisiez	conduirez	conduiriez
ils, elles	conduisent	conduisaient	conduiront	conduiraient

SUBJUNCTIVE

Simple Past		Present	Imperfect
je	*conduisis*	conduise	conduisisse
tu	*conduisis*	conduises	conduisisses
il, elle	*conduisit*	conduise	conduisît
nous	*conduisîmes*	conduisions	conduisissions
vous	*conduisîtes*	conduisiez	conduisissiez
ils, elles	*conduisirent*	conduisent	conduisissent

PAST PARTICIPLE	conduit		
PRESENT PARTICIPLE	conduisant		
	(tu)	(nous)	(vous)
IMPERATIVE	conduis	conduisons	conduisez
STEMS	condui-, conduis-, conduis- / condu**it** / *conduis**i**-* / conduir-		
REMARKS	Simple past stem differs from past participle stem: *condu**is**-* vs. *condu-*		
OTHER VERBS	verbs ending in *-duire, -(s)truire,* and *-cuire: déduire, introduire, produire, réduire, reproduire, séduire, traduire, construire, détruire, instruire, reconstruire, cuire, recuire,* etc.		

5-9B NUIRE TO HARM

INDICATIVE

	Present	Imperfect	Future	Conditional
je	nuis	nuisais	nuirai	nuirais
tu	nuis	nuisais	nuiras	nuirais
il, elle	nuit	nuisait	nuira	nuirait
nous	nuisons	nuisions	nuirons	nuirions
vous	nuisez	nuisiez	nuirez	nuiriez
ils, elles	nuisent	nuisaient	nuiront	nuiraient

Simple Past		SUBJUNCTIVE Present	SUBJUNCTIVE Imperfect
je	nuisis	nuise	nuisisse
tu	nuisis	nuises	nuisisses
il, elle	nuisit	nuise	nuisît
nous	nuisîmes	nuisions	nuisissions
vous	nuisîtes	nuisiez	nuisissiez
ils, elles	nuisirent	nuisent	nuisissent

PAST PARTICIPLE	*nui* (invariable)		
PRESENT PARTICIPLE	nuisant		
	(tu)	(nous)	(vous)
IMPERATIVE	nuis	nuisons	nuisez
STEMS	nui-, nuis-, nuis- / nu**i** / *nuis**i**-* / nuir-		
REMARKS	Conjugation analogous to *conduire,* except for past participle *nui*		
OTHER VERBS	verbs ending in *-nuire* and *-luire: s'entre-nuire* (or *s'entrenuire*), *luire, reluire*		

5-10 LIRE TO READ

INDICATIVE

	Present	Imperfect	Future	Conditional
je	lis	lisais	lirai	lirais
tu	lis	lisais	liras	lirais
il, elle	lit	lisait	lira	lirait
nous	lisons	lisions	lirons	lirions
vous	lisez	lisiez	lirez	liriez
ils, elles	lisent	lisaient	liront	liraient

Simple Past		SUBJUNCTIVE Prcsent	Imperfect
je	lus	lise	lusse
tu	lus	lises	lusses
il, elle	lut	lise	lût
nous	lûmes	lisions	lussions
vous	lûtes	lisiez	lussiez
ils, elles	lurent	lisent	lussent

PAST PARTICIPLE	lu		
PRESENT PARTICIPLE	lisant		
	(tu)	(nous)	(vous)
IMPERATIVE	lis	lisons	lisez
STEMS	li-, lis-, lis- / **lu** / **lu**- / lir-		
OTHER VERBS	*élire, réélire, relire*		

5-11 RIRE TO LAUGH

INDICATIVE

	Present	Imperfect	Future	Conditional
je	ris	riais	rirai	rirais
tu	ris	riais	riras	rirais
il, elle	rit	riait	rira	rirait
nous	rions	***riions***	rirons	ririons
vous	riez	***riiez***	rirez	ririez
ils, elles	rient	riaient	riront	riraient

Simple Past		SUBJUNCTIVE Present	Imperfect
je	ris	rie	risse
tu	ris	ries	risses
il, elle	rit	rie	rît
nous	rîmes	***riions***	rissions
vous	rîtes	***riiez***	rissiez
ils, elles	rirent	rient	rissent

PAST PARTICIPLE	ri (invariable)		
PRESENT PARTICIPLE	riant		
	(tu)	(nous)	(vous)
IMPERATIVE	ris	rions	riez
STEMS	ri-, ri-, ri- / **ri** / **ri**- / rir-		
REMARKS	(Regular) *-ii* in *nous r**ii**ons, vous r**ii**ez* (present indicative and subjunctive)		
OTHER VERBS	*sourire*		

5-12 (I) PLAINDRE TO PITY

INDICATIVE

	Present	Imperfect	Future	Conditional
je	plains	plaignais	plaindrai	plaindrais
tu	plains	plaignais	plaindras	plaindrais
il, elle	plaint	plaignait	plaindra	plaindrait
nous	plaignons	plaignions	plaindrons	plaindrions
vous	plaignez	plaigniez	plaindrez	plaindriez
ils, elles	plaignent	plaignaient	plaindront	plaindraient

Simple Past		SUBJUNCTIVE Present	Imperfect
je	plaignis	plaigne	plaignisse
tu	plaignis	plaignes	plaignisses
il, elle	plaignit	plaigne	plaignît
nous	plaignîmes	plaignions	plaignissions
vous	plaignîtes	plaigniez	plaignissiez
ils, elles	plaignirent	plaignent	plaignissent

PAST PARTICIPLE	plaint		
PRESENT PARTICIPLE	plaignant		
	(tu)	(nous)	(vous)
IMPERATIVE	plains	plaignons	plaignez
STEMS	plain-, plaign-, plaign- / plain**t** / plaign**i**- / plaindr-		
REMARKS	Conjugation analogous to *p**ei**ndre* and *j**oi**ndre*		
OTHER VERBS	*-aindre* verbs: *contraindre, craindre*		

5-12 (II) PEINDRE TO PAINT

INDICATIVE

	Present	Imperfect	Future	Conditional
je	peins	peignais	peindrai	peindrais
tu	peins	peignais	peindras	peindrais
il, elle	peint	peignait	peindra	peindrait
nous	peignons	peignions	peindrons	peindrions
vous	peignez	peigniez	peindrez	peindriez
ils, elles	peignent	peignaient	peindront	peindraient

Simple Past		SUBJUNCTIVE Present	Imperfect
je	peignis	peigne	peignisse
tu	peignis	peignes	peignisses
il, elle	peignit	peigne	peignît
nous	peignîmes	peignions	peignissions
vous	peignîtes	peigniez	peignissiez
ils, elles	peignirent	peignent	peignissent

PAST PARTICIPLE peint
PRESENT PARTICIPLE peignant

	(tu)	(nous)	(vous)
IMPERATIVE	peins	peignons	peignez

STEMS pein-, peign-, peign- / pein**t** / peign**i**- / peindr-
REMARKS Conjugation analogous to *pl**ai**ndre* and *j**oi**ndre*
OTHER VERBS *-eindre* verbs: *astreindre, atteindre, ceindre, dépeindre, déteindre, empreindre, enceindre, enfreindre, épreindre, éteindre, étreindre, feindre, geindre, repeindre, restreindre, retreindre* (or *rétreindre*), *teindre*

5-12 (III) JOINDRE TO JOIN

INDICATIVE

	Present	Imperfect	Future	Conditional
je	joins	joignais	joindrai	joindrais
tu	joins	joignais	joindras	joindrais
il, elle	joint	joignait	joindra	joindrait
nous	joignons	joignions	joindrons	joindrions
vous	joignez	joigniez	joindrez	joindriez
ils, elles	joignent	joignaient	joindront	joindraient

Simple Past		SUBJUNCTIVE Present	Imperfect
je	joignis	joigne	joignisse
tu	joignis	joignes	joignisses
il, elle	joignit	joigne	joignît
nous	joignîmes	joignions	joignissions
vous	joignîtes	joigniez	joignissiez
ils, elles	joignirent	joignent	joignissent

PAST PARTICIPLE joint
PRESENT PARTICIPLE joignant

	(tu)	(nous)	(vous)
IMPERATIVE	joins	joignons	joignez

STEMS join-, joign-, joign- / join**t** / joign**i**- / joindr-
REMARKS Conjugation analogous to *pl**ai**ndre* and *p**ei**ndre*
OTHER VERBS *-oindre* verbs: *adjoindre, disjoindre, enjoindre, oindre, poindre, rejoindre*

5-13A ABSOUDRE TO ABSOLVE

INDICATIVE

	Present	Imperfect	Future	Conditional
j'	absous	absolvais	absoudrai	absoudrais
tu	absous	absolvais	absoudras	absoudrais
il, elle	absout	absolvait	absoudra	absoudrait
nous	absolvons	absolvions	absoudrons	absoudrions
vous	absolvez	absolviez	absoudrez	absoudriez
ils, elles	absolvent	absolvaient	absoudront	absoudraient

	Simple Past	SUBJUNCTIVE Present	SUBJUNCTIVE Imperfect
j'	—	absolve	—
tu	—	absolves	—
il, elle	—	absolve	—
nous	—	absolvions	—
vous	—	absolviez	—
ils, elles	—	absolvent	—

PAST PARTICIPLE *absous* (m.), *absoute* (f.)
PRESENT PARTICIPLE absolvant

	(tu)	(nous)	(vous)
IMPERATIVE	absous	absolvons	absolvez

STEMS absou-, absolv-, absolv- / [see remark no. 1] / — / absoudr-
REMARKS 1. Feminine past participle not predictable from masculine
2. No simple past or imperfect subjunctive
OTHER VERBS *dissoudre*

5-13B RÉSOUDRE TO RESOLVE

INDICATIVE

	Present	Imperfect	Future	Conditional
je	résous	résolvais	résoudrai	résoudrais
tu	résous	résolvais	résoudras	résoudrais
il, elle	résout	résolvait	résoudra	résoudrait
nous	résolvons	résolvions	résoudrons	résoudrions
vous	résolvez	résolviez	résoudrez	résoudriez
ils, elles	résolvent	résolvaient	résoudront	résoudraient

Simple Past		SUBJUNCTIVE Present	Imperfect
je	résolus	résolve	résolusse
tu	résolus	résolves	résolusses
il, elle	résolut	résolve	résolût
nous	résolûmes	résolvions	résolussions
vous	résolûtes	résolviez	résolussiez
ils, elles	résolurent	résolvent	résolussent

PAST PARTICIPLE	(a) *résolu*	(b) *résous* (m.), *résoute* (f.)	
PRESENT PARTICIPLE	résolvant		
	(tu)	(nous)	(vous)
IMPERATIVE	résous	résolvons	résolvez
STEMS	résou-, résolv-, résolv- / [see remarks] / résol**u**- / résoudr-		
REMARKS	Conjugated like *absoudre,* apart from: (1) simple past (and imperfect subjunctive); and (2) two separate past participles: (a) in sense of "resolving a problem" (b) in sense of "to change or convert into" (rare)		

5-14 COUDRE TO SEW

INDICATIVE

	Present	Imperfect	Future	Conditional
je	couds	cousais	coudrai	coudrais
tu	couds	cousais	coudras	coudrais
il, elle	*cou**d***	cousait	coudra	coudrait
nous	cousons	cousions	coudrons	coudrions
vous	cousez	cousiez	coudrez	coudriez
ils, elles	cousent	cousaient	coudront	coudraient

Simple Past		SUBJUNCTIVE Present	Imperfect
je	cousis	couse	cousisse
tu	cousis	couses	cousisses
il, elle	cousit	couse	cousît
nous	cousîmes	cousions	cousissions
vous	cousîtes	cousiez	cousissiez
ils, elles	cousirent	cousent	cousissent

PAST PARTICIPLE	cousu		
PRESENT PARTICIPLE	cousant		
	(tu)	(nous)	(vous)
IMPERATIVE	couds	cousons	cousez
STEMS	coud-, cous-, cous- / cous**u** / cous**i**- / coudr-		
REMARKS	3rd person singular present indicative ends in *-d*		
OTHER VERBS	*découdre, recoudre*		

5-15 MOUDRE TO GRIND

INDICATIVE

	Present	Imperfect	Future	Conditional
je	mouds	moulais	moudrai	moudrais
tu	mouds	moulais	moudras	moudrais
il, elle	*mou**d***	moulait	moudra	moudrait
nous	moulons	moulions	moudrons	moudrions
vous	moulez	mouliez	moudrez	moudriez
ils, elles	moulent	moulaient	moudront	moudraient

Simple Past		SUBJUNCTIVE Present	Imperfect
je	moulus	moule	moulusse
tu	moulus	moules	moulusses
il, elle	moulut	moule	moulût
nous	moulûmes	moulions	moulussions
vous	moulûtes	mouliez	moulussiez
ils, elles	moulurent	moulent	moulussent

PAST PARTICIPLE	moulu		
PRESENT PARTICIPLE	moulant		
	(tu)	(nous)	(vous)
IMPERATIVE	mouds	moulons	moulez
STEMS	moud-, moul-, moul- / moul**u** / moul**u**- / moudr-		
REMARKS	3rd person singular present indicative ends in *-d*		

5-16A EXCLURE TO EXCLUDE

INDICATIVE

	Present	Imperfect	Future	Conditional
j'	exclus	excluais	exclurai	exclurais
tu	exclus	excluais	excluras	exclurais
il, elle	exclut	excluait	exclura	exclurait
nous	excluons	excluions	exclurons	exclurions
vous	excluez	excluiez	exclurez	excluriez
ils, elles	excluent	excluaient	excluront	excluraient

Simple Past		SUBJUNCTIVE Present	Imperfect
j'	exclus	exclue	exclusse
tu	exclus	exclues	exclusses
il, elle	exclut	exclue	exclût
nous	exclûmes	excluions	exclussions
vous	exclûtes	excluiez	exclussiez
ils, elles	exclurent	excluent	exclussent

PAST PARTICIPLE	exclu		
PRESENT PARTICIPLE	excluant		
	(tu)	(nous)	(vous)
IMPERATIVE	exclus	excluons	excluez
STEMS	exclu-, exclu-, exclu- / exclu / exclu- / exclur-		
OTHER VERBS	*conclure*		

5-16B INCLURE TO INCLUDE

PAST PARTICIPLE	*inclus*
STEMS	inclu-, inclu-, inclu- / inclus / inclu- / inclur-
REMARKS	Conjugated like *exclure,* except for past participle *inclus* (*-s* is **included** for *inclure*, **excluded** for *exclure*)
OTHER VERBS	*occlure*

5-17 BOIRE TO DRINK

INDICATIVE

	Present	Imperfect	Future	Conditional
je	bois	buvais	boirai	boirais
tu	bois	buvais	boiras	boirais
il, elle	boit	buvait	boira	boirait
nous	buvons	buvions	boirons	boirions
vous	buvez	buviez	boirez	boiriez
ils, elles	boivent	buvaient	boiront	boiraient

Simple Past		SUBJUNCTIVE Present	SUBJUNCTIVE Imperfect
je	bus	boive	busse
tu	bus	boives	busses
il, elle	but	boive	bût
nous	bûmes	buvions	bussions
vous	bûtes	buviez	bussiez
ils, elles	burent	boivent	bussent

PAST PARTICIPLE	bu		
PRESENT PARTICIPLE	buvant		
	(tu)	(nous)	(vous)
IMPERATIVE	bois	buvons	buvez
STEMS	boi-, buv-, boiv- / bu / bu- / boir-		

5-18 CROIRE TO BELIEVE

INDICATIVE

	Present	Imperfect	Future	Conditional
je	crois	*croyais*	croirai	croirais
tu	crois	*croyais*	croiras	croirais
il, elle	croit	*croyait*	croira	croirait
nous	*croyons*	*croyions*	croirons	croirions
vous	*croyez*	*croyiez*	croirez	croiriez
ils, elles	croient	*croyaient*	croiront	croiraient

Simple Past		SUBJUNCTIVE Present	Imperfect
je	crus	croie	crusse
tu	crus	croies	crusses
il, elle	crut	croie	crût
nous	crûmes	*croyions*	crussions
vous	crûtes	*croyiez*	crussiez
ils, elles	crurent	croient	crussent

PAST PARTICIPLE cru
PRESENT PARTICIPLE *croyant*

	(tu)	(nous)	(vous)
IMPERATIVE	crois	*croyons*	*croyez*

STEMS croi-, *croy-*, croi- / c**ru** / c**ru**- / croir-
REMARKS -*i* between two vowels → *y*, unless second vowel is *mute -e* (13 conjugations)

5-19A CROÎTRE TO GROW

INDICATIVE

	Present	Imperfect	Future	Conditional
je	*croîs*	croissais	croîtrai	croîtrais
tu	*croîs*	croissais	croîtras	croîtrais
il, elle	croît	croissait	croîtra	croîtrait
nous	croissons	croissions	croîtrons	croîtrions
vous	croissez	croissiez	croîtrez	croîtriez
ils, elles	croissent	croissaient	croîtront	croîtraient

Simple Past		SUBJUNCTIVE Present	Imperfect
je	***crûs***	croisse	***crûsse***
tu	***crûs***	croisses	***crûsses***
il, elle	***crût***	croisse	crût
nous	crûmes	croissions	***crûssions***
vous	crûtes	croissiez	***crûssiez***
ils, elles	***crûrent***	croissent	***crûssent***

PAST PARTICIPLE	***crû*** (crue, crus, crues)		
PRESENT PARTICIPLE	croissant		
	(tu)	(nous)	(vous)
IMPERATIVE	***croîs***	croissons	croissez
STEMS	*croî-*, croiss-, croiss-/cr**û**/cr**û**-/croîtr-		
REMARKS	"Regular" circumflex throughout on *-ît* (representing former *-ist*). In addition, there are circumflexes on *-i* and *-u* whenever the form would otherwise be identical to that of *croire* (total of 13).		

5-19B ACCROÎTRE TO INCREASE

INDICATIVE

	Present	Imperfect	Future	Conditional
j'	accrois	accroissais	accroîtrai	accroîtrais
tu	accrois	accroissais	accroîtras	accroîtrais
il, elle	*accroît*	accroissait	accroîtra	accroîtrait
nous	accroissons	accroissions	accroîtrons	accroîtrions
vous	accroissez	accroissiez	accroîtrez	accroîtriez
ils, elles	accroissent	accroissaient	accroîtront	accroîtraient

Simple Past		SUBJUNCTIVE Present	Imperfect
j'	accrus	accroisse	accrusse
tu	accrus	accroisses	accrusses
il, elle	accrut	accroisse	accrût
nous	accrûmes	accroissions	accrussions
vous	accrûtes	accroissiez	accrussiez
ils, elles	accrurent	accroissent	accrussent

PAST PARTICIPLE	accru		
PRESENT PARTICIPLE	accroissant		
	(tu)	(nous)	(vous)
IMPERATIVE	accrois	accroissons	accroissez
STEMS	accroi-, accroiss-, accroiss-/accr**u**/accr**u**-/accroîtr-		
REMARKS	General rule: *-i* has circumflex whenever followed by *-t* (including indicative singular 3s). No "extra" circumflexes.		
OTHER VERBS	*décroître*		

5-20 CONNAÎTRE TO KNOW

INDICATIVE

	Present	Imperfect	Future	Conditional
je	connais	connaissais	connaîtrai	connaîtrais
tu	connais	connaissais	connaîtras	connaîtrais
il, elle	*connaît*	connaissait	connaîtra	connaîtrait
nous	connaissons	connaissions	connaîtrons	connaîtrions
vous	connaissez	connaissiez	connaîtrez	connaîtriez
ils, elles	connaissent	connaissaient	connaîtront	connaîtraient

Simple Past		SUBJUNCTIVE Present	Imperfect
je	connus	connaisse	connusse
tu	connus	connaisses	connusses
il, elle	connut	connaisse	connût
nous	connûmes	connaissions	connussions
vous	connûtes	connaissiez	connussiez
ils, elles	connurent	connaissent	connussent

PAST PARTICIPLE	connu		
PRESENT PARTICIPLE	connaissant		
	(tu)	(nous)	(vous)
IMPERATIVE	connais	connaissons	connaissez
STEMS	connai-, connaiss-, connaiss-/conn**u**/conn**u**-/connaîtr-		
REMARKS	General rule: *-i* has circumflex whenever followed by *-t* (including indicative singular 3s)		
OTHER VERBS	*-aître* verbs **other than** *naître* and *renaître* (5-21): *apparaître, comparaître, disparaître, méconnaître, paître* (defective), *paraître, réapparaître, reconnaître, repaître, reparaître, transparaître*		

5-21 NAÎTRE TO BE BORN

INDICATIVE

	Present	Imperfect	Future	Conditional
je	nais	naissais	naîtrai	naîtrais
tu	nais	naissais	naîtras	naîtrais
il, elle	*naît*	naissait	naîtra	naîtrait
nous	naissons	naissions	naîtrons	naîtrions
vous	naissez	naissiez	naîtrez	naîtriez
ils, elles	naissent	naissaient	naîtront	naîtraient

Simple Past		SUBJUNCTIVE Present	Imperfect
je	naquis	naisse	naquisse
tu	naquis	naisses	naquisses
il, elle	naquit	naisse	naquît
nous	naquîmes	naissions	naquissions
vous	naquîtes	naissiez	naquissiez
ils, elles	naquirent	naissent	naquissent

PAST PARTICIPLE	né		
PRESENT PARTICIPLE	naissant		
	(tu)	(nous)	(vous)
IMPERATIVE	nais	naissons	naissez
STEMS	nai-, naiss-, naiss- / **né** / naqu**i**- / naîtr-		
REMARKS	General rule: *-i* has circumflex whenever followed by *-t* (including indicative singular 3s)		
OTHER VERBS	*renaître*		

5-22A PLAIRE TO PLEASE

INDICATIVE

	Present	Imperfect	Future	Conditional
je	plais	plaisais	plairai	plairais
tu	plais	plaisais	plairas	plairais
il, elle	*plaît*	plaisait	plaira	plairait
nous	plaisons	plaisions	plairons	plairions
vous	plaisez	plaisiez	plairez	plairiez
ils, elles	plaisent	plaisaient	plairont	plairaient

Simple Past		SUBJUNCTIVE Present	Imperfect
je	plus	plaise	plusse
tu	plus	plaises	plusses
il, elle	plut	plaise	plût
nous	plûmes	plaisions	plussions
vous	plûtes	plaisiez	plussiez
ils, elles	plurent	plaisent	plussent

PAST PARTICIPLE	plu (*invariable*)		
PRESENT PARTICIPLE	plaisant		
	(tu)	(nous)	(vous)
IMPERATIVE	plais	plaisons	plaisez
STEMS	plai-, plais-, plais- / pl**u** / pl**u**- / plair-		
REMARKS	1. Circumflex: *il plaît* (only) 2. *Il a plu, il plut, il plût*—identical for *plaire* and *pleuvoir* (4-4)		
OTHER VERBS	*complaire, déplaire*		

5-22B	TAIRE	TO KEEP QUIET (*SE TAIRE*)

INDICATIVE

	Present
je	tais
tu	tais
il, elle	*tait*
nous	taisons
vous	taisez
ils, elles	taisent

STEMS	tai-, tais-, tais- / **tu** / **tu**- / tair-
REMARKS	Conjugation analogous to *plaire,* except *il tait* does not have circumflex

5-23	FAIRE	TO DO, TO MAKE

INDICATIVE

	Present	Imperfect	Future	Conditional
je	fais	faisais	ferai	ferais
tu	fais	faisais	feras	ferais
il, elle	fait	faisait	fera	ferait
nous	faisons	faisions	ferons	ferions
vous	***faites***	faisiez	ferez	feriez
ils, elles	***font***	faisaient	feront	feraient

Simple Past		SUBJUNCTIVE Present	SUBJUNCTIVE Imperfect
je	fis	*fasse*	fisse
tu	fis	*fasses*	fisses
il, elle	fit	*fasse*	fît
nous	fîmes	*fassions*	fissions
vous	fîtes	*fassiez*	fissiez
ils, elles	firent	*fassent*	fissent

PAST PARTICIPLE	fait		
PRESENT PARTICIPLE	faisant		
	(tu)	(nous)	(vous)
IMPERATIVE	fais	faisons	***faites***
STEMS	fai-, fais-, ***font***- / fa**it** / **fi**- / fer-		
REMARKS	1. *Vous **faites**:* present indicative and imperative; *ils **font***		
	2. Irregular present subjunctive stem *fass-*		
OTHER VERBS	*contrefaire, défaire, redéfaire, refaire, satisfaire, surfaire*		
	defective: *forfaire, parfaire, stupéfaire*		

5-24 TRAIRE TO MILK

INDICATIVE

	Present	Imperfect	Future	Conditional
je	trais	*trayais*	trairai	trairais
tu	trais	*trayais*	trairas	trairais
il, elle	trait	*trayait*	traira	trairait
nous	*trayons*	*trayions*	trairons	trairions
vous	*trayez*	*trayiez*	trairez	trairiez
ils, elles	traient	*trayaient*	trairont	trairaient

	Simple Past	SUBJUNCTIVE Present	SUBJUNCTIVE Imperfect
je	—	traie	—
tu	—	traies	—
il, elle	—	traie	
nous	—	*trayions*	—
vous	—	*trayiez*	—
ils, elles	—	traient	—

PAST PARTICIPLE trait
PRESENT PARTICIPLE *trayant*

	(tu)	(nous)	(vous)
IMPERATIVE	trais	*trayons*	*trayez*

STEMS trai-, *tray-*, trai- / tra**it** / — / trair-

REMARKS
1. *-i* between two vowels → *y*, unless second vowel is *mute -e* (13 conjugations)
2. No simple past or imperfect subjunctive

OTHER VERBS *-raire* verbs: *abstraire, braire* (defective), *distraire, extraire, raire, rentraire, soustraire*

5-25 VAINCRE TO VANQUISH

INDICATIVE

	Present	Imperfect	Future	Conditional
je	vaincs	*vainquais*	vaincrai	vaincrais
tu	vaincs	*vainquais*	vaincras	vaincrais
il, elle	<u>vain**c**</u>	*vainquait*	vaincra	vaincrait
nous	*vainquons*	vainquions	vaincrons	vaincrions
vous	vainquez	vainquiez	vaincrez	vaincriez
ils, elles	vainquent	*vainquaient*	vaincront	vaincraient

Simple Past		SUBJUNCTIVE Present	Imperfect
je	vainquis	vainque	vainquisse
tu	vainquis	vainques	vainquisses
il, elle	vainquit	vainque	vainquît
nous	vainquîmes	vainquions	vainquissions
vous	vainquîtes	vainquiez	vainquissiez
ils, elles	vainquirent	vainquent	vainquissent

PAST PARTICIPLE	vaincu		
PRESENT PARTICIPLE	*vainquant*		
	(tu)	(nous)	(vous)
IMPERATIVE	vaincs	*vainquons*	vainquez
STEMS	vainc-, vainqu-, vainqu- / vainc**u** / vainqu**i** / vaincr-		
REMARKS	1. 3rd person singular present indicative ends in *-c* 2. *-qua, -quo* rather than "normal" orthography *-ca, -co,* hence contrast: *convain**qua**nt—convain**ca**nt* (past part.—adjective)		
OTHER VERBS	*convaincre*		

6-1 (I) PARTIR TO LEAVE

INDICATIVE

	Present	Imperfect	Future	Conditional
je	pars	partais	partirai	partirais
tu	pars	partais	partiras	partirais
il, elle	part	partait	partira	partirait
nous	partons	partions	partirons	partirions
vous	partez	partiez	partirez	partiriez
ils, elles	partent	partaient	partiront	partiraient

Simple Past		SUBJUNCTIVE Present	Imperfect
je	partis	parte	partisse
tu	partis	partes	partisses
il, elle	partit	parte	partît
nous	partîmes	partions	partissions
vous	partîtes	partiez	partissiez
ils, elles	partirent	partent	partissent

PAST PARTICIPLE	parti
PRESENT PARTICIPLE	partant
	(tu) (nous) (vous)
IMPERATIVE	pars partons partez
STEMS	par-, part-, part- / **parti** / parti- / partir-
REMARKS	Conjugation analogous to *sortir, sentir, servir, dormir*
OTHER VERBS	*départir, repartir*

6-1 (II) SORTIR TO GO OUT, TAKE OUT

INDICATIVE

	Present	Imperfect	Future	Conditional
je	sors	sortais	sortirai	sortirais
tu	sors	sortais	sortiras	sortirais
il, elle	sort	sortait	sortira	sortirait
nous	sortons	sortions	sortirons	sortirions
vous	sortez	sortiez	sortirez	sortiriez
ils, elles	sortent	sortaient	sortiront	sortiraient

Simple Past		SUBJUNCTIVE Present	Imperfect
je	sortis	sorte	sortisse
tu	sortis	sortes	sortisses
il, elle	sortit	sorte	sortît
nous	sortîmes	sortions	sortissions
vous	sortîtes	sortiez	sortissiez
ils, elles	sortirent	sortent	sortissent

PAST PARTICIPLE	sorti
PRESENT PARTICIPLE	sortant
	(tu) (nous) (vous)
IMPERATIVE	sors sortons sortez
STEMS	sor-, sort-, sort- / **sorti** / sorti- / sortir-
REMARKS	Conjugation analogous to *partir, sentir, servir, dormir*
OTHER VERBS	*ressortir*

6-1 (III) SENTIR TO SENSE, SMELL

INDICATIVE

	Present	Imperfect	Future	Conditional
je	sens	sentais	sentirai	sentirais
tu	sens	sentais	sentiras	sentirais
il, elle	sent	sentait	sentira	sentirait
nous	sentons	sentions	sentirons	sentirions
vous	sentez	sentiez	sentirez	sentiriez
ils, elles	sentent	sentaient	sentiront	sentiraient

Simple Past			SUBJUNCTIVE Present	Imperfect
je	sentis		sente	sentisse
tu	sentis		sentes	sentisses
il, elle	sentit		sente	sentît
nous	sentîmes		sentions	sentissions
vous	sentîtes		sentiez	sentissiez
ils, elles	sentirent		sentent	sentissent

PAST PARTICIPLE	senti		
PRESENT PARTICIPLE	sentant		
	(tu)	(nous)	(vous)
IMPERATIVE	sens	sentons	sentez
STEMS	sen-, sent-, sent-/sent**i**/sent**i**-/sentir-		
REMARKS	Conjugation analogous to *partir, sortir, servir, dormir*		
OTHER VERBS	verbs ending in *-entir,* **except** *ralentir* and *retentir* (2-1): *consentir, pressentir, ressentir, démentir, mentir, repentir*		

6-1 (IV) SERVIR TO SERVE

INDICATIVE

	Present	Imperfect	Future	Conditional
je	sers	servais	servirai	servirais
tu	sers	servais	serviras	servirais
il, elle	sert	servait	servira	servirait
nous	servons	servions	servirons	servirions
vous	servez	serviez	servirez	serviriez
ils, elles	servent	servaient	serviront	serviraient

Simple Past			SUBJUNCTIVE Present	Imperfect
je	servis		serve	servisse
tu	servis		serves	servisses
il, elle	servit		serve	servît
nous	servîmes		servions	servissions
vous	servîtes		serviez	servissiez
ils, elles	servirent		servent	servissent

PAST PARTICIPLE	servi		
PRESENT PARTICIPLE	servant		
	(tu)	(nous)	(vous)
IMPERATIVE	sers	servons	servez
STEMS	ser-, serv-, serv-/serv**i**/serv**i**-/servir-		
REMARKS	Conjugation analogous to *partir, sortir, sentir, dormir*		
OTHER VERBS	*desservir, resservir*		

6-1 (V) DORMIR TO SLEEP

INDICATIVE

	Present	Imperfect	Future	Conditional
je	dors	dormais	dormirai	dormirais
tu	dors	dormais	dormiras	dormirais
il, elle	dort	dormait	dormira	dormirait
nous	dormons	dormions	dormirons	dormirions
vous	dormez	dormiez	dormirez	dormiriez
ils, elles	dorment	dormaient	dormiront	dormiraient

	Simple Past	SUBJUNCTIVE Present	SUBJUNCTIVE Imperfect
je	dormis	dorme	dormisse
tu	dormis	dormes	dormisses
il, elle	dormit	dorme	dormît
nous	dormîmes	dormions	dormissions
vous	dormîtes	dormiez	dormissiez
ils, elles	dormirent	dorment	dormissent

PAST PARTICIPLE	dormi		
PRESENT PARTICIPLE	dormant		
	(tu)	(nous)	(vous)
IMPERATIVE	dors	dormons	dormez
STEMS	dor-, dorm-, dorm- / dormi / dormi- / dormir-		
REMARKS	Conjugation analogous to *partir, sortir, sentir, servir*		
OTHER VERBS	*endormir, rendormir*		

6-2 FUIR TO FLEE

INDICATIVE

	Present	Imperfect	Future	Conditional
je	fuis	*fuyais*	fuirai	fuirais
tu	fuis	*fuyais*	fuiras	fuirais
il, elle	fuit	*fuyait*	fuira	fuirait
nous	*fuyons*	*fuyions*	fuirons	fuirions
vous	*fuyez*	*fuyiez*	fuirez	fuiriez
ils, elles	fuient	*fuyaient*	fuiront	fuiraient

Simple Past		SUBJUNCTIVE Present	Imperfect
je	fuis	fuie	fuisse
tu	fuis	fuies	fuisses
il, elle	fuit	fuie	fuît
nous	fuîmes	*fuyions*	fuissions
vous	fuîtes	*fuyiez*	fuissiez
ils, elles	fuirent	fuient	fuissent

PAST PARTICIPLE	fui		
PRESENT PARTICIPLE	*fuyant*		
	(tu)	(nous)	(vous)
IMPERATIVE	fuis	*fuyons*	*fuyez*
STEMS	fui-, *fuy-*, fui- / fu**i** / fu**i**- / fuir-		
REMARKS	*-i* between two vowels → *y*, unless second vowel is *mute -e* (13 conjugations)		
OTHER VERBS	*s'enfuir*		

6-3 ACQUÉRIR TO ACQUIRE

INDICATIVE

	Present	Imperfect	Future	Conditional
j'	acquiers	acquérais	acquerrai	acquerrais
tu	acquiers	acquérais	acquerras	acquerrais
il, elle	acquiert	acquérait	acquerra	acquerrait
nous	acquérons	acquérions	acquerrons	acquerrions
vous	acquérez	acquériez	acquerrez	acquerriez
ils, elles	acquièrent	acquéraient	acquerront	acquerraient

Simple Past		SUBJUNCTIVE Present	Imperfect
j'	acquis	acquière	acquisse
tu	acquis	acquières	acquisses
il, elle	acquit	acquière	acquît
nous	acquîmes	acquérions	acquissions
vous	acquîtes	acquériez	acquissiez
ils, elles	acquirent	acquièrent	acquissent

PAST PARTICIPLE	acquis		
PRESENT PARTICIPLE	acquérant		
	(tu)	(nous)	(vous)
IMPERATIVE	acquiers	acquérons	acquérez
STEMS	acquier-, acquér-, acquièr- / acqu**is** / acqu**i**- / acquerr-		
OTHER VERBS	*-quérir* verbs: *conquérir, s'enquérir, reconquérir, requérir*		

6-4 COURIR TO RUN

INDICATIVE

	Present	Imperfect	Future	Conditional
je	cours	courais	courrai	courrais
tu	cours	courais	courras	courrais
il, elle	court	courait	courra	courrait
nous	courons	courions	courrons	courrions
vous	courez	couriez	courrez	courriez
ils, elles	courent	couraient	courront	courraient

	Simple Past	SUBJUNCTIVE Present	Imperfect
je	courus	coure	courusse
tu	courus	coures	courusses
il, elle	courut	coure	courût
nous	courûmes	courions	courussions
vous	courûtes	couriez	courussiez
ils, elles	coururent	courent	courussent

PAST PARTICIPLE	couru		
PRESENT PARTICIPLE	courant		
	(tu)	(nous)	(vous)
IMPERATIVE	cours	courons	courez
STEMS	cour-, cour-, cour-/cour**u**/cour**u**-/courr-		
OTHER VERBS	*-courir* verbs: *accourir, concourir, discourir, encourir, parcourir, recourir, secourir*		

6-5 MOURIR TO DIE

INDICATIVE

	Present	Imperfect	Future	Conditional
je	meurs	mourais	mourrai	mourrais
tu	meurs	mourais	mourras	mourrais
il, elle	meurt	mourait	mourra	mourrait
nous	mourons	mourions	mourrons	mourrions
vous	mourez	mouriez	mourrez	mourriez
ils, elles	meurent	mouraient	mourront	mourraient

Simple Past		SUBJUNCTIVE Present	Imperfect
je	mourus	meure	mourusse
tu	mourus	meures	mourusses
il, elle	mourut	meure	mourût
nous	mourûmes	mourions	mourussions
vous	mourûtes	mouriez	mourussiez
ils, elles	moururent	meurent	mourussent

PAST PARTICIPLE	mort		
PRESENT PARTICIPLE	mourant		
	(tu)	(nous)	(vous)
IMPERATIVE	meurs	mourons	mourez
STEMS	meur-, mour-, meur- / mor**t** / mour**u**- / mourr-		

6-6 VÊTIR TO DRESS

INDICATIVE

	Present	Imperfect	Future	Conditional
je	vêts	vêtais	vêtirai	vêtirais
tu	vêts	vêtais	vêtiras	vêtirais
il, elle	***vêt***	vêtait	vêtira	vêtirait
nous	vêtons	vêtions	vêtirons	vêtirions
vous	vêtez	vêtiez	vêtirez	vêtiriez
ils, elles	vêtent	vêtaient	vêtiront	vêtiraient

Simple Past		SUBJUNCTIVE Present	Imperfect
je	vêtis	vête	vêtisse
tu	vêtis	vêtes	vêtisses
il, elle	vêtit	vête	vêtît
nous	vêtîmes	vêtions	vêtissions
vous	vêtîtes	vêtiez	vêtissiez
ils, elles	vêtirent	vêtent	vêtissent

PAST PARTICIPLE	vêtu		
PRESENT PARTICIPLE	vêtant		
	(tu)	(nous)	(vous)
IMPERATIVE	vêts	vêtons	vêtez
STEMS	vêt-, vêt-, vêt- / vêt**u** / vêt**i**- / vêtir-		
REMARKS	3rd person singular present indicative ***vêt*** (not **vêt-t*)		
OTHER VERBS	*dévêtir, revêtir*		

6-7 (I) VENIR TO COME

INDICATIVE

	Present	Imperfect	Future	Conditional
je	viens	venais	viendrai	viendrais
tu	viens	venais	viendras	viendrais
il, elle	vient	venait	viendra	viendrait
nous	venons	venions	viendrons	viendrions
vous	venez	veniez	viendrez	viendriez
ils, elles	viennent	venaient	viendront	viendraient

Simple Past		SUBJUNCTIVE Present	Imperfect
je	vins	vienne	vinsse
tu	vins	viennes	vinsses
il, elle	vint	vienne	vînt
nous	vînmes	venions	vinssions
vous	vîntes	veniez	vinssiez
ils, elles	vinrent	viennent	vinssent

PAST PARTICIPLE	venu		
PRESENT PARTICIPLE	venant		
	(tu)	(nous)	(vous)
IMPERATIVE	viens	venons	venez
STEMS	vien-, ven-, vienn- / ven**u** / vinˆ- / viendr-		
REMARKS	Conjugated like *tenir*		
OTHER VERBS	*-venir* verbs: *advenir, circonvenir, contrevenir, convenir, devenir, disconvenir, intervenir, obvenir, parvenir, prévenir, provenir, redevenir, se ressouvenir, revenir, souvenir, subvenir, survenir*		

6-7 (II) TENIR TO HOLD

INDICATIVE

	Present	Imperfect	Future	Conditional
je	tiens	tenais	tiendrai	tiendrais
tu	tiens	tenais	tiendras	tiendrais
il, elle	tient	tenait	tiendra	tiendrait
nous	tenons	tenions	tiendrons	tiendrions
vous	tenez	teniez	tiendrez	tiendriez
ils, elles	tiennent	tenaient	tiendront	tiendraient

Simple Past		SUBJUNCTIVE Present	Imperfect
je	tins	tienne	tinsse
tu	tins	tiennes	tinsses
il, elle	tint	tienne	tînt
nous	tînmes	tenions	tinssions
vous	tîntes	teniez	tinssiez
ils, elles	tinrent	tiennent	tinssent

PAST PARTICIPLE	tenu		
PRESENT PARTICIPLE	tenant		
	(tu)	(nous)	(vous)
IMPERATIVE	tiens	tenons	tenez
STEMS	tien-, ten-, tienn- / ten**u** / tinˆ- / tiendr-		
REMARKS	Conjugated like *venir*		
OTHER VERBS	*-tenir* verbs: *s'abstenir, appartenir, contenir, détenir, entretenir, maintenir, obtenir, retenir, soutenir*		

7 ÊTRE TO BE

INDICATIVE

	Present	Imperfect	Future	Conditional
je	*suis*	*étais*	serai	serais
tu	*es*	*étais*	seras	serais
il, elle	*est*	*était*	sera	serait
nous	*sommes*	*étions*	serons	serions
vous	*êtes*	*étiez*	serez	seriez
ils, elles	*sont*	*étaient*	seront	seraient

Simple Past		SUBJUNCTIVE Present	Imperfect
je	fus	*sois*	fusse
tu	fus	*sois*	fusses
il, elle	fut	*soit*	fût
nous	fûmes	*soyons*	fussions
vous	fûtes	*soyez*	fussiez
ils, elles	furent	*soient*	fussent

PAST PARTICIPLE	été (invariable)		
PRESENT PARTICIPLE	*étant*		
	(tu)	(nous)	(vous)
IMPERATIVE	*sois*	*soyons*	*soyez*
STEMS	—, —, — / **été** / **fu**- / ser-		
REMARKS	Forms not predictable from stems: present indicative and subjunctive, imperfect, present participle, imperative (= subjunctive)		

8 AVOIR TO HAVE

INDICATIVE

	Present	Imperfect	Future	Conditional
j'	*ai*	avais	aurai	aurais
tu	*as*	avais	auras	aurais
il, elle	*a*	avait	aura	aurait
nous	avons	avions	aurons	aurions
vous	avez	aviez	aurez	auriez
ils, elles	*ont*	avaient	auront	auraient

Simple Past		SUBJUNCTIVE Present	Imperfect
j'	eus	*aie*	eusse
tu	eus	*aies*	eusses
il, elle	eut	*ait*	eût
nous	eûmes	*ayons*	eussions
vous	eûtes	*ayez*	eussiez
ils, elles	eurent	*aient*	eussent

PAST PARTICIPLE	eu		
PRESENT PARTICIPLE	*ayant*		
	(tu)	(nous)	(vous)
IMPERATIVE	*aie*	*ayons*	*ayez*
STEMS	—, av-, —/**eu**/**eu**-/aur-		
REMARKS	Forms not predictable from stems: present indicative (singulars and 3p), present subjunctive, present participle, imperative		

9 ALLER TO GO

INDICATIVE

	Present	Imperfect	Future	Conditional
je	*vais*	allais	irai	irais
tu	*vas*	allais	iras	irais
il, elle	*va*	allait	ira	irait
nous	allons	allions	irons	irions
vous	allez	alliez	irez	iriez
ils, elles	*vont*	allaient	iront	iraient

Simple Past		SUBJUNCTIVE Present	Imperfect
j'	allai	*aille*	allasse
tu	allas	*ailles*	allasses
il, elle	alla	*aille*	allât
nous	allâmes	allions	allassions
vous	allâtes	alliez	allassiez
ils, elles	allèrent	*aillent*	allassent

PAST PARTICIPLE	allé		
PRESENT PARTICIPLE	allant		
	(tu)	(nous)	(vous)
IMPERATIVE	*va*	allons	allez
STEMS	—, all-, —/all**é**/all**a**-/ir-		
REMARKS	Forms not predictable from stems: present indicative and subjunctive (singulars and 3p); imperative 2s (regularly derived from present)		

ANNEX B

Alphabetical Listing of 6,200 Verbs by Model Number

Essentially all of the verbs found in *Le Petit Robert* are included in this annex.[1] Alternate spellings of the same verb—listed in *Le Petit Robert* as separate verbs—are for the most part not listed separately but rather shown in parentheses; when the alternate spelling implies a different conjugation model, this is also shown in parentheses:

iodler (jodler)	1-1
gangrener (gangréner)	1-4 (1-5)

Thus "to yodel" in French can be spelled either *iodler* or *jodler,* both conjugated like *parler* (1-1); *gangrener* without a written accent is conjugated like *peser* (1-4), while with a written accent it is conjugated like *céder* (1-5). A number of verbs can optionally be written with a hyphen, in which case the hyphen is placed in parentheses. For example:

pique(-)niquer	*piqueniquer* or *pique-niquer*

In a small number of cases, a verb has two different conjugations corresponding to completely separate meanings. In such cases the verb is shown twice. For example:

ressortir	2-1	["to concern", "to be relative to"]
ressortir	6-1	["to go out again"]

Verbs which can only be used pronominally (reflexively) are shown with the reflexive pronoun *se* in parentheses: *évader (s'), repentir (se).*[2]

Model verbs—whose conjugations are presented in Annex A—are italicized. *Defective* verbs existing only in certain conjugations are signaled by "(DEF)". For example:

advenir (DEF)	6-7
choir	DEF

---

[1] Different verbs with identical spellings are treated as a single verb, so long as the conjugations are the same: e.g., *dépendre* ("to depend") and *dépendre* ("to unhang"), both conjugated like *rendre* (5-1a).

[2] In general, the *smaller* a dictionary is, the more likely it is that all of the definitions for a given verb will involve reflexive uses, and hence the more likely it is that the verb will be shown in its reflexive form. As an example, many dictionaries show *prosterner* and *souvenir* only in their reflexive forms (*se prosterner, se souvenir*), while others (including *Le Petit Robert*) present them in their "normal" forms.

Advenir follows the conjugation pattern of *venir* (6-7) but only exists in limited conjugations, as set forth in Annex C. The conjugation of *choir* is also set forth in Annex C; however, it does not follow precisely any of the models presented in Annex A. *Impersonal* verbs (e.g., "it rains", "it is necessary"), generally existing only in the third person singular, are signaled by "(IMP)".

Verb	Model #
abaisser	1-1
abandonner	1-1
abasourdir	2-1
abâtardir	2-1
abattre	5-3
abcéder	1-5
abdiquer	1-1b
abêtir	2-1
abhorrer	1-1
abîmer	1-1
abjurer	1-1
ablater	1-1
abolir	2-1
abominer	1-1
abonder	1-1
abonner	1-1
abonnir	2-1
aborder	1-1
aboucher	1-1
abouler	1-1
abouter	1-1
aboutir	2-1
aboyer	1-7a
abraser	1-1
abréger	1-6c
abreuver	1-1
abriter	1-1
abroger	1-2b
abrutir	2-1
absenter (s')	1-1
absorber	1-1
absoudre	*5-13a*
abstenir (s')	6-7
abstraire	5-24
abuser	1-1
accabler	1-1
accaparer	1-1
accastiller	1-1
accéder	1-5
accélérer	1-5
accentuer	1-1
accepter	1-1
accessoiriser	1-1
acclamer	1-1
acclimater	1-1
accoler	1-1
accommoder	1-1
accompagner	1-1
accomplir	2-1
accorder	1-1
accoster	1-1
accoter	1-1
accoucher	1-1
accouder (s')	1-1
accoupler	1-1
accourcir	2-1
accourir	6-4
accoutrer	1-1
accoutumer	1-1
accréditer	1-1
accrocher	1-1
accroire	DEF
accroître	*5-19b*
accroupir (s')	2-1
accueillir	3-2b
acculer	1-1
accumuler	1-1
accuser	1-1
acérer	1-5
acétifier	1-1c
achalander	1-1
acharner	1-1

Verb	Model #
acheminer	1-1
acheter	1-4
achever	1-4
achopper	1-1
achromatiser	1-1
acidifier	1-1c
aciduler	1-1
aciérer	1-5
acoquiner (s')	1-1
acquérir	*6-3*
acquiescer	1-2a
acquitter	1-1
actionner	1-1
activer	1-1
actualiser	1-1
adapter	1-1
additionner	1-1
adhérer	1-5
adjectiver	1-1
adjoindre	5-12
adjuger	1-2b
adjurer	1-1
admettre	5-4
administrer	1-1
admirer	1-1
admonester	1-1
adonner	1-1
adopter	1-1
adorer	1-1
adosser	1-1
adouber	1-1
adoucir	2-1
adresser	1-1
adsorber	1-1
aduler	1-1
adultérer	1-5
advenir (DEF)	6-7
aérer	1-5
affabuler	1-1
affadir	2-1
affaiblir	2-1
affairer (s')	1-1
affaisser	1-1
affaler	1-1
affamer	1-1
affecter	1-1
affectionner	1-1
affermer	1-1
affermir	2-1
afficher	1-1
affiler	1-1
affilier	1-1c
affiner	1-1
affirmer	1-1
affleurer	1-1
affliger	1-2b
afflouer	1-1
affluer	1-1
affoler	1-1
affouiller	1-1
affourcher	1-1
affourrager (affourager)	1-2b
affranchir	2-1
affréter	1-5
affriander	1-1
affrioler	1-1
affronter	1-1
affubler	1-1
affûter	1-1
africaniser	1-1
agacer	1-2a
agencer	1-2a
agenouiller (s')	1-1
agglomérer	1-5
agglutiner	1-1
aggraver	1-1
agioter	1-1
agir	2-1
agiter	1-1
agneler	1-4
agonir	2-1
agoniser	1-1
agrafer	1-1
agrandir	2-1
agréer	1-1
agréger	1-6c

Verb	Model #	Verb	Model #
agrémenter	1-1	alourdir	2-1
agresser	1-1	alpaguer	1-1a
agripper	1-1	alphabétiser	1-1
aguerrir	2-1	altérer	1-5
aguicher	1-1	alterner	1-1
ahaner (ahanner)	1-1	aluminer	1-1
ahurir	2-1	aluner	1-1
aider	1-1	alunir	2-1
aigrir	2-1	amadouer	1-1
aiguiller	1-1	amaigrir	2-1
aiguilleter	1-3b	amalgamer	1-1
aiguillonner	1-1	amariner	1-1
aiguiser	1-1	amarrer	1-1
ailler	1-1	amasser	1-1
aimanter	1-1	amatir	2-1
aimer	1-1	ambitionner	1-1
airer	1-1	ambler	1-1
ajointer	1-1	améliorer	1-1
ajourer	1-1	aménager	1-2b
ajourner	1-1	amender	1-1
ajouter	1-1	amener	1-4
ajuster	1-1	amenuiser	1-1
alanguir	2-1	américaniser	1-1
alarmer	1-1	amerrir	2-1
alcaliniser	1-1	ameublir	2-1
alcooliser	1-1	ameuter	1-1
alerter	1-1	amidonner	1-1
aléser	1-5	amincir	2-1
aleviner	1-1	amnistier	1-1c
aliéner	1-5	amocher	1-1
aligner	1-1	amodier	1-1c
alimenter	1-1	amoindrir	2-1
aliter	1-1	amollir	2-1
allaiter	1-1	amonceler	1-3a
allécher	1-5	amorcer	1-2a
alléger	1-6c	amortir	2-1
alléguer	1-5	amouracher (s')	1-1
aller	*9*	amplifier	1-1c
allier	1-1c	amputer	1-1
allonger	1-2b	amuïr (s')	2-1
allouer	1-1	amurer	1-1
allumer	1-1	amuser	1-1
alluvionner	1-1	analyser	1-1

Verb	Model #	Verb	Model #
anastomoser	1-1	appauvrir	2-1
anathématiser (anathémiser)	1-1	*appeler*	*1-3a*
ancrer	1-1	appendre	5-1a
anéantir	2-1	appertiser	1-1
anémier	1-1c	appesantir	2-1
anesthésier	1-1c	applaudir	2-1
anglaiser	1-1	appliquer	1-1b
angliciser	1-1	appointer	1-1
angoisser	1-1	apponter	1-1
anhéler	1-5	apporter	1-1
animer	1-1	apposer	1-1
aniser	1-1	apprécier	1-1c
ankyloser	1-1	appréhender	1-1
annexer	1-1	apprendre	5-2
annihiler	1-1	apprêter	1-1
annoncer	1-2a	apprivoiser	1-1
annoter	1-1	approcher	1-1
annualiser	1-1	approfondir	2-1
annuler	1-1	approprier	1-1c
anoblir	2-1	approuver	1 1
anodiser	1-1	approvisionner	1-1
ânonner	1-1	appuyer	1-7a
anordir	2-1	apurer	1-1
antéposer	1-1	arabiser	1-1
anticiper	1-1	araser	1-1
antidater	1-1	arbitrer	1-1
apaiser	1-1	arborer	1-1
apercevoir	4-2b	arc-bouter	1-1
apeurer	1-1	architecturer	1-1
apiquer	1-1b	archiver	1-1
apitoyer	1-7a	argenter	1-1
aplanir	2-1	arguer	1-1a
aplatir	2-1	argumenter	1-1
apostasier	1-1c	armer	1-1
apostiller	1-1	armorier	1-1c
apostropher	1-1	arnaquer	1-1b
apparaître	5-20	aromatiser	1-1
appareiller	1-1	arpéger	1-6c
apparenter	1-1	arpenter	1-1
apparier	1-1c	arquer	1-1b
apparoir	DEF	arracher	1-1
appartenir	6-7	arraisonner	1-1
appâter	1-1	arranger	1-2b

Verb	Model #	Verb	Model #
arrenter	1-1	asticoter	1-1
arrérager	1-2b	astiquer	1-1b
arrêter	1-1	astreindre	5-12
arriérer	1-5	atermoyer	1-7a
arrimer	1-1	atomiser	1-1
arriser (ariser)	1-1	atrophier	1-1c
arriver	1-1	attabler	1-1
arroger (s')	1-2b	attacher	1-1
arrondir	2-1	attaquer	1-1b
arroser	1-1	attarder	1-1
articuler	1-1	atteindre	5-12
ascensionner	1-1	atteler	1-3a
aseptiser	1-1	attendre	5-1a
asperger	1-2b	attendrir	2-1
asphalter	1-1	attenter	1-1
asphyxier	1-1c	atténuer	1-1
aspirer	1-1	atterrer	1-1
assagir	2-1	atterrir	2-1
assaillir	*3-2a*	attester	1-1
assainir	2-1	attiédir	2-1
assaisonner	1-1	attifer	1-1
assassiner	1-1	attiger	1-2b
assécher	1-5	attirer	1-1
assembler	1-1	attiser	1-1
assener (asséner)	1-4 (1-5)	attraper	1-1
asseoir	*4-9a/b*	attribuer	1-1
asservir	2-1	attrister	1-1
assiéger	1-6c	attrouper	1-1
assigner	1-1	auditer	1-1
assimiler	1-1	auditionner	1-1
assister	1-1	augmenter	1-1
associer	1-1c	augurer	1-1
assoiffer	1-1	auner	1-1
assombrir	2-1	auréoler	1-1
assommer	1-1	aurifier	1-1c
assortir	2-1	ausculter	1-1
assoupir	2-1	authentifier	1-1c
assouplir	2-1	authentiquer	1-1b
assourdir	2-1	autocensurer (s')	1-1
assouvir	2-1	autodétruire (s')	5-9a
assujettir	2-1	autofinancer	1-2a
assumer	1-1	autographier	1-1c
assurer	1-1	automatiser	1-1

Verb	Model #
autoproclamer (s')	1-1
autopsier	1-1c
autorépliquer (s')	1-1b
autoriser	1-1
avachir	2-1
avaler	1-1
avaliser	1-1
avancer	1-2a
avantager	1-2b
avarier	1-1c
aventurer	1-1
avérer (DEF)	1-5
avertir	2-1
aveugler	1-1
aveulir	2-1
avilir	2-1
aviser	1-1
avitailler	1-1
aviver	1-1
avoir	*8*
avoisiner	1-1
avorter	1-1
avouer	1-1
avoyer	1-7a
axer	1-1
axiomatiser	1-1
azurer	1-1
babiller	1-1
bâcher	1-1
bachoter	1-1
bâcler	1-1
badigeonner	1-1
badiner	1-1
bafouer	1-1
bafouiller	1-1
bâfrer	1-1
bagarrer	1-1
baguenauder	1-1
baguer	1-1a
baigner	1-1
bailler	1-1
bâiller	1-1
bâillonner	1-1
baiser	1-1
baisser	1-1
balader	1-1
balafrer	1-1
balancer	1-2a
balayer	1-7b
balbutier	1-1c
baliser	1-1
balkaniser	1-1
ballaster	1-1
baller	1-1
ballonner	1-1
ballotter	1-1
bambocher	1-1
banaliser	1-1
bancher	1-1
bander	1-1
bannir	2-1
banquer	1-1b
banqueter	1-3b
baptiser	1-1
baragouiner	1-1
baraquer	1-1b
baratiner	1-1
baratter	1-1
barber	1-1
barbifier	1-1c
barboter	1-1
barbouiller	1-1
barder	1-1
barguigner	1-1
barioler	1-1
barrer	1-1
barricader	1-1
barrir	2-1
basaner	1-1
basculer	1-1
baser	1-1
bassiner	1-1
baster	1-1
batailler	1-1
bateler	1-3a
bâter	1-1

Verb	Model #	Verb	Model #
batifoler	1-1	bigorner	1-1
bâtir	2-1	biler (se)	1-1
bâtonner	1-1	biner	1-1
battre	*5-3*	biologiser	1-1
bavarder	1-1	biper	1-1
bavasser	1-1	biscuiter	1-1
baver	1-1	biseauter	1-1
bayer (DEF)	1-1	biser	1-1
bazarder	1-1	bisquer	1-1b
béatifier	1-1c	bisser	1-1
bêcher	1-1	bistourner	1-1
bêcheveter	1-3b	bistrer	1-1
bécoter	1-1	biter (bitter)	1-1
becqueter (béqueter)	1-3b	bitumer	1-1
becter	1-1	biturer (se) (bitturer)	1-1
bedonner	1-1	bivouaquer	1-1b
béer (DEF)	1-1	bizuter	1-1
bégayer	1-7b	blablater	1-1
bégueter	1-4	blackbouler	1-1
bêler	1-1	blaguer	1-1a
bémoliser	1-1	blairer	1-1
bénéficier	1-1c	blâmer	1-1
bénir	2-1	blanchir	2-1
béquiller	1-1	blaser	1-1
bercer	1-2a	blasonner	1-1
berner	1-1	blasphémer	1-5
besogner	1-1	blatérer	1-5
bêtifier	1-1c	blêmir	2-1
bétonner	1-1	bléser	1-5
beugler	1-1	blesser	1-1
beurrer	1-1	blettir	2-1
biaiser	1-1	bleuir	2-1
biberonner	1-1	blinder	1-1
bicher	1-1	blistériser	1-1
bichonner	1-1	blondir	2-1
bidonner	1-1	bloquer	1-1b
bidouiller	1-1	blottir (se)	2-1
bienvenir	DEF	blouser	1-1
biffer	1-1	bluffer	1-1
bifurquer	1-1b	bluter	1-1
bigarrer	1-1	bobiner	1-1
bigler	1-1	bocarder	1-1
bigophoner	1-1	*boire*	*5-17*

Verb	Model #
boiser	1-1
boiter	1-1
boitiller	1-1
bombarder	1-1
bomber	1-1
bondir	2-1
bonifier	1-1c
bonimenter	1-1
border (bordurer)	1-1
borner	1-1
bornoyer	1-7a
bosseler	1-3a
bosser	1-1
bossuer	1-1
bostonner	1-1
botteler	1-3a
botter	1-1
boubouler	1-1
boucaner	1-1
boucharder	1-1
boucher	1-1
bouchonner	1-1
boucler	1-1
bouder	1-1
boudiner	1-1
bouffer	1-1
bouffir	2-1
bouffonner	1-1
bouger	1-2b
bougonner	1-1
bouillir	*3-2c*
bouillonner	1-1
bouillotter	1-1
boulanger	1-2b
bouler	1-1
bouleverser	1-1
boulocher	1-1
boulonner	1-1
boulotter	1-1
boumer	1-1
bouquiner	1-1
bourdonner	1-1
bourgeonner	1-1
bourlinguer	1-1a
bourreler	1-3a
bourrer	1-1
boursicoter	1-1
boursoufler	1-1
bousculer	1-1
bousiller	1-1
bouter	1-1
boutonner	1-1
bouturer	1-1
boxer	1-1
boyauter (se)	1-1
boycotter	1-1
braconner	1-1
brader	1-1
brailler	1-1
braire (DEF)	5-24
braiser	1-1
bramer	1-1
brancarder	1-1
brancher	1-1
brandir	2-1
branler	1-1
braquer	1-1b
braser	1-1
brasiller	1-1
brasser	1-1
brasseyer	1-1
braver	1-1
bredouiller	1-1
brêler	1-1
brésiller	1-1
bretteler (bretter)	1-3a (1-1)
breveter	1-3b
bricoler	1-1
brider	1-1
bridger	1-2b
briefer	1-1
briffer	1-1
briguer	1-1a
brillanter	1-1
brillantiner	1-1
briller	1-1

Verb	Model #
brimbaler	1-1
brimer	1-1
bringuebaler (brinquebaler)	1-1
briquer	1-1b
briqueter	1-3b
briser	1-1
brocanter	1-1
brocarder	1-1
brocher	1-1
broder	1-1
broncher	1-1
bronzer	1-1
brosser	1-1
brouetter	1-1
brouillasser (IMP)	1-1
brouiller	1-1
brouter	1-1
broyer	1-7a
bruiner (IMP)	1-1
bruire (DEF)	2-2
bruisser	1-1
bruiter	1-1
brûler	1-1
brunir	2-1
brusquer	1-1b
brutaliser	1-1
bûcher	1-1
budgétiser (budgéter)	1-1 (1-5)
buller	1-1
bureaucratiser	1-1
buriner	1-1
buter	1-1
butiner	1-1
butter	1-1
cabaler	1-1
cabaner	1-1
câbler	1-1
cabosser	1-1
caboter	1-1
cabotiner	1-1
cabrer	1-1
cabrioler	1-1
cacaber	1-1

Verb	Model #
cacarder	1-1
cacher	1-1
cacheter	1-3b
cachetonner	1-1
cadastrer	1-1
cadenasser	1-1
cadencer	1-2a
cadrer	1-1
cafarder	1-1
cafeter (DEF)	1-1
cafouiller	1-1
cafter	1-1
cahoter	1-1
cailler	1-1
caillouter	1-1
cajoler	1-1
calaminer (se)	1-1
calamistrer	1-1
calancher	1-1
calandrer	1-1
calciner	1-1
calculer	1-1
caler	1-1
caleter (DEF)	1-1
calfater	1-1
calfeutrer	1-1
calibrer	1-1
câliner	1-1
calligraphier	1-1c
calmer	1-1
calmir	2-1
calomnier	1-1c
calorifuger	1-2b
calquer	1-1b
calter	1-1
cambrer	1-1
cambrioler	1-1
camer (se)	1-1
camionner	1-1
camoufler	1-1
camper	1-1
canaliser	1-1
canarder	1-1

Verb	Model #	Verb	Model #
cancaner	1-1	carreler	1-3a
cancériser	1-1	carrer	1-1
candir (se)	2-1	carrosser	1-1
caner	1-1	carroyer	1-7a
canneler	1-3a	carter	1-1
canner	1-1	cartonner	1-1
cannibaliser	1-1	cascader	1-1
canoniser	1-1	caser	1-1
canonner	1-1	caserner	1-1
canoter	1-1	casquer	1-1b
cantonner	1-1	casse-croûter	1-1
canuler	1-1	casser	1-1
caoutchouter	1-1	castagner	1-1
caparaçonner	1-1	castrer	1-1
capeler	1-3a	cataloguer	1-1a
capeyer	1-1	catalyser	1-1
capitaliser	1-1	catapulter	1-1
capitonner	1-1	catastropher	1-1
capituler	1-1	catcher	1-1
capoter	1-1	catéchiser	1-1
capsuler	1-1	catir	2-1
capter	1-1	cauchemarder	1-1
captiver	1-1	causer	1-1
capturer	1-1	cautériser	1-1
caqueter	1-4	cautionner	1-1
caracoler	1-1	cavalcader	1-1
caractériser	1-1	cavaler	1-1
caramboler	1-1	caver	1-1
caraméliser	1-1	caviarder	1-1
carapater (se)	1-1	*céder*	*1-5*
carbonater	1-1	ceindre	5-12
carboniser	1-1	ceinturer	1-1
carburer	1-1	célébrer	1-5
carcailler	1-1	celer	1-4
carder	1-1	cémenter	1-1
carencer	1-2a	cendrer	1-1
caréner	1-5	censurer	1-1
caresser	1-1	centraliser	1-1
carguer	1-1a	centrer	1-1
caricaturer	1-1	centrifuger	1-2b
carier	1-1c	centupler	1-1
carillonner	1-1	cercler	1-1
carotter	1-1	cerner	1-1

Verb	Model #
certifier	1-1c
césariser	1-1
cesser	1-1
chagriner	1-1
chahuter	1-1
chaîner	1-1
chaloir	DEF
chalouper	1-1
chamailler	1-1
chamarrer	1-1
chambarder	1-1
chambouler	1-1
chambrer	1-1
chamoiser	1-1
champagniser	1-1
champlever	1-4
chanceler	1-3a
chancir	2-1
chanfreiner	1-1
changer	1-2b
chansonner	1-1
chanter	1-1
chantonner	1-1
chantourner	1-1
chaparder	1-1
chapeauter	1-1
chaperonner	1-1
chapitrer	1-1
chaponner	1-1
chaptaliser	1-1
charbonner	1-1
charcuter	1-1
charger	1-2b
charmer	1-1
charpenter	1-1
charrier	1-1c
charroyer	1-7a
chartériser	1-1
chasser	1-1
châtaigner	1-1
châtier	1-1c
chatonner	1-1
chatouiller	1-1
chatoyer	1-7a
châtrer	1-1
chauffer	1-1
chauler	1-1
chaumer	1-1
chausser	1-1
chauvir	DEF
chavirer	1-1
cheminer	1-1
chemiser	1-1
chercher	1-1
chérir	2-1
chevaler	1-1
chevaucher	1-1
cheviller	1-1
chevroter	1-1
chiader	1-1
chialer	1-1
chicaner	1-1
chier	1-1c
chiffonner	1-1
chiffrer	1-1
chigner	1-1
chiner	1-1
chinoiser	1-1
chiper	1-1
chipoter	1-1
chiquer	1-1b
chlinguer (schlinguer)	1-1a
chlorer	1-1
chloroformer	1-1
chlorurer	1-1
choir	DEF
choisir	2-1
chômer	1-1
choper	1-1
chopper	1-1
choquer	1-1b
chorégraphier	1-1c
chosifier	1-1c
chouchouter	1-1
chouiner (chougner)	1-1
chouraver	1-1

Verb	Model #
chourer	1-1
choyer	1-7a
christianiser	1-1
chromer	1-1
chronométrer	1-5
chuchoter	1-1
chuinter	1-1
chuter	1-1
cibler	1-1
cicatriser	1-1
ciller	1-1
cimenter	1-1
cinématographier	1-1c
cingler	1-1
cintrer	1-1
circoncire	*5-8d*
circonscrire	5-7
circonvenir	6-7
circuler	1-1
cirer	1-1
cisailler	1-1
ciseler	1-4
citer	1-1
civiliser	1-1
clabauder	1-1
claironner	1-1
clamecer (DEF)	1-6a
clamer	1-1
clamper	1-1
clamser	1-1
clapir	2-1
clapir (se)	2-1
clapoter	1-1
clapper	1-1
claquemurer	1-1
claquer	1-1b
claqueter	1-3b
clarifier	1-1c
classer	1-1
classifier	1-1c
claudiquer	1-1b
claustrer	1-1
claveter	1-3b

Verb	Model #
clayonner	1-1
clicher	1-1
cligner	1-1
clignoter	1-1
climatiser	1-1
cliquer	1-1b
cliqueter	1-3b
clisser	1-1
cliver	1-1
clochardiser	1-1
clocher	1-1
cloisonner	1-1
cloîtrer	1-1
cloner	1-1
clopiner	1-1
cloquer	1-1b
clore	DEF
clôturer	1-1
clouer	1-1
clouter	1-1
coacher	1-1
coaguler	1-1
coaliser	1-1
coasser	1-1
cocher	1-1
côcher	1-1
cochonner	1-1
cocotter (cocoter)	1-1
cocufier	1-1c
coder	1-1
codifier	1-1c
coéditer	1-1
coexister	1-1
coffrer	1-1
cofinancer	1-2a
cogérer	1-5
cogiter	1-1
cogner	1-1
cohabiter	1-1
coiffer	1-1
coincer	1-2a
coïncider	1-1
coïter	1-1

Verb	Model #	Verb	Model #
cokéfier	1-1c	compenser	1-1
collaborer	1-1	compiler	1-1
collapser	1-1	compisser	1-1
collationner	1-1	complaire	5-22a
collecter	1-1	compléter	1-5
collectionner	1-1	complexer	1-1
collectiviser	1-1	complexifier	1-1c
coller	1-1	complimenter	1-1
colleter	1-3b	compliquer	1-1b
colliger	1-2b	comploter	1-1
colloquer	1-1b	comporter	1-1
colmater	1-1	composer	1-1
coloniser	1-1	composter	1-1
colorer	1-1	comprendre	5-2
colorier	1-1c	compresser	1-1
coloriser	1-1	comprimer	1-1
colporter	1-1	compromettre	5-4
coltiner	1-1	comptabiliser	1-1
combattre	5-3	compter	1-1
combiner	1-1	compulser	1-1
combler	1-1	concasser	1-1
commander	1-1	concéder	1-5
commanditer	1-1	concélébrer	1-5
commémorer	1-1	concentrer	1-1
commencer	1-2a	conceptualiser	1-1
commenter	1-1	concerner	1-1
commercer	1-2a	concerter	1-1
commercialiser	1-1	concevoir	4-2b
commettre	5-4	conchier	1-1c
commissionner	1-1	concilier	1-1c
commotionner	1-1	conclure	5-16a
commuer	1-1	concocter	1-1
communaliser	1-1	concorder	1-1
communier	1-1c	concourir	6-4
communiquer	1-1b	concrétiser	1-1
commuter	1-1	concurrencer	1-2a
compacter	1-1	condamner	1-1
comparaître	5-20	condenser	1-1
comparer	1-1	condescendre	5-1a
comparoir	DEF	conditionner	1-1
compartimenter	1-1	*conduire*	*5-9a*
compasser	1-1	confectionner	1-1
compatir	2-1	confédérer	1-5

Verb	Model #	Verb	Model #
conférer	1-5	constiper	1-1
confesser	1-1	constituer	1-1
confier	1-1c	constitutionnaliser	1-1
configurer	1-1	construire	5-9a
confiner	1-1	consulter	1-1
confire	5-8b	consumer	1-1
confirmer	1-1	contacter	1-1
confisquer	1-1b	contagionner	1-1
confluer	1-1	contaminer	1-1
confondre	5-1a	contempler	1-1
conformer	1-1	conteneuriser	1-1
conforter	1-1	contenir	6-7
confronter	1-1	contenter	1-1
congédier	1-1c	conter	1-1
congeler	1-4	contester	1-1
congestionner	1-1	contingenter	1-1
conglomérer	1-5	continuer	1-1
conglutiner	1-1	contorsionner (se)	1-1
congratuler	1-1	contourner	1-1
congréer	1-1	contracter	1-1
conjecturer	1-1	contractualiser	1-1
conjuguer	1-1a	contraindre	5-12
conjurer	1-1	contrarier	1-1c
connaître	*5-20*	contraster	1-1
connecter	1-1	contre-attaquer	1-1b
connoter	1-1	contrebalancer	1-2a
conquérir	6-3	contrebattre	5-3
consacrer	1-1	contrebraquer	1-1b
conscientiser	1-1	contrebuter	1-1
conseiller	1-1	contrecarrer	1-1
consentir	6-1	contredire	5-8b
conserver	1-1	contrefaire	5-23
considérer	1-5	contreficher (se)	1-1
consigner	1-1	contrefoutre (se)	DEF
consister	1-1	contre-indiquer	1-1b
consoler	1-1	contre-manifester	1-1
consolider	1-1	contre-passer	1-1
consommer	1-1	contrer	1-1
conspirer	1-1	contresigner	1-1
conspuer	1-1	contre-tirer	1-1
constater	1-1	contrevenir	6-7
consteller	1-1	contribuer	1-1
consterner	1-1	contrister	1-1

Verb	Model #
contrôler	1-1
controverser	1-1
contusionner	1-1
convaincre	5-25
convenir	6-7
converger	1-2b
converser	1-1
convertir	2-1
convier	1-1c
convivialiser	1-1
convoiter	1-1
convoler	1-1
convoquer	1-1b
convoyer	1-7a
convulser	1-1
convulsionner	1-1
coopérer	1-5
coopter	1-1
coordonner	1-1
copermuter	1-1
copier	1-1c
copiloter	1-1
copiner	1-1
coposséder	1-5
coproduire	5-9a
copuler	1-1
coqueter	1-3b
cordeler	1-3a
corder	1-1
cordonner	1-1
cornaquer	1-1b
corner	1-1
correctionnaliser	1-1
corréler	1-5
correspondre	5-1a
corriger	1-2b
corroborer	1-1
corroder	1-1
corrompre	5-1b
corroyer	1-7a
corser	1-1
corseter	1-4
cosigner	1-1

Verb	Model #
cosmétiquer	1-1b
costumer	1-1
coter	1-1
cotiser	1-1
cotonner (se)	1-1
côtoyer	1-7a
couchailler	1-1
coucher	1-1
couder	1-1
coudoyer	1-7a
coudre	*5-14*
couillonner	1-1
couiner	1-1
couler	1-1
coulisser	1-1
coupailler (coupasser)	1-1
couper	1-1
coupler	1-1
courbaturer	1-1
courber	1-1
courir	*6-4*
couronner	1-1
courre	DEF
courroucer	1-2a
courser	1-1
courtauder	1-1
court-circuiter	1-1
courtiser	1-1
cousiner	1-1
coûter	1-1
couver	1-1
couvrir	*3-1*
cracher	1-1
crachiner (IMP)	1-1
crachoter	1-1
crachouiller	1-1
crailler	1-1
craindre	5-12
cramer	1-1
cramponner	1-1
crâner	1-1
cranter	1-1
crapahuter	1-1

Verb	Model #	Verb	Model #
crapoter	1-1	crouler	1-1
craqueler	1-3a	croupir	2-1
craquer	1-1b	croustiller	1-1
craqueter	1-3b	croûter	1-1
crasher (se)	1-1	crucifier	1-1c
cravacher	1-1	crypter	1-1
cravater	1-1	cryptographier	1-1c
crawler	1-1	cuber	1-1
crayonner	1-1	*cueillir*	*3-2b*
crécher	1-5	cuirasser	1-1
crédibiliser	1-1	cuire	5-9a
créditer	1-1	cuisiner	1-1
créer	1-1	cuiter (se)	1-1
crémer	1-5	cuivrer	1-1
créneler	1-3a	culbuter	1-1
créner	1-5	culer	1-1
créoliser	1-1	culminer	1-1
crêper	1-1	culotter	1-1
crépir	2-1	culpabiliser	1-1
crépiter	1-1	cultiver	1-1
crétiniser	1-1	cumuler	1-1
creuser	1-1	curer	1-1
crevasser	1-1	cureter	1-3b
crever	1-4	customiser	1-1
criailler	1-1	cuveler	1-3a
cribler	1-1	cuver	1-1
crier	1-1c	cyanoser	1-1
criminaliser	1-1	cylindrer	1-1
criser	1-1	dactylographier	1-1c
crisper	1-1	daigner	1-1
crisser	1-1	daller	1-1
cristalliser	1-1	damasquiner	1-1
criticailler	1-1	damasser	1-1
critiquer	1-1b	damer	1-1
croasser	1-1	damner	1-1
crocher	1-1	dandiner	1-1
crocheter	1-4	danser	1-1
croire	*5-18*	dansoter (dansotter)	1-1
croiser	1-1	darder	1-1
croître	*5-19a*	dater	1-1
croquer	1-1b	dauber	1-1
crosser	1-1	dealer	1-1
crotter	1-1	déambuler	1-1

Verb	Model #
débâcler	1-1
débagouler	1-1
débâillonner	1-1
déballer	1-1
déballonner (se)	1-1
débanaliser	1-1
débander	1-1
débaptiser	1-1
débarbouiller	1-1
débarder	1-1
débarquer	1-1b
débarrasser	1-1
débarrer	1-1
débâter	1-1
débâtir	2-1
débattre	5-3
débaucher	1-1
débecter	1-1
débenzoler	1-1
débiliter	1-1
débillarder	1-1
débiner	1-1
débiter	1-1
déblatérer	1-5
déblayer	1-7b
débloquer	1-1b
débobiner	1-1
déboguer	1-1a
déboiser	1-1
déboîter	1-1
débonder	1-1
déborder	1-1
débosseler	1-3a
débotter	1-1
déboucher	1-1
déboucler	1-1
débouler	1-1
déboulonner	1-1
débouquer	1-1b
débourber	1-1
débourrer	1-1
débourser	1-1
déboussoler	1-1
débouter	1-1
déboutonner	1-1
débraguetter	1-1
débrailler (se)	1-1
débrancher	1-1
débrayer	1-7b
débrider	1-1
débriefer	1-1
débrocher	1-1
débrouiller	1-1
débroussailler	1-1
débucher	1-1
débudgétiser	1-1
débureaucratiser	1-1
débusquer	1-1b
débuter	1-1
décacheter	1-3b
décaisser	1-1
décalaminer	1-1
décalcifier	1-1c
décaler	1-1
décalotter	1-1
décalquer	1-1b
décamper	1-1
décaniller	1-1
décanter	1-1
décapeler	1-3a
décaper	1-1
décapitaliser	1-1
décapiter	1-1
décapoter	1-1
décapsuler	1-1
décapuchonner	1-1
décarbonater	1-1
décarburer	1-1
décarcasser (se)	1-1
décarreler	1-3a
décatir	2-1
décauser	1-1
décavaillonner	1-1
décaver	1-1
décéder	1-5
déceler	1-4

Verb	Model #	Verb	Model #
décélérer	1-5	décolérer	1-5
décentraliser	1-1	décoller	1-1
décentrer	1-1	décolleter	1-3b
décercler	1-1	décoloniser	1-1
décérébrer	1-5	décolorer	1-1
décerner	1-1	décommander	1-1
décerveler	1-3a	décommettre	5-4
décevoir	4-2b	décommuniser	1-1
déchaîner	1-1	décompacter	1-1
déchanter	1-1	décompenser	1-1
déchaperonner	1-1	décomplexer	1-1
décharger	1-2b	décomposer	1-1
décharner	1-1	décompresser	1-1
déchaumer	1-1	décomprimer	1-1
déchausser	1-1	décompter	1-1
déchiffonner	1-1	déconcentrer	1-1
déchiffrer	1-1	déconcerter	1-1
déchiqueter	1-3b	déconditionner	1-1
déchirer	1-1	décongeler	1-4
déchlorurer	1-1	décongestionner	1-1
déchoir	DEF	déconnecter	1-1
déchristianiser	1-1	déconner	1-1
décider	1-1	déconseiller	1-1
décimaliser	1-1	déconsidérer	1-5
décimer	1-1	déconsigner	1-1
décintrer	1-1	déconstruire	5-9a
déclamer	1-1	décontaminer	1-1
déclarer	1-1	décontenancer	1-2a
déclasser	1-1	décontracter	1-1
déclassifier	1-1c	décorder	1-1
déclaveter	1-3b	décorer	1-1
déclencher	1-1	décorner	1-1
décléricaliser	1-1	décortiquer	1-1b
décliner	1-1	découcher	1-1
décliqueter	1-3b	découdre	5-14
décloisonner	1-1	découler	1-1
déclore	DEF	découper	1-1
déclouer	1-1	découpler	1-1
décocher	1-1	décourager	1-2b
décoder	1-1	découronner	1-1
décoffrer	1-1	découvrir	3-1
décoiffer	1-1	décrasser	1-1
décoincer	1-2a	décrédibiliser	1-1

Verb	Model #	Verb	Model #
décréditer	1-1	déferler	1-1
décrêper	1-1	déferrer	1-1
décrépir	2-1	défeuiller	1-1
décréter	1-5	défeutrer	1-1
décreuser	1-1	défibrer	1-1
décrier	1-1c	déficeler	1-3a
décrire	5-7	défier	1-1c
décrisper	1-1	défier (se)	1-1c
décrocher	1-1	défigurer	1-1
décroiser	1-1	défiler	1-1
décroître	5-19b	définir	2-1
décrotter	1-1	défiscaliser	1-1
décruer	1-1	déflagrer	1-1
décruser	1-1	défléchir	2-1
décrypter	1-1	défleurir	2-1
décuivrer	1-1	déflorer	1-1
déculasser	1-1	défolier	1-1c
déculotter	1-1	défoncer	1-2a
déculpabiliser	1-1	déforcer	1-2a
décupler	1-1	déforester	1-1
décuver	1-1	déformer	1-1
dédaigner	1-1	défouler	1-1
dédicacer	1-2a	défourailler	1-1
dédier	1-1c	défourner	1-1
dédifférencier (se)	1-1c	défraîchir	2-1
dédire	5-8b	défrayer	1-7b
dédommager	1-2b	défricher	1-1
dédorer	1-1	défriper	1-1
dédouaner	1-1	défriser	1-1
dédoubler	1-1	défroisser	1-1
dédramatiser	1-1	défroncer	1-2a
déduire	5-9a	défroquer	1-1b
défaillir	3-2a	défruiter	1-1
défaire	5-23	dégager	1-2b
défalquer	1-1b	dégainer	1-1
défatiguer	1-1a	déganter	1-1
défaufiler	1-1	dégarnir	2-1
défausser	1-1	dégauchir	2-1
défavoriser	1-1	dégazer	1-1
défendre	5-1a	dégazoliner (dégasoliner)	1-1
défenestrer	1-1	dégazonner	1-1
déféquer	1-5	dégeler	1-4
déférer	1-5	dégénérer	1-5

Verb	Model #
dégermer	1-1
dégivrer	1-1
déglacer	1-2a
déglinguer	1-1a
dégluer	1-1
déglutir	2-1
dégober	1-1
dégobiller	1-1
dégoiser	1-1
dégommer	1-1
dégonfler	1-1
dégorger	1-2b
dégoter (dégotter)	1-1
dégouliner	1-1
dégoupiller	1-1
dégourdir	2-1
dégoûter	1-1
dégoutter	1-1
dégrader	1-1
dégrafer	1-1
dégraisser	1-1
dégravoyer	1-7a
dégréer	1-1
dégrever	1-4
dégringoler	1-1
dégripper	1-1
dégriser	1-1
dégrosser	1-1
dégrossir	2-1
dégrouiller (se)	1-1
dégrouper	1-1
déguerpir	2-1
dégueulasser	1-1
dégueuler	1-1
déguiser	1-1
dégurgiter	1-1
déguster	1-1
déhaler	1-1
déhancher (se)	1-1
déharnacher	1-1
déhotter	1-1
déhouiller	1-1
déifier	1-1c
déjanter	1-1
déjauger	1-2b
déjeter	1-3b
déjeuner	1-1
déjouer	1-1
déjucher	1-1
déjuger (se)	1-2b
délabialiser	1-1
délabrer	1-1
délabyrinther	1-1
délacer	1-2a
délainer	1-1
délaisser	1-1
délaiter	1-1
délarder	1-1
délasser	1-1
délaver	1-1
délayer	1-7b
déléaturer	1-1
délecter	1-1
délégitimer	1-1
déléguer	1-5
délester	1-1
délibérer	1-5
délier	1-1c
délignifier	1-1c
délimiter	1-1
délinéamenter	1-1
délinéer	1-1
délirer	1-1
déliter	1-1
délivrer	1-1
délocaliser	1-1
déloger	1-2b
délurer	1-1
délustrer	1-1
déluter	1-1
démagnétiser	1-1
démaigrir	2-1
démailler	1-1
démailloter	1-1
démancher	1-1
demander	1-1

Verb	Model #	Verb	Model #
démanger	1-2b	démultiplier	1-1c
démanteler	1-4	démunir	2-1
démantibuler	1-1	démuseler	1-3a
démaquiller	1-1	démutiser	1-1
démarcher	1-1	démyéliniser	1-1
démarier	1-1c	démystifier	1-1c
démarquer	1-1b	démythifier	1-1c
démarrer	1-1	dénasaliser	1-1
démascler	1-1	dénationaliser	1-1
démasquer	1-1b	dénatter	1-1
démastiquer	1-1b	dénaturaliser	1-1
démâter	1-1	dénaturer	1-1
dématérialiser	1-1	dénazifier	1-1c
démédicaliser	1-1	dénébuler (dénébuliser)	1-1
démêler	1-1	déneiger	1-2b
démembrer	1-1	déniaiser	1-1
déménager	1-2b	dénicher	1-1
démener (se)	1-4	dénicotiniser	1-1
démentir	6-1	dénier	1-1c
démerder (se)	1-1	dénigrer	1-1
démériter	1-1	dénitrifier	1-1c
démettre	5-4	déniveler	1-3a
démeubler	1-1	dénombrer	1-1
demeurer	1-1	dénommer	1-1
démieller	1-1	dénoncer	1-2a
démilitariser	1-1	dénoter	1-1
déminer	1-1	dénouer	1-1
déminéraliser	1-1	dénoyauter	1-1
démissionner	1-1	dénoyer	1-7a
démobiliser	1-1	densifier	1-1c
démocratiser	1-1	denteler	1-3a
démoder	1-1	dénucléariser	1-1
démoduler	1-1	dénuder	1-1
démolir	2-1	dénuer (se)	1-1
démonétiser	1-1	dépailler	1-1
démonter	1-1	dépalisser	1-1
démontrer	1-1	dépanner	1-1
démoraliser	1-1	dépaqueter	1-3b
démordre	5-1a	déparasiter	1-1
démotiver	1-1	dépareiller	1-1
démoucheter	1-3b	déparer	1-1
démouler	1-1	déparier	1-1c
démoustiquer	1-1b	déparler	1-1

Verb	Model #
départager	1-2b
départementaliser	1-1
départir	6-1
dépasser	1-1
dépassionner	1-1
dépatouiller (se)	1-1
dépatrier	1-1c
dépaver	1-1
dépayser	1-1
dépecer	*1-6a*
dépêcher	1-1
dépeigner	1-1
dépeindre	5-12
dépénaliser	1-1
dépendre	5-1a
dépenser	1-1
dépérir	2-1
dépersonnaliser	1-1
dépêtrer	1-1
dépeupler	1-1
déphaser	1-1
déphosphorer	1-1
dépiauter	1-1
dépiler	1-1
dépiquer	1-1b
dépister	1-1
dépiter	1-1
déplacer	1-2a
déplafonner	1-1
déplaire	5-22a
déplanter	1-1
déplâtrer	1-1
déplier	1-1c
déplisser	1-1
déplomber	1-1
déplorer	1-1
déployer	1-7a
déplumer	1-1
dépoétiser	1-1
dépointer	1-1
dépoitrailler (se)	1-1
dépolariser	1-1
dépolir	2-1

Verb	Model #
dépolitiser	1-1
dépolluer	1-1
dépolymériser	1-1
déporter	1-1
déposer	1-1
déposséder	1-5
dépoter	1-1
dépouiller	1-1
dépoussiérer	1-5
dépraver	1-1
déprécier	1-1c
déprendre (se)	5-2
dépressuriser	1-1
déprimer	1-1
dépriser	1-1
déprogrammer	1-1
déprolétariser	1-1
déprotéger	1-6c
dépuceler	1-3a
dépulper	1-1
dépurer	1-1
députer	1-1
déqualifier	1-1c
déraciner	1-1
dérader	1-1
dérager	1-2b
déraidir	2-1
dérailler	1-1
déraisonner	1-1
déramer	1-1
déranger	1-2b
déraper	1-1
déraser	1-1
dératiser	1-1
dérayer	1-7b
déréaliser	1-1
déréglementer	1-1
dérégler	1-5
déresponsabiliser	1-1
dérider	1-1
dériver	1-1
dérober	1-1
dérocher	1-1

Verb	Model #
déroder	1-1
déroger	1-2b
dérougir	2-1
dérouiller	1-1
dérouler	1-1
dérouter	1-1
désabonner	1-1
désabuser	1-1
désaccentuer	1-1
désacclimater	1-1
désaccorder	1-1
désaccoupler	1-1
désaccoutumer	1-1
désacidifier	1-1c
désaciérer	1-5
désacraliser	1-1
désactiver	1-1
désadapter	1-1
désaérer	1-5
désaffecter	1-1
désaffectionner (se)	1-1
désaffilier	1-1c
désagrafer	1-1
désagréger	1-6c
désaimanter	1-1
désaisonnaliser	1-1
désajuster	1-1
désaliéner	1-5
désaligner	1-1
désalper	1-1
désaltérer	1-5
désambiguïser	1-1
désamianter	1-1
désamidonner	1-1
désaminer	1-1
désamorcer	1-2a
désapparier	1-1c
désappointer	1-1
désapprendre	5-2
désapprouver	1-1
désapprovisionner	1-1
désarçonner	1-1
désargenter	1-1
désarmer	1-1
désarrimer	1-1
désarticuler	1-1
désassembler	1-1
désassimiler	1-1
désassortir	2-1
désatomiser	1-1
désavantager	1-2b
désavouer	1-1
désaxer	1-1
desceller	1-1
descendre	5-1a
déséchouer	1-1
désectoriser	1-1
désembobiner	1-1
désembourber	1-1
désembourgeoiser	1-1
désembouteiller	1-1
désembuer	1-1
désemparer	1-1
désemplir	2-1
désencadrer (décadrer)	1-1
désenchaîner	1-1
désenchanter	1-1
désenclaver	1-1
désencombrer	1-1
désencrasser	1-1
désendetter (se)	1-1
désénerver	1-1
désenfler	1-1
désenfumer	1-1
désengager	1-2b
désengluer	1-1
désengorger	1-2b
désengourdir	2-1
désengrener	1-4
désenivrer	1-1
désennuyer	1-7a
désenrayer	1-7b
désensabler	1-1
désensibiliser	1-1
désensorceler	1-3a
désentoiler	1-1

Verb	Model #
désentortiller	1-1
désentraver	1-1
désenvaser	1-1
désenvenimer	1-1
désenverguer	1-1a
désenvoûter	1-1
désépaissir	2-1
déséquilibrer	1-1
déséquiper	1-1
déserter	1-1
désertifier (se)	1-1c
désespérer	1-5
désétatiser	1-1
désexciter	1-1
désexualiser	1-1
déshabiller	1-1
déshabituer	1-1
désherber	1-1
déshériter	1-1
déshonorer	1-1
déshuiler	1-1
déshumaniser	1-1
déshydrater	1-1
déshydrogéner	1-5
déshypothéquer	1-5
désigner	1-1
désillusionner	1-1
désincarner	1-1
désincruster	1-1
désindexer	1-1
désindustrialiser	1-1
désinfecter	1-1
désinformer	1-1
désinhiber	1-1
désinsectiser	1-1
désinstaller	1-1
désintégrer	1-5
désintéresser	1-1
désintoxiquer	1-1b
désinvestir	2-1
désirer	1-1
désister (se)	1-1
désobéir	2-1

Verb	Model #
désobliger	1-2b
désobstruer	1-1
désocialiser	1-1
désodoriser	1-1
désoler	1-1
désolidariser	1-1
désoperculer	1-1
désopiler	1-1
désorbiter	1-1
désorganiser	1-1
désorienter	1-1
désosser	1-1
désoxygéner	1-5
desquamer	1-1
dessabler	1-1
dessaisir	2-1
dessaler	1-1
dessangler	1-1
dessaper (désaper)	1-1
dessécher	1-5
desseller	1-1
desserrer	1-1
dessertir	2-1
desservir	6-1
dessiller	1-1
dessiner	1-1
dessoler	1-1
dessouder	1-1
dessoûler (dessaouler)	1-1
dessuinter	1-1
déstabiliser	1-1
déstaliniser	1-1
destiner	1-1
destituer	1-1
déstocker	1-1
déstructurer	1-1
désulfiter	1-1
désulfurer	1-1
désunir	2-1
désynchroniser	1-1
détacher	1-1
détailler	1-1
détaler	1-1

Verb	Model #
détartrer	1-1
détaxer	1-1
détecter	1-1
déteindre	5-12
dételer	1-3a
détendre	5-1a
détenir	6-7
déterger	1-2b
détériorer	1-1
déterminer	1-1
déterrer	1-1
détester	1-1
détirer	1-1
détoner	1-1
détonner	1-1
détordre	5-1a
détortiller	1-1
détourer	1-1
détourner	1-1
détoxiquer	1-1b
détracter	1-1
détraquer	1-1b
détremper	1-1
détromper	1-1
détrôner	1-1
détroquer	1-1b
détrousser	1-1
détruire	5-9a
dévaler	1-1
dévaliser	1-1
dévaloriser	1-1
dévaluer	1-1
devancer	1-2a
dévaster	1-1
développer	1-1
devenir	6-7
dévergonder (se)	1-1
déverguer	1-1a
dévernir	2-1
déverrouiller	1-1
déverser	1-1
dévêtir	6-6
dévider	1-1
dévier	1-1c
deviner	1-1
dévirer	1-1
dévirginiser	1-1
déviriliser	1-1
dévisager	1-2b
deviser	1-1
dévisser	1-1
dévitaliser	1-1
dévitrifier	1-1c
dévoiler	1-1
devoir	*4-2a*
dévolter	1-1
dévorer	1-1
dévouer	1-1
dévoyer	1-7a
diaboliser	1-1
diagnostiquer	1-1b
dialectiser	1-1
dialoguer	1-1a
dialyser	1-1
diamanter	1-1
diaphragmer	1-1
diaprer	1-1
dicter	1-1
diéser	1-5
diffamer	1-1
différencier	1-1c
différentier	1-1c
différer	1-5
diffracter	1-1
diffuser	1-1
digérer	1-5
digitaliser	1-1
digresser	1-1
dilacérer	1-5
dilapider	1-1
dilater	1-1
diligenter	1-1
diluer	1-1
dimensionner	1-1
diminuer	1-1
dîner	1-1

Verb	Model #
dinguer	1-1a
diphtonguer	1-1a
diplômer	1-1
dire	*5-8a*
diriger	1-2b
discerner	1-1
discipliner	1-1
discontinuer	1-1
disconvenir	6-7
discorder	1-1
discounter	1-1
discourir	6-4
discréditer	1-1
discrétiser	1-1
discriminer	1-1
disculper	1-1
discutailler	1-1
discuter	1-1
disgracier	1-1c
disjoindre	5-12
disjoncter	1-1
disloquer	1-1b
disparaître	5-20
dispatcher	1-1
dispenser	1-1
disperser	1-1
disposer	1-1
disputailler	1-1
disputer	1-1
disqualifier	1-1c
disséminer	1-1
disséquer	1-5
disserter	1-1
dissimuler	1-1
dissiper	1-1
dissocier	1-1c
dissoner	1-1
dissoudre	5-13a
dissuader	1-1
distancer	1-2a
distancier	1-1c
distendre	5-1a
distiller	1-1

Verb	Model #
distinguer	1-1a
distordre	5-1a
distraire	5-24
distribuer	1-1
divaguer	1-1a
diverger	1-2b
diversifier	1-1c
divertir	2-1
diviniser	1-1
diviser	1-1
divorcer	1-2a
divulguer	1-1a
documenter	1-1
dodeliner	1-1
dogmatiser	1-1
doigter	1-1
doler	1-1
domestiquer	1-1b
domicilier	1-1c
dominer	1-1
dompter	1-1
donner	1-1
doper	1-1
dorer	1-1
dorloter	1-1
dormir	*6-1*
doser	1-1
doter	1-1
double-cliquer	1-1b
doubler	1-1
doublonner	1-1
doucher	1-1
doucir	2-1
douer (DEF)	1-1
douiller	1-1
douter	1-1
dracher (IMP)	1-1
dragéifier	1-1c
drageonner	1-1
draguer	1-1a
drainer	1-1
dramatiser	1-1
draper	1-1

Verb	Model #	Verb	Model #
draver	1-1	écarteler	1-4
drayer	1-7b	écarter	1-1
dresser	1-1	échafauder	1-1
dribbler	1-1	échalasser	1-1
dribler	1-1	échancrer	1-1
driver	1-1	échanger	1-2b
droguer	1-1a	échantillonner	1-1
droper (dropper)	1-1	échapper	1-1
drosser	1-1	échardonner	1-1
duper	1-1	écharner	1-1
duplexer	1-1	écharper	1-1
dupliquer	1-1b	échauder	1-1
durcir	2-1	échauffer	1-1
durer	1-1	échelonner	1-1
duveter (se)	1-4	écheniller	1-1
dynamiser	1-1	écher	1-5
dynamiter	1-1	écheveler	1-3a
ébahir	2-1	échiner	1-1
ébarber	1-1	échoir	DEF
ébattre (s')	5-3	échopper	1-1
ébaucher	1-1	échouer	1-1
ébaudir	2-1	écimer	1-1
ébavurer	1-1	éclabousser	1-1
ébiseler	1-3a	éclaircir	2-1
éblouir	2-1	éclairer	1-1
éborgner	1-1	éclater	1-1
ébouillanter	1-1	éclipser	1-1
ébouler	1-1	éclisser	1-1
ébourgeonner	1-1	éclore	DEF
ébouriffer	1-1	écluser	1-1
ébourrer	1-1	écobuer	1-1
ébouter	1-1	écœurer	1-1
ébrancher	1-1	éconduire	5-9a
ébranler	1-1	économiser	1-1
ébraser	1-1	écoper	1-1
ébrécher	1-5	écorcer	1-2a
ébrouer (s')	1-1	écorcher	1-1
ébruiter	1-1	écorner	1-1
écacher	1-1	écornifler	1-1
écailler	1-1	écosser	1-1
écaler	1-1	écouler	1-1
écanguer	1-1a	écourter	1-1
écarquiller	1-1	écouter	1-1

Verb	Model #
écouvillonner	1-1
écrabouiller	1-1
écraser	1-1
écrémer	1-5
écrêter	1-1
écrier (s')	1-1c
écrire	*5-7*
écrivailler	1-1
écrivasser	1-1
écrouer	1-1
écrouir	2-1
écrouler (s')	1-1
écroûter	1-1
écuisser	1-1
écumer	1-1
écurer	1-1
écussonner	1-1
édenter	1-1
édicter	1-1
édifier	1-1c
éditer	1-1
éditionner	1-1
édulcorer	1-1
éduquer	1-1b
éfaufiler	1-1
effacer	1-2a
effarer	1-1
effaroucher	1-1
effectuer	1-1
efféminer	1-1
effeuiller	1-1
effiler	1-1
effilocher (effiloquer)	1-1 (1-1b)
effleurer	1-1
effleurir	2-1
effondrer	1-1
efforcer (s')	1-2a
effranger	1-2b
effrayer	1-7b
effriter	1-1
égailler (s')	1-1
égaler	1-1
égaliser	1-1

Verb	Model #
égarer	1-1
égayer	1-7b
égorger	1-2b
égosiller (s')	1-1
égoutter	1-1
égrapper	1-1
égratigner	1-1
égravillonner	1-1
égrener (égrainer)	1-4 (1-1)
égriser	1-1
égruger	1-2b
égueuler	1-1
éjaculer	1-1
éjecter	1-1
éjointer	1-1
élaborer	1-1
élaguer	1-1a
élancer	1-2a
élargir	2-1
électrifier	1-1c
électriser	1-1
électrocuter	1-1
électrolyser	1-1
élégir	2-1
élever	1-4
élider	1-1
élimer	1-1
éliminer	1-1
élinguer	1-1a
élire	5-10
éloigner	1-1
élonger	1-2b
élucider	1-1
élucubrer	1-1
éluder	1-1
éluer	1-1
émacier	1-1c
émailler	1-1
émanciper	1-1
émaner	1-1
émarger	1-2b
émasculer	1-1
emballer	1-1

Verb	Model #	Verb	Model #
embarbouiller	1-1	émietter	1-1
embarquer	1-1b	émigrer	1-1
embarrasser	1-1	émincer	1-2a
embarrer	1-1	emmagasiner	1-1
embastiller	1-1	emmailloter	1-1
embattre	5-3	emmancher	1-1
embaucher	1-1	emmêler	1-1
embaumer	1-1	emménager	1-2b
embellir	2-1	emmener	1-4
emberlificoter	1-1	emmerder	1-1
embêter	1-1	emmétrer	1-5
emblaver	1-1	emmieller	1-1
embobeliner	1-1	emmitoufler	1-1
embobiner	1-1	emmouscailler	1-1
emboîter	1-1	emmurer	1-1
embosser	1-1	émonder	1-1
emboucher	1-1	émorfiler	1-1
embouquer	1-1b	émotionner	1-1
embourber	1-1	émotter	1-1
embourgeoiser	1-1	émousser	1-1
embouteiller	1-1	émoustiller	1-1
embouter	1-1	émouvoir	4-3b
emboutir	2-1	empailler	1-1
embrancher	1-1	empaler	1-1
embraquer	1-1b	empanner	1-1
embraser	1-1	empaqueter	1-3b
embrasser	1-1	emparer (s')	1-1
embrayer	1-7b	empâter	1-1
embrever	1-4	empatter	1-1
embrigader	1-1	empaumer	1-1
embringuer	1-1a	empêcher	1-1
embrocher	1-1	empenner	1-1
embroncher	1-1	emperler	1-1
embrouiller	1-1	empeser	1-4
embroussailler	1-1	empester	1-1
embrumer	1-1	empêtrer	1-1
embuer	1-1	empierrer	1-1
embusquer	1-1b	empiéter	1-5
émécher	1-5	empiffrer (s')	1-1
émerger	1-2b	empiler	1-1
émeriser	1-1	empirer	1-1
émerveiller	1-1	emplafonner	1-1
émettre	5-4	emplir	2-1

Verb	Model #
employer	*1-7a*
empocher	1-1
empoigner	1-1
empoisonner	1-1
empoissonner	1-1
emporter	1-1
empoter	1-1
empourprer	1-1
empoussiérer	1-5
empreindre	5-12
empresser (s')	1-1
emprésurer	1-1
emprisonner	1-1
emprunter	1-1
empuantir	2-1
émuler	1-1
émulsifier	1-1c
émulsionner	1-1
enamourer (s') (énamourer)	1-1
encabaner	1-1
encadrer	1-1
encager	1-2b
encagouler	1-1
encaisser	1-1
encanailler (s')	1-1
encapsuler	1-1
encapuchonner	1-1
encaquer	1-1b
encarter (encartonner)	1-1
encaserner	1-1
encastrer	1-1
encaustiquer	1-1b
encaver	1-1
enceindre	5-12
encenser	1-1
encercler	1-1
enchaîner	1-1
enchanter	1-1
enchâsser	1-1
enchatonner	1-1
enchausser	1-1
enchemiser	1-1
enchérir	2-1
enchevaucher	1-1
enchevêtrer	1-1
enclaver	1-1
enclencher	1-1
encliqueter	1-3b
enclore	DEF
enclouer	1-1
encocher	1-1
encoder	1-1
encoller	1-1
encombrer	1-1
encorder (s')	1-1
encorner	1-1
encourager	1-2b
encourir	6-4
encrasser	1-1
encrer	1-1
encroûter	1-1
enculer	1-1
encuver	1-1
endenter	1-1
endetter	1-1
endeuiller	1-1
endêver	1-1
endiabler	1-1
endiguer	1-1a
endimancher (s')	1-1
endoctriner	1-1
endommager	1-2b
endormir	6-1
endosser	1-1
enduire	5-9a
endurcir	2-1
endurer	1-1
énerver	1-1
enfaîter	1-1
enfanter	1-1
enfariner	1-1
enfermer	1-1
enferrer	1-1
enficher	1-1
enfieller	1-1
enfiévrer	1-5

Verb	Model #	Verb	Model #
enfiler	1-1	enkyster (s')	1-1
enflammer	1-1	enlacer	1-2a
enfler	1-1	enlaidir	2-1
enfleurer	1-1	enlever	1-4
enfoncer	1-2a	enliasser	1-1
enfouir	2-1	enlier	1-1c
enfourcher	1-1	enliser	1-1
enfourner	1-1	enluminer	1-1
enfreindre	5-12	ennoblir	2-1
enfuir (s')	6-2	ennuager	1-2b
enfumer	1-1	ennuyer	1-7a
enfutailler	1-1	énoncer	1-2a
enfûter	1-1	enorgueillir	2-1
engager	1-2b	énouer	1-1
engainer	1-1	enquérir (s')	6-3
engazonner	1-1	enquêter	1-1
engendrer	1-1	enquiquiner	1-1
englober	1-1	enraciner	1-1
engloutir	2-1	enrager	1-2b
engluer	1-1	enrayer	1-7b
engober	1-1	enrégimenter	1-1
engommer	1-1	enregistrer	1-1
engoncer	1-2a	enrésiner	1-1
engorger	1-2b	enrhumer	1-1
engouer (s')	1-1	enrichir	2-1
engouffrer	1-1	enrober	1-1
engourdir	2-1	enrocher	1-1
engraisser	1-1	enrôler	1-1
engranger	1-2b	enrouer	1-1
engraver	1-1	enrouler	1-1
engrener	1-4	enrubanner	1-1
engrosser	1-1	ensabler	1-1
engueuler	1-1	ensacher	1-1
enguirlander	1-1	ensanglanter	1-1
enhardir	2-1	ensauvager	1-2b
enharnacher	1-1	enseigner	1-1
enherber	1-1	ensemencer	1-2a
enivrer	1-1	enserrer	1-1
enjamber	1-1	ensevelir	2-1
enjoindre	5-12	ensiler	1-1
enjôler	1-1	ensoleiller	1-1
enjoliver	1-1	ensorceler	1-3a
enjuiver	1-1	ensuivre (s') (DEF)	5-5

Verb	Model #
entabler	1-1
entacher	1-1
entailler	1-1
entamer	1-1
entarter	1-1
entartrer	1-1
entasser	1-1
entendre	5-1a
enténébrer	1-5
enter	1-1
entériner	1-1
enterrer	1-1
entêter	1-1
enthousiasmer	1-1
enticher	1-1
entoiler	1-1
entôler	1-1
entonner	1-1
entortiller	1-1
entourer	1-1
entraccuser (s')	1-1
entradmirer (s')	1-1
entraider (s')	1-1
entraîner	1-1
entrapercevoir	4-2b
entraver	1-1
entrebâiller	1-1
entrechoquer	1-1b
entrecouper	1-1
entrecroiser	1-1
entre(-)déchirer (s')	1-1
entre(-)détruire (s')	5-9a
entre(-)dévorer (s')	1-1
entr(e-)égorger (s')	1-2b
entrelacer	1-2a
entrelarder	1-1
entre(-)manger (s')	1-2b
entremêler	1-1
entremettre (s')	5-4
entre(-)nuire (s')	5-9b
entreposer	1-1
entreprendre	5-2
entrer	1-1
entre(-)regarder (s')	1-1
entretailler (s')	1-1
entretenir	6-7
entretoiser	1-1
entre(-)tuer (s')	1-1
entrevoir	4-1a
entrevoûter	1-1
entrouvrir	3-1
entuber	1-1
énucléer	1-1
énumérer	1-5
envahir	2-1
envaser	1-1
envelopper	1-1
envenimer	1-1
enverguer	1-1a
envider	1-1
envier	1-1c
environner	1-1
envisager	1-2b
envoiler (s')	1-1
envoler (s')	1-1
envoûter	1-1
envoyer	*1-8*
épaissir	2-1
épamprer	1-1
épancher	1-1
épandre	5-1a
épanneler	1-3a
épanouir	2-1
épargner	1-1
éparpiller	1-1
épater	1-1
épaufrer	1-1
épauler	1-1
épeler	1-3a
épépiner	1-1
éperonner	1-1
épeurer	1-1
épicer	1-2a
épier	1-1c
épierrer	1-1
épiler	1-1

Verb	Model #
épiloguer	1-1a
épincer (épinceter)	1-2a (1-3b)
épiner	1-1
épingler	1-1
épisser	1-1
éployer	1-7a
éplucher	1-1
épointer	1-1
éponger	1-2b
épontiller	1-1
épouiller	1-1
époumoner (s')	1-1
épouser	1-1
épousseter	1-3b
époustoufler	1-1
époutir	2-1
épouvanter	1-1
épreindre	5-12
éprendre (s')	5-2
éprouver	1-1
épucer	1-2a
épuiser	1-1
épurer	1-1
équarrir	2-1
équerrer	1-1
équeuter	1-1
équilibrer	1-1
équiper	1-1
équivaloir	4-5a
équivoquer	1-1b
éradiquer	1-1b
érafler	1-1
érailler	1-1
éreinter	1-1
ergoter	1-1
ériger	1-2b
éroder	1-1
érotiser	1-1
errer	1-1
éructer	1-1
esbigner (s')	1-1
esbroufer	1-1
escalader	1-1

Verb	Model #
escamoter	1-1
escher/aicher (écher)	1-1 (1-5)
esclaffer (s')	1-1
esclavager	1-2b
escompter	1-1
escorter	1-1
escrimer (s')	1-1
escroquer	1-1b
espacer	1-2a
espérer	1-5
espionner	1-1
esquicher	1-1
esquinter	1-1
esquisser	1-1
esquiver	1-1
essaimer	1-1
essanger	1-2b
essarter	1-1
essayer	1-7b
essorer	1-1
essoriller	1-1
essoucher	1-1
essouffler	1-1
essuyer	*1-7a*
estamper	1-1
estampiller	1-1
ester	DEF
estérifier	1-1c
esthétiser	1-1
estimer	1-1
estiver	1-1
estomaquer	1-1b
estomper	1-1
estoquer	1-1b
estourbir	2-1
estrapader	1-1
estrapasser	1-1
estropier	1-1c
établir	2-1
étager	1-2b
étalager	1-2b
étaler	1-1
étalinguer	1-1a

Verb	Model #	Verb	Model #
étalonner	1-1	évaluer	1-1
étamer	1-1	évangéliser	1-1
étamper	1-1	évanouir (s')	2-1
étancher	1-1	évaporer	1-1
étançonner	1-1	évaser	1-1
étarquer	1-1b	éveiller	1-1
étatiser	1-1	éventer	1-1
étayer	1-7b	éventrer	1-1
éteindre	5-12	évertuer (s')	1-1
étendre	5-1a	évider	1-1
éterniser	1-1	évincer	1-2a
éternuer	1-1	éviscérer	1-5
étêter	1-1	éviter	1-1
éthérifier	1-1c	évoluer	1-1
éthériser	1-1	évoquer	1-1b
ethniciser	1-1	exacerber	1-1
étinceler	1-3a	exagérer	1-5
étioler	1-1	exalter	1-1
étiqueter	1-3b	examiner	1-1
étirer	1-1	exaspérer	1 5
étoffer	1-1	exaucer	1-2a
étoiler	1-1	excaver	1-1
étonner	1-1	excéder	1-5
étouffer	1-1	exceller	1-1
étouper	1-1	excentrer	1-1
étourdir	2-1	excepter	1-1
étrangler	1-1	exciper	1-1
être	*7*	exciser	1-1
étrécir	2-1	exciter	1-1
étreindre	5-12	exclamer (s')	1-1
étrenner	1-1	*exclure*	*5-16a*
étrésillonner	1-1	excommunier	1-1c
étriller	1-1	excorier	1-1c
étriper	1-1	excréter	1-5
étriquer	1-1b	excursionner	1-1
étronçonner	1-1	excuser	1-1
étudier	1-1c	exécrer	1-5
étuver	1-1	exécuter	1-1
euphoriser	1-1	exemplifier	1-1c
européaniser	1-1	exempter	1-1
euthanasier	1-1c	exercer	1-2a
évacuer	1-1	exfiltrer	1-1
évader (s')	1-1	exfolier	1-1c

Verb	Model #	Verb	Model #
exhaler	1-1	exulcérer	1-5
exhausser	1-1	exulter	1-1
exhéréder	1-5	*fabriquer*	*1-1b*
exhiber	1-1	fabuler	1-1
exhorter	1-1	facetter	1-1
exhumer	1-1	fâcher	1-1
exiger	1-2b	faciliter	1-1
exiler	1-1	façonner	1-1
exister	1-1	facturer	1-1
exonder (s')	1-1	fagoter	1-1
exonérer	1-5	faiblir	2-1
exorciser	1-1	failler (se)	1-1
expatrier	1-1c	faillir	DEF
expectorer	1-1	fainéanter	1-1
expédier	1-1c	*faire*	*5-23*
expérimenter	1-1	faisander	1-1
expertiser	1-1	*falloir* (IMP)	*4-5c*
expier	1-1c	falsifier	1-1c
expirer	1-1	faluner	1-1
expliciter	1-1	familiariser	1-1
expliquer	1-1b	fanatiser	1-1
exploiter	1-1	faner	1-1
explorer	1-1	fanfaronner	1-1
exploser	1-1	fantasmer	1-1
exporter	1-1	farcir	2-1
exposer	1-1	farder	1-1
exprimer	1-1	farfouiller	1-1
exproprier	1-1c	fariner	1-1
expulser	1-1	farter	1-1
expurger	1-2b	fasciner	1-1
exsuder	1-1	fasciser	1-1
extasier (s')	1-1c	faseyer	1-1
exténuer	1-1	*fatiguer*	*1-1a*
extérioriser	1-1	faucarder	1-1
exterminer	1-1	faucher	1-1
externaliser	1-1	faufiler	1-1
extirper	1-1	fausser	1-1
extorquer	1-1b	fauter	1-1
extrader	1-1	favoriser	1-1
extraire	5-24	faxer	1-1
extrapoler	1-1	fayoter	1-1
extravaguer	1-1a	féconder	1-1
extravaser (s')	1-1	féculer	1-1

Verb	Model #
fédéraliser	1-1
fédérer	1-5
feindre	5-12
feinter	1-1
fêler	1-1
féliciter	1-1
féminiser	1-1
fendiller	1-1
fendre	5-1a
fenêtrer	1-1
férir	DEF
ferler	1-1
fermenter	1-1
fermer	1-1
ferrailler	1-1
ferrer	1-1
ferrouter	1-1
fertiliser	1-1
fesser	1-1
festonner	1-1
festoyer	1-7a
fêter	1-1
fétichiser	1-1
feuiller	1-1
feuilleter	1-3b
feuler	1-1
feutrer	1-1
fiabiliser	1-1
fiancer	1-2a
ficeler	1-3a
fiche	DEF
ficher	1-1
fidéliser	1-1
fienter	1-1
fier (se)	1-1c
figer	1-2b
fignoler	1-1
figurer	1-1
filer	1-1
fileter	1-4
filialiser	1-1
filigraner	1-1
filmer	1-1
filocher	1-1
filouter	1-1
filtrer	1-1
finaliser	1-1
financer	1-2a
financiariser	1-1
finasser	1-1
finir	*2-1*
fiscaliser	1-1
fissurer	1-1
fixer	1-1
flageller	1-1
flageoler	1-1
flagorner	1-1
flairer	1-1
flamber	1-1
flamboyer	1-7a
flancher	1-1
flâner	1-1
flanquer	1-1b
flasher	1-1
flatter	1-1
flécher	1-5
fléchir	2-1
flemmarder	1-1
flétrir	2-1
fleurer	1-1
fleurir	2-1
flexibiliser	1-1
flinguer	1-1a
flipper	1-1
fliquer	1-1b
flirter	1-1
floconner	1-1
floculer	1-1
flotter	1-1
flouer	1-1
fluctuer	1-1
fluer	1-1
fluidifier	1-1c
flûter	1-1
focaliser	1-1
foirer	1-1

Verb	Model #	Verb	Model #
foisonner	1-1	fourrer	1-1
folâtrer	1-1	fourvoyer	1-7a
folioter	1-1	foutre	DEF
folkloriser	1-1	fracasser	1-1
fomenter	1-1	fractionner	1-1
foncer	1-2a	fracturer	1-1
fonctionnariser	1-1	fragiliser	1-1
fonctionner	1-1	fragmenter	1-1
fonder	1-1	fraîchir	2-1
fondre	5-1a	fraiser	1-1
forcer	1-2a	framboiser	1-1
forcir	2-1	franchir	2-1
forclore	DEF	franchiser	1-1
forer	1-1	franciser	1-1
forfaire (DEF)	5-23	franger	1-2b
forger	1-2b	fransquillonner	1-1
forjeter	1-3b	frapper	1-1
forlancer	1-2a	fraterniser	1-1
forligner	1-1	frauder	1-1
forlonger	1-2b	frayer	1-7b
formaliser	1-1	fredonner	1-1
formater	1-1	frégater	1-1
former	1-1	freiner	1-1
formoler	1-1	frelater	1-1
formuler	1-1	frémir	2-1
forniquer	1-1b	fréquenter	1-1
fortifier	1-1c	fréter	1-5
fossiliser	1-1	frétiller	1-1
fouailler	1-1	fretter	1-1
foudroyer	1-7a	fricasser	1-1
fouetter	1-1	fricoter	1-1
fouger	1-2b	frictionner	1-1
fouiller	1-1	frigorifier	1-1c
fouiner	1-1	frimer	1-1
fouir	2-1	fringuer	1-1a
fouler	1-1	friper	1-1
fourbir	2-1	frire	DEF
fourcher	1-1	friser	1-1
fourgonner	1-1	frisotter	1-1
fourguer	1-1a	frissonner	1-1
fourmiller	1-1	friter (se)	1-1
fournir	2-1	fritter	1-1
fourrager	1-2b	froisser	1-1

Verb	Model #
frôler	1-1
froncer	1-2a
fronder	1-1
frotter	1-1
frouer	1-1
froufrouter	1-1
fructifier	1-1c
frustrer	1-1
fuguer	1-1a
fuir	*6-2*
fulgurer	1-1
fulminer	1-1
fumer	1-1
fumiger	1-2b
fureter	1-4
fuseler	1-3a
fuser	1-1
fusiller	1-1
fusionner	1-1
fustiger	1-2b
gabarier	1-1c
gâcher	1-1
gadgétiser	1-1
gaffer	1-1
gager	1-2b
gagner	1-1
gainer	1-1
galber	1-1
galéjer	1-5
galérer	1-5
galipoter	1-1
galonner	1-1
galoper	1-1
galvaniser	1-1
galvauder	1-1
gambader	1-1
gamberger	1-2b
gambiller	1-1
gangrener (gangréner)	1-4 (1-5)
ganser	1-1
ganter	1-1
garancer	1-2a
garantir	2-1
garder	1-1
garer	1-1
gargariser (se)	1-1
gargouiller	1-1
garnir	2-1
garrotter	1-1
gaspiller	1-1
gâter	1-1
gâtifier	1-1c
gauchir	2-1
gaufrer	1-1
gauler	1-1
gausser (se)	1-1
gaver	1-1
gazéifier	1-1c
gazer	1-1
gazonner	1-1
gazouiller	1-1
geindre	5-12
geler	1-4
gélifier	1-1c
géminer	1-1
gémir	2-1
gemmer	1-1
gendarmer (se)	1-1
gêner	1-1
généraliser	1-1
générer	1-5
gerber	1-1
gercer	1-2a
gérer	1-5
germaniser	1-1
germer	1-1
gésir	DEF
gesticuler	1-1
gicler	1-1
gifler	1-1
gigoter	1-1
gîter	1-1
givrer	1-1
glacer	1-2a
glairer	1-1
glaiser	1-1

Verb	Model #
glander (glandouiller)	1-1
glaner	1-1
glapir	2-1
glatir	2-1
glavioter	1-1
gléner	1-5
glisser	1-1
globaliser	1-1
glorifier	1-1c
gloser	1-1
glouglouter	1-1
glousser	1-1
glycériner	1-1
gober	1-1
goberger (se)	1-2b
godailler	1-1
goder	1-1
godiller	1-1
godronner	1-1
goinfrer (se)	1-1
gominer (se)	1-1
gommer	1-1
gondoler	1-1
gonfler	1-1
gorger	1-2b
gouacher	1-1
gouailler	1-1
goudronner	1-1
gouger	1-2b
goujonner	1-1
goupiller	1-1
gourer (se)	1-1
gourmander	1-1
gournabler	1-1
goûter	1-1
goutter	1-1
gouverner	1-1
gracier	1-1c
graduer	1-1
graffiter	1-1
grailler	1-1
graillonner	1-1
grainer	1-1

Verb	Model #
graisser	1-1
grammaticaliser	1-1
grandir	2-1
graniter	1-1
granuler	1-1
graphiter	1-1
grappiller	1-1
grasseyer	1-1
graticuler	1-1
gratifier	1-1c
gratiner	1-1
gratouiller (grattouiller)	1-1
gratter	1-1
graver	1-1
gravillonner	1-1
gravir	2-1
graviter	1-1
gréciser	1-1
grecquer	1-1b
gréer	1-1
greffer	1-1
grêler (IMP)	1-1
grelotter	1-1
grenailler	1-1
greneler	1-3a
grener	1-4
grenouiller	1-1
gréser	1-5
grésiller	1-1
grever	1-4
gribouiller	1-1
griffer	1-1
griffonner	1-1
grigner	1-1
grignoter	1-1
grillager	1-2b
griller	1-1
grimacer	1-2a
grimer	1-1
grimper	1-1
grincer	1-2a
gripper	1-1
grisailler	1-1

Verb	Model #
griser	1-1
grisoller	1-1
grisonner	1-1
griveler	1-3a
grognasser	1-1
grogner	1-1
grognonner	1-1
grommeler	1-3a
gronder	1-1
grossir	2-1
grossoyer	1-7a
grouiller	1-1
grouper	1-1
gruger	1-2b
grumeler (se)	1-3a
guéer	1-1
guérir	2-1
guerroyer	1-7a
guêtrer	1-1
guetter	1-1
gueuler	1-1
gueuletonner	1-1
guider	1-1
guigner	1-1
guillemeter	1-3b
guillocher	1-1
guillotiner	1-1
guincher	1-1
guinder	1-1
guiper	1-1
habiliter	1-1
habiller	1-1
habiter	1-1
habituer	1-1
hacher	1-1
hachurer	1-1
haïr	*2-3*
halener	1-4
haler	1-1
hâler	1-1
haleter	1-4
halluciner	1-1
halogéner	1-5
hameçonner	1-1
hancher	1-1
handicaper	1-1
hannetonner	1-1
hanter	1-1
happer	1-1
haranguer	1-1a
harasser	1-1
harceler	1-4
harder	1-1
harmoniser	1-1
harnacher	1-1
harponner	1-1
hasarder	1-1
hâter	1-1
haubaner	1-1
hausser	1-1
haver	1-1
héberger	1-2b
hébéter	1-5
hébraïser	1-1
héler	1-5
hélitreuiller	1-1
helléniser	1-1
hennir	2-1
herbager	1-2b
herboriser	1-1
hercher (herscher)	1-1
hérisser	1-1
hérissonner	1-1
hériter	1-1
herser	1-1
hésiter	1-1
heurter	1-1
hiberner	1-1
hiérarchiser	1-1
hisser	1-1
historier	1-1c
hiverner	1-1
hocher	1-1
holographier	1-1c
homogénéiser (homogénéifier)	1-1 (1-1c)

Verb	Model #
homologuer	1-1a
hongrer	1-1
hongroyer	1-7a
honnir	2-1
honorer	1-1
hoqueter	1-3b
hormoner	1-1
horrifier	1-1c
horripiler	1-1
hospitaliser	1-1
houblonner	1-1
houpper	1-1
hourder	1-1
houspiller	1-1
housser	1-1
hucher	1-1
huer	1-1
huiler	1-1
hululer (ululer)	1-1
humaniser	1-1
humecter	1-1
humer	1-1
humidifier	1-1c
humilier	1-1c
hurler	1-1
hybrider	1-1
hydrater	1-1
hydrofuger	1-2b
hydrogéner	1-5
hydrolyser	1-1
hypertrophier	1-1c
hypnotiser	1-1
hypostasier	1-1c
hypothéquer	1-5
idéaliser	1-1
identifier	1-1c
idolâtrer	1-1
ignifuger	1-2b
ignorer	1-1
illuminer	1-1
illusionner	1-1
illustrer	1-1
imaginer	1-1
imbiber	1-1
imbriquer	1-1b
imiter	1-1
immatriculer	1-1
immerger	1-2b
immigrer	1-1
immiscer (s')	1-2a
immobiliser	1-1
immoler	1-1
immortaliser	1-1
immuniser	1-1
impartir (DEF)	2-1
impatienter	1-1
impatroniser	1-1
imperméabiliser	1-1
impétrer	1-5
implanter	1-1
implémenter	1-1
impliquer	1-1b
implorer	1-1
imploser	1-1
importer	1-1
importuner	1-1
imposer	1-1
imprégner	1-5
impressionner	1-1
imprimer	1-1
improviser	1-1
impulser	1-1
imputer	1-1
inactiver	1-1
inaugurer	1-1
incarcérer	1-5
incarner	1-1
incendier	1-1c
incidenter	1-1
incinérer	1-5
inciser	1-1
inciter	1-1
incliner	1-1
inclure	*5-16b*
incomber (DEF)	1-1
incommoder	1-1

Verb	Model #
incorporer	1-1
incriminer	1-1
incruster	1-1
incuber	1-1
inculper	1-1
inculquer	1-1b
incurver	1-1
indemniser	1-1
indexer	1-1
indifférer	1-5
indigner	1-1
indiquer	1-1b
indisposer	1-1
individualiser	1-1
induire	5-9a
indurer	1-1
industrialiser	1-1
infantiliser	1-1
infatuer	1-1
infecter	1-1
inféoder	1-1
inférer	1-5
inférioriser	1-1
infester	1-1
infiltrer	1-1
infirmer	1-1
infléchir	2-1
infliger	1-2b
influencer	1-2a
influer	1-1
informatiser	1-1
informer	1-1
infuser	1-1
ingénier (s')	1-1c
ingérer	1-5
ingurgiter	1-1
inhaler	1-1
inhiber	1-1
inhumer	1-1
initialiser	1-1
initier	1-1c
injecter	1-1
injurier	1-1c
innerver	1-1
innocenter	1-1
innover	1-1
inoculer	1-1
inonder	1-1
inquiéter	1-5
inscrire	5-7
insculper	1-1
inséminer	1-1
insensibiliser	1-1
insérer	1-5
insinuer	1-1
insister	1-1
insoler	1-1
insolubiliser	1-1
insonoriser	1-1
inspecter	1-1
inspirer	1-1
installer	1-1
instaurer	1-1
instiguer	1-1a
instiller	1-1
instituer	1-1
institutionnaliser	1-1
instruire	5-9a
instrumentaliser	1-1
instrumenter	1-1
insuffler	1-1
insulter	1-1
insupporter	1-1
insurger (s')	1-2b
intailler	1-1
intégrer	1-5
intellectualiser	1-1
intensifier	1-1c
intenter	1-1
interagir	2-1
intercaler	1-1
intercéder	1-5
intercepter	1-1
interclasser	1-1
interconnecter	1-1
interdire	5-8b

Verb	Model #	Verb	Model #
intéresser	1-1	irriguer	1-1a
interférer	1-5	irriter	1-1
interfolier	1-1c	islamiser	1-1
intérioriser	1-1	isoler	1-1
interjeter	1-3b	italianiser	1-1
interligner	1-1	itérer	1-5
interloquer	1-1b	ixer	1-1
internationaliser	1-1	jabler	1-1
interner	1-1	jaboter	1-1
interpeller	1-1	jacasser	1-1
interpénétrer (s')	1-5	jacter	1-1
interpoler	1-1	jaillir	2-1
interposer	1-1	jalonner	1-1
interpréter	1-5	jalouser	1-1
interroger	1-2b	japoniser	1-1
interrompre	5-1b	japper	1-1
intervenir	6-7	jardiner	1-1
intervertir	2-1	jargonner	1-1
interviewer	1-1	jarreter	1-3b
intimer	1-1	jaser	1-1
intimider	1-1	jasper	1-1
intituler	1-1	jaspiner	1-1
intoxiquer	1-1b	jauger	1-2b
intriguer	1-1a	jaunir	2-1
intriquer	1-1b	javeler	1-3a
introduire	5-9a	javelliser	1-1
introniser	1-1	jerker	1-1
invaginer (s')	1-1	*jeter*	*1-3b*
invalider	1-1	jeûner	1-1
invectiver	1-1	jobarder	1-1
inventer	1-1	jogger	1-1
inventorier	1-1c	*joindre*	*5-12*
inverser	1-1	jointoyer	1-7a
invertir	2-1	joncer	1-2a
investir	2-1	joncher	1-1
inviter	1-1	jongler	1-1
invoquer	1-1b	joualiser	1-1
ioder	1-1	jouer	1-1
iodler (jodler)	1-1	jouir	2-1
ioniser	1-1	jouter	1-1
iriser	1-1	jouxter	1-1
ironiser	1-1	jubiler	1-1
irradier	1-1c	jucher	1-1

Verb	Model #
judaïser	1-1
judiciariser	1-1
juger	1-2b
juguler	1-1
jumeler	1-3a
juponner	1-1
jurer	1-1
justifier	1-1c
juter	1-1
juxtaposer	1-1
kératiniser	1-1
kidnapper	1-1
kifer	1-1
kilométrer	1-5
klaxonner	1-1
labelliser	1-1
labialiser	1-1
labourer	1-1
lacer	1-2a
lacérer	1-5
lâcher	1-1
laïciser	1-1
lainer	1-1
laisser	1-1
laitonner	1-1
laïusser	1-1
lambiner	1-1
lambrisser	1-1
lamenter	1-1
lamer	1-1
laminer	1-1
lamper	1-1
lancer	*1-2a*
lanciner	1-1
langer	1-2b
langueyer	1-1
languir	2-1
lanterner	1-1
laper	1-1
lapider	1-1
lapidifier	1-1c
lapiner	1-1
laquer	1-1b
larder	1-1
larguer	1-1a
larmoyer	1-7a
laryngectomiser	1-1
lasser	1-1
latiniser	1-1
latter	1-1
laver	1-1
layer	1-7b
lécher	1-5
légaliser	1-1
légender	1-1
légiférer	1-5
légitimer	1-1
léguer	1-5
lemmatiser	1-1
lénifier	1-1c
léser	1-5
lésiner	1-1
lessiver	1-1
lester	1-1
leurrer	1-1
lever	1-4
léviger	1-2b
léviter	1-1
levretter	1-1
lexicaliser (se)	1-1
lézarder	1-1
liaisonner	1-1
libeller	1-1
libéraliser	1-1
libérer	1-5
licencier	1-1c
licher	1-1
liciter	1-1
lier	1-1c
lifter	1-1
ligaturer	1-1
ligner	1-1
lignifier (se)	1-1c
ligoter	1-1
liguer	1-1a
limer	1-1

Verb	Model #	Verb	Model #
limiter	1-1	macadamiser	1-1
limoger	1-2b	macérer	1-5
limousiner	1-1	mâcher	1-1
liquéfier	1-1c	machiner	1-1
liquider	1-1	mâchonner	1-1
lire	*5-10*	mâchouiller	1-1
liserer (lisérer)	1-4 (1-5)	mâchurer	1-1
lisser	1-1	macler	1-1
lister	1-1	maçonner	1-1
liter	1-1	maculer	1-1
lithographier	1-1c	magasiner	1-1
livrer	1-1	magner (se)	1-1
lober	1-1	magnétiser	1-1
lobotomiser	1-1	magnétoscoper	1-1
localiser	1-1	magnifier	1-1c
locher	1-1	magouiller	1-1
lock(-)outer	1-1	maigrir	2-1
lofer	1-1	mailler	1-1
loger	1-2b	maintenir	6-7
longer	1-2b	maîtriser	1-1
lorgner	1-1	majorer	1-1
lotionner	1-1	malaxer	1-1
lotir	2-1	malléabiliser	1-1
louanger	1-2b	malmener	1-4
loucher	1-1	malter	1-1
louer	1-1	maltraiter	1-1
louper	1-1	manager	1-2b
lourder	1-1	mandater	1-1
lourer	1-1	mander	1-1
louveter	1-3b	*manger*	*1-2b*
louvoyer	1-7a	manier	1-1c
lover	1-1	manifester	1-1
lubrifier	1-1c	manigancer	1-2a
luger	1-2b	manipuler	1-1
luire	5-9b	manœuvrer	1-1
lustrer	1-1	manquer	1-1b
luter	1-1	manucurer	1-1
lutiner	1-1	manufacturer	1-1
lutter	1-1	manutentionner	1-1
luxer	1-1	mapper	1-1
lyncher	1-1	maquer	1-1b
lyophiliser	1-1	maquereauter	1-1
lyser	1-1	maquetter	1-1

Verb	Model #
maquignonner	1-1
maquiller	1-1
marabouter	1-1
marauder	1-1
marbrer	1-1
marchander	1-1
marcher	1-1
marcotter	1-1
marger	1-2b
marginaliser	1-1
marginer	1-1
margoter (margotter, margauder)	1-1
marier	1-1c
mariner	1-1
marivauder	1-1
marketer	1-3b
marmiter	1-1
marmonner	1-1
marmoriser	1-1
marmotter	1-1
marner	1-1
maronner	1-1
maroufler	1-1
marquer	1-1b
marrer (se)	1-1
marsouiner	1-1
marteler	1-4
martyriser	1-1
masculiniser	1-1
masquer	1-1b
massacrer	1-1
masser	1-1
massicoter	1-1
massifier	1-1c
mastiquer	1-1b
masturber	1-1
matelasser	1-1
mater	1-1
mâter	1-1
matérialiser	1-1
materner	1-1
mathématiser	1-1
mâtiner	1-1
matir	2-1
matraquer	1-1b
matricer	1-2a
maudire	*2-2*
maugréer	1-1
maximaliser	1-1
maximiser	1-1
mazouter	1-1
mécaniser	1-1
mécher	1-5
méconduire (se)	5-9a
méconnaître	5-20
mécontenter	1-1
médailler	1-1
médiatiser	1-1
médicaliser	1-1
médire	5-8b
méditer	1-1
méduser	1-1
méfier (se)	1-1c
mégir (mégisser)	2-1 (1-1)
mégoter	1-1
méjuger	1-2b
mélanger	1-2b
mêler	1-1
mémoriser	1-1
menacer	1-2a
ménager	1-2b
mendier	1-1c
mendigoter	1-1
mener	1-4
menotter	1-1
mensualiser	1-1
mentionner	1-1
mentir	6-1
menuiser	1-1
méprendre (se)	5-2
mépriser	1-1
mercantiliser	1-1
merceriser	1-1
merder	1-1
merdoyer	1-7a

Verb	Model #	Verb	Model #
meringuer	1-1a	mithridatiser	1-1
mériter	1-1	mitiger	1-2b
mésallier (se)	1-1c	mitonner	1-1
mésestimer	1-1	mitrailler	1-1
messeoir	DEF	mixer	1-1
mesurer	1-1	mixtionner	1-1
mésuser	1-1	mobiliser	1-1
métaboliser	1-1	modeler	1-4
métalliser	1-1	modéliser	1-1
métamorphiser	1-1	modérer	1-5
métamorphoser	1-1	moderniser	1-1
météoriser	1-1	modifier	1-1c
métisser	1-1	moduler	1-1
métrer	1-5	moirer	1-1
mettre	*5-4*	moiser	1-1
meubler	1-1	moisir	2-1
meugler	1-1	moissonner	1-1
meuler	1-1	moitir	2-1
meurtrir	2-1	molester	1-1
miauler	1-1	moleter	1-3b
michetonner	1-1	mollarder	1-1
microcopier	1-1c	mollir	2-1
microfilmer	1-1	momifier	1-1c
micro-injecter	1-1	monder	1-1
microniser	1-1	mondialiser	1-1
mignoter	1-1	monétiser	1-1
migrer	1-1	monnayer	1-7b
mijoter	1-1	monologuer	1-1a
militariser	1-1	monopoliser	1-1
militer	1-1	monter	1-1
mimer	1-1	montrer	1-1
minauder	1-1	moquer	1-1b
mincir	2-1	moquetter	1-1
miner	1-1	moraliser	1-1
minéraliser	1-1	morceler	1-3a
miniaturiser	1-1	mordancer	1-2a
minimiser	1-1	mordiller	1-1
minorer	1-1	*mordre*	*5-1a*
minuter	1-1	morfler	1-1
mirer	1-1	morfondre (se)	5-1a
miroiter	1-1	morigéner	1-5
miser	1-1	mortaiser	1-1
miter (se)	1-1	mortifier	1-1c

Verb	Model #
motiver	1-1
motoriser	1-1
motter (se)	1-1
moucharder	1-1
moucher	1-1
moucheronner	1-1
moucheter	1-3b
moudre	*5-15*
moufeter (DEF)	1-1
moufter	1-1
mouiller	1-1
mouler	1-1
mouliner	1-1
moulurer	1-1
mourir	*6-5*
mousser	1-1
moutonner	1-1
mouvementer	1-1
mouvoir	*4-3a*
moyenner	1-1
muer	1-1
mugir	2-1
multiplier	1-1c
municipaliser	1-1
munir	2-1
murer	1-1
mûrir	2-1
murmurer	1-1
musarder	1-1
muscler	1-1
museler	1-3a
muser	1-1
musiquer	1-1b
musser (mucher)	1-1
muter	1-1
mutiler	1-1
mutiner (se)	1-1
mutualiser	1-1
mystifier	1-1c
mythifier	1-1c
nacrer	1-1
nager	1-2b
naître	*5-21*

Verb	Model #
nanifier	1-1c
nantir	2-1
napper	1-1
narguer	1-1a
narrer	1-1
nasaliser	1-1
nasiller	1-1
nationaliser	1-1
natter	1-1
naturaliser	1-1
naviguer	1-1a
navrer	1-1
néantiser	1-1
nécessiter	1-1
nécroser	1-1
négliger	1-2b
négocier	1-1c
neiger (IMP)	1-2b
nervurer	1-1
nettoyer	1-7a
neutraliser	1-1
nicher	1-1
nickeler	1-3a
nidifier	1-1c
nieller	1-1
nier	1-1c
nimber	1-1
nipper	1-1
niquer	1-1b
nitrater	1-1
nitrer	1-1
nitrifier	1-1c
nitrurer	1-1
niveler	1-3a
noircir	2-1
noliser	1-1
nomadiser	1-1
nombrer	1-1
nominaliser	1-1
nommer	1-1
nordir	2-1
normaliser	1-1
noter	1-1

Verb	Model #
notifier	1-1c
nouer	1-1
nourrir	2-1
novéliser (novelliser)	1-1
nover	1-1
noyauter	1-1
noyer	1-7a
nuancer	1-2a
nucléariser	1-1
nuire	*5-9b*
numériser	1-1
numéroter	1-1
obéir	2-1
obérer	1-5
objecter	1-1
objectiver	1-1
obliger	1-2b
obliquer	1-1b
oblitérer	1-5
obnubiler	1-1
obombrer	1-1
obscurcir	2-1
obséder	1-5
observer	1-1
obstiner (s')	1-1
obstruer	1-1
obtempérer	1-5
obtenir	6-7
obturer	1-1
obvenir	6-7
obvier	1-1c
occasionner	1-1
occidentaliser	1-1
occire	DEF
occlure	5-16b
occulter	1-1
occuper	1-1
octavier	1-1c
octroyer	1-7a
octupler	1-1
œilletonner	1-1
œuvrer	1-1
offenser	1-1
officialiser	1-1
officier	1-1c
offrir	*3-1*
offusquer	1-1b
oindre	5-12
oiseler	1-3a
ombrager	1-2b
ombrer	1-1
omettre	5-4
ondoyer	1-7a
onduler	1-1
opacifier	1-1c
opaliser	1-1
opérer	1-5
opiner	1-1
opiniâtrer (s')	1-1
opposer	1-1
oppresser	1-1
opprimer	1-1
opter	1-1
optimiser (optimaliser)	1-1
oraliser	1-1
orbiter	1-1
orchestrer	1-1
ordonnancer	1-2a
ordonner	1-1
organiser	1-1
organsiner	1-1
orienter	1-1
originer (s')	1-1
ornementer	1-1
orner	1-1
orthographier	1-1c
osciller	1-1
oser	1-1
ossifier	1-1c
ôter	1-1
ouater	1-1
ouatiner	1-1
oublier	1-1c
ouiller	1-1
ouïr	DEF
ourdir	2-1

Verb	Model #
ourler	1-1
outiller	1-1
outrager	1-2b
outrepasser	1-1
outrer	1-1
ouvrer	1-1
ouvrir	3-1
ovationner	1-1
ovuler	1-1
oxyder	1-1
oxygéner	1-5
ozoniser	1-1
pacager	1-2b
pacifier	1-1c
pacquer	1-1b
pacser	1-1
pactiser	1-1
paganiser	1-1
pagayer	1-7b
paginer	1-1
pagnoter (se)	1-1
paillassonner	1-1
pailler	1-1
pailleter	1-3b
paître (DEF)	5-20
palabrer	1-1
palanquer	1-1b
palataliser	1-1
palettiser	1-1
pâlir	2-1
palissader	1-1
palisser	1-1
palissonner	1-1
pallier	1-1c
palper	1-1
palpiter	1-1
pâmer (se)	1-1
panacher	1-1
paner	1-1
panifier	1-1c
paniquer	1-1b
panneauter	1-1
panoramiquer	1-1b
panosser	1-1
panser	1-1
panteler	1-3a
pantoufler	1-1
papillonner	1-1
papilloter	1-1
papoter	1-1
parachever	1-4
parachuter	1-1
parader	1-1
paraffiner	1-1
paraître	5-20
paralyser	1-1
paramétrer	1-5
parangonner	1-1
parapher (parafer)	1-1
paraphraser	1-1
parasiter	1-1
parcelliser	1-1
parcheminer	1-1
parcourir	6-4
pardonner	1-1
parementer	1-1
parer	1-1
paresser	1-1
parfaire (DEF)	5-23
parfiler	1-1
parfondre	5-1a
parfumer	1-1
parier	1-1c
parjurer (se)	1-1
parlementer	1-1
parler	*1-1*
parodier	1-1c
parquer	1-1b
parqueter	1-3b
parrainer	1-1
parsemer	1-4
partager	1-2b
participer	1-1
particulariser	1-1
partir (DEF)	2-1
partir	*6-1*

Verb	Model #	Verb	Model #
partouzer (partouser)	1-1	pendiller	1-1
parvenir	6-7	pendouiller	1-1
passementer	1-1	pendre	5-1a
passepoiler	1-1	penduler	1-1
passer	1-1	pénétrer	1-5
passionner	1-1	penser	1-1
pasteuriser	1-1	pensionner	1-1
pasticher	1-1	pépier	1-1c
patauger	1-2b	percer	1-2a
patienter	1-1	percevoir	4-2b
patiner	1-1	percher	1-1
pâtir	2-1	percuter	1-1
pâtisser	1-1	*perdre*	*5-1a*
patoiser	1-1	perdurer	1-1
patouiller	1-1	pérenniser	1-1
patronner	1-1	perfectionner	1-1
patrouiller	1-1	perforer	1-1
pâturer	1-1	perfuser	1-1
paumer	1-1	péricliter	1-1
paumoyer	1-7a	périmer (se)	1-1
paupériser	1-1	périphraser	1-1
pauser	1-1	périr	2-1
pavaner (se)	1-1	perler	1-1
paver	1-1	permanenter	1-1
pavoiser	1-1	permettre	5-4
payer	*1-7b*	permuter	1-1
peaufiner	1-1	pérorer	1-1
pêcher	1-1	peroxyder	1-1
pécher	1-5	perpétrer	1-5
pédaler	1-1	perpétuer	1-1
peigner	1-1	perquisitionner	1-1
peindre	*5-12*	persécuter	1-1
peiner	1-1	persévérer	1-5
peinturer	1-1	persifler	1-1
peinturlurer	1-1	persister	1-1
peler	1-4	personnaliser	1-1
peller	1-1	personnifier	1-1c
pelleter	1-3b	persuader	1-1
peloter	1-1	perturber	1-1
pelotonner	1-1	pervertir	2-1
pelucher (plucher)	1-1	pervibrer	1-1
pénaliser	1-1	*peser*	*1-4*
pencher	1-1	pester	1-1

Verb	Model #
pétarader	1-1
péter	1-5
pétiller	1-1
petit-déjeuner	1-1
pétitionner	1-1
pétrarquiser	1-1
pétrifier	1-1c
pétrir	2-1
pétuner	1-1
peupler	1-1
phagocyter	1-1
philosopher	1-1
phosphater	1-1
phosphorer	1-1
photocopier	1-1c
photographier	1-1c
phraser	1-1
piaffer	1-1
piailler	1-1
pianoter	1-1
piauler	1-1
picoler	1-1
picorer	1-1
picoter	1-1
piéger	1-6c
piéter	1-5
piétiner	1-1
pieuter (se)	1-1
pifer (piffer)	1-1
pigeonner	1-1
piger	1-2b
pigmenter	1-1
pignocher	1-1
piler	1-1
piller	1-1
pilonner	1-1
piloter	1-1
pimenter	1-1
pinailler	1-1
pincer	1-2a
pindariser	1-1
pinter	1-1
piocher	1-1

Verb	Model #
pioncer	1-2a
piper	1-1
pique(-)niquer	1-1b
piquer	1-1b
piqueter	1-3b
pirater	1-1
pirouetter	1-1
pisser	1-1
pister	1-1
pistonner	1-1
pitonner	1-1
pivoter	1-1
placarder	1-1
placardiser	1-1
placer	1-2a
plafonner	1-1
plagier	1-1c
plaider	1-1
plaindre	*5-12*
plaire	*5-22a*
plaisanter	1-1
planchéier	1-1c
plancher	1-1
planer	1-1
planifier	1-1c
planquer	1-1b
planter	1-1
plaquer	1-1b
plasmifier	1-1c
plastifier	1-1c
plastiquer	1-1b
plastronner	1-1
platiner	1-1
plâtrer	1-1
plébisciter	1-1
pleurer	1-1
pleurnicher	1-1
pleuvasser (IMP)	1-1
pleuviner (IMP)	1-1
pleuvoir (IMP)	*4-4*
pleuvoter (pleuvioter) (IMP)	1-1
plier	1-1c
plisser	1-1

Verb	Model #	Verb	Model #
plomber	1-1	porter	1-1
plonger	1-2b	portraiturer	1-1
ployer	1-7a	poser	1-1
plumer	1-1	positionner	1-1
pluviner (IMP)	1-1	positiver	1-1
pocharder (se)	1-1	posséder	1-5
pocher	1-1	postdater	1-1
podzoliser	1-1	poster	1-1
poêler	1-1	postériser	1-1
poétiser	1-1	postfacer	1-2a
poignarder	1-1	postillonner	1-1
poiler (se)	1-1	postposer	1-1
poinçonner	1-1	postsynchroniser	1-1
poindre	5-12	postuler	1-1
pointer	1-1	potasser	1-1
pointiller	1-1	potentialiser	1-1
poireauter	1-1	potiner	1-1
poisser	1-1	poudrer	1-1
poivrer	1-1	poudroyer	1-7a
polariser	1-1	pouffer	1-1
polémiquer	1-1b	pouliner	1-1
policer	1-2a	pouponner	1-1
polir	2-1	pourchasser	1-1
polissonner	1-1	pourfendre	5-1a
politiquer	1-1b	pourlécher	1-5
politiser	1-1	pourrir	2-1
polluer	1-1	poursuivre	5-5
polycopier	1-1c	*pourvoir*	*4-1c*
polymériser	1-1	pousser	1-1
pommader	1-1	poutser	1-1
pommeler (se)	1-3a	*pouvoir*	*4-6*
pommer	1-1	praliner	1-1
pomper	1-1	pratiquer	1-1b
pomponner	1-1	préaviser	1-1
poncer	1-2a	précariser	1-1
ponctionner	1-1	précautionner	1-1
ponctuer	1-1	précéder	1-5
pondérer	1-5	préchauffer	1-1
pondre	5-1a	prêcher	1-1
ponter	1-1	précipiter	1-1
pontifier	1-1c	préciser	1-1
populariser	1-1	précompter	1-1
poquer	1-1b	préconiser	1-1

Verb	Model #	Verb	Model #
prédestiner	1-1	prétexter	1-1
prédéterminer	1-1	*prévaloir*	*4-5b*
prédiquer	1-1b	prévariquer	1-1b
prédire	*5-8b*	prévenir	6-7
prédisposer	1-1	*prévoir*	*4-1b*
prédominer	1-1	*prier*	*1-1c*
préempter	1-1	primer	1-1
préétablir	2-1	priser	1-1
préexister	1-1	privatiser	1-1
préfacer	1-2a	priver	1-1
préférer	1-5	privilégier	1-1c
préfigurer	1-1	procéder	1-5
préfixer	1-1	proclamer	1-1
préformer	1-1	procréer	1-1
préjudicier	1-1c	procurer	1-1
préjuger	1-2b	prodiguer	1-1a
prélasser (se)	1-1	produire	5-9a
prélever	1-4	profaner	1-1
préluder	1-1	proférer	1-5
préméditer	1-1	professer	1-1
prémunir	2-1	professionnaliser	1-1
prendre	*5-2*	profiler	1-1
prénommer	1-1	profiter	1-1
préoccuper	1-1	programmer	1-1
préparer	1-1	progresser	1-1
prépayer	1-7b	prohiber	1-1
préposer	1-1	projeter	1-3b
prérégler	1-5	prolétariser	1-1
présager	1-2b	proliférer	1-5
prescrire	5-7	prolonger	1-2b
présélectionner	1-1	promener	1-4
présenter	1-1	promettre	5-4
préserver	1-1	promotionner	1-1
présider	1-1	*promouvoir*	*4-3b*
pressentir	6-1	promulguer	1-1a
presser	1-1	prôner	1-1
pressurer	1-1	prononcer	1-2a
pressuriser	1-1	pronostiquer	1-1b
présumer	1-1	propager	1-2b
présupposer	1-1	prophétiser	1-1
présurer	1-1	proportionner	1-1
prétendre	5-1a	proposer	1-1
prêter	1-1	propulser	1-1

Verb	Model #	Verb	Model #
proroger	1-2b	quittancer	1-2a
proscrire	5-7	quitter	1-1
prospecter	1-1	rabâcher	1-1
prospérer	1-5	rabaisser	1-1
prosterner	1-1	rabattre	5-3
prostituer	1-1	rabibocher	1-1
protéger	*1-6c*	rabioter	1-1
protester	1-1	raboter	1-1
prouver	1-1	rabougrir (se)	2-1
provenir	6-7	rabouter	1-1
provigner	1-1	rabrouer	1-1
provisionner	1-1	raccommoder	1-1
provoquer	1-1b	raccompagner	1-1
psalmodier	1-1c	raccorder	1-1
psychanalyser	1-1	raccourcir	2-1
psychiatriser	1-1	raccrocher	1-1
publier	1-1c	racheter	1-4
puddler	1-1	raciner	1-1
puer	1-1	racketter	1-1
puiser	1-1	racler	1-1
pulluler	1-1	racoler	1-1
pulvériser	1-1	raconter	1-1
punaiser	1-1	racornir	2-1
punir	2-1	rader	1-1
purger	1-2b	radicaliser	1-1
purifier	1-1c	radier	1-1c
putréfier	1-1c	radiner	1-1
pyramider	1-1	radiobaliser	1-1
pyrograver	1-1	radiodiffuser	1-1
quadriller	1-1	radiographier	1-1c
quadrupler	1-1	radioguider	1-1
qualifier	1-1c	radoter	1-1
quantifier	1-1c	radouber	1-1
quarderonner	1-1	radoucir	2-1
quartager	1-2b	raffermir	2-1
quémander	1-1	raffiner	1-1
quereller	1-1	raffoler	1-1
quérir	DEF	rafistoler	1-1
questionner	1-1	rafler	1-1
quêter	1-1	rafraîchir	2-1
queuter	1-1	ragaillardir	2-1
quintessencier	1-1c	rager	1-2b
quintupler	1-1	ragréer	1-1

Verb	Model #
raguer	1-1a
raidir (roidir)	2-1
railler	1-1
rainer	1-1
rainurer	1-1
raire (réer)	5-24 (1-1)
raisonner	1-1
rajeunir	2-1
rajouter	1-1
rajuster	1-1
ralentir	2-1
râler	1-1
ralinguer	1-1a
raller	1-1
rallier	1-1c
rallonger	1-2b
rallumer	1-1
ramager	1-2b
ramasser	1-1
ramender	1-1
ramener	1-4
ramer	1-1
rameuter	1-1
ramifier (se)	1-1c
ramollir	2-1
ramoner	1-1
ramper	1-1
rancarder (rencarder)	1-1
rancir	2-1
rançonner	1-1
randomiser	1-1
randonner	1-1
ranger	1-2b
ranimer	1-1
rapatrier	1-1c
rapatronner	1-1
râper	1-1
rapetasser	1-1
rapetisser	1-1
rapiécer	*1-6b*
rapiner	1-1
raplatir	2-1
rapointir	2-1

Verb	Model #
rappareiller	1-1
rapparier	1-1c
rappeler	1-3a
rapper (raper)	1-1
rappliquer	1-1b
rappointir	2-1
rapporter	1-1
rapprendre	5-2
rapprocher	1-1
rapproprier	1-1c
raquer	1-1b
raréfier	1-1c
raser	1-1
rassasier	1-1c
rassembler	1-1
rasseoir	4-9a/b
rasséréner	1-5
rassir	DEF
rassurer	1-1
ratatiner	1-1
râteler	1-3a
rater	1-1
ratiboiser	1-1
ratifier	1-1c
ratiner	1-1
ratiociner	1-1
rationaliser	1-1
rationner	1-1
ratisser	1-1
ratonner	1-1
rattacher	1 1
rattraper	1-1
raturer	1-1
rauquer	1-1b
ravager	1-2b
ravaler	1-1
ravauder	1-1
ravigoter	1-1
raviner	1-1
ravir	2-1
raviser (se)	1-1
ravitailler	1-1
raviver	1-1

Verb	Model #	Verb	Model #
ravoir	DEF	rebuter	1-1
rayer	1-7b	recacheter	1-3b
rayonner	1-1	recalcifier	1-1c
razzier	1-1c	recaler	1-1
réabonner	1-1	récapituler	1-1
réabsorber	1-1	recarreler	1-3a
réaccoutumer	1-1	recaser	1-1
réactiver	1-1	recauser	1-1
réactualiser	1-1	recéder	1-5
réadapter	1-1	receler (recéler)	1-4 (1-5)
réadmettre	5-4	recenser	1-1
réaffirmer	1-1	recentrer	1-1
réagir	2-1	receper	1-4
réajuster	1-1	recéper	1-5
réaléser	1-5	réceptionner	1-1
réaliser	1-1	recercler	1-1
réaménager	1-2b	*recevoir*	*4-2b*
réanimer	1-1	réchampir (rechampir)	2-1
réapparaître	5-20	rechanger	1-2b
réapprendre	5-2	rechanter	1-1
réapprovisionner	1-1	rechaper	1-1
réargenter	1-1	réchapper	1-1
réarmer	1-1	recharger	1-2b
réarranger	1-2b	rechasser	1-1
réassigner	1-1	réchauffer	1-1
réassortir	2-1	rechausser	1-1
réassurer	1-1	rechercher	1-1
rebaisser	1-1	rechigner	1-1
rebaptiser	1-1	rechristianiser	1-1
rebâtir	2-1	rechuter	1-1
rebattre	5-3	récidiver	1-1
rebeller (se)	1-1	réciproquer	1-1b
rebiffer (se)	1-1	réciter	1-1
rebiquer	1-1b	réclamer	1-1
reboiser	1-1	reclasser	1-1
rebondir	2-1	reclouer	1-1
reborder	1-1	recoiffer	1-1
reboucher	1-1	récoler	1-1
rebouter	1-1	recoller	1-1
reboutonner	1-1	récolter	1-1
rebraguetter	1-1	recommander	1-1
rebroder	1-1	recommencer	1-2a
rebrousser	1-1	récompenser	1-1

Verb	Model #	Verb	Model #
recomposer	1-1	redécouvrir	3-1
recompter	1-1	redéfaire	5-23
réconcilier	1-1c	redéfinir	2-1
reconduire	5-9a	redemander	1-1
réconforter	1-1	redémarrer	1-1
reconnaître	5-20	redescendre	5-1a
reconquérir	6-3	redevenir	6-7
reconsidérer	1-5	redevoir	4-2a
reconsolider	1-1	rediffuser	1-1
reconstituer	1-1	rédiger	1-2b
reconstruire	5-9a	rédimer	1-1
reconvertir	2-1	redire	5-8a
recopier	1-1c	rediscuter	1-1
recorder	1-1	redistribuer	1-1
recorriger	1-2b	redonner	1-1
recoucher	1-1	redorer	1-1
recoudre	5-14	redoubler	1-1
recouper	1-1	redouter	1-1
recouponner	1-1	redresser	1-1
recourber	1-1	réduire	5-9a
recourir	6-4	réédifier	1-1c
recouvrer	1-1	rééditer	1-1
recouvrir	3-1	rééduquer	1-1b
recracher	1-1	réélire	5-10
recréer	1-1	réembaucher (rembaucher)	1-1
récréer	1-1	réemployer	1-7a
recrépir	2-1	réensemencer	1-2a
recreuser	1-1	réentendre	5-1a
récrier (se)	1-1c	rééquilibrer	1-1
récriminer	1-1	réescompter	1-1
récrire (réécrire)	5-7	réessayer	1-7b
recristalliser	1-1	réévaluer	1-1
recroqueviller	1-1	réexaminer	1-1
recruter	1-1	réexpédier	1-1c
rectifier	1-1c	réexporter	1-1
recueillir	3-2b	refaire	5-23
recuire	5-9a	refendre	5-1a
reculer	1-1	référencer	1-2a
reculotter	1-1	référer	1-5
récupérer	1-5	refermer	1-1
récurer	1-1	refiler	1-1
récuser	1-1	réfléchir	2-1
recycler	1-1	refléter	1-5

Verb	Model #
refleurir	2-1
refluer	1-1
refonder	1-1
refondre	5-1a
reformer	1-1
réformer	1-1
reformuler	1-1
refouiller	1-1
refouler	1-1
refourguer	1-1a
refoutre	DEF
réfracter	1-1
refréner (réfréner)	1-5
réfrigérer	1-5
refroidir	2-1
réfugier (se)	1-1c
refuser	1-1
réfuter	1-1
regagner	1-1
régaler	1-1
regarder	1-1
regarnir	2-1
régater	1-1
regeler	1-4
régénérer	1-5
régenter	1-1
regimber	1-1
régionaliser	1-1
régir	2-1
réglementer	1-1
régler	1-5
régner	1-5
regonfler	1-1
regorger	1-2b
regratter	1-1
regréer	1-1
regreffer	1-1
régresser	1-1
regretter	1-1
regrimper	1-1
regrossir	2-1
regrouper	1-1
régulariser	1-1
réguler	1-1
régurgiter	1-1
réhabiliter	1-1
réhabituer	1-1
rehausser	1-1
réhydrater	1-1
réifier	1-1c
réimperméabiliser	1-1
réimplanter	1-1
réimporter	1-1
réimposer	1-1
réimprimer	1-1
réincarcérer	1-5
réincarner (se)	1-1
réincorporer	1-1
réinfecter	1-1
réinjecter	1-1
réinscrire	5-7
réinsérer	1-5
réinstaller	1-1
réintégrer	1-5
réinterpréter	1-5
réintroduire	5-9a
réinventer	1-1
réinviter	1-1
réitérer	1-5
rejaillir	2-1
rejeter	1-3b
rejoindre	5-12
rejointoyer	1-7a
rejouer	1-1
réjouir	2-1
relâcher	1-1
relaisser (se)	1-1
relancer	1-2a
relater	1-1
relativiser	1-1
relaver	1-1
relaxer	1-1
relayer	1-7b
reléguer	1-5
relever	1-4
relier	1-1c

Verb	Model #
relire	5-10
reloger	1-2b
relooker	1-1
relouer	1-1
reluire	5-9b
reluquer	1-1b
remâcher	1-1
remanger	1-2b
remanier	1-1c
remaquiller	1-1
remarcher	1-1
remarier	1-1c
remarquer	1-1b
remastiquer	1-1b
remballer	1-1
rembarquer	1-1b
rembarrer	1-1
remblayer	1-7b
rembobiner	1-1
remboîter	1-1
rembourrer	1-1
rembourser	1-1
rembrunir	2-1
rembucher	1-1
remédier	1-1c
remembrer	1-1
remémorer	1-1
remercier	1-1c
remettre	5-4
remeubler	1-1
remilitariser	1-1
remiser	1-1
remmailler (remailler)	1-1
remmener	1-4
remodeler	1-4
remonter	1-1
remontrer	1-1
remordre	5-1a
remorquer	1-1b
remouiller	1-1
rempailler	1-1
rempaqueter	1-3b
rempiéter	1-5
rempiler	1-1
remplacer	1-2a
remplier	1-1c
remplir	2-1
remployer	1-7a
remplumer	1-1
rempocher	1-1
rempoissonner	1-1
remporter	1-1
rempoter	1-1
remprunter	1-1
remuer	1-1
rémunérer	1-5
renâcler	1-1
renaître	5-21
renauder	1-1
rencaisser	1-1
renchérir	2-1
rencogner	1-1
rencontrer	1-1
rendormir	6-1
rendosser	1-1
rendre	*5-1a*
renégocier	1-1c
reneiger (IMP)	1-2b
rénetter	1-1
renfermer	1-1
renfiler	1-1
renflammer	1-1
renfler	1-1
renflouer	1-1
renfoncer	1-2a
renforcer	1-2a
renformir	2-1
renfrogner (se)	1-1
rengager	1-2b
rengainer	1-1
rengorger (se)	1-2b
rengréner (rengrener)	1-5 (1-4)
renier	1-1c
renifler	1-1
renommer	1-1
renoncer	1-2a

Verb	Model #
renouer	1-1
renouveler	1-3a
rénover	1-1
renquiller	1-1
renseigner	1-1
rentabiliser	1-1
renter	1-1
rentoiler	1-1
rentraire (rentrayer)	5-24 (1-7b)
rentrer	1-1
renverser	1-1
renvider	1-1
renvoyer	1-8
réoccuper	1-1
réopérer	1-5
réorchestrer	1-1
réorganiser	1-1
réorienter	1-1
repairer	1-1
repaître	5-20
répandre	*5-1a*
reparaître	5-20
réparer	1-1
reparler	1-1
repartir	6-1
répartir	2-1
repasser	1-1
repaver	1-1
repayer	1-7b
repêcher	1-1
repeindre	5-12
repenser	1-1
repentir (se)	6-1
repercer	1-2a
répercuter	1-1
reperdre	5-1a
repérer	1-5
répertorier	1-1c
répéter	1-5
repeupler	1-1
repiquer	1-1b
replacer	1-2a
replanter	1-1

Verb	Model #
replâtrer	1-1
repleuvoir (IMP)	4-4
replier	1-1c
répliquer	1-1b
replonger	1-2b
reployer	1-7a
repolir	2-1
répondre	*5-1a*
reporter	1-1
reposer	1-1
repositionner	1-1
repousser	1-1
reprendre	5-2
représenter	1-1
réprimander	1-1
réprimer	1-1
repriser	1-1
reprocher	1-1
reproduire	5-9a
reprogrammer	1-1
reprographier	1-1c
réprouver	1-1
répudier	1-1c
répugner	1-1
réputer	1-1
requalifier	1-1c
requérir	6-3
requinquer	1-1b
réquisitionner	1-1
resaler	1-1
resalir	2-1
rescinder	1-1
réséquer	1-5
réserver	1-1
résider	1-1
résigner	1-1
résilier	1-1c
résiner	1-1
résister	1-1
resituer	1-1
résonner	1-1
résorber	1-1
résoudre	*5-13b*

Verb	Model #
respectabiliser	1-1
respecter	1-1
respirer	1-1
resplendir	2-1
responsabiliser	1-1
resquiller	1-1
ressaigner	1-1
ressaisir	2-1
ressasser	1-1
ressauter	1-1
ressembler	1-1
ressemeler	1-3a
ressemer (resemer)	1-4
ressentir	6-1
resserrer	1-1
resservir	6-1
ressortir	2-1
ressortir	6-1
ressouder	1-1
ressourcer	1-2a
ressouvenir (se)	6-7
ressuer	1-1
ressusciter	1-1
ressuyer	1-7a
restaurer	1-1
rester	1-1
restituer	1-1
restreindre	5-12
restructurer	1-1
résulter (DEF)	1-1
résumer	1-1
resurgir (ressurgir)	2-1
rétablir	2-1
retailler	1-1
rétamer	1-1
retaper	1-1
retapisser	1-1
retarder	1-1
retâter	1-1
retéléphoner	1-1
retendre	5-1a
retenir	6-7
retenter	1-1
retentir	2-1
retercer	1-2a
réticuler	1-1
retirer	1-1
retisser	1-1
retomber	1-1
retordre	5-1a
rétorquer	1-1b
retoucher	1-1
retourner	1-1
retracer	1-2a
rétracter	1-1
retraduire	5-9a
retraiter	1-1
retrancher	1-1
retranscrire	5-7
retransmettre	5-4
retravailler	1-1
retraverser	1-1
rétrécir	2-1
retreindre (rétreindre)	5-12
retremper	1-1
rétribuer	1-1
rétroagir	2-1
rétrocéder	1-5
rétrograder	1-1
retrousser	1-1
retrouver	1-1
retuber	1-1
réunifier	1-1c
réunir	2-1
réussir	2-1
réutiliser	1-1
revacciner	1-1
revaloir	4-5a
revaloriser	1-1
revancher (se)	1-1
rêvasser	1-1
réveiller	1-1
réveillonner	1-1
révéler	1-5
revendiquer	1-1b
revendre	5-1a

Verb	Model #	Verb	Model #
revenir	6-7	riposter	1-1
rêver	1-1	*rire*	*5-11*
réverbérer	1-5	risquer	1-1b
reverdir	2-1	rissoler	1-1
révérer	1-5	ristourner	1-1
revernir	2-1	ritualiser	1-1
reverser	1-1	rivaliser	1-1
revêtir	6-6	river	1-1
revigorer	1-1	riveter	1-3b
réviser	1-1	rober	1-1
revisiter	1-1	robotiser	1-1
revisser	1-1	rocher	1-1
revitaliser	1-1	rocouer	1-1
revivifier	1-1c	rôdailler	1-1
revivre	5-6	roder	1-1
revoir	4-1a	rôder	1-1
revoler	1-1	rogner	1-1
révolter	1-1	rognonner	1-1
révolutionner	1-1	romancer	1-2a
révolvériser	1-1	romaniser	1-1
révoquer	1-1b	*rompre*	*5-1b*
revoter	1-1	ronchonner	1-1
revouloir	4-8	ronéotyper (ronéoter)	1-1
révulser	1-1	ronfler	1-1
rewriter	1-1	ronger	1-2b
rhabiller	1-1	ronronner	1-1
rhumer	1-1	roquer	1-1b
ribouler	1-1	roser	1-1
ricaner	1-1	rosir	2-1
ricocher	1-1	rosser	1-1
rider	1-1	roter	1-1
ridiculiser	1-1	rôtir	2-1
rifler	1-1	roucouler	1-1
rigidifier	1-1c	rouer	1-1
rigoler	1-1	rougeoyer	1-7a
rimailler	1-1	rougir	2-1
rimer	1-1	rouiller	1-1
rincer	1-2a	rouir	2-1
ringarder	1-1	rouler	1-1
ringardiser	1-1	roupiller	1-1
ripailler	1-1	rouscailler	1-1
riper	1-1	rouspéter	1-5
ripoliner	1-1	roussir	2-1

Verb	Model #
roustir	2-1
router	1-1
rouvrir	3-1
rubaner	1-1
rucher	1-1
rudoyer	1-7a
ruer	1-1
rugir	2-1
ruiler	1-1
ruiner	1-1
ruisseler	1-3a
ruminer	1-1
ruser	1-1
russifier	1-1c
rustiquer	1-1b
rutiler	1-1
rythmer	1-1
sabler	1-1
sablonner	1-1
saborder	1-1
saboter	1-1
sabouler	1-1
sabrer	1-1
saccader	1-1
saccager	1-2b
saccharifier	1-1c
sacquer (saquer)	1-1b
sacraliser	1-1
sacrer	1-1
sacrifier	1-1c
safraner	1-1
saietter	1-1
saigner	1-1
saillir	DEF
saisir	2-1
salarier	1-1c
saler	1-1
salifier	1-1c
salir	2-1
saliver	1-1
saloper	1-1
saluer	1-1
sanctifier	1-1c
sanctionner	1-1
sanctuariser	1-1
sandwicher	1-1
sangler	1-1
sangloter	1-1
saper	1-1
saponifier	1-1c
sarcler	1-1
sarmenter	1-1
sasser	1-1
satelliser	1-1
satiner	1-1
satiriser	1-1
satisfaire	5-23
saturer	1-1
saucer	1-2a
saucissonner	1-1
saumurer	1-1
sauner	1-1
saupoudrer	1-1
saurer	1-1
sauter	1-1
sautiller	1-1
sauvegarder	1-1
sauver	1-1
savoir	*4-7*
savonner	1-1
savourer	1-1
scalper	1-1
scandaliser	1-1
scander	1-1
scanner	1-1
scarifier	1-1c
sceller	1-1
scénariser	1-1
schématiser	1-1
schlitter	1-1
scier	1-1c
scinder	1-1
scintiller	1-1
scléroser (se)	1-1
scolariser	1-1
scorifier	1-1c

Verb	Model #	Verb	Model #
scotcher	1-1	sévir	2-1
scotomiser	1-1	sevrer	1-4
scratcher	1-1	sextupler	1-1
scruter	1-1	sexualiser	1-1
sculpter	1-1	shampouiner (shampooiner)	1-1
sécher	1-5	shooter	1-1
seconder	1-1	shunter	1-1
secouer	1-1	sidérer	1-5
secourir	6-4	siéger	1-6c
secréter	1-5	siffler	1-1
sécréter	1-5	siffloter	1-1
sectionner	1-1	signaler	1-1
sectoriser	1-1	signaliser	1-1
séculariser	1-1	signer	1-1
sécuriser	1-1	signifier	1-1c
sédentariser	1-1	silhouetter	1-1
sédimenter	1-1	siliconer	1-1
séduire	5-9a	sillonner	1-1
segmenter	1-1	similiser	1-1
ségréguer (ségréger)	1-5 (1-6c)	simplifier	1-1c
séjourner	1-1	simuler	1-1
sélecter	1-1	singer	1-2b
sélectionner	1-1	singulariser	1-1
seller	1-1	siniser	1-1
sembler	1-1	sinuer	1-1
semer	1-4	siphonner	1-1
semoncer	1-2a	siroter	1-1
sensibiliser	1-1	situer	1-1
sentir	*6-1*	skier	1-1c
seoir	DEF	slalomer	1-1
séparer	1-1	slaviser	1-1
septupler	1-1	slicer	1-2a
séquencer	1-2a	smasher	1-1
séquestrer	1-1	smurfer	1-1
sérancer	1-2a	snifer (sniffer)	1-1
serfouir	2-1	snober	1-1
sérier	1-1c	socialiser	1-1
seriner	1-1	sodomiser	1-1
sermonner	1-1	soigner	1-1
serpenter	1-1	solder	1-1
serrer	1-1	solenniser	1-1
sertir	2-1	solfier	1-1c
servir	*6-1*	solidariser	1-1

Verb	Model #
solidifier	1-1c
soliloquer	1-1b
solliciter	1-1
solubiliser	1-1
solutionner	1-1
somatiser	1-1
sombrer	1-1
sommeiller	1-1
sommer	1-1
somnoler	1-1
sonder	1-1
songer	1-2b
sonnailler	1-1
sonner	1-1
sonoriser	1-1
sophistiquer	1-1b
sortir (DEF)	2-1
sortir	*6-1*
soucier	1-1c
souder	1-1
soudoyer	1-7a
souffler	1-1
souffleter	1-3b
souffrir	*3-1*
soufrer	1-1
souhaiter	1-1
souiller	1-1
soulager	1-2b
soûler (saouler)	1-1
soulever	1-4
souligner	1-1
soumettre	5-4
soumissionner	1-1
soupçonner	1-1
souper	1-1
soupeser	1-4
soupirer	1-1
souquer	1-1b
sourciller	1-1
sourdre (DEF)	5-1a
sourire	5-11
souscrire	5-7
sous-employer	1-7a
sous-entendre	5-1a
sous-estimer	1-1
sous-évaluer	1-1
sous-exposer	1-1
sous-louer	1-1
sous-payer	1-7b
sous-tendre	5-1a
sous-titrer	1-1
soustraire	5-24
sous-traiter	1-1
sous-virer	1-1
soutacher	1-1
soutenir	6-7
soutirer	1-1
souvenir	6-7
soviétiser	1-1
spatialiser	1-1
spécialiser	1-1
spécifier	1-1c
spéculer	1-1
speeder	1-1
spiritualiser	1-1
spolier	1-1c
sponsoriser	1-1
sporuler	1-1
sprinter	1-1
squatter (squattériser)	1-1
squeezer	1-1
stabiliser	1-1
staffer	1-1
stagner	1-1
standardiser	1-1
stariser (starifier)	1-1 (1-1c)
stationner	1-1
statuer	1-1
statufier	1-1c
sténographier	1-1c
stérer	1-5
stériliser	1-1
stigmatiser	1-1
stimuler	1-1
stipendier	1-1c
stipuler	1-1

Verb	Model #	Verb	Model #
stocker	1-1	suiffer	1-1
stopper	1-1	suinter	1-1
stranguler	1-1	*suivre*	*5-5*
stratifier	1-1c	sulfater	1-1
stresser	1-1	sulfurer	1-1
striduler	1-1	superposer	1-1
strier	1-1c	superviser	1-1
stripper	1-1	supplanter	1-1
structurer	1-1	suppléer	1-1
stupéfaire (DEF)	5-23	supplémenter	1-1
stupéfier	1-1c	supplicier	1-1c
stuquer	1-1b	supplier	1-1c
styliser	1-1	supporter	1-1
subdéléguer	1-5	supposer	1-1
subdiviser	1-1	supprimer	1-1
subir	2-1	suppurer	1-1
subjuguer	1-1a	supputer	1-1
sublimer	1-1	surabonder	1-1
submerger	1-2b	surajouter	1-1
subodorer	1-1	suralimenter	1-1
subordonner	1-1	surarmer	1-1
suborner	1-1	surbaisser	1-1
subroger	1-2b	surcharger	1-2b
subsister	1-1	surchauffer	1-1
substantiver	1-1	surclasser	1-1
substituer	1-1	surcomprimer	1-1
subsumer	1-1	surcontrer	1-1
subtiliser	1-1	surcouper	1-1
subvenir	6-7	surélever	1-4
subventionner	1-1	surenchérir	2-1
subvertir	2-1	surentraîner	1-1
succéder	1-5	suréquiper	1-1
succomber	1-1	surestimer	1-1
sucer	1-2a	surévaluer	1-1
suçoter	1-1	surexciter	1-1
sucrer	1-1	surexploiter	1-1
suer	1-1	surexposer	1-1
suffire	*5-8c*	surfacer	1-2a
suffixer	1-1	surfacturer	1-1
suffoquer	1-1b	surfaire	5-23
suggérer	1-5	surfer	1-1
suggestionner	1-1	surfiler	1-1
suicider (se)	1-1	surgeler	1-4

Verb	Model #
surgeonner	1-1
surgir	2-1
surhausser	1-1
surimposer	1-1
suriner	1-1
surinvestir	2-1
surir	2-1
surjaler	1-1
surjeter	1-3b
surjouer	1-1
surligner	1-1
surmédicaliser	1-1
surmener	1-4
surmonter	1-1
surmouler	1-1
surnager	1-2b
surnommer	1-1
suroxyder	1-1
surpasser	1-1
surpayer	1-7b
surpiquer	1-1b
surplomber	1-1
surprendre	5-2
surproduire	5-9a
surprotéger	1-6c
sursauter	1-1
sursemer	1-4
surseoir	*4-9c*
surstocker	1-1
surtaxer	1-1
surtondre	5-1a
surveiller	1-1
survenir	6-7
survirer	1-1
survivre	5-6
survoler	1-1
survolter	1-1
susciter	1-1
suspecter	1-1
suspendre	5-1a
sustenter	1-1
susurrer	1-1
suturer	1-1
swinguer	1-1a
symboliser	1-1
sympathiser	1-1
synchroniser	1-1
syncoper	1-1
syncristalliser	1-1
syndicaliser	1-1
syndiquer	1-1b
synthétiser	1-1
syntoniser	1-1
systématiser	1-1
tabasser	1-1
tabler	1-1
tabouiser	1-1
tacher	1-1
tâcher	1-1
tacheter	1-3b
tacler	1-1
taguer	1-1a
taillader	1-1
tailler	1-1
taire	*5-22b*
taler	1-1
taller	1-1
talocher	1-1
talonner	1-1
talquer	1-1b
tambouriner	1-1
tamiser	1-1
tamponner	1-1
tancer	1-2a
tanguer	1-1a
taniser (tanniser)	1-1
tanner	1-1
tapager	1-2b
taper	1-1
tapiner	1-1
tapir (se)	2-1
tapisser	1-1
tapoter	1-1
taquer	1-1b
taquiner	1-1
tarabiscoter	1-1

Verb	Model #
tarabuster	1-1
tarauder	1-1
tarder	1-1
tarer	1-1
targuer (se)	1-1a
tarifer	1-1
tarir	2-1
tartiner	1-1
tartir	2-1
tasser	1-1
tâter	1-1
tâtonner	1-1
tatouer	1-1
tauder	1-1
taxer	1-1
tayloriser	1-1
tchatcher	1-1
techniciser	1-1
technocratiser	1-1
teiller (tiller)	1-1
teindre	5-12
teinter	1-1
télécharger	1-2b
télécommander	1-1
télédiffuser	1-1
télégraphier	1-1c
téléguider	1-1
téléphoner	1-1
télescoper	1-1
téléviser	1-1
télexer	1-1
témoigner	1-1
tempérer	1-5
tempêter	1-1
temporiser	1-1
tenailler	1-1
tendre	5-1a
tenir	*6-7*
tenonner	1-1
ténoriser	1-1
tenter	1-1
tergiverser	1-1
terminer	1-1
ternir	2-1
terrasser	1-1
terreauter	1-1
terrer	1-1
terrifier	1-1c
terroriser	1-1
terser	1-1
tester	1-1
tétaniser	1-1
téter	1-5
texturer	1-1
théâtraliser	1-1
théoriser	1-1
thésauriser	1-1
tiédir	2-1
tiercer (tercer)	1-2a
timbrer	1-1
tinter	1-1
tintinnabuler	1-1
tiquer	1-1b
tirailler	1-1
tire(-)bouchonner	1-1
tirer	1-1
tisonner	1-1
tisser	1-1
titiller	1-1
titrer	1-1
tituber	1-1
titulariser	1-1
toiletter	1-1
toiser	1-1
tolérer	1-5
tomber	1-1
tomer	1-1
tondre	5-1a
tonifier	1-1c
tonitruer	1-1
tonner	1-1
tonsurer	1-1
tontiner	1-1
toper	1-1
toquer	1-1b
torcher	1-1

Verb	Model #	Verb	Model #
torchonner	1-1	tranchefiler	1-1
tordre	5-1a	trancher	1-1
toréer	1-1	tranquilliser	1-1
toronner	1-1	transbahuter	1-1
torpiller	1-1	transborder	1-1
torréfier	1-1c	transcender	1-1
torsader	1-1	transcoder	1-1
tortiller	1-1	transcrire	5-7
tortorer	1-1	transférer	1-5
torturer	1-1	transfigurer	1-1
tosser	1-1	transfiler	1-1
totaliser	1-1	transformer	1-1
toucher	1-1	transfuser	1-1
touer	1-1	transgresser	1-1
touiller	1-1	transhumer	1-1
toupiller	1-1	transiger	1-2b
toupiner	1-1	transir	2-1
tourber	1-1	transistoriser	1-1
tourbillonner	1-1	transiter	1-1
tourmenter	1-1	translittérer	1-5
tournailler	1-1	transmettre	5-4
tournebouler	1-1	transmigrer	1-1
tourner	1-1	transmuer (transmuter)	1-1
tournicoter	1-1	transparaître	5-20
tourniquer	1-1b	transpercer	1-2a
tournoyer	1-7a	transpirer	1-1
toussailler	1-1	transplanter	1-1
tousser	1-1	transporter	1-1
toussoter	1-1	transposer	1-1
trabouler	1-1	transsuder	1-1
tracasser	1-1	transvaser	1-1
tracer	1-2a	transvider	1-1
tracter	1-1	traquer	1-1b
traduire	5-9a	traumatiser	1-1
traficoter	1-1	travailler	1-1
trafiquer	1-1b	travailloter	1-1
trahir	2-1	traverser	1-1
traînailler	1-1	travestir	2-1
traînasser	1-1	trébucher	1-1
traîner	1-1	tréfiler	1-1
traire	*5-24*	treillager	1-2b
traiter	1-1	treillisser	1-1
tramer	1-1	trémater	1-1

Verb	Model #
trembler	1-1
trembloter	1-1
trémousser (se)	1-1
tremper	1-1
trémuler	1-1
trépaner	1-1
trépasser	1-1
trépider	1-1
trépigner	1-1
tressaillir	3-2a
tressauter	1-1
tresser	1-1
treuiller	1-1
trévirer	1-1
trianguler	1-1
triballer	1-1
tricher	1-1
tricoter	1-1
trier	1-1c
trifouiller	1-1
triller	1-1
trimarder	1-1
trimballer (trimbaler)	1-1
trimer	1-1
tringler	1-1
trinquer	1-1b
triompher	1-1
tripatouiller	1-1
tripler	1-1
tripoter	1-1
trisser	1-1
triturer	1-1
tromper	1-1
trompeter	1-3b
tronçonner	1-1
trôner	1-1
tronquer	1-1b
tropicaliser	1-1
troquer	1-1b
trotter	1-1
trottiner	1-1
troubler	1-1
trouer	1-1

Verb	Model #
trousser	1-1
trouver	1-1
truander	1-1
trucider	1-1
truffer	1-1
truquer	1-1b
trusquiner	1-1
truster	1-1
tuber	1-1
tuer	1-1
tuméfier	1-1c
turbiner	1-1
turlupiner	1-1
tuteurer	1-1
tutoyer	1-7a
tuyauter	1-1
twister	1-1
tympaniser	1-1
typer	1-1
typographier	1-1c
tyranniser	1-1
ulcérer	1-5
unifier	1-1c
uniformiser	1-1
unir	2-1
universaliser	1-1
urbaniser	1-1
urger	1-2b
uriner	1-1
user	1-1
usiner	1-1
usurper	1-1
utiliser	1-1
vacciner	1-1
vaciller	1-1
vacuoliser	1-1
vadrouiller	1-1
vagabonder	1-1
vagir	2-1
vaguer	1-1a
vaincre	*5-25*
valdinguer	1-1a
valider	1-1

Verb	Model #
valoir	*4-5a*
valoriser	1-1
valser	1-1
vamper	1-1
vampiriser	1-1
vandaliser	1-1
vanner	1-1
vanter	1-1
vaporiser	1-1
vaquer	1-1b
varapper	1-1
varier	1-1c
varloper	1-1
vaseliner	1-1
vaser (IMP)	1-1
vasouiller	1-1
vaticiner	1-1
vautrer (se)	1-1
végéter	1-5
véhiculer	1-1
veiller	1-1
veiner	1-1
vêler	1-1
velouter	1-1
vendanger	1-2b
vendre	5-1a
vénérer	1-5
venger	1-2b
venir	*6-7*
venter (IMP)	1-1
ventiler	1-1
verbaliser	1-1
verdir	2-1
verdoyer	1-7a
vérifier	1-1c
verjuter	1-1
vermiller	1-1
vermillonner	1-1
vernir	2-1
vernisser	1-1
verrouiller	1-1
verser	1-1
versifier	1-1c
vesser	1-1
vétiller	1-1
vêtir	*6-6*
vexer	1-1
viabiliser	1-1
viander	1-1
vibrer	1-1
vibrionner	1-1
vicier	1-1c
vidanger	1-2b
vider	1-1
vidimer	1-1
vieillir	2-1
vieller	1-1
vilipender	1-1
villégiaturer	1-1
vinaigrer	1-1
viner	1-1
vinifier	1-1c
violacer	1-2a
violenter	1-1
violer	1-1
violoner	1-1
virer	1-1
virevolter	1-1
viriliser	1-1
viroler	1-1
viser	1-1
visionner	1-1
visiter	1-1
visser	1-1
visualiser	1-1
vitrer	1-1
vitrifier	1-1c
vitrioler	1-1
vitupérer	1-5
vivifier	1-1c
vivoter	1-1
vivre	*5-6*
vocaliser	1-1
vociférer	1-5
voguer	1-1a
voiler	1-1

Verb	Model #
voir	*4-1a*
voisiner	1-1
voiturer	1-1
volatiliser	1-1
voler	1-1
voleter	1-3b
voliger	1-2b
volleyer	1-1
volter	1-1
voltiger	1-2b
vomir	2-1
voter	1-1
vouer	1-1
vouloir	*4-8*
vousoyer (voussoyer)	1-7a
voûter	1-1
vouvoyer	1-7a
voyager	1-2b
vriller	1-1
vrombir	2-1
vulcaniser	1-1
vulgariser	1-1
warranter	1-1
yoyoter (yoyotter)	1-1
zapper	1-1
zébrer	1-5
zézayer	1-7b
zieuter (zyeuter)	1-1
zigouiller	1-1
zigzaguer	1-1a
zinguer	1-1a
zinzinuler	1-1
zipper	1-1
zoner	1-1
zoomer	1-1
zouker	1-1
zozoter	1-1

ANNEX C

Defective Verbs

"Defective" verbs are normally defined as those which do not possess complete conjugations. By this definition, several of the model verbs presented in Annex A would also qualify, notably:

absoudre (5-13a), traire (5-24)

as well as the "impersonal" verbs *pleuvoir* (4-4) and *falloir* (4-5c).

The verbs listed in this annex are generally used infrequently, in a number of cases only in special contexts or expressions. There is occasionally disagreement between various sources as to which forms actually exist.

Several classical verbs formerly of everyday use are found in this "graveyard", replaced at various stages by competing verbs offering more regular conjugations. Chief among these are:

(a) *choir* ("to fall") replaced by *tomber*
(b) *clore* ("to close") replaced by *fermer*
(c) *occire* ("to kill") replaced by *tuer*
(d) *ouïr* ("to listen")—origin of English *"Oyez, oyez, oyez* the court is now in session!"—replaced by *entendre* (and *écouter*)

In the presentation which follows:

(1) *3rd persons* means that conjugations exist only for the third person singular and plural; *participles* means that both present and past participles exist.
(2) When the past participle exists, the verb is also normally used in the associated compound tenses (*passé composé, past perfect,* etc.).
(3) No specific mention is made of imperatives; these follow the conjugations of the corresponding present indicatives.
(4) Grammatical persons are referred to as *1s, 2s, 3s, 1p, 2p, 3p: je, tu, il, nous, vous, ils.*

accroire	to deceive	Infinitive only.
advenir	to happen	3rd persons, participles, model *venir* (6-7).
apparoir	to be evident	3s indicative present only: *il appert.*
avérer	to prove to be	3rd persons, participles, model *céder* (1-5).
bayer	to gape	Theoretically like *parler* (1-1); only in expression *bayer aux corneilles* ("to gape").

béer	to gape	Theoretically like *parler* (1-1); in practice most commonly present participle *béant* and in fixed expression (*être*) *bouche bée* ("to be with gaping mouth", in astonishment, admiration, etc.).
bienvenir	to make welcome	Infinitive only.
braire	to bray	3rd persons, participles, model *traire* (5-24).
bruire	to rustle	3rd persons, present participle, model *maudire* (2-2).
cafeter	to denounce	Not used in 1s-2s-3s-3p present indicative or subjunctive, otherwise conjugated like *parler* (1-1). Regular variant is *cafter.*
caleter	to flee	Not used in 1s-2s-3s-3p present indicative or subjunctive, otherwise conjugated like *parler* (1-1). Regular variant is *calter.*
chaloir		Essentially only 3s present indicative in expression *peu me chaut* ("it matters little to me"), *peu lui chaut,* etc.; old past participle *chalant* appears in Eng./Fr. *nonchalant.*
chauvir	to prick (up)	Conjugated like *partir* (6-1), except for 1s-2s-3s present indicative conjugated like *finir* (2-1); in practice appears only in expression *chauvir les oreilles,* speaking of the ears of a mule, donkey, or horse.
choir	to fall	Conjugation presented at end of this section (D-1a); in practice limited to infinitive (preceded by *faire* or *laisser*) and past participle *chu.*
clamecer	to die	Theoretically follows model of *dépecer* (1-6a), except: (a) present indicative and subjunctive has only 1p/2p; (b) there is no future or conditional. Generally replaced by the regular verb *clamser.*
clore	to close	Conjugation presented at end of this section (D-2).
comparoir	to appear (legal)	Infinitive only; and past participle *comparant* used as adjective or noun referring to a person or persons appearing in a judicial proceeding.
contrefoutre (se)	to mock	Follows conjugation of *foutre* (see below).
courre	to hunt	Infinitive only; old form of *courir,* used only in hunting language: *chasse à courre* (on horses, with dogs).
déchoir	to deprive (of right)	Conjugation presented at end of this section (D-1b).

déclore	to remove fence	In practice, only past participle (*déclos*) is used.
douer	to endow	Only past participle *doué.*
échoir	to fall due	Conjugation presented at end of this section (D-1c).
éclore	to hatch, bloom	Conjugated like *clore* (D-2), except 3s present indicative has no circumflex (*éclot*). Generally only 3rd persons.
enclore	to enclose	Conjugated like *clore,* except: (a) 1p-2p present indicatives exist (*enclosons, enclosez*); (b) no circumflex on 3s present indicative (*enclot*).
ensuivre (s')	to ensue	3rd persons, participles, model *suivre* (5-5).
ester	to be (legal)	Infinitive only; legal term *ester en justice, ester en jugement.*
faillir	to almost (nearly) do something, fail, fall short	Normally only simple past (*failli-*) and past participle (*failli*), although some sources indicate complete conjugation exists as per model *finir* (2-1). Archaic forms *je faux . . . nous faillons . . .* sometimes found.
férir		Infinitive only, in expression *sans coup férir* ("without meeting the least resistance", "without difficulty").
ficher/fiche		In sense "to put something on file" or "to drive into" (e.g., a nail), conjugation is regular, model *parler* (1-1); in more colloquial senses (e.g., *je m'en fiche,* "I don't give a damn"), past participle is *fich**u**,* there is no simple past, and infinitive is frequently *fiche.*[1]
forclore	to exclude, foreclose	In practice, only past participle (*forclos*) is used.
forfaire	to forfeit[2]	Only past participle *forfait.*
foutre	to do[3]	The six key stems are: fou-, fout-, fout- / fout**u** / —/ foutr- There is no simple past.
frire	to fry	Normally only past participle *frit;* can also be used in 1s-2s-3s present indicative (*je fris, tu fris, il frit*), all futures, and conditionals (stem *frir-*). "Missing" conjugations are supplied by the combination *faire frire* (e.g., *nous faisons frire, je faisais frire,* etc.).

[1] Representing the only French infinitive not ending in *-er, -oir, -re,* or *-ir.* The irregular past participle *fichu* is due to contamination with the like-meaning verb *foutre* (pp. *foutu*).

[2] Also in the sense of "to transgress against, violate".

[3] *Foutre* has historically been the equivalent of the English "f-word". However, this use is now considered obsolete, and *foutre* has developed a range of "informal" uses similar to those of *ficher:* e.g., *Il ne fout rien de la journée* ("He does nothing all day").

gésir	to be lying (down)	Only forms in use are present indicative, imperfect, and present participle. Conjugations are analogous to *lire* (5-10), apart from circumflex in 3s present indicative.

present	imperfect	present participle
je gis	je gisais	gisant
tu gis	tu gisais	
il *gît*	il gisait	
nous gisons	nous gisions	
vous gisez	vous gisiez	
ils gisent	ils gisaient	

Old French 3s present (*il gist*) is source of English noun *gist*.

impartir	to impart, accord (a delay to)	Present indicative and past participle, model *finir* (2-1).
importer		In transitive sense of importing goods, conjugation is complete, model *parler* (1-1); in intransitive sense of "to matter", "to be important", only 3rd persons and present participle.
incomber	to fall to	3rd persons and participles, model *parler* (1-1).
messeoir	to not sit well with	Like *seoir* (D-4) but with only one form for present participle (*messéant*).
moufeter	to protest	Only past participle *moufeté;* in practice replaced by regular verb *moufter.*
occire	to kill	Only past participle *occis.*
ouïr	to listen, hear	Conjugation presented at end of this section (D-3); in practice, only past participle *ouï* (*ouï-dire* is a noun meaning "hearsay") and in the tongue-in-cheek imperative (*oyez, braves gens!*).
paître	to graze, pasture	No simple past or past participle, model *connaître* (5-20).
parfaire	to perfect	Past participle *parfait* only.
partir		In the sense "to leave", conjugation is regular, model *partir* (6-1); in the sense "to share" or "to separate into parts", infinitive only, essentially restricted to the expression *avoir maille à partir (avec quelqu'un),* "to have a disagreement or dispute (with someone)".[4]

[4] In medieval France, a *maille* was the coin of least value, so that the sense is literally "to have a centime to divide".

quérir	to seek, fetch	Infinitive only.
rassir	to go stale	Past participle *rassis* only.
ravoir	to have again, get back	Infinitive only.
refoutre	to put back, return	Follows conjugation of *foutre* (see above).
résulter	to result from	3rd persons, participles, model *parler* (1-1).
saillir		Generally only 3rd persons and participles. In the sense "to mate/couple" conjugated like *finir* (2-1). In sense "to jut out/bulge", generally conjugated like *assaillir* (3-2a) but in literary use can be found conjugated like *finir* (2-1).
seoir		In sense "to sit well with" (i.e., to suit), conjugation presented at end of this section (D-4). In sense "to be situated", only present (*séant*) and past (*sis*) participles.
sortir		In the sense "to go out", conjugation is regular, model *partir* (6-1); in the legal sense "to obtain", only 3rd persons and participles, model *finir* (2-1).
sourdre	to surge, seep out	3rd persons present indicative and imperfect, no participles, model *rendre* (5-1a).
stupéfaire	to stupefy, bemuse, amaze	3s present indicative (*stupéfait*), past participle (*stupéfait*). Corresponding regular verb is *stupéfier*.

D-1A CHOIR TO FALL

INDICATIVE

	Present	Imperfect	Future	Conditional
je	chois	—	choirai, cherrai	choirais, cherrais
tu	chois	—	choiras, cherras	choirais, cherrais
il, elle	choit	—	choira, cherra	choirait, cherrait
nous	—	—	choirons, cherrons	choirions, cherrions
vous	—	—	choirez, cherrez	choiriez, cherriez
ils, elles	choient	—	choiront, cherront	choiraient, cherraient

	Simple Past	SUBJUNCTIVE Present	SUBJUNCTIVE Imperfect
je	chus	—	—
tu	chus	—	—
il, elle	chut	—	chût
nous	chûmes	—	—
vous	chûtes	—	—
ils, elles	churent	—	—

PAST PARTICIPLE	chu		
PRESENT PARTICIPLE	—		
	(tu)	(nous)	(vous)
IMPERATIVE	—	—	—
STEMS	choi-, —, choi- / ch**u** / ch**u**- / choir- (or cherr-)		

D-1B DÉCHOIR TO DEPRIVE (OF RIGHT), TO DEMEAN (ONESELF)

INDICATIVE

	Present	Imperfect	Future	Conditional
je	déchois (*rare*)	—	déchoirai	déchoirais
tu	déchois	—	déchoiras	déchoirais
il, elle	déchoit	—	déchoira	déchoirait
nous	déchoyons (*rare*)	—	déchoirons	déchoirions
vous	déchoyez (*rare*)	—	déchoirez	déchoiriez
ils, elles	déchoient	—	déchoiront	déchoiraient

	Simple Past	SUBJUNCTIVE Present	SUBJUNCTIVE Imperfect
je	déchus	déchoie	déchusse
tu	déchus	déchoies	déchusses
il, elle	déchut	déchoie	déchût
nous	déchûmes	déchoyions	déchussions
vous	déchûtes	déchoyiez	déchussiez
ils, elles	déchurent	déchoient	déchussent

PAST PARTICIPLE	déchu		
PRESENT PARTICIPLE	—		
	(tu)	(nous)	(vous)
IMPERATIVE	—	—	—
STEMS	déchoi-, *déchoy-*, déchoi- / déch**u** / déch**u**- / déchoir-		
REMARKS	There is an alternative, albeit archaic, future stem *décherr-*		

D-1C ÉCHOIR TO FALL DUE

INDICATIVE

	Present	Imperfect	Future	Conditional
je	—	—	—	—
tu	—	—	—	—
il, elle	échoit	échoyait	échoira	échoirait
nous	—	—	—	—
vous	—	—	—	—
ils, elles	échoient	échoyaient	échoiront	échoiraient

Simple Past		SUBJUNCTIVE Present	Imperfect
je	—	—	—
tu	—	—	—
il, elle	échut	échoie	échût
nous	—	—	—
vous	—	—	—
ils, elles	échurent	échoient	échussent

PAST PARTICIPLE	échu		
PRESENT PARTICIPLE	échéant		
	(tu)	(nous)	(vous)
IMPERATIVE	—	—	—
STEMS	échoi-, —, échoi- / éch**u** / éch**u**- / échoir-		
REMARKS	There are also alternative (archaic) present (*échet, échéent*) and future/conditional (*écherr-*) forms		

D-2 CLORE TO CLOSE

INDICATIVE

	Present	Imperfect	Future	Conditional
je	clos	—	clorai	clorais
tu	clos	—	cloras	clorais
il, elle	*clô**t***	—	clora	clorait
nous	—	—	clorons	clorions
vous	—	—	clorez	cloriez
ils, elles	closent	—	cloront	cloraient

Simple Past		SUBJUNCTIVE Present	Imperfect
je	—	close	—
tu	—	closes	—
il, elle	—	close	—
nous	—	closions	—
vous	—	closiez	—
ils, elles	—	closent	—

PAST PARTICIPLE	clos		
PRESENT PARTICIPLE	closant (rare)		
	(tu)	(nous)	(vous)
IMPERATIVE	clos	—	—
STEMS	clo- ,—, clos- / clo**s** / — / clor-		
REMARKS	3rd person singular present has circumflex: *clôt*		

D-3 OUÏR TO LISTEN, HEAR

INDICATIVE

	Present	Imperfect	Future	Conditional
j'	ois	*oyais*	ouïrai, oirai	ouïrais, oirais
tu	ois	*oyais*	ouïras, oiras	ouïrais, oirais
il, elle	oit	*oyait*	ouïra, oira	ouïrait, oirait
nous	*oyons*	*oyions*	ouïrons, oirons	ouïrions, oirions
vous	*oyez*	*oyiez*	ouïrez, oirez	ouïriez, oiriez
ils, elles	oient	*oyaient*	ouïront, oiront	ouïraient, oiraient

	Simple Past	SUBJUNCTIVE Present	Imperfect
j'	ouïs	oie	ouïsse
tu	ouïs	oies	ouïsses
il, elle	ouït	oie	ouït
nous	ouïmes	*oyions*	ouïssions
vous	ouïtes	*oyiez*	ouïssiez
ils, elles	ouïrent	oient	ouïssent

PAST PARTICIPLE	ouï		
PRESENT PARTICIPLE	*oyant*		
	(tu)	(nous)	(vous)
IMPERATIVE	ois	*oyons*	*oyez*
STEMS	oi-, *oy-*, oi-/ouï/ouï-/ouïr-, oir-		
REMARKS	*-i* between two vowels → *y*, unless second vowel is *mute -e*. There is also a third (archaic) future stem *orr-*.		

D-4 SEOIR TO SIT WELL WITH, TO SUIT

INDICATIVE

	Present	Imperfect	Future	Conditional
je	—	—	—	—
tu	—	—	—	—
il, elle	sied	seyait	siéra	siérait
nous	—	—	—	—
vous	—	—	—	—
ils, elles	siéent	seyaient	siéront	siéraient

	Simple Past	SUBJUNCTIVE Present	Imperfect
je	—	—	—
tu	—	—	—
il, elle	—	siée	—
nous	—	—	—
vous	—	—	—
ils, elles	—	siéent	—

PAST PARTICIPLE	—		
PRESENT PARTICIPLE	séant / seyant		
	(tu)	(nous)	(vous)
IMPERATIVE	—	—	—
STEMS	sied-, [sey-], sié- / — / — / siér-		

Selected References

Bourciez, E., and J. Bourciez. 1967. *Phonétique française, étude historique.* Paris: Klincksieck.

Brunot, Ferdinand, and Charles Bruneau. 1937. *Précis de grammaire historique de la langue française.* Paris: Masson.

Chevalier, Jean-Claude, Claire Blanche-Benveniste, Michel Arrivé, and Jean Peytard. 2002. *Grammaire du français contemporain.* Paris: Larousse.

Colin, Jean-Paul. 2002. *Dictionnaire des difficultés du français.* Paris: Robert.

Dubois, Jean, and René Lagane. 2001. *La nouvelle grammaire du français.* Paris: Larousse.

Ewert, Alfred. 1969. *The French Language.* London: Faber and Faber.

Girodet, Jean. 2003. *Dictionnaire Bordas des pièges et difficultés de la langue française.* Paris: Bordas.

Guides Le Robert & Nathan: Conjugaison. 2001. Paris: Nathan.

Guides Le Robert & Nathan: Grammaire. 2001. Paris: Nathan.

Lanly, André. 2002. *Morphologie historique des verbes français.* Paris: Champion.

Le Goffic, Pierre. 1997. *Les formes conjugées du verbe français, oral et écrit.* Paris: Ophrys.

Le Petit Robert, dictionnaire de la langue française (CD-Rom Version 2.1). 2001. Paris: Dictionnaires Le Robert.

Thomas, Adolphe V. 1997. *Dictionnaire des difficultés de la langue française.* Paris: Larousse-Bordas.

Walter, Henriette. 1988. *Le français dans tous les sens.* Paris: Robert Laffont. (Also available in English: *French Inside Out.* London: Routledge, 1994.)